"From his deep experience in both Mennonite and Catholic circles, Gerald Schlabach explores well the transforming initiative of the church's evolving 'turn to active nonviolence' and offers a challenging reflection on the messy complexity of the just war framework's 'traditional righteousness.' This book should be required reading for all of us involved in the Catholic Nonviolence Initiative."

— Marie Dennis
Co-President of Pax Christi International (2007–2019)
Executive Committee of Pax Christi's Catholic Nonviolence Initiative

"More than any book on active nonviolence and peacemaking, Gerald Schlabach's *A Pilgrim People* offers a profound and solid theological foundation for this essential Christian mission. It shows that active nonviolence is demanded not only by the process of globalization but also, and more urgently, by Christ's command to his disciples to cross borders of all types to bring about God's reign of justice, peace, and love. It is a must-read for social activists as well as scholars. A timelier book for our Age of Migration can hardly be found."

— Peter C. Phan
Ellacuría Chair of Catholic Social Thought
Georgetown University

A Pilgrim People

Becoming a Catholic Peace Church

Gerald W. Schlabach

LITURGICAL PRESS
ACADEMIC

Collegeville, Minnesota
www.litpress.org

Cover design by Ann Blattner. Photo © 2014 *Arizona Daily Star*. Used with permission.

Scripture quotations are from New Revised Standard Version Bible © 1989 National Council of the Churches of Christ in the United States of America. Used by permission. All rights reserved worldwide.

Excerpts from documents of the Second Vatican Council are from *Vatican Council II: Constitutions, Decrees, Declarations; The Basic Sixteen Documents*, edited by Austin Flannery, OP, © 1996. Used with permission of Liturgical Press, Collegeville, Minnesota.

Excerpts from the Magisterium of Pope Francis and John Paul II © Libreria Editrice Vaticana. Used with permission.

© 2019 by Order of Saint Benedict, Collegeville, Minnesota. All rights reserved. No part of this book may be used or reproduced in any manner whatsoever, except brief quotations in reviews, without written permission of Liturgical Press, Saint John's Abbey, PO Box 7500, Collegeville, MN 56321-7500. Printed in the United States of America.

Library of Congress Cataloging-in-Publication Data

Names: Schlabach, Gerald, author.
Title: A pilgrim people : becoming a Catholic peace church / Gerald W. Schlabach.
Description: Collegeville : Liturgical Press, 2019. | Includes bibliographical references and index. | Summary: "Explores the trend in Roman Catholic teaching toward a commitment to active non-violence and how to become a truly catholic global peace church in which peacemaking is church-wide and parish-deep, Catholics should recognize that they have always properly been a diaspora people with an identity that transcends tribe and nation-state"—Provided by publisher.
Identifiers: LCCN 2019012510 (print) | ISBN 9780814644546 (pbk.)
Subjects: LCSH: Church. | Peace—Religious aspects—Catholic Church. | Nonviolence—Religious aspects—Catholic Church. | Reconciliation—Religious aspects—Catholic Church. | Catholics—Religious identity. | Christian sociology—Catholic Church. | Catholic Church—Doctrines.
Classification: LCC BX1746 .S2925 2019 (print) | LCC BX1746 (ebook) | DDC 261.8/73088282—dc23
LC record available at https://lccn.loc.gov/2019012510
LC ebook record available at https://lccn.loc.gov/2019980676

Dedicated to the legacy of
Dom Hélder Câmara,
Archbishop of Olinda and Recife, Brazil, 1964–1985,
whose stirring call, "Abrahamic minorities unite!"
invited me on pilgrimage from
my Mennonite origins
toward my Catholic horizon

Contents

Acknowledgments ix

Chapter 1
Introduction:
Key Terms, Assumptions, and Other Preliminaries 1

PART I:
Becoming Catholic Again for the First Time 29

Chapter 2
Taking Catholic Social Teaching into Diaspora 31

Chapter 3
We've Been Expecting This:
Christian Love Stretches beyond Borders 64

Chapter 4
We're All in Diaspora Now:
Being Global Church in an Age of Globalization 95

PART II:
Tent Stakes for a Pilgrim People 131

Chapter 5
Abrahamic Community as the Grammar of Gospel 133

Chapter 6
The Church as Sacrament of Human Salvation 162

PART III:
Maps for Peacebuilding by a Pilgrim People 197

Chapter 7
  Guesthood and the Politics of Hospitality 199

Chapter 8
  Escaping Our Vicious Cycles 236

Chapter 9
  Normative Nonviolence and the Unity of the Church 274

Notes 295

Bibliography 368

Index 396

Acknowledgments

Authors regularly worry out loud on pages like these that they will fail to acknowledge everyone to whom they owe the intellectual and personal debts that have made their books possible. For me the exercise is especially fraught. As I have been writing this book I have sometimes joked to friends that "I am trying to synthesize every Mennonite and Catholic thought I've had over the last thirty-five years." Where, then, to start or stop? In chapter 7, I will cite Cardinal Peter Turkson's definition of justice as "respect [for] the demands of the relationships in which we live." I doubt I can do justice to all the relationships with mentors, influencers, and debating partners that have helped shape this book. What I hope at least to do is to chart my pilgrimage through many clusters of relationships and conversations, trusting that all those whom I should also have named will at least recognize themselves in their networks. Whatever the contributions I have been able to make as a peace practitioner, scholar, and teacher, it has been a rich life. Simply to trace in rough chronological order my journey through the clusters of relationships that have formed me will hint at both my intellectual and spiritual journeys through an expanding web that obviously began in Mennonite community, but that soon extended inexorably outward. To say even this much prompts me to acknowledge—first and above all—my gratitude to God.

No doubt the deepest imprint of the creative "Abrahamic" tension running throughout salvation history that I name and celebrate repeatedly in these pages came from being part of a family, in a community, in a generation endeavoring with quiet urgency to discern how to be faithful to its Anabaptist-Mennonite identity as a peaceable people, while offering "alternative service" to the larger social order.

When my father, Theron F. Schlabach—the first in his family not only to go to college but to earn a doctorate—had a letter published prominently in a Madison, Wisconsin, newspaper in the early 1960s explaining why he did not let me or my brothers play with toy guns, he was doing both. When he and my mother, Sara Kauffman Schlabach, led a unit for Goshen (Indiana) College of what, to the best of our knowledge, was the first international studies program in the United States that was required of all students (giving me my start in Latin America, by the way) they were doing both. Indeed, for more than a century the motto of Goshen College, where my father dedicated his career, has reflected the hope of its stream of Mennonites that they could serve their Lord more faithfully precisely by engaging "culture for service."

A couple of years after graduating from Goshen College myself, I sought to put this legacy into practice by entering voluntary service with Mennonite Central Committee—the relief, development, and peacebuilding arm of Mennonites, first in North America and now global. Two years at its Pennsylvania headquarters working in its Information Services department gave me an informal master's degree of sorts in all kinds of issues in development ethics, international Christian solidarity, and the politics of social change. International program directors Edgar Stoesz and Herman Bontrager then entrusted my new wife, Joetta Handrich, and me with a formidable task that took us to Nicaragua and Honduras for five years—to represent the organization, and in a way the tradition, by figuring out how to hold out hope for nonviolent means of working for justice and peace amid revolutionary situations throughout the Central American region in the 1980s. We were still in our mid-twenties. Perhaps we needed to be young, adventurous, and idealistic to take on such a challenge, but still, what were we thinking? Those five years were some of the most difficult of our lives—but also the most formative. I am especially grateful to the Honduran Mennonite Church—especially Ovidio Flores, Isaías Flores, and Juan Angel Ochoa—and to the leadership of the then-fledgling Central American Mennonite seminary SEMILLA, based in Guatemala—especially Gilberto Flores and Rafaél Escobar—for the support and encouragement that made our work realistic and fruitful after all, rather than merely idealistic. Key ideas in these pages were forged in the cauldron of those years.

The very shape of the work drew us into wider and wider ecumenical relationships, after all, and in retrospect I recognize that even as a Mennonite, the Roman Catholic Church of the Second Vatican Council was already defining the horizon of my Christian life. Along with Mennonite churches in the region, primary partners were in Nicaragua's Protestant organization CEPAD, then under the leadership of the late Dr. Gustavo Parajón and Gilberto Aguirre. But among our best expatriate friends in Nicaragua were Maryknoll sisters and lay missioners, while Catholic nonviolence activists soon became close associates. With Nicaraguan Moravian Church leaders such as the Rev. Norman Bent, we founded a local chapter of Servicio Paz y Justicia (SERPAJ); aiding us were consultants Creuza Maciel from Brazil and Hildegard Goss-Mayr, the veteran Catholic peace activist who played a key role behind the scenes at the Second Vatican Council, along with her husband, Jean, and others, encouraging the church to begin reappraising its attitude toward war.[1] Collaboration in the founding months of the organization for nonviolent solidarity, Witness for Peace, led to continuing work with Catholic peace activist Philip McManus and to the book that he and I eventually coedited on nonviolent movements in Latin America, *Relentless Persistence*.[2] Just as auspicious was the archbishop I never met in person but did meet in print in these years, Dom Hélder Câmara of Brazil; to his legacy I have dedicated this book.

It was not until a few years later at the University of Notre Dame that I began to weave my growing number of Catholic connections into the longer threads of the Catholic tradition. Here my guides were Jean Porter and John Cavadini especially, along with Todd Whitmore, Blake Leyerle, and the late Catherine LaCugna. Porter and LaCugna introduced me to Thomas Aquinas; Leyerle and Cavadini to patristics. Porter and Cavadini guided me into the deeper engagement with Augustine that persists, even in this book, against the tide of his ill-repute in Catholic peace activist circles.[3] Of my difficult but unavoidably influential relationship with the late John Howard Yoder, leading Mennonite theologian of his generation then at Notre Dame, I will say more in a bit.

Though I had gone to Notre Dame because Catholicism seemed a far more interesting conversation partner than mainline Protestantism, not because I was consciously exploring becoming Catholic, I did increasingly come to think of myself as a "Catholic Mennonite"—until in 2004 at the Pentecost Vigil, I flipped noun and adjective to become a "Mennonite Catholic" and enter into full communion with the Roman Catholic Church. To say only that much is to abbreviate greatly, of course, but I have written of the process of discernment elsewhere.[4] What is especially relevant to this book is the companionship that the grassroots organization for Mennonite-Catholic dialogue, Bridgefolk, has offered along the way. My fellow cofounders, Marlene Kropf, Weldon Nisly, and above all my dear friend the late Ivan Kauffman, deserve special mention, along with Abbot John Klassen and Fr. William Skudlarek of Saint John's Abbey in Minnesota, Margie Pfeil, and the late Alan Kreider. Another way that I was able to bridge Mennonite and Catholic communities in these years was participation on the international Peace Committee of Mennonite Central Committee, which was gracious enough to let me continue on the committee and do major work on peace theology even as my move into Catholicism became public; thanks go especially to Robert and Judy Zimmerman Herr, Alain Epp-Weaver, and Duane Friesen.[5] Also supplying key materials for bridging traditions was the late Glen Stassen, a Christian ethicist in the Baptist (but also *Anabaptist*) tradition, whose help will be quite evident in my final two chapters.

By now, to be sure, many of my most constant conversation partners are fellow Catholics. Fr. Drew Christiansen, SJ, and I occasionally joke that we have become a tag team in our insistence that if Catholics are to take church teaching seriously, peacemaking must become "church-wide and parish-deep." Christiansen is currently the Distinguished Professor of Ethics and Global Human Development in Georgetown's School of Foreign Service and a senior research fellow at the Berkley Center for Religion, Peace, and World Affairs. No one has done more to tease out the development of papal teaching concerning peace and war, and the emergence of nonviolence as a clear norm for the church, than Fr. Christiansen. As will be especially evident in chapter 2, despite a few ongoing disagreements I have learned much from him and cannot imagine having written this book without his direct and indirect help. Tobias Winright, a peer in graduate studies at Notre Dame who now holds the Hubert Mäder Endowed Chair at Saint Louis University, has continued to be a regular conversation partner despite a bit of friendly sparring about how best to frame and promote the notion of "just policing." Gerard Powers, who coordinates the Catholic Peacebuilding Network (CPN) as part of his portfolio at Notre Dame's Kroc Institute for International Peace Studies, and who previously directed the Office of International Justice and Peace of the U.S. Conference of Catholic Bishops, welcomed me on to the CPN coordinating committee a few years ago and has become a good friend. That committee in turn introduced me to veteran peace activist Marie Dennis, copresident of Pax Christi International, who has steadily drawn me into what is now known as the Catholic Nonviolence Initiative (CNI), which in conversation with the Vatican's Pontifical Council for Justice and Peace—now folded into the Dicastery for Promoting Integral Human Development—has been spurring fresh debate over the adequacy of the Catholic just-war tradition. The CNI has also provided the context for conversation and collaboration with Eli McCarthy, who teaches peace studies at Georgetown University and directs the justice and peace office of the Conference of Major Superiors of Men in the United States, and with Lisa Sowle Cahill, the J. Donald Monan, S.J., Professor at Boston College.

Of course, my colleagues in the Theology Department at the University of St. Thomas in Minnesota have offered invaluable support since I joined them in 2000. Bernard Brady, Paul Wojda, John Boyle, Kimberly Vrudny, and Michael Hollerich have first of all been good friends, but also always available to bat around ideas and suggest resources. William Cavanaugh has now moved on to DePaul University, and Massimo Faggioli to Villanova University, but they have also played these roles. To John Martens and Corrine Carvalho, I owe specific debts for helping me double-check my biblical scholarship at points, and to my former colleague Tisha Rajendra, now at Loyola University Chicago, I am indebted for a critical review of my chapter on immigration issues. I am also grateful to faculty in the Department of Justice and Peace Studies with whom I was associated for a few years—Jack Nelson-Pallmeyer, Michael Klein, and Amy Finnegan.

Without the financial and logistical support of three institutions, this book almost certainly could not have come to fruition. The Faculty Development office of the University of St. Thomas channeled institutional funding at various stages of this project, first by facilitating a sabbatical, and later through a major University Scholars Grant. For generous external funding that allowed that sabbatical to extend for a full year, I am grateful to the Louisville Institute. Providing an ideal location and camaraderie with fellow scholars was the Collegeville Institute, an apostolic ministry of Saint John's Abbey in Minnesota.

Another kind of support—technical, though always somewhat more than that—has come from the scrappy company that built an elegant tool for scholarship years ago when I was just beginning my scholarly career, and that has continued perfecting it ever since: The Nota Bene word processor, bibliographic organizer, and note indexer has streamlined and structured my work for over three decades, and allowed an intuitive, big-picture thinker like me to act as though he had an eye for details. Gratitude goes both to Steve Siebert, its creator, and to the erudite community of Nota Bene users around the world that has kept this irreplaceable tool alive and helped it get better and better.

But now I must turn to that more freighted acknowledgment of my debt to the late John Howard Yoder, one of my teachers at both the Anabaptist Mennonite Biblical Seminary in Elkhart, Indiana,[6] and ten years later at Notre Dame. At the time, he was a towering figure in Anabaptist-Mennonite theology and a leading spokesman for Christian pacifism ecumenically. Today his legacy is rightly suspect— as in, subject to trenchant hermeneutics of suspicion—due to his now-well-documented sexual abuse, which he used his brilliant theological mind to rationalize.[7]

If I knew how to expunge all traces of Yoder's influence, I would. I have broken with him in various ways that might give me an excuse, after all. He was not particularly pleased when I turned to Augustine to solve the central problematic of my doctoral dissertation. I knew enough about the reasons for his estrangement from Mennonite Church leadership before details began to become public during my years at Notre Dame in the early 1990s that I began even then to deepen my own hermeneutic of suspicion about how his abuses might have vitiated his ecclesiology with regard to pastoral leadership.[8] Our personal relationship was strained at Notre Dame; though he served on my dissertation committee, almost all communication went by way of my adviser, Jean Porter. I was writing one of the most important articles in my early career at the time of his death in December 1997; in it I questioned the explanatory power of "Constantinianism" as what seemed in Yoder's thought to be the most basic problem for Christian social ethics.[9] Even at the point where he advocated for a "Jeremianic" model of Christian social engagement and thus influenced my turn to "diaspora ecclesiology" in this book, a reader who knows his thought well might notice the ways that I stretch his thought toward greater appreciation for Christian vocations of governance. Yet however convenient it would be to distance myself from Yoder still further, to expunge all traces of his thought would be to commit a sin of my own—the scholarly one of plagiarism.

Make no mistake. John Howard Yoder betrayed many—none more than the survivors of his sexual abuse, but also those of us who had learned breakthrough concepts from him. Still, as I have written elsewhere concerning my relationship with Yoder and his legacy, "only those we need can betray us."[10] (To explain by way of contrast, prominent Protestant theologian Paul Tillich was also an egregious sexual predator. But while his abuses were surely scandalous and tragic, for me they do not constitute a *betrayal* because I am not at all a Tillichian who needs his words to trace or understand my own.) Few have done more than Yoder to show why and how even Christian pacifists should engage just-war thinking. None was more persistent in rebutting the claims of Reinhold Niebuhr that to renounce recourse to war and other forms of nation-state violence necessarily means rendering oneself politically irrelevant, nor did more to enumerate alternative forms of power by which a "creative minority" that does so might actually do more to serve the common good. These are the matters that have always interested me the most and that pertain to this book. Yoder's willful blindness to still other forms of power that he himself wielded to the great harm of those women who are his survivors deserves all the scrutiny and critique that it is receiving. But while I would be glad to stand corrected, to the best of my self-awareness I do not believe that the building blocks in this book that owe something to Yoderian thought lie in the vicinity of Yoder's intellectual mistakes or moral failings. If I am wrong, I hope that I have at least been intellectually honest and transparent enough to allow readers to decide, and for the painful conversation about what we do with Yoder's legacy to go forward.

Finally, and more happily, I must of course thank my wonderful wife of nearly four decades, Joetta Handrich Schlabach. Our interests, styles, and vocations have been close enough to allow us to support one another richly, yet different enough to allow our relationship to be a welcome reprieve when necessary. We traveled and worked together through those difficult-but-formative years in Central America. We have been partners in the great adventure of raising our delightful sons, Gabriel and Jacob, then welcoming their own life partners, Valerie and Angie, into our family. Joetta's hospitality has drawn me out of my bookish introversion as surely as it has drawn others into new circles of friendship. Whatever else it may accomplish for me to finish this book and send it out to God's pilgrim people, I am especially glad that we can now look forward to new adventures together.

Chapter 1

Introduction: Key Terms, Assumptions, and Other Preliminaries

> We shall not cease from exploration
> And the end of all our exploring
> Will be to arrive where we started
> And know the place for the first time.
> —T. S. Eliot, "Little Gidding,"

I might as well be forthcoming. The pages of this book aim to do nothing less than tweak and prod and shift the worldview of Christian readers, particularly Roman Catholic ones, until ultimately their worldview is transformed. That does not at all mean that the aim of these pages is to introduce a new, novel, modern, or more cutting-edge theology. Rather—as I will summarize later—the aim is to help us become Catholic again for the first time.

Dear to the Catholic heart is a yearning for Christian unity. Yet for centuries, our worldviews and too often our explicit theologies have allowed us to put national and tribal identities ahead of our baptismal identities as citizens in the worldwide people called church. In other words, we are prepared to kill one another. And sometimes we actually do. Wars of religion in the sixteenth century. Battlefield trenches with Christians on both sides in World War I. Nationalistic ideologies trumping Christian solidarity in World War II, and then the Cold War. Christian Hutus massacring Christian Tutsis and moderate Christian Hutus in Rwanda. At a time when many lament how sex-abuse scandals have turned people away from Christianity and the church has lost its moral force, the scandal of Christians not being able to avoid war even against one another—to say nothing of others—is a scandal that keeps on taking.

Yet also dear to the Catholic heart is a conviction grounded in the doctrine of the Incarnation and trained in sacramental practice, namely: God's grace works through and transforms the ordinary stuff of our lives in the body. And that means our lives in families, places, and nations. Grace perfects nature, as St. Thomas Aquinas put it. The Gospel requires inculturation, as the Second Vatican Council indicated and Pope Paul VI explained. Not only does God care about these realities, but we know God through these material, historical realities. No wonder, then, that we want to protect and defend the natural communities that have given us life, in all its particularity.

Somehow we must find our way through all of these concerns and convictions simultaneously. Thankfully, the Second Vatican Council pointed a way by retrieving an ancient theme that runs through Scripture and tradition: The church, the people of God, is a people on a continuing pilgrimage through history, a pilgrim people. Pilgrims make their journeys because particular places matter. Yet they also hold lightly to places, traveling as guests. To be a pilgrim people, therefore, requires becoming a people of peace. That becoming is our very journey of transformation.

To make this particular journey a little easier, let me begin by unpacking the terms in my title, *A Pilgrim People: Becoming a Catholic Peace Church*. Each word encodes assumptions, starting points, or markers that may help readers know what to expect from the outset, and thus keep their bearings as we proceed.

"Church"

This book is as much about ecclesiology—the nature and theology of the church—as it is about peace or peacemaking or peacebuilding. Yet it is no less about peace or peacemaking or peacebuilding for that reason. Its core argument builds on the assumption that peacemaking and being church are not really different things. This is certainly not to say that only Christians, or only Christians working through church structures, can build peace. It is to say that *working* for peace is inseparable from becoming a *people* of peace. It is to say that the fruit of peacebuilding is not to become one undifferentiated mass of individuals spread across the globe, but rather a community of peoples, each striving, as Gandhi said—and I will regularly quote—to "be the change they seek in the world." To be formed into a people of peace is not simply to become more fervent peace activists or more savvy policymakers, therefore. It is to be a people whose very life and presence in the world constitutes a steady, persistent, embodied contribution to the common good of the world and all its peoples.

I am a Christian. To be part of the change I long for in the world, therefore, means ever to begin with the Christian community. And so I must also always be the change I long for in the church. Stubbornly, mindfully, and joyfully out of sync with those who imagine it is even possible to be "spiritual but not religious" by following Jesus apart from church participation both locally and globally, I could not be a Christian if I lost all hope in the church. Religion, Christianity, and Catholicism are deeply suspect to many, I know. Loyalty to traditions and communal identities has been going out of fashion for centuries (except for the covert traditions of fleeting fashion that try to brand us for capitalist fun and profit). It would require another kind of book to answer those deep suspicions; and besides, in a way I have already written such a book.[1] So I will not try to prove the necessity of the church for God's purposes here. Yet by arguing *from* that axiom if not *toward* that axiom, I hope I will at least make it more intelligible.

Certainly my ultimate faith is in God, made flesh in Jesus Christ, gracing us back into relationship through the power and presence of the Holy Spirit. And certainly I know all too well—not just through historical study but in painful personal relationship—the scandals and shames and failings of the church down through the centuries, down into the pews, and up front at the altar. Yet the God I recognize in the long arc of church history and personal struggle is the God who was already proving faithful to Israel according to the Hebrew Scriptures, amid their very wanderings. As I read both "Old" and New Testaments, the indispensable (though not exclusive) way that God seeks to work for truly transformative social change is by forming a people whose life bears witness to the way of the LORD (cf. Gen 18:17-19, elaborating on 12:1-3)—"*imprescindible*," to use a not-quite-translatable Spanish word. Whatever else God does in history, God's people are never left behind, nor the social strategy in which they are key: God has called out and struggled with children of Abraham and communities of Jesus because none less than God has recognized that the salvation that is transformative social change always requires a creative minority—a distinctive people at work *within* and *for* the whole.

Imperfect? Scandalously unfaithful at times? Unworthy to bear the name of Christ? No doubt. But the very struggle together in community—the hanging together, the wrestling with God and one another—is the place where God forms us together as peacemakers, who are learning how to conflict nonviolently. What would be the point if God and God's people were so closed and inhospitable that thoroughly human people (aka sinful and still-being-formed people) could never join the centuries-long movement of learning and discerning together? I understand why disappointment with one's church can lead a person to look to other churches and movements for new homes that offer hope and support. But I am convinced that starting over often looks attractive mainly because new movements and churches have barely begun to face the challenges that will soon begin to present themselves in their second or third generation. Precisely because I am "progressive" in my longing for just and sustainable social change, I am also unapologetically conservative. "Sustainable" must include the hard-won wisdom of past generations. "Social" must draw in even the sisters and brothers with whom I have been in conflict. "Just" cannot dismiss their contributions, much less demean their persons. Far too often, the understandable impulse to start over from scratch merely resets the clock and postpones the hard work.

That this is a book about ecclesiology and the formation of a people also means that it must risk disappointing readers who come to the book from at least two opposite directions. To employ a useful though always problematic shorthand, its arguments will not align neatly with expectations from either left or right. Christian peace activists who want knock-down arguments to take into their advocacy work to stop whatever current war or injustice presses urgently upon them will be disappointed. But Christians who think that the work of such activism is a distraction from the true "spiritual" work of the church, or who think they can safely leave temporal matters to realistic and tough-minded protectors of "our" national security will be uncomfortable too.

I hope the latter will find it impossible to put this book aside because it takes church—and for that matter church teaching—at least as seriously as they. And I hope the former will find it impossible to put the book aside because I propose something at least as radical as they do. The two often seem to differ greatly over the nature of peace and the conditions that favor it. Yet they easily share an assumption that the most crucial work of peacemaking and promoting the common good gets done in the capitals of nation-states. For as much as they may differ over policies, readers from both of these directions tend to assume that policymaking is where they should either dedicate their governing skills or direct their prophetic critique, for that, they presume, is the crucial fulcrum by which to move history. Without minimizing the importance of policy decisions that can indeed affect millions or sometimes billions, my assumption is that policymaking is always, ultimately, derivative. What Christians should do or say in Washington or Geneva or Nairobi or Manila or Santiago is a matter of tactics and available tools, and of course we do well to refine such tools. But we will only do so wisely and ethically if we are formed within a people that has taught us our primary identity as followers of Christ in solidarity with one another across the globe. The formation of such a people is no mere tactic. It is God's own strategy of social transformation.

"Peace"

From its highest levels, the Roman Catholic Church has been making increasingly clear in recent decades that God has given every Christian the duty and the vocation of working for peace.[2] As Pope John Paul II proclaimed in a World Day of Peace message that had special significance, given that it opened Jubilee Year 2000,

> the Church vividly remembers her Lord and intends to confirm her vocation and mission to be in Christ a "sacrament" or *sign and instrument of peace in the world and for the world*. For the Church, to carry out her evangelizing mission means to work for peace. For the Catholic faithful, the commitment to build peace and justice is not secondary but essential.[3]

This is one reason to be sure we do well to frame Christian peace theology widely as first a question of ecclesiology. If we believe that Catholic peacemaking must be "church-wide and parish-deep," as I have argued elsewhere,[4] we should avoid the impression that peacemaking is just for people of a certain disposition, a particular personality type, a specific vocation, or those who are "into that kind of thing."

To hold up fervent peace activists as normative will inspire and mobilize some, but may then begin to have diminishing returns. I am certainly grateful for role models such as Dorothy Day, Peter Maurin, Daniel Berrigan, SJ, Jean and Hildegard Goss-Mayr, and my hero Dom Hélder Câmara, former archbishop of Recife, Brazil. We certainly need organizations like Bread for the World, Pax Christi, and Christian Peacemaker Teams. And we benefit especially from examples of transformation that were initially counterintuitive, such as Thomas Merton inspiring others from the seclusion of a Trappist monastery, or Oscar Romero defying all the expectations he brought into the office of archbishop of San Salvador as a bookish priest of traditionalist piety. I know from the classroom how important their stories can be for piquing the imaginations of young people who had not known that such lives of courage were possible, or that so many networks of action are already available. Yet stories of extraordinary lives may eventually leave us wondering whether *our* quite ordinary lives can make a difference. If the activist answer *seems* to be to move constantly from one issue to another—from letter-writing campaign to protest to the constant churning of social media—we introduce subtle dangers. Even those who take up the cause may eventually face burnout, often from the intense pace of activity, coupled with a discouragingly slow pace of change. But many Christians who watch them may never even begin because we have associated "peacemaking" with that narrow but frenetic band of activities. Thus we need a wider community and a longer story.

But there is another reason that the call for all Christians to be peacemakers too often falls on deaf ears: namely, "peace" can evoke a utopian state of perfect harmony. So it is also important to be clear, right up front, about what I mean by peace.

On one hand, it is helpful to begin with the Hebrew notion of *shalom*, and to allow it to color every use of the otherwise flat English word "peace." Holding up Hebrew *shalom* will keep tones from Greek *eirene* or Latin *pax* from bleeding into our working conception of peace. Greek *eirene* too easily suggests interior peace alone, while Latin *pax* easily connotes the mere suppression of conflict, perhaps even through violence. In Hebrew, *shalom* can translate not only as peace but as health, wholeness, true prosperity, right social relationships. *Shalom* thus resonates easily with the rich vision of healthy interdependent human relationships in many traditional cultures—*ubuntu* or *umunthu* in Southern Africa, *yamni* among the Miskito Indians of Central America, and so on. Yet it also resonates with classical concepts that have deep roots in Catholic moral and philosophical reflection—human thriving, the *bonum* or good, especially the *common* good—which in turn are basic to Catholic social teaching in the modern era on social justice. The concept of *shalom* constantly reminds us of this lesson; therefore, we can only work for peace by working for all the social, economic, spiritual, and environmental conditions that make for peace. That is why recent popes have insisted that the "new word for peace is development,"[5] that "if you want peace, work for justice,"[6] or that there is "no peace without justice; no justice without forgiveness."[7] All this should help avoid the impression that only those with an activist disposition can be peacemakers. Every condition that makes for peace is calling out our human talents, in all their diversity. There is plenty to do. All vocations are welcome.

But on the other hand, our consideration of *shalom* begins to open up such an extensive concept of peace and such an expansive vista for peacemaking—really involving every part of life and social relationships—that even if it is not utopian, it might still seem quite overwhelming. So in defining peace, let us quickly pair the lesson of *shalom* with another: *Peace is entirely compatible with conflict.*

As the Second Vatican Council insisted in its Pastoral Constitution on the Church in the Modern World, *Gaudium et Spes*—and as successive popes as well as regional conferences of bishops have reiterated—"peace is more than the absence of war"; it is not a mere "balance of power between opposing forces."[8] Rather, it requires constant reordering and restructuring; "it depends in the concrete upon circumstances that change as time goes on; consequently, peace will never be achieved once and for all, but must be built up continually."[9] This offers a helpful reminder on many fronts, to which we will return with some regularity in the coming pages. For now, what we should notice is this: If peace is a continual project, our operative understanding of peace need not and cannot be one of utopian harmony or blissful calm, free of all social friction. Such perfect peace may offer the ultimate horizon for a Christian worldview and its promise of full communion with God and one another at the end. But while the ultimate horizon of God's purposes will always orient Christian social ethics and Catholic social teaching, our purpose for now must be to take up the challenges of our present life and times.[10] We must allow the Christian message and its ever-strange victory through resurrection-only-after-cross to stretch our expectation as to what is realistic. But the point is never to be unrealistic; it is to be more realistic.

Our operative definition of peace, therefore, should include the absence of *war* as well as much else, yet should not imply the absence of all *conflict*. Rather, I would propose and will work from the following definition:

> Peace is the *presence* of creative processes by which human communities become ever more skillful and habituated at working through their conflicts without recourse to violence and without demeaning one another's dignity.

Lest my earlier insistence on moving our focus away from nation-state capitals and policymaking seem to have sounded like a rejection of politics, it is worth noting that this understanding of peace as creative conflict transformation is eminently political. The ideal of peace for which we can realistically work is actually the extension and deepening of politics, as skillful practitioners become many, at many levels, with less and less need even to consider recourse to violence. It is because peace requires more politics, not less, that I assume the church must come to recognize itself as a transnational people of peace—with all the storytelling and character formation and skillset development and proper rule of law and creative transformation of Christianity's own conflicts that this entails. It is in becoming a Christian people of peace opened out toward the world— a Catholic peace church—that we indispensably learn to contribute as wise policymakers and relentless peacemakers to the peace of the world.

"Peace church"

Another working assumption follows from what I have said both about *church* and about *peace*. Namely, we should not begin by assuming that "peace church" must mean "pacifist church." At least not at the outset, as a precondition for participating in a people of that peace which is "the presence of creative processes by which human communities become ever-more skillful and habituated at working through their conflicts without recourse to violence and without demeaning one another's dignity." To participate in a process of forming peaceable people who are learning the skills and habits needed to discover creative alternatives to violence is not yet to have reached its goal. As I said about the church, "What would be the point if God and God's people were so closed and inhospitable that thoroughly human people—aka sinful and still-being-formed people—could never join the centuries-long movement of learning and discerning together?"

Don't get me wrong. I am indeed a Christian pacifist, committed to principled active nonviolence. For years my daily prayer has been "for the unity and nonviolence of all Christians." I am a Christian pacifist not because I have an answer for how to overturn every injustice nonviolently, nor because I am sure of my capacity to respond nonviolently when put to the test. I am a Christian pacifist because Jesus Christ has taken my life captive. *Kyrios Christos*. Believing as I do the classic claims of Christianity that Jesus of Nazareth is none less than God, the Word Incarnate and Second Person of the Trinity, I cannot but conclude that in Jesus, God, the deepest reality of the universe, has shown nonviolent suffering love to be the strongest power *of* the universe. No more than any other believer or theologian have I learned all that this means, or *how* it all means, much less how to live it out in every circumstance. In fact, nonviolent vulnerability to the tragic challenges of others paradoxically requires me at least to entertain possible exceptions to absolute pacifism.[11] One way I have done this has been to explore "just policing" as an agenda for convergence between just-war and pacifist Christians, at risk that this will lead some of my fellow pacifists to question my pacifism.[12] Commitment to peaceableness and peacemaking requires me, I believe, to do business with the best arguments for just-war theory rather than cynically dismiss it on the basis of its most dubious motives or worst outcomes. Even so, I can only risk doing any of this from the core identity of one whom Jesus Christ continues to disciple through Scripture, community, liturgy, and Spirit.

The final chapter in this book will offer an argument based in none other than Jesus' Sermon on the Mount as to how and why just-war and pacifist Christians can recognize themselves as part of the same church.[13] This may not seem like such an obvious question for Catholic theology. Christians renouncing recourse to violence and departing from just-war tradition once risked the label of heretics, but since the Second Vatican Council, this has not been the case. Authoritative Catholic statements on war and peace now speak of just war and active nonviolence as twin legitimate traditions. But for church traditions that believe active nonviolence or pacifism to be a "confessional" matter—in other words, so near to the core of Christian faith itself as to be essential to Christian identity—no Christian or church that approves the very use of violence or war-making that Jesus rejected can be considered faithful to their Lord. To be sure, in an age of greater ecumenical generosity and mutual recognition between church bodies, few theologians or ethicists from these traditions may wish to be so impolite as to claim that theirs is the only true church. But the work of theologians in these "historic peace churches" still puts a question mark over the legitimacy of churches that have imagined that wars could be just—to say nothing of churches approving of Crusades and conquest in the name of God. At the very least, therefore, peace churches might want to reserve to pacifists and principled practitioners of active nonviolence that label, "peace church."

The terms "peace church" and "historic peace church" are accidents of history, though. They are not fixed, agreed-upon terms. That accident of history was the need for Mennonites, Quakers or Friends, and the Church of the Brethren to band together in a coalition to lobby for legal recognition of conscientious objection to military service in the United States as World War II loomed. Seeking to present a coherent position before the U.S. Congress and the Roosevelt administration, what they said they had in common was that they were "historic peace churches." They knew that politically they could only hope to win recognition for those who refused to participate in any war whatsoever. It thus made sense to seek recognition together as churches that had consistently taught their members to refuse participation in war—in season and out of season, *historically*.

Not only did that designation cover over important differences between the three groups, however; this was a coalition formed for one particular moment in history, and it ignored other churches whose histories might also have qualified them as historic peace churches at some other time in history, or might yet in another.[14] Until the previous century, for example, Moravians had expected their members to refuse military service as combatants. At the very time the historic peace church coalition was forming, many Pentecostal groups taught against combatant military service, at least officially, but they were not part of the coalition. A few decades later, the general synod of the United Church of Christ in the United States would vote to explore what it might mean to affirm itself as a peace church, and in 1985 after further study designated itself a "just-peace church."

The term "peace church" continues to be in flux, and thus open for debate and discernment. When delegations from the Vatican and Mennonite World Conference engaged in a first-ever international dialogue from 1998–2003, one of their early topics for discussion was precisely the question, "What is a peace church?" In the weeklong meeting dedicated to this theme, a Mennonite delegate from Guatemala, Mario Higueros, surprised everyone by arguing that the Catholic Church's defense of human rights and justice for the poor during years of repression in his country had made it more of a peace church than the churches of cautious and pietistic brothers and sisters with whom he himself was affiliated.[15]

It seems as fair as it is necessary, therefore, to treat the question of what it means to be a peace church as a matter for continuing ecumenical discernment. Certainly we must give pride of place to the witness and reflection of historic peace churches amid this discernment. As I will recount in the closing section of chapter 2, the Vatican itself has been doing exactly this.[16] The definition of "peace church" certainly cannot be so up-for-grabs that it loses all continuity with the historic witness of the historic peace churches. If a Christian community were to call itself a "peace church" while blessing the actions of its members no matter what means they chose, so long as they seemed well-intentioned and claimed that peace was their end or goal, it would render the term simply vacuous. Discernment is only meaningful if a definition remains open-ended enough for debate to proceed around the edges—but it is also only meaningful if *what* we are trying to discern means roughly the same thing to all conversation partners.

Accordingly, my working definition of a "peace church" may reflect more but certainly will reflect no less than the consensus that Vatican and Mennonite World Conference representatives were able to reach in their 1998–2003 dialogue. Their final report, *Called Together to be Peacemakers*,[17] never supplies a definitive joint answer to the question of what constitutes a peace church.[18] It does note solid agreement that "the Church is *called* to be a peace church," and that any such church will be a *"peacemaking* church" (§175, emphasis mine). But how best and most faithfully to make peace amid tragic circumstances is precisely what has divided Christians through the centuries. So while a narrowing gap between representatives of these quite different Christian traditions has been momentous to the point of miraculous, disagreement remains. On the one hand, *Called Together* marks agreement that the church as founded by Christ is "called to be a living sign and an effective instrument of peace," which actively works for reconciliation among all peoples, resists all forms of "ethnic and inter-religious hatred and violence," and engages the world on behalf of international peace (§175). But on the other hand, whether the work of peacemaking ever allows or requires Christians to participate in the use of military force, or at least police force, under the sort of exceptional circumstances that the just-war theory seeks to identify yet limit, is precisely the question on which Mennonites and Catholics continue to diverge (§187). If Catholic and Mennonite dialogue partners did not claim to have agreed on what a peace church is or should be, they were commendably and simply being honest.

Nonetheless, what Mennonite and Catholic representatives *did* agree upon in *Called Together* provides a floor for continuing to discern what it will take for a church to fulfill that calling to *become* a people of peace, a peace church. I speak of a "floor" here both as a minimum criterion below which no church can meaningfully call itself a peace church, and as a platform upon which to build what further deliberation might come to identify as a more demanding standard. That floor—that minimum but also that grounding—is what I will call *normative nonviolence*.

The shared theological ground concerning peace, justice, and nonviolence in *Called Together to Be Peacemakers* is astoundingly deep and solid. After centuries of alienation between Mennonites and Catholics, their global representatives here insisted that active nonviolence must be the normative ethic and strategy for all Christian lives and all of the church's work for peace and justice.[19] Basing its summary of shared convictions concerning peace and justice in that biblical word *shalom*, *Called Together* notes agreement that "the Gospel's vision of peace includes active non-violence for the defence of human life and human rights, for the promotion of economic justice for the poor, and in the interest of fostering solidarity among peoples" (§177–78). In fact, "We hold the conviction in common that reconciliation, nonviolence, and active peacemaking belong to the heart of the Gospel (§179). The implication that this must shape the vocations of all Christians as well as to the ministry of the church as a whole is clear: "Christian peace witness belongs integrally to our walk as followers of Christ and to the life of the Church as 'the household of God' and 'a dwelling place of God in the Spirit'" (§181). Such a conclusion is unavoidable, since

> discipleship, understood as following Christ in life in accordance with the teaching and example of Jesus, is basic to the Christian life. The earthly existence of Jesus is normative for human well being. . . . The decisions Jesus made and the steps he took leading to his crucifixion reveal the centrality of love, including love of enemy, in human life. (§180)

To be sure, saying that something is a norm does leave open the possibility of legitimate exceptions, and that of course is what the Catholic Church continues to do by affirming that war and military action may sometimes be justifiable in defense of the innocent (§187). But nothing in the consensus that *Called Together to be Peacemakers* names can justify exceptions to the call to follow Christ as disciples, to the vocation of peacemaking, or to the obligation to learn and practice active nonviolence as first resort and persistent response.

The working, minimal definition of a peace church that I propose to get us started, then, is this:

> A church that wishes to affirm its identity as a peace church must be striving to make active nonviolence normative in both the moral and the sociological senses of that word. In its teaching it

must be making clear that active nonviolence in the face of evil and injustice is morally normative for all Christians. And in its programming it must be cultivating the skillsets and virtues needed for active nonviolence to start becoming sociologically and statistically normative in*deed*.

This is not to suggest that the Roman Catholic Church may already dare to call itself a peace church. But it is to suggest the sense in which it may already be on its way to becoming a peace church. And it is to say that for now, on the way to becoming a peace church, resolving centuries of debate over whether Christian participation in warfare can ever be justifiable is *not* the most urgent Catholic task. For there is really no point debating whether a church can claim to be peace church yet allow for the justified use of violence in exceptional circumstances, unless and until such a church at least has the skills and sociology to make "exceptional" recourse to violence truly exceptional.[20] It must be a community in which peacemaking is becoming "church-wide and parish-deep." Becoming such a church, such a people of peace, is our primary task.

In any case, however much Christian pacifists either outside or inside the Roman Catholic Church may lament its long association with the just-war theory, a frontal attack in hopes of outright renunciation may not be wise and is probably not even necessary. What is far more likely to happen—and arguably is happening already—is that the just-war theory go the way of capital punishment. In theory, according to Pope John Paul II, capital punishment may have been legitimate in some historical circumstances where societies have had no other way to protect themselves. But that "may be" was effectively a past-tense "might have been," because the church's authoritative teachers could no longer imagine circumstances in modern societies where such conditions obtain.[21] Indeed, Pope Francis has now ruled out capital punishment altogether.[22] The theory justifying capital punishment may long have lingered, but in the modern world it became an empty set. We got a snapshot of this same process at work in relation to war when Cardinal Joseph Ratzinger, the future Pope Benedict XVI, suggested that because modern weaponry so seldom limits its destruction to combatants alone, "today we should be asking ourselves if it is still licit to admit the very existence of a 'just war.'"[23]

"Catholic"

To be sure, I bear no illusions about the cultural and theological inertia that the Roman Catholic Church must overcome if it is to become a globally catholic peace church in its normative practice as well as its normative teaching. But I still believe this is possible. And certainly I hear the magisterium or teaching authority of the church calling us to go there. I write primarily in service to the *Catholic* Church, therefore—my fellow Catholic Christians, our pastors, our bishops, and our shared witness.

Still, my hopes are also more widely *catholic*, in two ways. First, I hope that what I write will prove helpful and persuasive to other Christians as well. At one point I played with the idea of making the subtitle of this book "becoming a catholic peace church," with a lowercase *catholic* as a way to echo and extend my years of regular prayer "for the unity and nonviolence of all Christians." Eventually I dismissed this idea not only because it seemed a little too cute, but because it seemed a little less than honest. I would not be a Roman Catholic if I did not believe that the ministry of the bishop of Rome plays a unique role as sign and instrument of unity among all Christians. The second way that my hope is *catholic*, therefore, is indirect. All that the Roman Catholic Church does to become a global peace church—whether in its leadership or whether from its grassroots—will contribute in unique and indispensable ways to the shared catholic witness of all Christians and to greater unity among their churches.

Thus I will not be overly fastidious about when I am attending to the Roman *Catholic Church* and when to Christ's *Church Catholic*. Nor will I make it my task to take a stand concerning the exact relationship between these two overlapping realities. The Roman Catholic Church is on a still-unfinished pilgrimage, of course, and not just because the Second Vatican Council described the church theologically as a pilgrim people. Always aware of itself as an international body crossing ethnic, cultural, and political boundaries to in some way embrace the *katholikos* or universal whole, in the modern world Catholicism is confronting more than ever the realities of globalization and its own reality as a global church. It struggles as never before to figure out how to inculturate the Gospel—that is, express and embody the Christian message in ways appropriate to specific cultures—while also naming and embodying the oneness that churches in all cultures share. It has committed itself to deepening church unity through ecumenical dialogue, cooperation, and mutual admonition with other Christian churches. And it knows that its journey of widening relationships both among Christians and with all people of good will across the globe requires concrete practices of solidarity in the context of human need and struggle for dignity. Learning how to do inculturation, ecumenism, and solidarity well as a global community often feels disquieting on the inside and looks messy from the outside. But that is part of the pilgrimage.

This messy process of pilgrimage is itself the work of peacemaking and constitutes a witness. Sometimes despite themselves, therefore, all but the most fundamentalist and anti-Catholic Christians in other traditions often care deeply about what happens in the Roman Catholic Church. Vatican II was a global event. Each in his own way, all popes in the Vatican-II era have been world figures, alternately as prophets challenging the world's cultures of death or as pastors inspiring efforts to build cultures of life and peace among nations. Catholic liberation theology has inspired Christians across many traditions in their own struggles for social justice; Catholic insistence on respect for human life from conception to natural death has inspired Christians across many traditions as well. Holding all such issues together in defense of human dignity, Catholic social teaching has called Christians inside and outside of the Catholic fold toward that consistency to which we all need to hold ourselves accountable if we are to practice a consistent ethic of life. So as a friend of mine has observed, "People often say that the Catholic Church moves at a glacial pace, but when glaciers move they reshape the face of the earth."

To envision and contribute to the day when the Roman Catholic Church will more decisively and self-consciously become a globally catholic peace church, therefore, is one of the most important things any Christian peacebuilder or Christian peace theologian can do in hopes of a united Christian witness for peace. Certainly this work should help overcome specific church divisions at least vis-à-vis the historic peace churches. But it should also contribute more generally to a global Christian solidarity that creates conditions for the possibility that Christianity as a whole might yet constitute a catholic peace church.

"Becoming"

The most important story of "becoming" in this book is communitarian and ecclesial, not individual. It is the story of how the Roman Catholic Church has been becoming a peace church on its pilgrimage through the modern world, and how it might best continue that pilgrimage. Its genre is decidedly first-person plural, therefore, not first-person singular.

Still, I would not be telling that story if I had not found myself well positioned to witness it, to serve now as a witness *to* it, and perhaps to extend it. One of the subplots to this story has been an emerging conversation with one historic peace church, the Mennonites. And I am a Mennonite who, without burning my bridges back from the tradition that formed me, has become a Roman Catholic. I am in fact a cofounder of Bridgefolk, a movement for grassroots ecumenical dialogue between Mennonites and Catholics. Bridgefolk has dedicated itself above all to an "exchange of gifts" between the two traditions. So although the preoccupations I have carried with me in becoming a "Mennonite Catholic" are not the story here, and this book is hardly a memoir, recognizing those preoccupations may help situate the reader, as they have situated me, to trace out the church's larger and still unfinished story of becoming.

Mennonites are now spread throughout many cultures around the globe, with Mennonite service and peacemaking projects extending well beyond their own churches. Thus it can be misleading to summarize what Mennonites have often referred to as their "peace position" by citing their best-known North American theologians alone. And yet one important driver for that very global extension has been the desire of those in churches sometimes known as "the quiet in the land" to prove they could be faithful to their identity in a way less quiet and less withdrawn. For these Mennonites, a distinctively countercultural commitment to follow Jesus did not have to mean withdrawing from engagement with larger societal engagement or service to the world. That has often been the accusation against them, after all. In times of military conflict, general pressures to assimilate have taken on a particular edge in the charge that if they remained pacifists and conscientious objectors, Mennonites would be "shirkers." In response, legally recognized forms of alternative service during times of military conscription have coupled with the psychological need for Mennonites to prove themselves. These dynamics have in turn fueled various forms of mission work, relief and development work, on-the-ground peacebuilding, and eventually political advocacy for justice and peace.

One particular version of the "shirker" charge, however, has especially haunted Mennonite theologians and other intellectuals—that of the influential American Protestant thinker Reinhold Niebuhr. Something of a pacifist as a young pastor, Niebuhr changed his mind and went on to argue that any Christian who would renounce the power politics, coercive tools, and threat of violence that govern the life of all but the smallest face-to-face societies must also renounce any hope of being political relevant or claim to be socially responsible.[24] Unlike many theologians through the centuries who had concluded that Christians might be justified in taking up lethal arms in some situations, Niebuhr did not try to deny that Jesus' ethic of love taught otherwise; he simply argued that Jesus had not anticipated all the moral questions his followers would face if their movement lasted for centuries, and that ethics was not the core message of Christianity anyway. This left Mennonites with a conundrum: unlike centuries of persecutors and other opponents, Niebuhr complimented them for essentially interpreting Jesus' teachings aright— but the price for accepting this compliment would be to admit that they really had no place speaking to public affairs and should accept that they were socially irresponsible.

Niebuhr's challenge has shaped the careers of three successive generations of Mennonite thinkers—and counting. Guy F. Hershberger provided the core Mennonite response already in the 1940s. As a sociologist and historian, Hershberger accepted much of Niebuhr's social analysis, but he argued that the charge of social irresponsibility was unwarranted. There were many ways that a church committed to Jesus' nonviolent ethic of love could actually be more rather than less socially responsible, after all, by providing a laboratory for new responses to social needs and by contributing to the moral texture of society that nurtured democratic values. Hershberger's student John Howard Yoder continued to elaborate on this core response as Mennonites began to participate in coalitions with other kinds of nonviolent activists in opposing racial injustice, a succession of wars, and the nuclear arms race. Yoder pointed to empirically verifiable ways in which, as he put it, "those who bear crosses are working with the grain of the universe."[25] Groups lacking access to the reins of power are often the true agents of social change. The apparent powerlessness of their minority status allows them to forge creative pilot projects, which demonstrate patterns of equity and reconciliation or service for the common good that society-at-large may later adopt. The success of these prophetic or creative minorities is not guaranteed, of course; the very power of their witness may elicit a reaction on the part of those who benefit from status quo structures of power. But to hold fast to the ways of justice without resorting to violence in the defense of one's cause, thus suffering unjustly, is to unleash yet another recognizable form of power—the power of martyrdom—by which the witness of a small committed group or even a single individual will sometimes do more to turn the tide of history than all the battalions arrayed to stifle them, as they hold fast to their moral convictions even at the cost of their own death.[26] Yet another generation of Mennonite thinkers has noted that even in times that do not immediately demand moral heroism, the work of maintaining public order and true security arguably belongs far less to warriors than to all the quieter unobtrusive actors who knit together and sustain bonds of social trust based not on the logic of scarcity or threat but abundance and generosity.[27]

All of this I found convincing as a Mennonite and continue to find convincing as a Catholic. It has helped that figures such as the Rev. Dr. Martin Luther King Jr. persuaded Hershberger that Gandhian nonviolence could faithfully express the Jesus ethic. Thus, succeeding generations of more progressive Mennonites at least have shifted the accent in what Hershberger had called "biblical nonresistance" to "active nonviolence."[28] And if anything, encounters with Catholic social thought have deepened my confidence in the transformative social power of creative minorities—especially since I met it in the ringing call by Brazilian Archbishop Dom Hélder Câmara that "Abrahamic minorities unite!"[29] Whatever the sectarian tendencies of Mennonites historically, then, I do not believe either that sectarianism is essential to Mennonite theology and social ethics or that a commitment to principled nonviolence must necessarily render a Christian community socially irresponsible at all.

No, the problem with Mennonite social ethics lies not then in failure but in success—the challenge all social movements face when they actually start to win, a challenge that Mennonites now share as they move into coalitions with broader movements for peace and social justice. This challenge is a largely unacknowledged lacuna in peace studies and nonviolent social theory. While mainstream history and political science have too often ignored the track record by which nonviolent strategies have been key to overthrowing tyrannies of all sorts in the twentieth century,[30] what to do the next day is less clear. Proponents of active nonviolence have shown that they can successfully carry out the double negative of resisting evil, but have rarely faced the question of how they will positively govern without at least a circumscribed last resort to lethal force by the police. If anything, activists can get so used to the double-negative work of "deconstructing" ideologies of oppression, critiquing from the margin, and being prophetic, that they go through a serious identity crisis when they "speak truth to power" and the powerful actually start to listen. Without accounting for the positive role that institutions generally and government particularly have to play in building peaceful societies that share in the common good, Christian pacifists and others committed to principled nonviolence become disoriented when they have a chance to roll up their sleeves and help administer the very changes for which they have been calling. If my own "becoming" has drawn me toward the wider resources of Catholic social teaching, forced me to explore the need at least for "just policing," and fruitfully complicated the question of how Christians are to situate themselves in the world, this is part of why I find it both possible to remain Mennonite in very important ways, yet impossible to be only Mennonite. Precisely in seeking to be faithful to the Mennonite tradition—not in rejecting it—I have found myself becoming both catholic and Catholic.

Many different developments from the Catholic side have made this possible, of course. Though I entered the Catholic Church at Pentecost 2004, in retrospect the worldwide church that gathered through its bishops at the Second Vatican Council had become the horizon of my Christian life decades before. Pope John XXIII's prayer for Pentecostal renewal as he opened the council, liturgical reform as it both impacted other communions and made the Eucharist comprehensible to someone like me, continuing development of Catholic social teaching in the face of modern challenges, fresh reflection on how the Gospel takes shape in diverse cultures not just Western ones—all this offered me hope and guidance already as a Mennonite. But one particular change at Vatican II was critical. The way into full communion with the Roman Catholic Church would probably not have opened for me at all were it not for the council's invitation that the church "undertake a completely fresh reappraisal of war."[31] One thread running through all of these developments, both Mennonite and Catholic, has been a widening global consciousness. With it has come a deepening sense of the reality but also the challenge of being a global church. The challenge is to deepen bonds of solidarity across borders and cultures, of course. But it is also to do this while avoiding the local devastations that too often come in the name of globalism.

"Think globally, work locally" is a good slogan for encouraging global consciousness, not least because it hints at a crucial warning. To think globally but then to set out to work *globally rather than locally* can actually be a quite dangerous wellspring of injustice. As essayist Scott Russell Sanders once stated matters so eloquently,

> If you are not yourself *placed*, then you wander the world like a sightseer, a collector of sensations, with no gauge for measuring what you see. Local knowledge is the grounding for global knowledge. Those who care about nothing beyond the confines of their parish are in truth parochial, and are at least mildly dangerous to their parish; on the other hand, those who *have* no parish, those who navigate ceaselessly among postal zones and area codes, those for whom the world is only a smear of highways and bank accounts and stores, are a danger not just to their parish but to the planet.[32]

The greatest injustices of the last century have come in the name of total, universal solutions. Regimes bearing the label of totalitarianism have only been the most famous and obvious. After all, the system of global capitalism that has succeeded them may be all the more totalizing precisely because it is subtler; in the name of freedom it seems able to corrode and homogenize traditional communities and their particular cultural identities in every crevice of every continent. Because my own pilgrimage and preoccupations began in the particularity of a religious community with a strong sense of communal identity that sought to resist assimilation—yet whose very narrative of Christian service to other communities also impelled it out into widening relationships of global solidarity—local- and global-mindedness have combined into a passionate sensitivity to the vulnerability of other traditional communities as well.

So if I am seeking to integrate Mennonite and Catholic ethics and ecclesiologies, doing either or both requires the integration of much more as well. If I have any particular theological methodology, it is to practice theology as a ministry of reconciliation. It is to exercise a hermeneutic of suspicion when necessary but a hermeneutic of charity always. Thus it is to explore how we might reconcile the truths embedded even in positions and traditions one may find suspect. Specifically in the present project, it is to ask how best to hold together:

- an ethic of witness too often dismissed as sectarian

- with an ethic of responsibility too easily discounted as establishmentarian;

- the practice of missionary proclamation and service

- with respect for cultural integrity;

- a globalism that avoids being blindsided by its own covert imperialism

- with local particularities that are rich, thick, and loyal yet that avoid both tribalism and the repression of their members in the name of group conformity;

- practices of peacemaking grounded in Christ's call to love our enemies

- with a nonviolence toward the truth that extends even to those who differ about how to treat enemies.

All of this would be overly ambitious if I thought I had to forge syntheses myself in order to reconcile each of these tensive pairs. But somehow in my early theological formation, Archbishop Câmara's clarion call for Abrahamic minorities to unite answered my Mennonite searching—and seized me with a simple yet complex idea. *Abrahamic community.* The call of Abraham in Genesis 12:1-3 marks God's very launching of salvation history, according to many scholars. Abraham and his children are called out and blessed, yet God's pur-

Introduction: Key Terms, Assumptions, and Other Preliminaries 23

pose remains the blessing of all families of the earth. Thus, the deep grammar of the biblical drama gets set. As I wrote many years ago,

> An Abrahamic community is one that celebrates the calling and grace that has shaped its identity, yet knows instinctively that it cannot hoard this "blessing" for itself without losing that identity. After all, God calls it to be a people-for-others as its Lord was the person-for-others. It negotiates the path of faithfulness between the twin temptations of exclusiveness and dissipation [or assimilation]. It must engage boldly in the world without acculturating so fully that it no longer has anything distinct to offer. Yet it must not maintain its distinction by barricading itself against the challenges, needs, and needy ones for whom God has called it together. Ultimately it finds and sustains its identity by "dying to itself," by putting its very identity at risk through its service to other communities.[33]

This call is what continues to set God's people on pilgrimage. It is the deep grammar that guides their pilgrimage. It is the pattern that allows them—indeed requires them—to hold many creative tensions together. One of those tensions is between the "already" and the "not yet" of their incomplete pilgrimage, of course. In their not-yet-ness they so often find such tension uncomfortable and latch on to only one pole of a creative tension. But in their already-ness, they become a visible sign of that invisible reality that Jesus proclaimed as the kingdom of God. In other words, they become what Vatican II called the sacrament of human salvation. And in this meantime, I believe, it is the very grammar of Abrahamic community that holds apparently contending Christian impulses and traditions together.

"Pilgrim people" aka diaspora

And that in turn is why I employ a final concept. There is a sociological term for the kind of "in but not of" existence that participates in the common good of larger societies even while celebrating a distinct identity and resisting the assimilation that would fritter away what a community has most to contribute. But it also is a historical term that taps into precisely the narrative of pilgrim peoplehood that has formed the people called church. That term is *diaspora*.

Even some of my most sympathetic readers have asked whether I should look for a more immediately accessible and inviting term than "diaspora." The history into which it taps is of course that of the Jewish people, the archetypal diaspora that has lent other diasporas the name. As contemporary Jewish thinkers Daniel and Jonathan Boyarin have written, Judaism's centuries of life in diaspora over the last two millennia reflect something basic to its very character—an analogue and an extension of the nomadic life in which Judaism was formed. Territorial control, statehood, and even the biblical Davidic monarchy have been experiments and exceptions, not norms, the Boyarins have argued, for there is "a sense in which Israel was born in exile."[34] Yet that is why even a friendly reader may worry that a call for Christians to recognize themselves also as properly a diaspora people might be off-putting. Exile is never initially welcome. If Jewish diaspora is the archetypical diaspora that many associate first with the word, well, who wants to be hounded around various continents, over many centuries, bereft of an abiding homeland?

What gets lost in that first reaction is how rich a place of social and cultural creativity life in diaspora turns out to be. To be sure, the word *diaspora* has carried ambivalence and paradox with it from the beginning. Linguistically, that beginning is Deuteronomy 28:25 in the Greek translation from Hebrew known as the Septuagint. The passage warns Israel of all the calamities it will suffer if it is unfaithful to God's Law, including flight in every direction, such that the people become a scattering, dispersal—or in Greek, a *diaspora*—among all the kingdoms of the earth. A tough pill to swallow, in the first instance, no doubt. And we should never forget that exile and diaspora have often been forced upon the Jewish people by oppressive and anti-Semitic regimes, including "Christian" ones. Yet here is the creative paradox: Whatever its tragic beginnings, diaspora is often a place of rich cultural life.

We have the Hebrew Scripture or *Tanakh* itself, for example, because Jewish scholars began to codify their oral traditions in exile in Babylon in the sixth and fifth centuries BCE. In turn the Septuagint translation into Greek responded a few centuries later to the needs of diaspora communities spread throughout the Mediterranean, from their intellectual center in Alexandria, Egypt. Still later, in the first

Introduction: Key Terms, Assumptions, and Other Preliminaries   25

centuries of the Common Era, the final compilation of rabbinical commentary and debates known as the *Talmud* was the product of Jewish scholarship in Babylon. The rich and often feisty literary traditions of this first "people of the book" have in turn issued in an exceptional level of Jewish contributions to artistic, musical, and philosophical culture not least in the very European civilization that so often despised it.

My considered judgment, then, is that "diaspora" is simply and unavoidably the best and most accurate term—conceptually, theologically, sociologically, and globally—for framing who we are, where we are, and where we need to go as a Christian people.

Conceptually, "diaspora" summarizes and holds together so many of the creative "both-and" tensions that Christian social ethics must map if we are to understand our situation and our calling in the world. Christian theologians have engaged in long-standing debates over particulars and universals; over the disruptive message of the biblical narrative with a cross at its center and the natural law by which this message nonetheless responds to the deepest human longings of all peoples; over how "Christ" transforms "culture"; over how to hold convictions firmly while opening to the truths of others generously; and on and on. Reflecting the deep grammar of the biblical narrative while responding to the contemporary tasks of the church in a globalizing world, "diaspora" commends itself with the elegance of a conceptual framework that has the power to interlace what is right about all of these theological emphases and concerns.

Theologically, though, there always comes a point in Christian proclamation when we must face for ourselves and proclaim to others a call to repentance. "The mere fact of [the church] being a diaspora on this planet has had to be gradually admitted," wrote leading Catholic theologian Karl Rahner, SJ, already in the early 1960s. Yet, he continued, Christians "have still not fully wakened from our dream of a homogeneous Christian West. . . . It seems to me that much depends on our fully and freely recognizing this fact and courageously accepting its consequences."[35] Yes, a call for Catholics and other Christians to embrace life in diaspora on their way to becoming a truly catholic peace church will be disruptive and discomforting at points. But if we are to be honest about the Gospel, the good news we claim to bear, none of the packaging we rightly do in order to make the Gospel inviting and accessible dare hide the pain we sometimes need to accept on the way to fresh opportunities and indeed to new life. Thankfully, we can still, always, do so in hope and mercy because the promise of resurrection lies on the other side of the cross. In this faith we save our life by risking its loss for Christ, we receive by giving, and we find our true selves by living our baptisms in the stripping off of self-deceived selves. And yet find, receive, and live we do.

Sociologically, one specific reason that repentance is necessary on the way to peace is that the Christians of Christendom in many of its historic forms only *seem* to have settled, and wrongly dare to think of their settled states as normative Christianity. This is the false settledness that comes to identify Christian faith, culture, and community with one's own nation, kind, or tribe. To embrace life in diaspora, therefore, is to loosen the grip of that force that has most often turned Christians away from the call to be a peaceable, peacemaking people—the tribalistic and nationalistic identities that come to trump our baptismal citizenship in the transnational people called church and to override our primary loyalty to its Lord, the Suffering Servant of all peoples.

And *globally*, Christians of the Global South are reminding us more pointedly than ever that the settledness of older Western forms of Christendom cannot be the norm. Christians of the Global South have their own temptations, of course. The great scandal of the genocide in Rwanda of the 1990s, for example, is that in a country that is one of the most Christianized in Africa, tribal identities trumped Christian identity. Still, what historian Philip Jenkins has called "the next Christendom"[36] is well on its way, as the axis of global Christianity shifts decisively toward the Southern hemisphere. How new bonds of global Christian society—which is the proper, abiding meaning of "Christendom"—will take shape, we are only beginning to fathom. But almost surely, they will have to take shape not as territories but as overlapping communities and networks that cross the borders of nation-states. As I will argue, we are all in diaspora anyway now, so we might as well make sense of it.

That said, it would certainly be presumptuous of me to claim that what follows speaks from and for the situation of Christians in the Global South. My perspective is more Western than I might like, and inevitably I have been shaped more than I might wish by debates among North American Christians. Still, I am pretty sure that, far from being put off by a formulation of Christian social ethics and a reading of Catholic social teaching that uses "diaspora" as a framing device, many leaders from churches of the Global South will find it recognizable and appropriate. As I elaborate upon diaspora, therefore, my hope is that I am at least exercising solidarity from my part of the global Catholic Church to others.

PART I

Becoming Catholic Again for the First Time

My thesis is this: In so far as our outlook is really based on today and looking towards tomorrow, the present situation of Christians can be characterized as that of a diaspora; and this signifies, in terms of the history of salvation, a "must," from which we may and must draw conclusions about our behavior as Christians.

—Karl Rahner, SJ, "The Present Situation of Christians" (1961)

Above all the Gospel must be proclaimed by witness. Take a Christian or a handful of Christians who, in the midst of their own community, show their capacity for understanding and acceptance, their sharing of life and destiny with other people, their solidarity with the efforts of all for whatever is noble and good. Let us suppose that, in addition, they radiate in an altogether simple and unaffected way their faith in values that go beyond current values, and their hope in something that is not seen and that one would not dare to imagine. Through this wordless witness these Christians stir up irresistible questions in the hearts of those who see how they live. . . . Such a witness is already a silent proclamation of the Good News and a very powerful and effective one. Here we have an initial act of evangelization. The above questions will [be asked, whether by] people to whom Christ has never been proclaimed, or baptized people who do not practice, or people who live as nominal Christians but according to principles that are in no way Christian. . . .

All Christians are called to this witness, and in this way they can be real evangelizers. We are thinking especially of the responsibility incumbent on immigrants in the country that receives them.

—Pope Paul VI, *Evangelii Nuntiandi* (1975)

Chapter 2

Taking Catholic Social Teaching into Diaspora

> Above all the Gospel must be proclaimed by witness. Take a Christian or a handful of Christians who, in the midst of their own community, show their capacity for understanding and acceptance, their sharing of life and destiny with other people, their solidarity with the efforts of all for whatever is noble and good. . . . All Christians are called to this witness, and in this way they can be real evangelizers. *We are thinking especially of the responsibility incumbent on immigrants in the country that receives them.*
>
> Pope Paul VI, *Evangelii Nuntiandi* §21 (emphasis added)

Pope Paul VI would seem to have left us something of an "Easter egg." For computer programmers, filmmakers, and their aficionados, an Easter egg has come to refer to a hidden message or feature, the promise of which entices dedicated users to go deep into a game, or viewers to pay keen attention. The papal puzzle is this: As Paul VI penned an apostolic exhortation in 1975 to guide the church's evangelization and mission work, his thoughts turned "especially" to immigrant Christian communities and their special responsibilities. Why?

The occasion for Pope Paul's *Evangelii Nuntiandi*—or in English, *Evangelization in the Modern World*—provides certain clues. Significantly, the release date for the apostolic exhortation was December 8, 1975, a decade to the day after the close of the Second Vatican Council, that momentous gathering of bishops from around the world that had sought to guide the Roman Catholic Church into a new relationship with the modern world. Vatican II had indeed opened up the church in various ways, but after ten years of changes both invigorating and disorienting for Catholics, it was time for some clarifications. The council's declaration committing the church to interreligious dialogue, *Nostra Aetate*, had assured people of other faiths that it recognized all that was true in their religious traditions, and affirmed that those faiths can aid anyone who authentically seeks a saving relationship with God.[1] So then, did Catholics still need to proclaim the Gospel, and if so, how to do so in a respectful manner? Likewise, the council's Pastoral Constitution on the Church in the Modern World, *Gaudium et Spes*, had promised to accompany humankind "unreservedly" in a spirit of solidarity amid the exciting discoveries and troubling perplexities of modern life.[2] But didn't friendly accompaniment and a willingness to affirm all that was life-giving about the exciting discoveries of modern culture sometimes require the church to resist modernity too, at points? The twentieth century had shown that technological achievement could "recoil" against humanity, after all, and accelerate ancient patterns of violence and exploitation.[3] In these and many other cases, the challenge for Christians was to simultaneously challenge and affirm—to somehow be both countercultural and pro-cultural at the same time.

Paul VI left other clues as to why he may have been thinking "especially" of immigrant Christian communities as a preeminent model for all Christian witness in *Evangelii Nuntiandi*. The only footnote in section 21, where he left us his Easter egg of a remark, takes us back to challenges facing Christian communities in the centuries before they gained official acceptance from the Roman emperor Constantine. Early Christian apologists such as Tertullian and Minucius Felix, to whom the footnote referred, had needed to explain the faith and practice of fledgling Christian communities in the face of questions both curious and scandalized. Likewise, according to Pope Paul, the ways that a Christian community embodies its faith and mutual love today through acts of solidarity, both within churches and within the larger society that hosts them, should continue to provide occasions for verbalizing and explaining the Christian faith. To make that point, however, Pope Paul had mined near a deep vein in early Christian thought, in which some of the most influential of Christian thinkers (the "church fathers" or "patristic" theologians) had explicitly thought of themselves as a people living as though in exile, spread through many nations, yet all the more loyal to the one commonwealth of humanity as a whole.[4]

And so—whether deliberately or inadvertently or through the mysterious inspiration of the Holy Spirit—Pope Paul VI had diaspora on his mind. Appropriating words of Jesus (John 17:11 paired with John 15:19) Christians have often spoken of themselves as called to be "in the world but not of the world." An appropriate aphorism for all Christians, this in-but-not-of experience is daily, concrete, and existential for any new immigrant community, Christian or otherwise, at least when it continues to identify with a homeland elsewhere. This is what diaspora is. Derived from the Greek word for "dispersal," diaspora is the social pattern by which members of a community, ethnic group, or even a nation that is separated from (or that never has had) a nation-state of its own, now lives scattered among many nations, yet seeks to maintain some kind of group cohesion.[5] Unless its members are trying to assimilate and melt into another society as quickly as they can, their challenge is to structure their common life in hundreds of ways, small and large, according to the primary allegiance of one identity, while respecting and winning the respect of a host society that has its own laws, customs, and expectations. Sometimes this means conflict. Sometimes this means service. Always it requires faithful narration of the community's story, and careful navigation of competing demands.

Could this be a clue? Indeed it is—a clue for how *all* Christian communities, not just immigrant communities, are to be a living witness to the Gospel, a people of peace that serves the world in justice, a people that knows how to explain itself to itself and to others, a people with a supple and coherent social ethic, a people that knows and celebrates its primary identity as a community of redeemed disciples of Jesus Christ, a people nonetheless aware that to follow a crucified Lord means that the faithful can only preserve such an identity by putting it at risk on behalf of others as they travel through the many times and cultures of history. A pilgrim people.

Four interlocking theses

Indeed, only a church that embraces life in diaspora can be a global Catholic peace church. An adequately Catholic theology of peace depends on deepening the church's self-identification as a truly global people that has loosened every nationalistic loyalty, sees itself as living in diaspora among other nations, but is all the more prepared to serve the common good of every nation thereby. Amid all the interlocking arguments in the pages that follow, and all of the ethical practices to which they will point, these convictions will serve as their guiding center.

And become a peace church more truly we must. Reflecting on how the heroic nonviolent witness of "many Pastors, entire Christian communities, individual members of the faithful, and other people of good will" had unexpectedly ended the Cold War, brought down a totalitarian empire in 1989, and offered hope of peaceful change around the world through "dialogue and solidarity, rather than . . . struggle to destroy the enemy through war," Pope John Paul II insisted that actually, such efforts are not simply for a heroic few at all: "This is, in fact, a responsibility which falls not only to the citizens of the countries in question, but to all Christians and people of good will."[6] Bishops in one part of the world captured that conviction in a pastoral letter soon afterward when they wrote,

> Our biblical heritage and our body of tradition make the vocation of peacemaking mandatory. Authentic prayer, worship and sacramental life challenge us to conversion of our hearts and summon us to works of peace. These concerns are obviously not ours alone, but are the work of the entire community of faith and of all people of good will.[7]

So how shall a distinct "community of faith" work together with "all people of good will" for peace? The beauty and possibility of life in diaspora is that it simultaneously grounds a people in their core identity *and* opens them up to cultural engagement in endlessly and wonderfully diverse settings. More than either scriptural proof-text or rational syllogism, what will thus offer the ultimate warrant for the theology and ethics in this book will be the overarching coherence of the interlocking arguments and the practical wisdom that these pages offer as they demonstrate the capacity to guide Christians through multiple puzzles and life situations. Appropriate to life in diaspora, the argumentation that follows must necessarily be at once complex yet simple[8]—wide-ranging yet looping back home.

The simplicity-within-complexity of what follows should be quite manageable for readers if they notice now, and then continue to bear in mind, how our core thesis works in tandem with three others:

> Christian moral theology in general, and Catholic social teaching in particular, has always been stretching toward the challenges of global solidarity; this may only have become obvious in the age of globalization, but that is now merely *obvious*, not *new*.
>
> For a church that calls itself catholic and names its very presence in the world as the sacrament of human salvation, how to be a global church in the age of globalization and how to *be* a social ethic in accord with Catholic social teaching are virtually the same question.
>
> In order to be Catholic in deed and not just in name, a global church must be a peace church, committed to engendering the virtues necessary to practice normative nonviolence and extend active love to enemies.

So it is that we loop back to the core thesis:

> *Only a church that embraces life in diaspora can be a global Catholic peace church—or really a truly catholic Catholic Church at all.*

Indeed, as we embark, the burden of the book's opening chapters will be to show why each of these four theses entails the others. Globalization is merely making obvious something that has always been true of Christ's church: Namely, we are properly a diaspora people and must embrace this identity in order to practice Christian love of neighbor through global solidarity in all the ways to which Catholic social teaching has been calling us, thus to become a catholic peace church.

In one way, therefore, this book is an introduction to what Catholic social teaching has always been about. But in another way it is a constructive proposal for how Catholic social teaching must work itself out in practice. New appropriations of ancient Christian insights are especially necessary, after all, considering that "close ties of dependence between individuals and peoples are on the increase world-wide nowadays," as the Second Vatican Council described globalization before that term came into wide circulation.[9]

In one way, this book is very much in the genre of Christian social ethics. But in another way, this book's very approach to social ethics requires it to anticipate inculturating the fullness of the Gospel by learning to be church in many and diverse cultures, and thus "the sacrament of human salvation" within history.

In one way, this book builds that proposal by arguing that the only viable way both to be a global church and a peace church is through a social ethic that embraces life amid diaspora. Indeed, it invites us to do so in celebratory rather than grudging fashion. Such a calling invites us to share the peace of Christ in the world by working actively and nonviolently in collaboration with all people of good will, while keeping our primary loyalty clear. For in another way, this book builds that proposal by arguing that the Vatican and the Catholic faithful alike will be following through on the trajectory of recent popes who have been leading them to confirm their age-old calling to be a people of peace.

Catholic peace theology: quiet, relentless, developing

"Once again, no one noticed." Hinting at frustration, so remarked Drew Christiansen, SJ, in 2008 as he surveyed the developing commitment to peacemaking within Catholic social teaching. In a 1991 encyclical commemorating a hundred years of such teaching in the modern Catholic Church as well as the events that led to the end of the Soviet empire in 1989, Pope John Paul II had recognized active nonviolence as the decisive factor in those events, and endorsed it as relevant to public affairs—"but no one seemed to notice." Two years later, Catholic bishops in the United States had followed up with a pastoral letter that "identified nonviolence as the foundation of Catholic teaching on war and peace and argued it should be the basis of a state ethic as well as of personal witness." This was nothing short of "a genuine shift in teaching." But "once again, no one noticed."[10]

Of course, that is not quite right. Christiansen himself had noticed. As former director of the Office of International Justice and Peace for the U.S. Conference of Catholic Bishops, and later editor-in-chief of the influential Jesuit magazine *America*, few people have traced the subtle yet remarkable changes in official Catholic teaching with regard to the ethics of war and the Christian vocation of peacemaking more carefully than he.¹¹ Since the role of the *magisterium* (or teaching authority) in the Roman Catholic Church is usually to ratify a doctrinal or moral consensus that has emerged from the grassroots of the church and benefited from experiences in many locales, Christiansen did not believe that Catholic peacebuilders should expect an encyclical or other high-level papal document to provide an authoritative teaching on peace and war just yet.¹² Still, having traced a clear line of official teaching that has been developing since decades prior to the Second Vatican Council in the early 1960s, Christiansen had no doubt that a significant evolution is underway.

The Vatican has, if anything, led the way toward an increasingly restrictive use of the church's tradition of just-war analysis, Christiansen has argued. Active nonviolence as a means of resisting evil has gained increasing respect and urgency. Indeed, a presumption against war and in favor of nonviolence is the common ground that undergirds what Christiansen sees as "a hybrid of just-war and nonviolent components, with the honest exhaustion of nonviolent means a necessary requirement for use of force in the last resort."¹³ If the use of violent military force is ever justifiable, the only clear reason that remains for intervention appears to be to thwart genocide and other egregious violations of human rights. While the Vatican does continue to recognize the right of nation-states to defend themselves through military means, national self-defense is receiving far less emphasis. And if active nonviolence has a role to play not only among individuals and in social movements but in public affairs, so too does forgiveness, however reluctant governments are to apologize or vindictive cultures to forgive.

The Vatican II watershed

As with much else in the twentieth-century Roman Catholic Church, the Second Vatican Council that gathered the world's bishops from 1962 through 1965 was a watershed for Catholic peace theology. Multiple streams flow into and shape any watershed, however, then exit in a wider stream or even a new river. The devastations of two world wars and the specter of nuclear war had already led Popes Pius XII and John XXIII to condemn "total war" as morally indefensible, given its indiscriminate effects on entire populations and not simply combatants.¹⁴ In the very weeks of 1962 in which the council opened, the Cuban Missile Crisis brought the world as close to the brink of nuclear annihilation as ever before or since. As men who had come of age amid world war, leading cardinals at the council had witnessed firsthand the horrors of modern warfare. Even the leader of a conservative bloc of cardinals famous for resisting most Vatican II developments—Cardinal Alfredo Ottaviani, head of the Holy Office and successor to the Inquisition—passionately urged the council to make the strongest possible condemnation of modern war and drew a long, thunderous applause.[15]

To be sure, when the council formally called for "the avoidance of war" in its pastoral constitution, *Gaudium et Spes*, it was far from ready to reject its long-standing tradition of thinking deliberately about what might or might not justify warfare. That framework of just-war theory is quite sufficient to offer a devastating critique of the devastations of modern war. Saturation bombing of entire cities during World War II had already demonstrated the indiscriminate character of modern warfare, even before the advent of the atomic age.[16] And when warfare fails to meet criteria needed to qualify as just war, it really can bear no other name than murder, thus joining together with "all offenses against life itself" that the council lamented as all too characteristic of the modern world—including "genocide, abortion, euthanasia," and "all violations of the integrity of the human person," from torture to degrading living conditions, to slavery, human trafficking, and exploitative working conditions that turn human beings into "mere tools for profit."[17] So although Vatican II otherwise eschewed the genre of anathema that had so often characterized earlier councils throughout the history of the church, it issued one of the single most forceful condemnations in the entire corpus of conciliar documents when it joined with recent popes to declare most solemnly:

> Every act of war directed to the indiscriminate destruction of whole cities or vast areas with their inhabitants is a crime against God and humanity, which merits firm and unequivocal condemnation.[18]

That council fathers continued to work within a just-war framework should not obscure other streams flowing into and out of the Vatican II watershed, however. Despite precedents from the earliest centuries of Christianity, Catholic theologians of recent centuries had sometimes treated Christian pacifism as nothing short of heretical.[19] A movement of Catholic pacifists had grown in the twentieth century nonetheless, and some of its best representatives—such as Dorothy Day, Gordon Zahn, and Hildegard and Jean Goss-Mayr—attended the council as observers working behind the scenes not only for the condemnation of weapons of mass destruction, but for recognition of pacifism and conscientious objection to military participation. In the end, the council fathers did indeed express "admiration for all who forgo the use of violence to vindicate their rights and have recourse to those other means of defence," and called for "laws [that] make humane provision for the case of conscientious objectors who refuse to carry arms, provided they accept some other form of community service."[20] To be sure, as Christiansen has noted, at this point the sort of principled nonviolence that the church was prepared to honor was essentially the witness of personal holiness and heroism, not an ethic or a strategy that might guide action in the public arena, much less affairs of state.

Ultimately most momentous, then, is the way that council fathers invited further debate and discernment to flow out from the Vatican II watershed. When the Roman Catholic Church speaks at its highest levels, as it did in the Second Vatican Council, it hardly ever makes pronouncements unless they represent settled understandings that have formed through a long and careful deliberative process. It is all the more striking, therefore, that on the matter of war the Second Vatican Council departed from long-standing practice and deeply Catholic sensibilities in order to *launch* a churchwide process of discernment instead. After surveying the growing violence and potential for catastrophe wrought by modern warfare, the bishops famously declared:

> All these factors force us to undertake a completely fresh reappraisal of war.[21]

Even in the pursuit of justice, the world's bishops thus endorsed the view of Pope John XXIII that war was becoming obsolete as a means to vindicate human rights.[22] If the means to abolish and prevent war were less than clear in a sinful world that is easily tempted to false rather than true hope,[23] that simply meant that "it is our clear duty to spare no effort" to work both for alternatives to war as a means to resolve conflict and for the social, economic, and cultural conditions necessary to prevent war.[24] Precisely in this context the bishops promised: "The church . . . intends to propose to our age over and over again, in season and out of season, the apostle's message: 'Behold, now is the acceptable time' for a change of heart; 'behold, now is the day of salvation.'"[25]

The work of Catholic peace theology was only just beginning.

Reevaluating war amid challenges to peace

"Peace is more than the absence of war," the council fathers recognized; it grows from more than a balance of power for it is the fruit of righteousness and justice, as human beings order every part of their lives and society through "the deliberate practice of friendliness."[26] This "more than" of peace is crucial to the still-unfolding story of Catholic peace theology. Whenever war presents itself as a means to resolve our human conflicts, its allure is its promise that through the one grand action of a military campaign or strike, we might somehow set the billiard balls of history rolling in such a way that all our other problems begin to fall into place. Peacebuilding, however, does not simply wage a military campaign through a different grand strategy. Rather, it anticipates the need for many means. It is really peace-nurturing—something far more organic than the mechanistic causality of billiard balls.[27] Far from one grand action, peacebuilding requires thousands upon thousands of actions, many behind the scenes and away from media attention. Indeed, peace is really the fruit of all that makes for healthy thriving human communities. *Shalom*, the Hebrew word for "peace" bespeaks this dynamic far better than our English word, for it can just as easily be translated "health," "well-being," or even "prosperity" in the full sense of "thriving."

Thus, in the twenty-five years that followed the Second Vatican Council's call for a fresh reappraisal of war and untiring work for peace, in and out of season, that work proceeded in multiple ways. Pope Paul VI captured the need to combat poverty and ensure social conditions that favor peace, for example, when he proclaimed in his 1967 encyclical *Populorum Progressio* that "development is the new name for peace."[28] But when long-standing patterns of oppression stifle the social, cultural, and economic development of those whose land and labor the privileged are exploiting, changes in the very structure of society may be required. Only a few years later, therefore, in his 1972 World Day of Peace message, Pope Paul captured that wider reality with an additional catchphrase: "If you want peace, work for justice." This message implicitly endorsed at least some versions of "liberation theology" that were emerging in the so-called Third World or Global South, especially Latin America, in response to Vatican II inspiration on one hand, and obstacles besetting a global push for development in the 1960s on the other hand.

Complicating yet accentuating the need to work for both peace and justice, of course, was the Cold War between the capitalist West and the communist East, led by the United States and the Soviet Union, respectively. For decades this global civilizational conflict between competing ideologies and visions of human progress dominated every other challenge to peacemakers, from the global imperative of nuclear disarmament at one level, to the smaller regional yet interconnected challenges of Third World poverty and oppression at other levels. Even as geopolitical competition made the same players into "freedom fighters" to some and "terrorists" or "subversives" to others, Catholic leaders, commentators, and activists thus found themselves debating which were authentic movements for liberation and which were misguided at best. The church's continuing use of just-war analysis allowed for violence as a last resort—but when was violence justifiable for the oppressed and not just for national self-defense? Meanwhile, an accumulating set of historical experiences, such as the Gandhian-inspired but Catholic-led People Power Revolution in the Philippines of 1986, elicited growing confidence that campaigns of active nonviolence could overthrow petty tyrants and even military dictatorships. Still, nonviolence could never overthrow a totalitarian empire such as that of the Soviet Union, could it? Could it?

Amid this geopolitical complex, at least three major questions shaped efforts to "undertake a completely fresh reappraisal of war" in the 1960s–'80s, thus tending to define the challenge of becoming a Catholic peace church in this period.

Though the term "globalization" was only beginning to circulate in these years, the first question was simply how to respond to all the tectonic shifts that globalization was bringing to human existence. It is an underlying question so large yet basic that we may take it for granted—and initially it presented itself in other terms. Pope John XXIII and the documents of the Second Vatican Council posed the question in terms of the increasing "interdependence" of nations, economies, cultures, and peoples, thanks to the new links that technology was making possible.[29] But the question is the same, and the need for the church to respond was one of the very reasons Pope John convoked the council.[30] As the Vatican II document *Gaudium et Spes* put it:

> Because of the increasingly close interdependence which is gradually extending to the entire world, we are today witnessing an extension of the role of the common good, which is the sum total of social conditions which allow people, either as groups or as individuals, to reach their fulfillment more fully and more easily. The resulting rights and obligations are consequently the concern of the entire human race. Every group must take into account the needs and legitimate aspirations of every other group, and even those of the human family as a whole.[31]

This widening of human interdependence that we now call globalization was not uniformly positive in its results. The technological progress that was making globalization possible could "recoil" against humanity—as this same world-befriending document captured the paradox of modernity in a single word.[32] Meanwhile, the "increased exchange between cultures" often put vulnerable peoples and their cultures at risk rather than leading to a "fruitful dialogue" among peoples.[33]

This first and most basic question concerning globalization, then, underlies almost every other question concerning the tasks of justice and the challenge of peacebuilding in the modern world. Is globalization making true international community or a "civilization of love" imaginable? Or is it simply giving dominant nations and cultures the tools they need to perfect their power of cultural infiltration, economic exploitation, and geopolitical domination? Or if somehow both, what might a sober hope look like in practice?

Catholic social thought in principle holds the task and institutions of governance in esteem, as a preeminent way, though certainly not the only way, that Christians and all people of good will are called to work for the common good. The bishops gathered at the Second Vatican Council thus translated that positive view of the role of government in human societies into an abiding hope for "the establishment of a universally acknowledged public authority vested with the effective power to ensure security for all, regard for justice, and respect for law."[34] In Catholic social teaching, the peace toward which the human family must strive, the disarmament needed on the way to that peace, and any ultimate abolition of war must all entail some such international system of governance. And yet the bishops also knew that such a system could only emerge if it emerged bottom-up, "born of mutual trust between peoples instead of being forced on nations through dread of arms."[35] In turn, "if peace is to be established, the first condition is to root out those causes of discord between people which lead to wars, especially injustice."[36]

And so the challenge of peacebuilding that our second and third questions will share is this: Can we get there from here?

Ultimately, the first and abiding role of pope and council in the modern world has been to hold up the hope that we can indeed. "Never again war, never again war! It is peace, peace, that has to guide the destiny of the nations of all mankind!" proclaimed Pope Paul VI in a speech to the United Nations in 1965—a proclamation that successive popes have regularly repeated.[37] But if this is to be more than merely a stirring but idealistic vision, how? Regionally, can peoples long-oppressed through institutionalized forms of violence throw off their yokes without yet another loop around cycles of violence? And internationally, can a world system whose dysfunctionality has given it no semblance of peace except through rough balances of power and mutual threats of terror ever really transform itself into a system of cooperative interdependence?

The second question that made it challenging to "undertake a completely fresh reappraisal of war," then, was this: If just war is possible, is just revolution legitimate and under what circumstances? At least since Thomas Aquinas, the just-war tradition has contemplated the right to resist tyrants, but always done so with reserve. When the suffering cry out, yet programs of social reform meet with systematic repression, a pastor in the just-war tradition will struggle to promote nonviolent social change even while recognizing some possibility of just but violent revolution. This was Pope Paul's challenge, and with him many of the pastors and activists he sought to guide within the church. Writing midway through his encyclical on the development of peoples, *Populorum Progressio*, in 1967, the pontiff almost seemed to grow impatient with his own carefully reasoned prose, for suddenly he interjected:

> We must make haste: too many are suffering, and the distance is growing that separates the progress of some [along with] the stagnation, not to say the regression, of others.[38]

True, he paused, hasty agrarian reform or industrialization can produce their own hardships and run counter to human values. Nonetheless,

> there are certainly situations whose injustice cries to heaven. When whole populations destitute of necessities live in a state of dependence barring them from all initiative and responsibility, and all opportunity to advance culturally and share in social and political life, [then] recourse to violence, as a means to right these wrongs to human dignity, is a grave temptation.[39]

And so the pontiff chose his words carefully, embedding the exceptional possibility of just revolution deep within his warning:

> We know, however, that a revolutionary uprising—save where there is manifest, long-standing tyranny which would do great damage to fundamental personal rights and dangerous harm to the common good of the country—produces new injustices, throws more elements out of balance and brings on new disasters. A real evil should not be fought against at the cost of greater misery.[40]

In one way, the excruciating dilemma here is simply the one that has always faced practitioners of the just-war theory—how to allow for truly exceptional exceptions to the consistent practice of nonviolent peacemaking that should be regular for Christians and indeed all people of good will—without normalizing resort to war. Especially in the midst of competing Cold War claims of ideology and clashing self-interests that were both locally entrenched and geopolitical, it is no wonder that Christians found themselves deeply conflicted over what in fact are "the things that make for peace" (Luke 19:42).

So too with a third historical marker amid the challenge of becoming a Catholic peace church in the quarter century following Vatican II: How to work realistically within the international system as it is, while taking seriously the stirring papal call, "No, never again war"?[41] Perhaps the most vivid example of this challenge is the profoundly troubling moral puzzle of nuclear deterrence. As Catholic bishops in the United States prepared the pastoral letter in the early 1980s on war and peace that would become *The Challenge of Peace: God's Promise and Our Response*, they took up many issues, but this one was the thorniest, most controversial, and most divisive. As terrifying as the prospect of nuclear annihilation has been in the modern era, in the view of many strategists that terror has brought the very rough peace of a relatively stable standoff to the world, at least among the "great powers" whose competition had so recently given humanity two world wars. The system, however, requires each side to deter the other with threats to do what they recognize as morally reprehensible. So is it moral to continue policies that threaten a morally unspeakable "mutually assured destruction" (also known as "MAD") if those policies have apparently helped create a measure of peace at least between the so-called great powers?

U.S. Catholic bishops in the early 1980s were at first inclined to say no. But when they circulated the first draft of what was to become *The Challenge of Peace* and solicited feedback, pressure from U.S. government officials, including prominent Catholics, led to consultation with the Vatican and a guarded affirmation. *The Challenge of Peace* deemed deterrence policy acceptable so long as it was transitional and nuclear powers beginning with the United States were committing themselves to disarmament negotiations on the way to a truer and more sustainable peace. After all, Pope John Paul II himself had judged "that deterrence may still be judged morally acceptable, 'certainly not as an end in itself but as a step on the way toward a progressive disarmament,'" even as he warned of "the fragility and complexity of the deterrence relationship among nations."[42]

What is striking about the bishops' elaboration of a guarded acceptance of nuclear deterrence policy in light of the criteria of just-war theory, however, is that they not only insisted repeatedly on the "moral limits to deterrence policy as well as to policy regarding [actual] use" of nuclear weapons but expressed "factual concerns" about how and whether such policy could or would realistically be implemented.[43] A further statement by John Paul that they cited is hardly a confident endorsement either of deterrence policy or the policy-thinking around it, perhaps including the church's own:

> Up to the present, we are told that nuclear arms are a force of dissuasion which have prevented the eruption of a major war. And that is probably true. Still, we must ask if it will always be this way.[44]

The bishops could apply specific just-war criteria only in very guarded ways, after all. Government officials assured them that the United States was not intentionally targeting civilian population centers, which is one of the most essential of all requirements for a war to be morally justifiable according to leading accounts of just-war thinking.[45] But then another criterion arises, that of proportionality, the requirement that "the damage to be inflicted and the costs incurred by war must be proportionate to the good expected by taking up arms."[46] Even a well-targeted nuclear attack is likely to be indiscriminate in its disproportionate effects, spreading far beyond any legitimate military target alone. And then the danger that even a limited nuclear strike will escalate into all-out nuclear war makes proportionality even more difficult to calculate.[47]

What the bishops offered, therefore, was at most "a strictly conditioned moral acceptance of nuclear deterrence. We cannot consider it adequate as a long-term basis for peace."[48] Indeed, to many readers, the very straining that they needed to do to reach even this guarded conclusion constitutes an argument against that very conclusion. At one point the bishops in effect admitted the problem. In discussing one particular military strategy they noted that although it might do more to protect civilians than some other strategies, it "is often joined with a declaratory policy which conveys the notion that nuclear war is subject to precise rational and moral limits. We have already expressed our severe doubts about such a concept."[49]

But that can apply to the document itself. Even a reader who supports nuclear deterrence policy must admit that its argumentation is tortured. And for skeptics, the very list of criteria that the bishops proposed for guiding nuclear deterrence policy itself "conveys"—in its very attempt at precision—that same dubious "notion that nuclear war is subject to precise rational and moral limits."

The problem is that an argument for realism must itself be realistic about the likelihood that anyone has the knowledge, predictive capacity, or strategic control to carry out the dictates of just-war theory. Other systems of thought named capital-R Realism exist. Christian Realism is a school of thought in social ethics, and political Realism is a school of thought in the fields of political science and international relations. When they take up the morality of war, what they have in common is far less confidence that precise and rational moral judgment concerning warfare is even possible, and far more willingness to anticipate that sometimes "necessity" may drive people to do what is immoral in order to survive.[50] According to the specifically Christian version of this thinking, one will simply need to ask forgiveness, and the very expectation that one can act morally in war, the hope for which just-war thinking holds out, is itself sinfully proud.

Thus a skeptical reader of *The Challenge of Peace* on nuclear deterrence has reason to ask two questions: (1) While the bishops understandably wanted to bring small-c realism into their deliberations in order to help us "get there from here"—get, that is, to a more peaceful international system using the capacities of the international system as it is—did they not need to import some rather unrealistic expectations in order to make their arguments? And (2), if *The Challenge of Peace* did indeed need to draw upon capital-R Political Realism or even Christian Realism in order to make its case, was it actually importing an ethic of war into Catholicism that is neither its longstanding tradition of just-war deliberation, nor the pacifist Christian ethic of active nonviolence that the church has started to recognize as a legitimate option for Catholics—but instead a rival third position?[51]

In any case, as we step away from the moral puzzle of nuclear deterrence itself, this much seems clear: Readers may evaluate the arguably tortured argumentation concerning the ethics of nuclear deterrence in *The Challenge of Peace* differently. But the bishops' conclusion that despite their own "strictly conditioned moral acceptance of nuclear deterrence," they could not "consider it a long-term basis for peace"[52] is indicative. For such a conclusion uses just-war deliberation to point beyond the just-war tradition, and tells us to look further for an adequate Catholic response to the challenge of peace. Even by the lights of the just-war tradition, in other words, that tradition itself must be transitional. As John the Baptist said of Jesus, "He must increase and I must decrease." Insofar as just-war thinking may offer Christians a legitimate service, it must serve a much larger project. It must aid in developing the theology, ecclesial social ethic, and concrete peacebuilding practices needed to become a Catholic peace church indeed.

Thankfully, in other ways, *The Challenge of Peace* marked steady development in that direction.

John Paul II's answer to the challenge of peace

The nuclear standoff of the Cold War may have prompted *The Challenge of Peace* and forced upon U.S. Catholic bishops their most hotly debated deliberations, but it was not uniquely or primarily about that one particular challenge. Pages of context first laid out a biblical, theological, and ethical framework for specific policy issues, thus reinforcing and extending key developments in Catholic peace theology. Indeed, the extended attention that the U.S. bishops gave to the biblical and theological foundations of their thought—in contrast to an overbearing tendency in previous eras to rely almost exclusively on the philosophical elaboration of "natural law"—was itself a significant reinforcement and extension of Vatican II developments.

Drawing upon the Vatican II discussion of peace and war in *Gaudium et Spes*, U.S. bishops in close consultation with Rome not only reiterated the legitimacy of principled nonviolence or pacifism for Catholics, but they both elaborated on its basis in Catholic tradition and extended its purview. So long as pacifist nonviolence did not constitute mere passivity in the face of evil, its tradition stood alongside the just-war tradition in a necessary twin:

> Both find their roots in the Christian theological tradition; each contributes to the full moral vision we need in pursuit of a human peace. We believe the two perspectives support and

complement one another, each preserving the other from distortion. Finally, in an age of technological warfare, analysis from the viewpoint of non-violence and analysis from the viewpoint of the just-war teaching often converge and agree in their opposition to methods of warfare which are in fact indistinguishable from total warfare.[53]

Yes, the two traditions "diverge on some specific conclusions, but they share a common presumption against the use of force as a means of settling disputes."[54] One implication was that nonviolence was no longer simply a matter of essentially personal holiness, as in its first modern affirmation at Vatican II. Indeed, *The Challenge of Peace* outlines an impressive list of ways that strategies of active nonviolence can offer alternative forms of popular resistance to tyrants and even wage national self-defense, together with the nonviolence of sustained diplomacy and conflict resolution.[55] Thus, in the end, what Christian pacifism at its best shares with the just-war tradition at its best is not simply a negative presumption *against* war, according to *The Challenge of Peace*. Rather, it shares a positive stance toward life, through bonds of human solidarity, ultimately directed toward the kingdom of God.[56]

U.S. Catholic bishops would continue a trajectory toward greater recognition of nonviolence and more stringent application of just-war principles a decade later when they issued a pastoral letter of further reflections on peace and war, as they marked the tenth anniversary of *The Challenge of Peace*. Titled *The Harvest of Justice Is Sown in Peace*, the 1993 document is shorter, and its developments initially seem subtler, yet they mark changes in Catholic peace theology that may be nothing short of momentous. To the theological and biblical foundations that *The Challenge of Peace* had laid out, *The Harvest of Justice* adds the role of spirituality in forming the personal and communal virtues needed for Christians to be peacemakers. By 1993, in fact, the bishops had come to speak of peacemaking as a vocation to which God calls all Christians.

And in the practice of peacemaking in pursuit of justice, nonviolence was no longer simply one tradition next to that of just war, according to *The Harvest of Justice*. Now, at last, it clearly took priority. Arguably, this was always the logic of the just-war theory. After all, the requirement of "last resort" implies that political authorities will only turn to the use of force (and as little violent force as possible at that) "when sustained attempts at nonviolent action fail to protect the innocent against fundamental injustice," as *The Harvest of Justice* puts it.[57] Thus—and this reflects yet another subtle but significant development—the practice of nonviolence must be relevant and indeed obligatory for public officials in their governmental roles. In Catholic social teaching, it has now extended from the realm of the personal in *Gaudium et Spes*, to the realm of social activists in *The Challenge of Peace*, to the public arena of governments and nation-states itself.

For by now, another watershed in global Catholicism, another world-shaking event, had taken place: The 1989 Revolution had brought down the Soviet empire. Pope John Paul II himself had been a leading figure in that event, which began in 1980 with the emergence of Solidarność, the first independent trade union within the Soviet bloc, in the Gdańsk shipyards of the pope's native Poland. At least for Catholics, he was the best-placed interpreter of the 1989 Revolution and the dynamics that led to its success. And whom did he credit? Not himself. Not geopolitical titans such as U.S. President Ronald Reagan or Soviet President Mikhail Gorbachev. Not the military might of the West, nor the economic costs to the East of trying to compete. Rather: Pope John Paul II gave credit for the 1989 Revolution that had so recently seemed unimaginable to the people who had waged nonviolent struggle for liberation, human rights, and democratization, above all simply by bearing witness to the truth and living accordingly. Nonviolence could never overthrow a totalitarian empire such as that of the Soviet Union, could it? But it had. No one had thought so. But now it had.

An opportunity for John Paul's definitive reflection on the 1989 Revolution and the historical dynamics that led to it throughout the 1980s came in 1991, as he penned an encyclical titled *Centesimus Annus*. That title—"One Hundred Years"—refers to the anniversary that occasioned it, the hundredth anniversary of another groundbreaking encyclical by Pope Leo XIII, *Rerum Novarum*. Leo XIII had launched the modern era of Catholic social teaching by taking up the "new things" of modern industrialization and social reorganization that were dislocating so many nineteenth-century workers, leaving them and their families in degrading social conditions, and prompting class struggle. *Centesimus Annus*, therefore, surveys broadly the historical crises of the twentieth century and the ways that Catholic social teaching had responded. For as John Paul remarked at one point in the encyclical, although the "events of 1989 took place principally in the countries of Eastern and Central Europe . . ., they have worldwide importance because they share positive and negative consequences which concern the whole human family."[58]

As he surveyed history in *Centesimus Annus*, then, John Paul highlighted violations of human dignity through militarism and exaggerated nationalism, totalitarianism, and Western-backed "national security states" alike, along with unfettered "savage capitalism," a culture of consumerism amid world poverty, and the ambiguities of globalization. Giving hope, however, was the "general movement among workers and other people of good will for the liberation of the human person and for the affirmation of human rights"; this was "a movement which today has spread to many countries, and which, far from opposing the Catholic Church, looks to her with interest."[59] Indeed, as the pope in turn surveyed ways that Catholic social teaching had sought to prompt and guide responses to the century's threats against human dignity, he took up many more hopeful themes, many of which we will return to in coming chapters—the need to ground peace in justice if it is to be more than the absence of war, relationship of the state and its citizens, the necessary link between freedom and truth, the priority of religious freedom, the especially relevant truth of the human person as created and fulfilled in solidarity with others, and the call to create a culture of peace.

As often happens in the reception of papal teaching, commentators of divergent political tendencies have sometimes sought to pull *Centesimus Annus* in rightward or leftward directions. Some have emphasized John Paul's critique of atheistic communism and the way that its very economic model required a totalitarian management of human beings that fundamentally violates the truth that we are created to respond to God in freedom and work in the world with a corresponding creativity. In contrast, others have emphasized John Paul's critique of unfettered "savage capitalism" that exploits the work and degrades the dignity of others in the name of freedom, while offering false promises of human fulfillment through consumerism.

In turn, divergent approaches and priorities for the work of peacemaking often align with these divergent socioeconomic emphases. Yet what should be most instructive is that in *Centesimus Annus*, the pope integrated all of these concerns, often with a telling seamlessness that should rebuke all of us when we try to pull his thought apart.

Take sections 17 and 18 of *Centesimus Annus*. A broad range of "socioeconomic consequences," totalitarian violations of human dignity, and ideologically sanctioned hatreds had resulted from the very error of which Pope Leo had warned a century before, that of delinking freedom from obedience to truth:

> As has been mentioned, this error consists in an understanding of human freedom which detaches it from obedience to the truth, and consequently from the duty to respect the rights of others. The essence of freedom then becomes self-love carried to the point of contempt for God and neighbor, a self-love which leads to an unbridled affirmation of self-interest and which refuses to be limited by any demand of justice.[60]

When a fundamental error expresses itself in a totalizing political system, the temptation is to seek to defend ourselves or overturn it through violent counterforce, and to assume we are on the side of God's angels when we do. Whatever form of self-defense may be legitimate, however, military victory over a system grounded in fundamental error will never constitute a sufficient response. John Paul made this clear as he moved directly from his insistence on the relationship between truth and freedom into a reflection on the implications of the principle that peace is more than the absence of war. Yes, since 1945 and the victory over fascism in World War II, "weapons have been silent on the European continent." But "it must be remembered that true peace is never simply the result of military victory, but rather implies both the removal of the causes of war and genuine reconciliation between peoples."[61] In saying that true peace requires removal of the causes of war and genuine reconciliation, John Paul was reading the historical events of previous decades empirically—dare we say realistically?—yet employing theological categories grounded in Christian hope. No Christian can hear the words "true peace" and "genuine reconciliation," after all, without gospel resonances, for ultimately, Christian faith recognizes these as the work of Christ in history, to which the church is called to be a living sign and foretaste. As John Paul continued his descriptive reflections on historical events between 1945 and 1989, therefore, he was also making normative claims about the kind of peace to which all people of good will—but surely Christians—ought to aspire. And he was making normative claims about how to get there from here.

John Paul's highlighting of the role of active nonviolence in the 1989 Revolution must be recognized as serving exactly this purpose. Military victory over fascism in World War II may have been welcome, yet it left the world not only at a standoff between two great superpowers, but at an ideological impasse about how to respond. Simply as an economic system—the pope continued in subsequent sections—Marxist systems of the Eastern Bloc had failed because they denied the truth of the human person, whose work must express itself in dignity and creativity, not treat both person and work as a commodity. But when Western opponents had responded by putting in place "national security states," they too had "run the grave risk of destroying the freedom and values of the person, the very things for whose sake it is necessary to oppose Communism."[62]

Active nonviolence had offered a path through this impasse in power and ideology precisely because it depended on the force of truth—truth told, truth lived—and because it invited reconciliation between peoples. Even in a putatively just war (we might pause to note before we read John Paul's celebration of active nonviolence), military victory alone cannot bring "true peace" because violence does not need the truth at all, often rides roughshod over the true causes of war, and easily creates new resentments that make reconciliation all the harder. Whatever military victory may achieve even at its most justifiable, therefore, it always requires more, but so often undercuts that more. If peace is indeed more than the absence of war, then, we will not create the cultural, economic, and social conditions needed for peace if we cannot be honest. Hence the need to speak the truth. But when all sides have at least some legitimate grievances, we cannot respond to all the contrary implications of their truths nor discover the undivided truth that integrates them, without hard listening, deep humility, and growing trust. Hence the need for the work of reconciliation. Creative and confrontational protest is only one part of any overarching strategy of active nonviolence, sometimes necessary to win recognition of hard truths or to even a balance of power so that negotiations in hope of conflict resolution will be possible and fair. But vulnerability to the truth and openness to reconciliation are *always* necessary simply to recognize the conditions that will make for peace, to say nothing of treating once-estranged potential partners in the task of peacebuilding with the dignity they require to join in the task as collaborators.[63]

Thus, as Pope John Paul II analyzed the various factors that had led to the fall of repressive regimes in the 1989 Revolution, one was especially "worthy of emphasis":

> the fact that the fall of this kind of "bloc" or empire was accomplished almost everywhere by means of peaceful protest, using only the weapons of truth and justice. While Marxism held that only by exacerbating social conflicts was it possible to resolve them through violent confrontation, the protests which led to the collapse of Marxism tenaciously insisted on trying every avenue of negotiation, dialogue, and witness to the truth, appealing to the conscience of the adversary and seeking to reawaken in him a sense of shared human dignity.[64]

It had seemed that nothing but another war could alter the standoff that post-World War II treaties had sanctioned, offering the rough peace of a balance of power but subjugating whole peoples in that vast bloc.

> Instead, it has been overcome by the non-violent commitment of people who, while always refusing to yield to the force of power, succeeded time after time in finding effective ways of bearing witness to the truth. This disarmed the adversary, since violence always needs to justify itself through deceit, and to appear, however falsely, to be defending a right or responding to a threat posed by others.[65]

Perhaps because the 1989 Revolution had seemed so unexpected as to have been a miracle, here the pope paused to "thank God for having sustained people's hearts amid difficult trials." Yet as he continued, his prayer made clear that human agency and initiative were quite compatible with divine intervention:

> I pray that this example will prevail in other places and other circumstances. May people learn to fight for justice without violence, renouncing class struggle in their internal disputes, and war in international ones.

Indeed, the spiritual vacuum of atheism was another on the pope's list of factors contributing to the 1989 Revolution.[66] Throughout *Centesimus Annus*, after all, John Paul was insisting upon respect for the fundamental truth of the human person as created with an "essential 'capacity for transcendence.'"[67] The pope's critique of atheism, however, was hardly a mandate for militaristic counternarratives of the Cold War or the collapse of the Soviet empire. Nor was it a justification for continuing countermeasures against enemies, countermeasures that are themselves immoral yet are so-called "necessities" because only they offer "realistic" ways to defend freedom in the face of godless communism or other new threats. Quite to the contrary, "The events of 1989 are an example of the success of willingness to negotiate and of the Gospel spirit in the face of an adversary determined not to be bound by moral principles."[68]

The pope certainly wished to be realistic about human limitations—given the "wound of original sin"—and to distance himself from any idealism that might confuse the sort of political society that is possible in this world with the kingdom of God.[69] But 1989 had shown that political Realism as a core worldview is if anything not realistic enough, for it underestimates the power of moral force in human affairs, to say nothing of the power of cruciform yet courageous witness to God's nonviolent power as revealed in Jesus Christ:

> These events are a warning to those who, in the name of political realism, wish to banish law and morality from the political arena. Undoubtedly, the struggle which led to the changes of 1989 called for clarity, moderation, suffering and sacrifice. In a certain sense, it was a struggle born of prayer, and it would have been unthinkable without immense trust in God, the Lord of history, who carries the human heart in his hands. It is by uniting his own sufferings for the sake of truth and freedom to the sufferings of

Christ on the Cross that man is able to accomplish the miracle of peace and is in a position to discern the often narrow path between the cowardice which gives in to evil and the violence which, under the illusion of fighting evil, only makes it worse.[70]

As he surveyed the world that was changing and realigning in the wake of 1989, John Paul II discussed much else in *Centesimus Annus* as well, of course. Ultimately, every question of economics, politics, social organization, and international relations met in the question of culture. After all, "All human activity takes place within a culture and interacts with culture."[71] And that is where the Christian Church has its greatest role to play, by speaking to each human heart and helping form whole persons who will exercise "creativity, intelligence, and knowledge of the world and of people," while displaying the "capacity for self-control, personal sacrifice, solidarity and readiness to promote the common good."[72] Personal conversion, cultural formation, and just societal change each loops around to the others in the pope's vision; need for any one of them is never an excuse from the others. For even if we focus on the need for individuals to change, the core Christian duty of love for neighbor demands of each person nothing less than "a shared responsibility for all of humanity."[73] As we will see in the next chapter when we return to the papal call to build a "civilization of love," Christian love can never be "limited to one's own family, nation or state, but extends progressively to all humankind, since no one can consider himself extraneous or indifferent to the lot of another member of the human family."[74]

Precisely here, however, Pope John Paul II turned again to the priority of active peacemaking both to avoid war and to create the positive conditions that make for peace, thus fostering a culture of peace. With previous popes he had consistently joined his voice to cry, " 'Never again war!' " So now, again, he must repeat:

> No, never again war, which destroys the lives of innocent people, teaches how to kill, throws into upheaval even the lives of those who do the killing and leaves behind a trail of resentment and hatred, thus making it all the more difficult to find a just solution of the very problems which provoked the war. Just as the time has finally come when in individual States a system of private vendetta and reprisal has given way to the rule of law, so too a

similar step forward is now urgently needed in the international community. Furthermore, it must not be forgotten that at the root of war there are usually real and serious grievances: injustices suffered, legitimate aspirations frustrated, poverty, and the exploitation of multitudes of desperate people who see no real possibility of improving their lot by peaceful means.[75]

Such an expansive vision of global transformation might lead some to conclude that in fact "you *can't* get there from here"—yet it also contains key clues about how to find our way: Though the vision is all-encompassing, it cannot repeat the totalitarian sin of attempting to manage our way to a better world, only to manage human beings themselves as though they are nothing more than material objects. Though the vision requires a fundamental respect for human freedom, it cannot endorse the capitalist sin of confusing freedom with endless consumer choice, only to manipulate some human beings as though the only path to meaning is the fulfillment of their desires (while exploiting other human beings so we can do so). And though the vision expects Christians to be deeply embedded in the shared work of humanity in building and sustaining institutions that serve the common good, the church must clearly do its own work of cultural transformation within itself if it is to play that special role which John Paul II named—that of fostering a culture of peace through the work of well-formed Christian persons at work in the world, and indeed through the witness of its own shared life as a global community.

In short, Catholic peace theology cannot *first* be about what to *do* in the world. It must be about more than better techniques in the growing field of Catholic peacebuilding, or more fervent activism for justice and peace, or more astute and timely policy proposals, or even more savvy and consistent application of active nonviolence. It must first be about how to be in the world as a Christian community. Then-Methodist theologian Stanley Hauerwas once asserted famously: "The church does not have a social ethic; the church is a social ethic."[76] Catholic peace theology, in that sense, must be as much about sacrament and ecclesiology as about social ethics or even Catholic social teaching, narrowly construed. Its first and deepest concern must be the question of how to be a Christian people together in the world, in service to all peoples of the world.

The Vatican mandate to learn from a historic peace church[77]

The day: January 24, 2002. The place: Assisi. In the wake of the 9/11 attacks on the World Trade Center in New York and on the Pentagon in Washington, DC, as well as war in Afghanistan and the sense of many that the world was living through a "clash of civilizations," Pope John Paul II had convened leaders from the world's most prominent religions and from across Christian traditions to converge, pray, and rededicate themselves to peace in the hometown of one of Christianity's most beloved and peaceable saints: St. Francis.[78] The differing religious communities had gone to separate sites in order to pray for peace, simultaneously if not quite together. Afterward, they returned for a closing ceremony to solemnly renounce any use of violence in the name of religion and urge humanity to embrace the work of peace. One by one, leaders from Catholic, Eastern Orthodox, Protestant, Sikh, Islamic, Confucian, Buddhist, and Jewish communities rose to so pledge, each in their own spiritual idiom. In a moment the pope himself would bring the litany and the day to its climax as he mustered all the force that his Parkinson's disease-ravished voice would allow, in order to call out:

> Violence never again! War never again! Terrorism never again!
> In the name of God, may every religion bring upon the earth Justice and Peace, Forgiveness and Life, Love![79]

But first, one last Christian leader spoke up for the global communion he represented, and for all of the religious traditions who had just then preceded him. That leader was a Mennonite, Dr. Mesach Krisetya of Indonesia, president of Mennonite World Conference:

> We, as persons of different religious traditions, will tirelessly proclaim that peace and justice are inseparable, and that peace in justice is the only path which humanity can take towards a future of hope. In a world with ever more open borders, shrinking distances and better relations as a result of a broad network of communications, we are convinced that security, freedom and peace will never be guaranteed by force but by mutual trust. May God bless these our resolutions and grant justice and peace to the world.[80]

That Vatican choreographers had chosen the smallest of all the religious bodies represented on stage to finalize the solemn promises of all representatives would be a remarkable enough signal. But what is more, at its highest levels of leadership the Roman Catholic Church was attending with utmost seriousness to the centuries-long witness of peace and nonviolence by Mennonites. And behind the scenes there was even more to this staging, with signals to follow in the years to come.

This was the second time that John Paul II had convened such a gathering in Assisi, after all. Compared to the role of the Mennonite World Conference (MWC) president at the first World Day of Prayer for Peace in Assisi in 1986, Krisetya's role in 2002 could not have been more strikingly different. The Mennonite family of faith now includes more than 2.1 million believers, 60 percent of whom are African, Asian, or Latin American. It traces its roots back to the Anabaptist or Radical Reformation movement in sixteenth-century Europe. In 1525, only a few years after Martin Luther sparked the Protestant Reformation in 1517, Anabaptist groups began breaking away from both Luther's movement and from the Reformed movement in Switzerland that would soon find its leader in John Calvin. The Anabaptists believed that by tying the pace and direction of their reform to the sponsorship of town councils and princes, the "magisterial" (i.e., princely) Reformers were compromising their commitment to biblical authority and distancing themselves from the nonviolent path by which Christians were to follow their crucified Lord as disciples. To reject infant baptism and baptize adults upon confession of faith instead was not just a matter of biblical precedent or sacramental propriety for Anabaptists but a necessity if Christians were to align their allegiance to Christ through a church distinct from the civil community or nation-state. Even though Anabaptist/Mennonite theology has arguably remained closer to Catholicism in key ways than to mainline Reformers,[81] it has been easy to see the Mennonite tradition as a double distancing—a break first from Roman Catholicism and then from newly established Protestant churches.

At the first Assisi gathering in 1986, then, the seating arrangement had seemed to assume exactly this double departure. The distance between the then-president of MWC, Paul Kraybill, and Pope John Paul II—along with the symbolic distance between the Christian communions they represented—could not have been greater. Seated in a line extending from one side of the papal chair had been leaders of non-Christian religions. Seated in another line extending from the other side of the papal chair had been leaders of Christian communions, with a final seat reserved for a leading Jewish rabbi, in light of the special relationship between Judaism and Christianity.[82] Seated next to the rabbi was Kraybill, the Mennonite, as far from the pope as a Christian tradition apparently could be.

Something had dramatically changed in just sixteen years. Likely impelled by John Paul II's own passionate commitment to peacemaking and his own experience with the power of active nonviolence,[83] the Vatican had been taking an interest in interchurch dialogue with Mennonites that was totally out of proportion with their numbers. For although Mennonites are hardly the only church family that traces its ancestry back to sixteenth-century Anabaptists, and although they often stand with the Society of Friends (Quakers) and Church of the Brethren as the three most commonly listed "historic peace churches," the Anabaptist-Mennonite tradition regularly serves in both scholarly and ecumenical circles as paradigmatic for both the Radical Reformation tradition and historic peace church theology. One explanation for why Mennonites, above all, have played this role may be that in North America and Europe they have acculturated more than their Amish, Hutterite, and other "Old Order" cousins, yet not so much as Quakers or the Church of the Brethren, at least until recently. The result in the twentieth century was Mennonite intellectual leaders educated enough to produce leading historians and theologians while retaining a distinctive voice. Their historians have sought to recover the record and wisdom of their tradition using modern tools of scholarship, while their leading theologians have both engaged the larger culture and dialogued with ecumenical partners, even while retaining a particularly strong sense of distinct collective identity.[84] Meanwhile, the much-respected work of the relief, development, and peacebuilding organization Mennonite Central Committee has placed Mennonites into collaborative relationships with other Christian peacemakers and justice advocates in countless on-the-ground situations of conflict and human need around the world, beginning in 1920 and with increasing urgency throughout the latter half of the twentieth century and beyond. A papacy impassioned to strengthen the work and witness of the Catholic Church on behalf of world peace in the face of what John Paul II called a modern "culture of death" seems to have turned to Mennonites as a dialogue partner and even as a teacher of sorts.

In 1998, therefore, the Pontifical Council for Promoting Christian Unity had joined with Mennonite World Conference to launch a five-year international dialogue. Since the Second Vatican Council sealed its commitment to ecumenical dialogue, the Catholic Church had engaged in approximately fifteen such sessions, none with a worldwide communion as small as the Mennonites. From 1998 to 2003, delegations of roughly seven people from the two communions met once a year for a full week. They prayed, studied, discussed, debated, and visited one another's local congregations, parishes, and religious communities. "The general purpose of the dialogue was to learn to know one another better, to promote better understanding of the positions on Christian faith held by Catholics and Mennonites, and to contribute to the overcoming of prejudices that have long existed between them."[85] Participants later reported that "the atmosphere in the meetings was most cordial. Each side presented its views on the theological issues as clearly and forcefully as possible, seeking to foster an honest and fruitful dialogue." As usual in such ecumenical dialogues, the task was for conversation partners to clearly state their views, so that it would be "possible to begin to see which parts of the Christian heritage are held in common by both Mennonites and Catholics, and where they have strong differences."[86] Indeed, discussions could be frank and probing:

> In presenting their respective views on history, dialogue members did not refrain from allowing one another to see clearly the criticism each communion has traditionally raised against the other. At the same time, dialogue participants did this with the kind of self-criticism that is needed if an authentic search for truth is to take place. The constant hope was that clarifications in both areas of study, historical and theological, might contribute to a healing of memories between Catholics and Mennonites.[87]

The most obvious result of the international dialogue has been its groundbreaking final report, *Called Together to Be Peacemakers*, issued a year after the 2002 Assisi event. The report gives sustained attention not only to peacemaking theology but also to key historical watersheds in the fourth and sixteenth centuries, to ecclesiology or theology of the church, to understandings of the sacraments or church ordinances, and to repentance for past persecutions and recriminations. Commentators occasionally remark that Catholic social teaching is Catholicism's "best kept secret"; be that as it may, Mennonite-Catholic dialogue, the final report of its first international round, and its implications for Catholic peace teaching are an even better kept secret. Nowhere else in the corpus of its authoritative teaching[88] has the Catholic magisterium so definitively endorsed active nonviolence as normative, at least until Pope Francis's 2017 World Day of Peace message.[89]

Following through on both the commitment that many faiths made to peace at Assisi in 2002 and to the specific ways that Mennonites and Catholics affirmed themselves "called together to be peacemakers," representatives of the two world communions went on to join in a most unprecedented shared witness, in 2007. Even while Mennonite-Catholic dialogue had been unfolding, Mennonites and other historic peace church leaders were also having an impact on more Protestant ecumenical conversations. Among other things, they had convinced the World Council of Churches to launch a "Decade to Overcome Violence" project (2001–2010) to find a fresh consensus about truly Christian ways to work for human security that might transcend centuries-old debates between just-war and pacifist Christians. As it prepared to draft an "Ecumenical Call to Just Peace" for a final international peace convocation scheduled to take place in Jamaica in May 2011, the WCC's general secretary invited input from church bodies around the world. Although a number of academic institutions, Christian peace groups, and congregations responded, only two wider confessional bodies did so—Mennonite and Catholic.

And they did so together. As one way to follow up on their international dialogue, the Vatican's Pontifical Council for Promoting Christian Unity invited a delegation of Mennonite World Conference representatives to Rome in October 2007. Participants took the opportunity to finalize a joint "contribution" to the WCC's Decade to Overcome Violence that offered a biblical/theological foundation for peace and peacemaking, a spirituality of Christian discipleship following the Prince of Peace, and suggestions for action and continued discussion. Building on *Called Together to Be Peacemakers*, the theology of the joint contribution to the WCC project was even more seamless, with differing Catholic or Mennonite emphases hard to discern. "The Church is called to be a peace church," Catholics and Mennonites affirmed together. "This calling is based on the conviction we hold in common as Catholics and Mennonites, that the Church, founded by Christ, is to be a living sign and an effective instrument of peace." Few people and fewer Christians would say that they oppose peace, of course; debates are always centered on how to get there. The document is honest about continuing differences concerning the means to peace, noting, for example, that "for both Catholics and Mennonites the ultimate personal and ecclesial challenge is to spell out the consequences of the cross for our teaching on peace and war, and for our response in the face of injustice and violence." But simply to center ongoing debates around the cross already marks out a fresh new consensus. For Catholics, after all, joining a cross-centered consensus represents movement away from their traditional tendency to use "natural law" approaches to think about war and violence. But Mennonites, too, have had to move historically in order to affirm that "in the absence of justice and human rights, peace is a mirage," and "the Gospel's vision includes active nonviolence for defense of human life and human rights, economic justice for the poor, and solidarity among peoples."[90]

The bottom line: "Reconciliation, nonviolence, and active peacemaking belong to the heart of the Gospel." Not an add-on. Not just an option for particularly heroic saints or particularly dedicated activists. Not simply a this-worldly concern but at "the heart of the Gospel." When Mennonites and Catholics can say that—"together," to the world, and to all who claim the name of Christ—then something is happening that deserves far greater attention. The choreography of Assisi 2002 was hardly a fluke.

Chapter 3

We've Been Expecting This: Christian Love Stretches beyond Borders

> For if you love those who love you, what reward do you have? Do not even the tax collectors do the same? And if you greet only your brothers and sisters, what more are you doing than others? Do not even the Gentiles do the same?
>
> —Matthew 5:46-47

If all Christians are "called together to be peacemakers"[1] because "reconciliation, nonviolence, and active peacemaking belong to the heart of the Gospel,"[2] that calling invites us to share the peace of Christ in the world by working actively and nonviolently in collaboration with all people of good will. Praying fervently for those who work to "eliminate the havoc of war," the Second Vatican Council promised its support to all diplomats and peacemakers of good will regardless of faith or nationality. Such work, after all, required a courageous movement of imagination beyond the confines of national self-interest:

> In our day, this work [to eliminate war and build a lasting peace] demands that they enlarge their thoughts and their spirit beyond the confines of their own country, that they put aside nationalistic selfishness and ambitions to dominate other nations, and that they cultivate deep reverence for the whole of humanity which is painstakingly advancing towards greater maturity.[3]

Five years later, Pope Paul VI began to speak of the goal as building a "civilization of love," a term to which his successor John Paul II would return repeatedly. Christian social ethics and Catholic peace theology apparently can stop nowhere short of such a vision.

Christian moral theology at the borders

Whatever John Paul II meant with his sweeping vision of a "civilization of love," the phrase itself is telling: Christian moral concern must stretch until it embraces the good of every distant neighbor, or even, in some way, every creature. And because the good of every human neighbor is entwined and interdependent both with other humans and with the natural world that provides their homes and sustenance, Christian moral practice must translate into far more than well-meaning but vague concern. It must take on the enduring, concrete, and hard work of ordering human relations well and justly, in that vast complex of culture, agriculture, hearth, craft, and industry that aspires to deserve the name of civilization. Whether or not most so-called civilizations have been sustainable or even as civilized as they have claimed is another question. The point is this: Whenever Christians reflect deeply upon the love that is at the center of both their faith and their lived response to the One who loved them first, that oft-abused, sadly cliched word "love" cannot help but call and cajole them further and further out into the world, and ever more deeply into its work. That is why Christian ethics can never just be personal ethics but must always be social ethics. That is why Christian social ethics and Catholic social teaching have always stretched toward the challenges of global solidarity, long before anyone had begun to speak of "globalization."

> "'You shall love the Lord your God with all your heart, and with all your soul, and with all your mind.' This is the greatest and first commandment. And a second is like it: 'You shall love your neighbor as yourself.' On these two commandments hang all the law and the prophets." (Matt 22:37-40; cf. Mark 12:28-34; Luke 10:25-28)

Jesus spoke these words because skeptics were challenging him to demonstrate that he was a faithful rabbi or teacher of Israel. Judging from the way his questioners responded to his answer in the

Gospels of Mark and Luke, he was. Indeed, despite many Christian attempts to suppress this fact, the very Jewishness of Jesus arguably turns out to be key to a Christian ethic that faithfully engages culture and society. Always recognizing at least some continuity, Christian theologians both ancient and contemporary have often put Jesus' twofold love commands at the core of Christian ethics, but also matched them up with the two tables of the "Ten Commandments" or Decalogue that summarizes the Law of Moses.[4] Thoroughgoing love for God corresponds with the first table of commandments that recognizes God as our liberator, rejects the worship of any other gods or idols, insists on keeping the name of the true God holy, and guides us to worship rightly by resting trustfully on the day of Sabbath. Likewise, love of neighbor corresponds with the second table of commandments about honoring one's parents and rejecting murder, adultery, theft, lying or false witness in court, and covetousness or greed.

The only reality that goes even deeper into the core of Jewish and Christian faith—for indeed, Christianity proclaims that its faith points to the very *core* of reality—is God's *own* liberating and saving love. Human love for God and neighbor is ultimately but a fitting response and witness to God's prior all-embracing love. In fact, if Christians have sometimes misinterpreted the "Ten Commandments" that were given first to the fleeing Hebrew slaves whom their gracious liberator now sought to form into a people, the Christian mistake may have been to call them *commandments* in the first place. Christians would do better to follow Jewish practice and instead call them The Ten Words, thus avoiding the legalistic or arbitrary overtones that modern folks, at least, hear in the words "command" or "commandment." As Judaism has traditionally numbered the Decalogue, after all, the first "word" is not even a commandment. Rather, it is a reminder that God always goes first by freely saving, before we can even attempt to earn our own salvation through obedience: The First Word is that "I am the LORD your God, who brought you out of the land of Egypt, out of the house of bondage" (Exod 20:2). All that follows from the human side then is really a "therefore" not a "should." For as the writer of the First Letter of John succinctly put it: "We love, because he first loved us" (1 John 4:19).

With such a clear overarching framework to integrate faith and work, one might almost wonder why we need a distinctive discipline called Christian ethics or moral theology. But one will not wonder long. For no one will seek to follow the teachings of Jesus about the two commandments of love that fulfill the Law of Moses or heed the Prophets of Israel without quickly encountering two major challenges.

Two challenges for love of neighbor

The first challenge is well known: We have many neighbors of course, and loving more than one at a time requires that we coordinate our response to their multiple needs in a way that is fair. This leads immediately to questions of justice, and soon to questions of *social justice*. To see why, consider this thought experiment:

Imagine someone who has lived in such a bubble in a suburb or small town that she has never heard of homelessness. (Unlikely, but again, this is a thought experiment.) Upon encountering a homeless person for the first time, she buys him a meal, asks how he manages to survive on the city streets, and is so taken with his struggle that soon she is volunteering at a homeless shelter with a soup kitchen. In other words, she has responded to human need with basic charity work that is innocent to the point of naive, but well-intentioned. What she soon finds in the soup kitchen is rules to make sure that those who are first in line only take their fair share, so that enough will remain for those last in line.

Matters become even more complicated when a cold snap sets in. Proud but homeless men who preferred to sleep on the street now ask for beds, but there are not enough to go around. Our new volunteer may "just want to help" but doesn't know what to think as she sits in on a staff meeting. The shelter's managers have to decide how to prioritize. First come, first served? Prioritize families? Prioritize single mothers with children? Prioritize women who have fled abusive relationships because they need extra protection? Prioritize military veterans who served their country but continue to fight the war in their heads? Prioritize people who are looking for work, or maybe even working-poor families whose houses have just been foreclosed, because they seem more "deserving"? Or prioritize those with the most abject need?

Even on the simple scale of one small institution serving a few hundred people at a time, then, questions of fairness and justice are arising. And there are hints of still larger issues of justice at a societal level—social justice, in other words. What is it about the economic system that led to foreclosure and loss of a home even for hardworking families? What is it about the culture that has fostered domestic abuse? Why are so many people homeless in the first place? And if that is not enough, the plight of wounded warriors hints at still-wider international questions of justice. If our well-meaning volunteer truly wants to help, she and her colleagues are going to have to coordinate their responses to many neighbors in ever-widening circles. Inevitably, they will face some tough decisions about how to organize society in such a way that as many people as possible share fairly in the distribution of resources and opportunities. Social. Justice.

A second challenge has received less attention but goes far to explain why nice-sounding proposals for a "love ethic" often lead to our most protracted debates in Christianity. Namely, what, if any, are the limits of love? It seems that love of God and neighbor really cannot stop without embracing the common good of humanity and the planet that is our home. Yet justice for neighbors close at hand seems to require that we protect them from the intruding claims of outsiders or their potentially violent threats. Whatever else justice may mean, surely it must require special protection for the innocent children of one's neighbors, no? But if Jesus' second love command is like the first—if love of neighbor must take on some of the sweep that is essential to loving God with all one's heart, soul, and mind—then who is not also a neighbor, far beyond our geographical neighbors and kin?

Christian teachers and ethicists down through the centuries have regularly concluded that "love your neighbor" applies to every other human being, however distant. So our second challenge—that of naming the limits of love—turns out to be quite challenging indeed. After all, if love of neighbor must "likewise" extend to distant neighbors, then just when we think we have worked out hard-nosed rules of justice in order to distribute and protect scarce resources within our family, community, or nation, the question of *global solidarity* whispers a reminder: There are distant neighbors too. Immigrants, legally here or not. Struggling factory workers, making our running shoes and electronic gadgets in subhuman conditions. Poor people we thought we knew how to help, still scratching out a living on the land of a fickle plantation owner or looking for work in sprawling urban slums, despite decades of economic development projects around the world. In our frustration we may have long ago given up and latched on to ideologies that rationalize our nagging guilt. But for anyone whom God's love has grasped, the whispering call to somehow live in solidarity with every global neighbor remains.

St. Augustine on the ordering of multiple loves

Saint Augustine illustrates these two challenges, and—given his formative role in the Christian tradition at least of the West—offers much else as well. For many, the fourth-and-fifth-century Christian apologist, bishop, and theologian has been one of the most durable guides through the hidden complexities of love for God and multiple neighbors. Autobiographically, Augustine's long reflections on Christian love actually began with the grief-stricken problem of how to love the beautiful but fragile and fleeting goods of the world. The problem with love for things that exist in time—temporal goods—is not that they are evil or seductive in themselves. No, it is because the world is so good and beautiful that we desperately desire to hold on to them and control them for ourselves. Augustine seems to have begun to learn this in the wake of the death of a close friend when both were in their teens; that event in any case provided the occasion for some of his most poignant reflections on how to love (*Confessions* 4.8.13– 4.14.23). The only way to love the world and its goods rightly, amid all their flux and mortality, must be to love them "in God" their Creator, praising God for their beauty and goodness in order to receive them as a gift that only God the eternal one can preserve and sustain: "Blessed is he who loves you, and loves his friend in you and his enemy for your sake. He alone loses no one dear to him, to whom all are dear in the One who is never lost" (*Confessions* 4.9.14).

Midway between a misdirected love for temporal goods, and a properly centered and centering love for God, was love for human beings—the neighbor and the self. The fourfold framework that resulted was both simple and complex, and Augustine used it consistently throughout his career.[5] Every kind of relationship with every possible being could be analyzed as a relationship of either well-ordered or misguided love for God, neighbor, self, or temporal goods.

Love of God? We rightly love God with a love that *enjoys*. This, in other words, is a love that finds our ultimate joy and happiness in relationship with God.

Temporal goods? These we can love in some limited sense so long as we do not fixate upon them. Instead we must recognize that their proper role is to serve as mere tools on the journey that is an ever-deepening relationship with God. This is a love of *use* not enjoyment.

Love of neighbor? Human beings are less than God but infinitely more valuable than other material and temporal beings; thus proper love for them is a complex hybrid that says "both . . . and . . ." Since every other human being is created for a life-giving relationship with God as surely as I am, I dare not simply "use" them in the sense of manipulating or domineering them for my own ends. Paradoxically, that would actually be to expect from them an ultimately futile source of joy, a wrongful enjoyment that we will find only in relationship to God. In another sense, however, we rightly do both use and enjoy our neighbors. We use the aid they offer us on our journey toward God, and we enjoy them as companions on the journey into that deeper love of God that we cannot know at all without sharing.

What about love of self? Augustine was certainly aware that self-love could be pernicious and egotistical. But Jesus' second great love command did imply this third kind of love, insofar as one is called to love the neighbor *as* the self. Encoded in that "as" was the conviction for Augustine that the ultimate good of every human being is to be found not in what either the neighbor or I my*self* may egotistically seek, but in a relationship with God. To love one's neighbors was to wish that good for them and to aid them in every possible way on their journey toward that good. To love oneself rightly, then, was to wish precisely this same good for oneself. One must love the neighbor as the self, in other words, but also love the self as one rightly loves the neighbor.[6] The equal dignity of all human beings as creatures whom God is equally calling and wooing into relationship is an elegantly simple lesson that we must never forget when we work through the puzzles of justice and the complexities of love.

And that *is* always a temptation, even for the most elegant of moral theories and theological frameworks. Augustine has illustrated our first challenge, the need to coordinate multiple loves simultaneously.

His fourfold theory of love, ordered according to the contrasting modes of use and enjoyment, offers Christians much guidance, especially at the psychological and vocational levels in which everyone must test their desires and recognize their life priorities according to a proper hierarchy of goods.

But in other ways, Augustine left the subsequent Christian tradition unsettled. For he also illustrates our second challenge—the difficulty of setting any neat and manageable limits to a love so sweeping as this "likewise" Christian love. That is not necessarily a criticism, because God's love is supposed to leave our own loves unsettled. But if Augustine provides an illustration, he may also serve as a warning. For as helpful as this framework is both for illustrating and guiding us through our first challenge, that of coordinating multiple loves, its very elegance invites a second challenge.

St. Augustine on the stretching of love

When "a lawyer stood up to test Jesus" in Luke 10:25 by asking what he must do to inherit eternal life, after all, there was nothing intrinsically wrong with his ethical framework. He and Jesus quickly found agreement precisely where we have come to expect it, in the twofold command to love God and love neighbor as self. But the lawyer wanted to use this framework to trace out the obligations of love with the kind of juridical precision that would allow him to limit those obligations and so "to justify himself." He thus asked Jesus to clarify exactly who was his neighbor precisely so that he would know who was *not* his neighbor. When Jesus called his bluff, the result was that famous parable that we (not Jesus or the gospel writer) have come to title "The Good Samaritan":

> Jesus replied, "A man was going down from Jerusalem to Jericho, and fell into the hands of robbers, who stripped him, beat him, and went away, leaving him half dead. Now by chance a priest was going down that road; and when he saw him, he passed by on the other side. So likewise a Levite, when he came to the place and saw him, passed by on the other side. But a Samaritan while traveling came near him; and when he saw him, he was moved with pity. He went to him and bandaged his wounds, having

poured oil and wine on them. Then he put him on his own animal, brought him to an inn, and took care of him. The next day he took out two denarii, gave them to the innkeeper, and said, 'Take care of him; and when I come back, I will repay you whatever more you spend.' Which of these three, do you think, was a neighbor to the man who fell into the hands of the robbers?" He said, "The one who showed him mercy." Jesus said to him, "Go and do likewise." (Luke 10:30-37)

Indeed, Jesus was stretching the lawyer's love of neighbor in two ways. For one thing, Jesus cleverly refused the lawyer's question simply by turning it on its head. To Jesus, the real question was not who was the lawyer's neighbor but whether or not the lawyer himself was neighborly. That much is clear simply from the structure of the story, without any historical background about titles like "priest," "Levite," or "Samaritan."

Knowing who the Samaritans were, however, helps us recognize a second way in which Jesus was stretching the lawyer's love. For pious and loyal Jews, the Samaritans were half-breeds and heretics. In many ways more irksome than clearly non-Jewish foreigners or Gentiles, they were seen as the product of dubious intermarriages; they worshipped the right God but in the wrong place and in the wrong ways.[7] What if Jesus had identified the robbery victim as a pathetic Samaritan and told the lawyer that he too deserved help? The lawyer might have had some trouble stretching love of neighbor, yet could probably have managed to *pity* him under the *guise* of love. But no, Jesus stretched further. A Samaritan was to be the lawyer's exemplar and mentor! Implicitly, the lawyer's love would have to recognize the Samaritan's dignity through a respect that went far beyond pity. The lawyer must "go and do likewise" by helping, sure. But he must do so by breaking through the common-sense categories and the borders that usually limit our love. Luke's inclusion of this story in the gospel has thus told all Christians ever since: Likewise "do likewise."

The problem with common-sense categories is that instead of unsettling our loves whenever they become too limited and complacent, "common sense" may *re*-settle a Christian ethic too quickly—even or especially a teaching on love that is as penetrating as Augustine's.

Notice what Augustine's overarching fourfold framework of loves has *not* yet told us, after all. It has told us how to prioritize love for God, others, self and temporal goods—but it has not yet told us how to coordinate love for multiple neighbors simultaneously.

Again, this is not necessarily a criticism. All the really tough issues of interpersonal relationships and social justice trace back to exactly this juncture. But an overarching framework can only do so much. It can serve as a map, but in and of itself a map cannot do our on-the-ground, location-specific work of navigation for us. In Catholic moral theology and other virtue-oriented approaches to ethics, this is why even the most carefully formulated rules can never supplant the need for prudence, rightly understood as the artful ability not only to recognize and do the right thing, but to do so in the right way at the right time.

Still, it is telling that Augustine's justifiable influence on later Christian traditions has proven most controversial and arguably most problematic precisely at those points where he sought to adjudicate competing claims for multiple neighbors.

St. Augustine in the stretch: neighbors near, distant, and estranged

One of Augustine's most basic tools for weighing the claims of multiple neighbors was the common sense one that all of us inevitably use. "Neighbor" literally means one who is near, and it seems obvious that we are best positioned to love those who literally are nearest to us—a bit *too* obvious. Ethicists call this "proximate love." Augustine put it this way: "All people are to be loved equally; but since you cannot be of service to everyone, you have to take greater care of those who are more closely joined to you by a turn, so to say, of fortune's wheel, whether by occasion of place or time, or any other circumstance."[8] Elsewhere he elaborated on the particular responsibilities one has to household and family "both in the order of nature and in the framework of human society," while citing the biblical injunction in 1 Timothy 5:8 to take care of one's own people, lest one prove worse than an unbeliever.[9]

Doubtless even the most idealistic Christian, or even the most radical advocate of global solidarity with the poor and hungry around the world, will have to make many—indeed most—decisions in just this way. In healthy families, for example, no one is more suited to care for a child than the child's own parents. But the same principle operates elsewhere: My university has about 5,500 undergraduates and I will be glad to help any one of them who knocks on my door, but of course my academic advisees and the students in my own classes are the ones who knock most often. Likewise, those who distinguish a proper duty of patriotism from jingoistic nationalism do so by rejecting appeals to love their country based on any sense of superiority to all others, and instead simply note that all people should love their nation as an extension of the love owed to the land and communities nearest to them. The principle is so common sense as to be banal. If it needs elaboration, that may actually be because arguably we could often use *more* "proximate love" not less. For in a culture of unprecedented mobility, in which people become increasingly accustomed to maintaining social ties through "virtual" communities using technology to bypass the limitations of geography and locale, we dare not lose the habits we need to relate to those whose real-time, real-space proximity makes them impossible simply to tune out, click off, or "de-friend" when we find ourselves in conflict.[10]

Augustine himself was uneasy about allowing proximate love to limit Christ's own love, however. The love of Christ himself, he recognized, is at work in the world creating that new worldwide social reality which is the church itself. In a homily on John 13:34-35, where Jesus told his disciples that he was giving them the "new commandment" that they love one another as he has loved them, Augustine took pains to distinguish such love from natural human loves, including between family members. Uniquely, he insisted, Christ's love is reflected in the mutual love of those who follow him, as it creates a new people who sing the "new song" of which Old Testament prophets spoke. It is this love alone "that is now renewing the nations, and from among the universal race of man, which overspreads the whole world, is making and gathering together a new people, the body of the newly married spouse of the only-begotten Son of God."[11]

Still, according to Jesus himself, love that partakes of the character of his heavenly Father must stretch further still—to enemies. As Oliver O'Donovan has observed, the common-sense obligations of proximate relations will present a problem for *any* theory of universal love.[12] And Jesus has upped the ante further still, both by identifying love for enemies as the distinguishing mark of God's own love and by anticipating that this very kind of love is what will distinguish those who are truly to be known as God's children. Lest there be any doubt, Jesus underscored his point by insisting that actually, proximate love is really quite unremarkable and humdrum:

> You have heard that it was said, "You shall love your neighbor and hate your enemy." But I say to you, Love your enemies and pray for those who persecute you, so that you may be children of your Father in heaven; for he makes his sun rise on the evil and on the good, and sends rain on the righteous and on the unrighteous. For if you love those who love you, what reward do you have? Do not even the tax collectors do the same? And if you greet only your brothers and sisters, what more are you doing than others? Do not even the Gentiles do the same? Be perfect [i.e., consistent, undiscriminating, and fully developed in your love], therefore, as your heavenly Father is perfect. (Matt 5:43-48)

Augustine knew this as well as anyone. But how to be faithful to the inevitable human duties of proximate love while doing better than the merely human morality of proximate love? This remained unsettling for Augustine. He and his community had very real and threatening enemies, after all. A competing church in North Africa, the Donatists, was aligned with an extremist guerrilla faction. Augustine lived long enough to see the so-called "barbarians" who were fighting for greater recognition in the Roman Empire reach the gates of the city where he lay on his deathbed. His were violent times. He thus strove mightily—even heroically—to guide Christian and civic leaders toward a way of responding to the threats of enemies while loving them as Jesus called and God's love required. But it is hardly surprising, then, that the traditions of Western Christianity that Augustine has so influenced have remained unsettled, and his legacy has been most controversial, precisely here at the borders where lines of identity, human recognition, and estrangement run.[13]

In the face of practical pastoral challenges, Augustine's love ethic both allowed him and forced him to hold multiple considerations in tension. Having recognized the biblical neighbor not simply as the proximate neighbor but as every human being, Augustine not only had to include enemies in the circle of neighbors, but to see in love of enemies the ultimate test of neighbor love. But just how *does* one love enemies? Augustine was surely right that discipline can and must be compatible with love—this is why we expect parents to exercise "tough love" for the good of their children. But Augustine then used this argument to justify religious coercion as a kind of loving correction that aimed to incentivize conversion. Fewer and fewer Christians defend such coercion today, and at the Second Vatican Council the Catholic Church decisively embraced principles of religious freedom with its 1965 declaration *Dignitatis Humanae*.

Less controversially, arguments similar to Augustine's help justify Christian involvement in governance for the sake of the common good through the exercise of civil authority. Not until modern times would a distinction between the roles of policing and soldiering begin to emerge, however, so in Augustine's mind these were also arguments for why Christians could participate in just wars. In all of this, Augustine still strove to be accountable to Jesus' call to love our enemies. Indeed, we know much about how he thought through these issues precisely because he so often used his sermons to plead with his congregations to treat the Donatists *generously*, and so often used his letters to cajole Christians in positions of power to be *lenient and merciful*. In their mercy, civil authorities should refuse recourse to the death penalty. If they were indeed acting from a true desire for peace, as they should, military men should resist every temptation toward cruelty and hatred.

If love of enemy was the ultimate test of neighbor love, however, many doubt that Augustine passed that test. For if Augustine would have us trace all of our moral decisions back to love of God and love of neighbor as to self—including the decisions Christians make as they exercise civil authority and participate in just wars—then what can possibly justify the killing of a threatening criminal in flight or an enemy on the battlefield except for love? Some critics accuse Augustine of imagining that it is possible to love enemies while killing them. They are almost right, and rightly unsettled at such a jarring counterintuitive. In fact, Augustine never said this in so many words. He certainly called rulers to rule and soldiers to fight out of a motivation of love for others that pursues the common good of society. And again, all of Augustine's moral counsel must trace its way back to love of God and neighbor as self.

What Augustine did not quite say is whether those who bear the sword could be expected and called to love the actual enemy one might have to kill in the process of acting out of love for still others. Yet it is hard to infer any other conclusion when we see so much of what he tried to hold in tension converging in the following paragraphs to Marcellinus, a devout Christian who was one of Rome's highest officials in North Africa:

> We must, then, always keep those precepts of patience in the disposition of the heart, and we must always have benevolence in the will so that we do not return evil for evil. But we also have to do many things, even against the will of people who need to be punished with a certain kind harshness, for we have to consider their benefit rather than their will. . . . For in rebuking a child, no matter how harshly, a father's love is surely never lost; he nonetheless does what the son does not want and causes pain to the son who, despite his unwillingness, he judges must be healed by pain. And for this reason, if this earthly state keeps the Christian commandments, even wars will not be waged without goodwill in order more easily to take into account the interests of the conquered with a view to a society made peaceful with piety and justice. For a person whose freedom for wickedness is taken away is conquered to his own benefit. . . . [Thus] good men would wage wars even with mercy, if this were possible, in order that by taming licentious passions they might destroy these vices that a just empire ought either to wipe out or to suppress. For, if Christian doctrine condemned all wars, it would rather be said in the gospel to the soldiers who sought advice about their salvation that they could cast aside their weapons and completely withdraw from the army. . . .[14]

Defenders of Augustine will want to jump in to explain, and then critics will push back—but that is my point. Augustine is arguably the most influential theologian of Western Christianity. Many Catholic thinkers will now cite Thomas Aquinas more often, while Protestant thinkers will cite Martin Luther and John Calvin, but all of these in turn saw themselves as faithful interpreters of Augustine, and even thinkers in dissenting traditions have felt his influence. Augustine also stood near the beginning of acceptance by many Christians of what they hope will be just wars, and he helped to cement the close cooperation between church and state that had begun to develop a few decades before, when the emperor Constantine legalized Christianity and sought help from Christian bishops in stabilizing imperial society. Augustine has thus left an unsettling legacy.

But if Augustine's thought is unsettled, that is because the Gospel itself unsettles. Critics should recognize his heroic efforts to remain truly accountable to Jesus' teachings in the face of tough ethical challenges. Defenders should recognize how his (and their own) straining to hold together love for proximate, distant, and estranged neighbors testifies to the way that Christlike love must ever stretch Christians in directions they do not naturally want to go. For no Christian ethical deliberation can change the character of the One who is its very foundation. The Father of Jesus Christ is one who makes rain and sunshine fall on the just and unjust alike, on friends and enemies, on neighbors near and far—both far as in distant strangers and far as in profoundly estranged. The very debate over Augustine's legacy thus makes clear the one point we most need to agree upon in order to proceed:

Love of neighbor has been stretching toward global solidarity all along.

Quietly yet relentlessly, gospel love of neighbor just keeps yearning and calling Christians to care actively for distant neighbors across cultures and around the globe, even including enemies, in the embrace of human solidarity. The priorities of the proximate cannot be dismissed, but neither can they serve as a singularly reliable guide. For even the best philosophical or theological clarity about how to order justly the duties of Christian love can never alter the character at its core. The trinitarian wellspring of Christian love must ever be expected to stretch and break out of even our most elegant categories. After all,

- the loving God and Creator of *all* creation . . .

- revealed preeminently in Jesus of Nazareth who linked the very character of his heavenly Father with love of enemies, and who himself died for "them" as well as "us" when we too were estranged . . .

- keeps beckoning and cajoling God's pilgrim people called church to embrace their unexpected others, through the Holy Spirit who is the very bond of God's own mutual love.

To build a civilization of love

Christian social ethics and Catholic social teaching, apparently, cannot help but risk charges of idealism. Addressing the General Assembly of the United Nations on the occasion of its fiftieth anniversary in 1995, Pope John Paul II implicitly acknowledged the risk of such charges but refused to accept them: "None of this should appear an unattainable utopia," he insisted.[15] And what was his "this"? It was the visionary call that he and his predecessor, Pope Paul VI, had been making for the world community to transform itself into a *civilization of love*.

If the notion of a civilization of love could draw charges of idealism, the reason may simply be that it is elusive—suggestive but elusive. For those who know the history of actual civilizations and the way they have risen through domination of the natural world, class stratification, and imperial conquest of subject peoples, the word "civilization" bespeaks the *hard* language of political Realism. After all, even the positive civility that civilization at best makes possible always seems to be a tenuous space carved out through the harsh realities of power for some and violence against others. The word "love," however, strikes many as *soft* language, so that to speak of a civilization of love must appear to reintroduce political Idealism. Which is it, then, realism or idealism? Are we to sing nationalistic anthems or "Kumbaya?"

(The elusiveness of the term "civilization of love" also may go far to explain why it has yet to catch on either among Catholic social thinkers and activists or in the wider Catholic imagination. This despite John Paul's steadily increasing employment of the term throughout his papacy in relation to a wide range of political, economic, cultural, and social issues.[16] Indeed, the 2004 *Compendium of the Social Doctrine of the Church*, published scarcely a year before the pope's death, unmistakably signals the role that "the civilization of love" is supposed to play in summarizing the whole of Catholic social teaching; its final summary chapter bears the title "For a Civilization of Love," and the chapter itself concludes with a section titled "Building the Civilization of Love."[17])

It reflects no criticism either of John Paul II, or of his predecessor, Paul VI, who first introduced the term in 1970,[18] if we recognize that the pontiff did not know exactly what the civilization of love must look like either—if by that we are expecting him to have elaborated a full cultural, economic, and political program. Catholic social teaching often takes pains to clarify that in their role as authoritative teachers of the Catholic Christian faith (the role known as that of the *magisterium*), popes and bishops are not attempting to endorse any one political or economic model or work out all the policy implications of their teaching. Rather the role of the magisterium with regard to Catholic social teaching is to lay out those broad and necessary moral principles that any system must follow if it is to be humane and just. Differing societies, in their freedom, must work out the specific institutional patterns that are appropriate to their cultures. And within the church itself, it is the laity that is to play the leading role in helping work out those specifics as part of its vocation to "seek the Kingdom of God by engaging in temporal affairs and ordering them according to the plan of God."[19]

Still, at least eight principles are discernible in John Paul II's 1995 address to the United Nations General Assembly. These must not only guide all true work to build a civilization of love, it turns out, but may also help navigate the shoals and puzzles of globalization.

1. *Christian concern seeks and embraces the good of all human beings.* Though the first and most basic of guidelines for building a civilization of love that we may discern in John Paul's address is not particularly original, its very unoriginality reminds us again of the stretch toward global solidarity that has been inherent in Christianity from the beginning. If John Paul could stop nowhere short of such an all-encompassing concept as "civilization of love," that simply reflects the character of Christian love of neighbor itself. As he himself noted, John Paul was addressing the United Nations precisely because the Vatican's role in international diplomacy is supposed to reflect something far greater than national self-interest. The Holy See or Vatican foreign ministry, "in virtue of its specifically spiritual mission, [is] concerned for the integral good of every human being."[20] Later in the speech he elaborated: "Because of the radiant humanity of Christ,

nothing genuinely human fails to touch the hearts of Christians. . . . Love of Christ does not distract us from interest in others, but rather invites us to responsibility for them, to the exclusion of no one and indeed, if anything, with a special concern for the weakest and the suffering."[21]

2. *The accelerated global quest for freedom that distinguishes our time reflects universal human rights that we must recognize as grounded in the nature and dignity of the human person.* If faith in Christ stretches Christian love in ever-widening circles, it also reveals a reality that must have been present all along, with or without faith. Namely, whether or not people ancient or modern have recognized themselves as created by a loving God, all and each of them indeed enjoys human dignity. The United Nations' 1948 Universal Declaration of Human Rights had been a response to the "outrages against human dignity" in the previous decades, but it has "remain[ed] one of the highest expressions of the human conscience of our time."[22] Recognition of human dignity, noted the pope, has become irrepressible:

> On the threshold of a new millennium we are witnessing an extraordinary global acceleration of that quest for freedom which is one of the great dynamics of human history. This phenomenon is not limited to any one part of the world, nor is it the expression of any single culture. Men and women throughout the world, even when threatened by violence, have taken the risk of freedom, asking to be given a place in social, political, and economic life which is commensurate with their dignity as free human beings. This universal longing for freedom is truly one of the distinguishing marks of our time.[23]

Indeed, "the non-violent revolutions of 1989" that toppled totalitarian regimes throughout Central Europe and dismantled the Soviet empire had "demonstrated that the quest for freedom cannot be suppressed."[24]

3. *Truly human freedom is found, however, neither in libertarian license nor through imperialistic imposition, but through active nonviolence and social solidarity.* Though the quest for freedom is insuppressible, it is nonetheless subject to misunderstanding and ideological manipulation. Thus, insisted John Paul, we need to grasp the "inner structure"

of the worldwide movement for freedom and universal human rights.²⁵ Any culture of freedom will have an "inner architecture," a "moral structure," that encourages both persons and societies to use their freedom responsibly.²⁶

> Freedom is not simply the absence of tyranny or oppression. Nor is freedom a licence to do whatever we like. Freedom has an inner "logic" which distinguishes it and ennobles it: *freedom is ordered to the truth*, and is fulfilled in man's quest for truth and in man's living in the truth. Detached from the truth about the human person, freedom deteriorates into license in the lives of individuals, and, in political life, it becomes the caprice of the most powerful and the arrogance of power.²⁷

Note the pontiff's paired warnings against the abuse of freedom both by individuals and in political life. At least in the West, and perhaps especially in the United States, there is a tendency to decry the abuse of freedom in one of these areas while winking at the other—or while accepting it in the name of realism, or even while celebrating it. The tendency on "the left" is to underplay the role of personal and sexual self-discipline in a healthy society, for example, while seeing the benefits of economic and workplace regulation. The tendency on "the right" is to underplay the role of economic regulation in disciplining the marketplace for the common good, while emphasizing the benefits of thrift for those who expect to get ahead, as well as sexual propriety for the sake of strong and well-ordered families. Internationally, both "left" and "right" have been willing to intervene and impose their values on other nations in the name of freedom—despite the inherent contradictions in any attempt to *impose* freedom!—but each exercises greater indulgence toward the abuses of regimes whose stated values roughly match their own balance of economic or social priorities. The "architecture" of Catholic social teaching undergirds neither of these biases. Because the truth of the human person is that we are always who we are through relationship with God and one another, our thoroughgoing interdependence means we can only really be free together. And being free together requires the practiced inculcation of shared habits. Social solidarity is thus both the goal toward which we are to exercise our freedom and the moral discipline that makes us truly free.

The 1989 Revolution had shown that to struggle nonviolently toward a new order of social solidarity opened up altogether realistic alternatives to both dubious libertarian and violently coercive paths to "freedom." John Paul had been a leading figure on the world stage amid the events that led to the 1989 Revolution. From his vantage point, the decisive cause of the collapse of the Soviet empire had been neither the threat of relentless military buildup led by U.S. President Ronald Reagan in the 1980s nor even the way John Paul had set off a chain reaction by inspiring the Solidarność labor movement in his homeland of Poland. Rather it was the dedication of ordinary people in such movements using strategies of active nonviolence and envisioning a new order of social solidarity:

> The revolutions of 1989 were made possible by the commitment of brave men and women inspired by a different, and ultimately more profound and powerful, vision: the vision of man as a creature of intelligence and free will, immersed in a mystery which transcends his own being and endowed with the ability to reflect and the ability to choose—and thus capable of wisdom and virtue. A decisive factor in the success of those non-violent revolutions was the experience of social solidarity. . . .[28]

In other words, the only way to build rather than impose a civilization of love is through active nonviolence. Further, the only way to exercise a freedom that enhances rather than impinges on the freedom of others is through social solidarity. However a civilization of love may take shape, therefore, it can be neither a libertarian project, nor an imperialist project, nor that strange and contradictory mix by which some claim to be extending democracy and free markets when they expand their spheres of geopolitical influence through military means.

4. *For social solidarity to be concrete, the quest for freedom and universal rights must translate into just economic relationships.* The quest for freedom is not really advancing, after all, if it is simply "freeing" some to use others as tools to advance their own interests. The approach to ethics and policy-making known as *utilitarianism* is so widely assumed across the cultural and political spectrum that as John Paul elaborated on the inner architecture of freedom, he rejected it by

name. At least when understood as "the doctrine which defines morality not in terms of what is good but of what is advantageous," utilitarianism "threatens the freedom of individuals and nations and obstructs the building of a true culture of freedom." It is precisely such an approach to international politics that "inspires an aggressive nationalism on the basis of which the subjugation, for example, of a smaller or weaker nation is claimed to be a good thing solely because it corresponds to the national interest." But "*economic* utilitarianism" also leads to consequences that are "no less grave" and "devastating," for it "drives more powerful countries to manipulate and exploit weaker ones."[29]

Indeed—the pontiff pointed out—economic and nationalistic utilitarianism often work in tandem. This was why the post-colonial era had proven so disappointing to the nations of the Global South. Political independence had left them just as dependent economically on the Global North, if not more, as they struggled simply to satisfy "the essential needs of their people." "Such situations offend the conscience of humanity and pose a formidable moral challenge to the human family." The answer, however, "cannot be conceived exclusively in terms of help and assistance, or even by considering the eventual returns on the resources provided." Instead, true and just economic development will require both South and North to take responsibility. Developing countries must guarantee "proper management . . . as well as respect for human rights, by replacing where necessary unjust, corrupt, or authoritarian forms of government with participatory and democratic ones" if they hope to "unleash the best civil and economic energies of their people." But developed countries must also change their approach by "renounc[ing] strictly utilitarian approaches and develop[ing] new approaches inspired by greater justice and solidarity."[30]

> Yes, distinguished Ladies and Gentlemen! The international economic scene needs an ethic of solidarity, if participation, economic growth, and a just distribution of goods are to characterize the future of humanity. . . . When millions of people are suffering from a poverty which means hunger, malnutrition, sickness, illiteracy, and degradation, we must not only remind ourselves that no one has a right to exploit another for his own

advantage, but also and above all we must recommit ourselves to that solidarity which enables others to live out, in the actual circumstances of their economic and political lives, the creativity which is a distinguishing mark of the human person and the true source of the wealth of nations in today's world.[31]

5. *Human communities, not simply individuals, enjoy rights.* We now come to a most crucial point, both for grasping John Paul's vision of a civilization of love and for navigating the shoals and puzzles of globalization. Even though many resist the implications, it is not *too* hard to recognize that Catholic social teaching in general, and the papal call to build a civilization of love in particular, do not fit neatly onto a standard left-right political continuum, for by turns they alternately challenge and buttress arguments all along a continuum of socialist, regulated, social-welfare, entrepreneurial, and free-market economic models. But why?

Why does a Catholic social vision not quite coincide with our standard political categories, much less endorse any one economic model? One key reason is that in the modern world we are so in the habit of framing our debates and choices around the relative claims, rights, and responsibilities of individuals on the one hand, and national governments or nation-states on the other hand, that we have trouble hearing proposals or imagining models that focus elsewhere. While arguing fiercely for the rights and dignity of every individual human person from conception to natural death, however, Catholic social teaching does not exactly endorse *individualism*. And while it certainly expects national governments and international bodies such as the United Nations to play crucial roles in service to the common good of humanity even as they especially protect "the weakest and the suffering," Catholic social teaching resists overbearingly nationalistic claims too. Its vision is certainly not totalitarian, but neither is it that of liberalism in either its economic or social forms.

Rather, the freedom, liberty, and liberation that John Paul was celebrating resides in communities that inhabit social spaces in between the individual and the nation-state, yet face both directions through positive engagement. It would thus enable the individual persons who constitute those communities to thrive, while serving the common good of other communities who together constitute "society" and civilization. Such a vision is neither anti-government in the name of individualism, nor large-government in the name of total solutions. It is communitarian.

6. *Nation-states and the international system represented by the United Nations have a role to play in building a civilization of love, but are not the key.* We may miss the crucial communitarian point as it surfaces in John Paul's address to the United Nations, however, unless we also notice how he used the word "nation." No sooner had he celebrated the global quest for freedom in the twentieth century, and those who take risks for it, than the pontiff paused to remind his listeners that this quest "has engaged not only individuals but nations as well." After all, the violations that had first provoked World War II and then prompted the founding of the United Nations itself in the hope of avoiding future wars had been *"violations of the rights of nations."* In other words, "Many of those nations suffered grievously for no other reason than that they were deemed 'other.' Terrible crimes were committed in the name of lethal doctrines which taught the 'inferiority' of some nations and cultures" precisely as groups.[32] So pause to notice, said the pope: The United Nations had "spoke[n] eloquently of the rights of persons; but *no similar international agreement has yet adequately addressed the rights of nations*. This situation must be carefully pondered, for it raises urgent questions about justice and freedom in the world today."[33]

Key to what needed pondering, however, were the issues of identity amid globalization that require us to rethink the very definition of those nations whose communal rights deserve recognition, John Paul II pointed out. In previous centuries, ethicists, jurists, and statesmen had defended the rights of vulnerable nations to exist as independent nation-states, from Central Europe to the so-called New World. But globalization and the blurring of borders now presented new challenges to nationalities seeking to preserve their communal identities:

> Today the problem of nationalities forms part of a new world horizon marked by a great "mobility" which has blurred the ethnic and cultural frontiers of the different peoples, as a result of a variety of processes such as migrations, mass-media and the globalization of the economy. And yet, precisely against this

horizon of universality we see the powerful re-emergence of a certain ethnic and cultural consciousness, as it were an explosive need for identity and survival, a sort of counterweight to the tendency toward uniformity.[34]

The impulse to preserve communal identity "must not be underestimated or regarded as a simple left-over of the past." Far from reflecting some kind of primal or retrograde tribalism that the modern world would eventually get over—the pope seemed to be saying—this phenomenon "demands serious interpretation, and a closer examination on the levels of anthropology, ethics and law."[35]

Intrinsic to the human condition, after all, is a "tension between the particular and the universal." Sharing the same human nature, "people automatically feel that they are members of one great family" and indeed they are. But as historical creatures, our shared humanity always takes concrete historical shape, so that human beings "are necessarily bound in a *more intense* way to particular human groups, beginning with the family and going on to the various groups to which they belong and up to the whole of their ethnic and cultural group, which is called, not by accident, a 'nation', from the Latin word 'nasci': 'to be born.'" Any adequate anthropology or understanding of the human condition must hold the two poles of universality and particularity in a "vital" and "inevitable" tension, and any social ethic or global politics must embrace that tension as a fruitful one if we are to live it out "in a calm and balanced way." Exactly how the claims of individuals, nations, and nation-states are to be synchronized may be difficult and require serious study. But what should be clear from this anthropological foundation is that upon it rests "the 'rights of nations,' which are nothing but 'human rights' fostered at the specific level of community life."[36]

In any case, key both to John Paul's argument here, and to the continuing study he called for, is the recognition that nations are not the same as nation-states. Indeed, they often exist independently of nation-states and are never simply coterminous with them. John Paul's native Poland had survived as a nation despite losing statehood and disappearing from maps for over a century. What complicates any study of "the rights of nations," admitted the pope, is "the difficulty of defining the very concept of 'nation.'" But this much was clear, he insisted: it "cannot be identified a priori and necessarily with the State." Every nation has a right to exist—he insisted emphatically—and none can deprive another of that right for any reason. But this "fundamental right to existence does not necessarily call for sovereignty as a state." We should speak instead of a "kind of fundamental spiritual 'sovereignty' " by which every nation "enjoys the right to its own language and culture." And thus, so long as it does not abuse basic human rights or oppress other minorities, "[e]very nation therefore has also the right to shape its life according to its own traditions."[37]

7. *Globalization must not mean homogenization, therefore.* Here then is the puzzle that we will grapple with for many pages, but whose unlocking may open the way toward a deeply Catholic theology of peace: How are we to build a just and peaceful social order extending around the world—whether we loftily call it a "civilization of love" or not—that avoids decimating vulnerable peoples, economies, and cultures through its very spread and unintended consequences? Globalization often proceeds in the name of noble goals of freedom and prosperity but ends up favoring the strong, while corroding the cultural identities of the weak, as it alternately requires and seduces them into smoothing out their differences and trivializing their traditions in order to participate in global systems.

It is no accident that John Paul II addressed the United Nations General Assembly not as "the people of the world" but as a "family of peoples."[38] The first phrase would have allowed for that very cultural homogenization which globalization too often seems to entail. The pope's alternative implied a more complex diversity-within-universality. One reflection of that complex was his pairing, in a single paragraph,[39] of the universality of human rights and the continuing insistence of Catholic social teaching that "there is no single model for organizing the politics and economics of human freedom," since "different cultures and different historical experiences give rise to different institutional forms of public life in a free and responsible society." Furthermore, reflected John Paul in yet another section, the very nature of a family is that of "a community based on mutual trust, mutual support and sincere respect. In an authentic family the strong do not dominate; instead, the weaker members, because of their very weakness, are all the more welcomed and served." The role of a body such as the United Nations, therefore, was to help create the conditions that would allow the nations of the world not only to relate organizationally but at a "more 'organic' level" as it fostered "a fruitful exchange of gifts, primarily for the good of the weaker nations but even so, [as] a clear harbinger of greater good for everyone."[40]

Christianity itself had a crucial role to play precisely here. "Unhappily, the world has yet to learn how to live with diversity. . . . The fact of 'difference,' and the reality of 'the other,' can sometimes be felt as a burden, or even as a threat," leading to "a denial of the very humanity of 'the other': with the result that people fall into a cycle of violence in which no one is spared, not even the children."[41] Respect for diverse cultures must begin with the recognition that no culture is *merely* a culture, for at a profound level, each

> is an effort to ponder the mystery of the world and in particular of the human person: it is a way of giving expression to the transcendent dimension of human life. The heart of every culture is its approach to the greatest of all mysteries: the mystery of God. . . . Thus the 'difference' which some find so threatening can, through respectful dialogue, become the source of a deeper understanding of the mystery of human existence.[42]

This prompted the pontiff to underscore generally "*the fundamental right to freedom of religion and freedom of conscience,* as one of the cornerstones in the structure of human rights and the foundation of every truly free society."[43] But the particularity of faith in Jesus Christ must lead the church itself still further away from intolerance and toward respectful dialogue:

> Faith in Christ does not impel us to intolerance. On the contrary, it obliges us to engage others in a respectful dialogue. Love of Christ does not distract us from interest in others, but rather invites us to responsibility for them, to the exclusion of no one and indeed, if anything, with a special concern for the weakest and the suffering. Thus, . . . the Church asks only to be able to propose respectfully this message of salvation, and to be able to promote, in charity and service, the solidarity of the entire human family.[44]

And although an address before the United Nations was not the place to address matters of ecclesiology internal to Christianity itself, other formative resources from the post-conciliar era allow us to extrapolate: The very way that the church itself embodies diversity-within-unity would have to be among its greatest contributions to respectful globalization, insofar as the church "passes the peace" among formerly estranged peoples when it allows the Gospel to take distinctive shape within many cultures. Any Christian social ethic or Catholic peace theology that hopes to rise to the challenges of globalization will thus need to attend to the Vatican II mandate to welcome appropriate models of "inculturation" that invite Christians to become a truly catholic global church.

8. *Only by risking strategies of active nonviolence will we build a civilization of love.* The lessons of the 1989 Revolution were not just that no system—not even a totalitarian system—could thwart the aspiration of all peoples for freedom, nor that the United Nations must respond by redoubling its efforts to institutionalize respect for universal human rights. For if, as the pontiff noted, utilitarianism can be a dangerous temptation, then the *means* of struggling for freedom matter as much as the *end* for freedom. The intrinsic connection that John Paul II drew between freedom, solidarity, and nonviolence thus bears repeating.

John Paul's overarching hope as he looked ahead to the year 2000, and indeed the hope among the gathered nations of the world to which he appealed, was that "a *century of violent coercion* [would] be succeeded by a *century of persuasion.*"[45] Learning to engage in dialogue between cultures and nations based on recognition of universal human rights was of course essential to such a transition. But his repeated references to the 1989 Revolution serve to remind us that one may not always be able to move from violent coercion to persuasion through talk alone. Social struggle is often necessary. Power may be required in order to persuade the powerful to come to the table. So what kind of power maintains respect for adversaries and their freedom too, their dignity too, their humanity and human rights too, even amid social struggle? Only a form of struggle and an exercise of power that depends upon rather than tatters the webs of human solidarity.

The 1989 Revolution in Central Europe that had toppled Soviet totalitarianism was John Paul II's model for many reasons, but this one was crucial. Again, it was not just that he himself had been a player in, and inspiration for, that global event. It was not just that as a Pole and a Polish bishop he had experienced the devastations and degradations of Soviet rule firsthand. No, just as in his encyclical *Centesimus Annus*, the pontiff's focus was not on himself or his own experiences but on that "commitment of brave men and women inspired by a different, and ultimately more profound and powerful, vision" of social change that comes by living out the fullness of their humanity:

> A decisive factor in the success of those non-violent revolutions was the experience of social solidarity: in the face of regimes backed by the power of propaganda and terror, that solidarity was the moral core of the "power of the powerless," a beacon of hope and an enduring reminder that it is possible for man's historical journey to follow a path which is true to the finest aspirations of the human spirit.[46]

And those same values—that same moral architecture which means *we* cannot achieve freedom unless we struggle in a way that preserves solidarity with *them* and their humanity too—was what linked recent "people's liberation movements and many of the moral commitments inscribed in the United Nations Charter."[47] In other words, the moral structure shaping nonviolent social movements from below must continue being institutionalized at national and global levels. By implication, John Paul II was recognizing active nonviolence as essential for building a civilization of love. This, after all, was his heartfelt appeal:

> Inspired by the example of all those who have taken the *risk of freedom*, can we not recommit ourselves also to taking the *risk of solidarity*—and thus the *risk of peace*?

Welcome home away from home

Along with much else—but key to much else—John Paul II has reminded us that a "tension between the particular and the universal" has always been intrinsic to human existence. Human beings are all part of one universal family, yet can only live out their shared humanity in particular families, communities, cultures, nations, histories. Our very "human condition thus finds itself between these two poles—universality and particularity—with a vital tension between them." That tension, however, will be "singularly fruitful if they are lived in a calm and balanced way."[48]

"Singularly fruitful." Which is to say that in building a "civilization of love" nothing will be more fruitful. Which is to say that in building peace both locally and globally—nothing will be more fruitful. For however abstract the "two poles" of "universality and particularity" may sound at first, together they name the dogged problem that bedevils every project for building more just, peaceful, and truly humane human communities. Yet the promise of a fruitful tension between them also names a path, a strategy, a social posture for doing so. Indeed, as I will argue in chapter 5, they name nothing short of God's own "Abrahamic" strategy for working within history to save humanity.

The dogged, bedeviling problem is how to do two things simultaneously: How are we to practice universality without imperialism? But then how are we to celebrate particularity without tribalism?

The first side of the problematic may not be obvious to those who are trying to live out the implications of universalism until it is too late, though it may be obvious immediately to the recipients of their poorly practiced good intentions. As we have seen, true Christian love must stretch beyond the borders of proximate love in order to serve the good of those who bear many other identities, and really has nowhere to stop stretching until it reaches the universal good of all humanity and the planet that sustains us. At their best, other religions, too, invoke universal regard and compassion. And partly in reaction to the failure of Christians as well as other believers to rise above our own historical tribalisms, modern philosophers, at least since the so-called Enlightenment, have offered their own projects in the name of reason and universal human rights. But one after another, and often reacting one to another, universalizing projects have taken imperialist turns. Christian missionary work over the centuries has too often gone hand in hand with geographical conquest and colonialism. But Enlightenment liberal projects have just as easily gone hand in hand with economic or cultural conquest and neo-colonialism as well. Just as "the white man's burden" once motivated *both* generous efforts to uplift others through educational, medical, and economic development *and* cynical efforts to "civilize" "backward races," a new white woman's burden rightly advocates universal education of girls but thus offers the best face for wars in the Islamic world. The point is not to dismiss any of these or other benevolent efforts out of hand, but to recognize their shared challenge of practicing universal regard without turning imperialistic.

The flip side of the problematic, after all, may arise as we recognize the mistakes of these well-meaning incursions into the cultures of others, or they may start closer to home. Believers who insist on the need to preserve a specifically Catholic or Christian identity, for example, are not wrong. In order to serve the world and promote the common good of humanity precisely as Christians, we have to know who we are and keep our primary loyalties clear. And as we have just seen, this side of the problematic does not go away at all when a sense of vocation impels Christians qua Christians into solidarity with other faith communities and "all people of goodwill" in pursuit of human development and peace with justice. For on whichever side of the problematic we begin, the Golden Rule as translated into intercommunal relations would insist that we respect the cultural integrity of other peoples as we would have them respect ours. And yet our valid mutual fear is that efforts to preserve communal identity—whether theirs or ours or both—will express themselves in the very opposite of solidarity. This is what we name and fear when we speak of tribalism. In tribalism we are back to the all-too-easy human tendency to prefer our own kind over the needs of distant neighbors, to say nothing of our inclination to love our own kind rather than to love our enemies. Hopefully we can recognize that cultural integrity and communal cohesion is itself a human need. But now we both recognize a temptation in ourselves, and fear it in others—namely, that we or they will use violence or cultural repression to defend the borders of clan, ethnicity, race, nation, or religion.

Hence the tension between particularity and universality proves almost brutally concrete, not abstract at all. Particularity sins against universal concern when it issues in tribalism. Universality sins against respect for particular communities and cultures when it issues in imperialism, overt and covert alike. No Christian social ethic, or outworking of Catholic social teaching, or proposal for peace theology will prove adequate unless it can navigate through both sides of this problematic.

Yet this is exactly the problematic through which God has been trying to guide God's people since launching Abraham, Sarah, and their children as a pilgrim people who would celebrate the blessing of a covenanted identity while being a blessing to all the families of the earth. A pilgrim people entering into relationship with families throughout the earth must always have an ambivalent, tenuous relationship to land and territory. As much as anyone else, they need the harvest of the land to live. Yet territorial control so easily subverts their very identity as a people on pilgrimage through history and culture. The only safe defense for any quasi-nomadic pilgrim community therefore will always be a repertoire of skills at peacemaking and hospitality. Diaspora must be their identity; diaspora must be the gift they give. Arguably, living out the only social posture that holds particularity and universality together in fruitful tension, that turns love into realism, and that actually stands a chance of building a civilization of love—diaspora is such a people's very home. It is always a home away from home, to be sure. But for Christians to welcome life in diaspora is to *return* home to what church always was supposed to be.

That a globalizing world may now be forcing us to struggle with what it means to be a global church—in other words a truly catholic Catholic Church—does not make any of this new. It simply makes it obvious. God is welcoming us home away from home. God is leading us to become Catholic again for the first time.

Chapter 4

We're All in Diaspora Now: Being Global Church in an Age of Globalization

> The mere fact of [the church] being a diaspora on this planet has had to be gradually admitted. . . . Indeed, we are undoubtedly in an era which is going to see an increase in this diaspora character, no matter what causes we may assign to it. . . . It seems to me that much depends on our fully and freely recognizing this fact and courageously accepting its consequences.
>
> —Karl Rahner, SJ[1]

> I believe that in this saying about the lord who should serve others, and also in Jesus' own actions in doing so himself [e.g. by washing his disciples' feet], we see the true revolution that can and should change the world. . . . God, who is absolute power itself, doesn't want to trample on us, but kneels down before us so as to exalt us. The mystery of the greatness of God is seen precisely in the fact that he can be small. He doesn't always have to take the highest place or the box seats. God is trying in this way to wean us away from our ideas of power and domination.
>
> —Joseph Cardinal Ratzinger
> (soon to become Pope Benedict XVI)[2]

To many readers, of course, the Roman Catholic Church—with its ancient stones, artistic treasures, conquering past, and continuing prominence on the world stage—hardly seems to constitute a people in diaspora.

For critics, the Catholic Church seems the epitome of Christian institutional power, having once been the official religion of the Roman Empire, and then provided cultural and religious glue for Western civilization, and then become the established church of many nations, especially in Europe and Latin America. Even today in countries such as the United States, with its separation of church and state, Catholics are in positions of prominence; if anything they seem to have moved decisively out of diaspora, from marginalized immigrant communities to influential halls of power.[3]

For some Catholic thinkers, the prospect of diaspora will prompt objections from an opposite direction. Certain kinds of Catholic apologists will be loath to relinquish the very vision of a church militant that critics fear. For them, exercising cultural and political power in order to preserve or reinstate Christian values is not a regret but a responsibility. Meanwhile, other Catholics may recoil at such militancy, yet still worry that diaspora could imply a sectarian withdrawal from cultural engagement. For them, to embrace life in diaspora would mean capitulating to voices in the church that are already calling for an adversarial "Christ-against-culture" posture toward society, thus trading away a Catholic genius for cultural engagement in service to the common good in favor of a countercultural siege mentality.

Prescient words from Karl Rahner, SJ, as early as 1961 should give pause to skeptics on all sides.[4] Many consider the German Jesuit to have been "the most prominent and influential Catholic theologian of the twentieth century."[5] As Rahner was erudite, a student not just of classical Catholic theology but of the early twentieth-century philosopher Martin Heidegger, and among the most prominent unofficial advisers as the Second Vatican Council sought to guide the Catholic Church into rapprochement with the modern world, none can accuse him of shrinking from deep engagement with the world, its thought, or its historical trends. If anything, Rahner's influence has waned somewhat in recent decades as some Catholic commentators have worried that he was *too* generous toward secular experience, toward other religions, and toward modernity in general. Perhaps. But precisely because Rahner engaged culture in the world so broadly, he recognized earlier than most theologians that by going global, Christianity was becoming what it always claimed to be, and could no longer pretend to express itself fully through any one culture, much less control the social order.

Diaspora was for Rahner both a descriptive "fact," therefore, and a normative or imperative "must."[6] "My thesis is this," he wrote:

> In so far as our outlook is really based on today and looking towards tomorrow, the present situation of Christians can be characterized as that of a diaspora; and this signifies, in terms of the history of salvation, a "must," from which we may and must draw conclusions about our behavior as Christians.[7]

Older forms of Christendom were gone or going: "the Christendom of the Middle Ages" was obviously gone, but early modern and baroque forms of Christendom ("peasant and individualistic petty-bourgeois" versions were the way he named them) were also "going to disappear with ever-increasing speed."[8] Whether or not European countries should be considered mission-sending countries or mission fields had become "an open question."[9]

So Rahner was blunt. Christians simply had to face the fact that they were no longer in control:[10]

> The mere fact of being a diaspora on this planet has had to be gradually admitted. . . . [T]hat there are no longer any Christian countries . . . is a fact. Christianity (though in very varying proportions) exists *everywhere* in the world, and everywhere as a diaspora. It is effectually, *in terms of numbers*, a minority everywhere; nowhere does it fill such a role of effective leadership as would permit it to set upon the age, with any force or clarity, the stamp of a Christian ideal. Indeed, we are undoubtedly in an era which is going to see an increase in this diaspora character, no matter what causes we may assign to it.[11]

And really, Christians should never have expected otherwise. After all, "that we are a diaspora throughout the world is not merely a fact to be recognized *a posteriori* [as a matter of descriptive reality] and with dismay." For while Christians should desire what "ought" to be and wish that none need live in diaspora because all people know Christ and live according to God's will,[12] the church's own founder promised nothing at all like a straight line toward institutional success, free of paradox or cross. Rather, the very one whom Christians call Lord promised that Christianity would in some way or another always be a "sign of contradiction."[13] Persecution from without the church, and waning love within the church, are always possibilities we must anticipate. Inversely, we should not expect to manage and reform our way to the kingdom of God. For according to the Gospel—proclaimed by the one who founded Christianity precisely through the logic of cross and resurrection, not the logic of cause and effect—"the victory of Christianity would not be the fruit of immanent development and widening and a steady, progressive leavening of the world but would come as the act of God coming in judgment to gather up world history into its wholly unpredictable and unexpected end."[14]

Rahner knew that the reality of life in diaspora would not find easy acceptance among Christians: "We have still not fully wakened from our dream of a homogeneous Christian West. It often leads us to react furiously and in a false context when something happens to shake us out of the dream." Assuming we live in a different sociohistorical situation than we actually do, and trying desperately to hold on to the ideal of Christian hegemony, we use "inappropriate means" attempting to achieve misguided ends.[15] Wide recognition that the Christian community would have to live, grow, and preserve itself "in an indifferent or hostile environment" as "a Church of the diaspora, now and for the foreseeable future" was thus not automatic. Nonetheless, "much depends on our fully and freely recognizing this fact and courageously accepting its consequences."[16]

For in fact, diaspora presented the church above all with opportunity. While some Catholics might be tempted to respond to the historical fact of life everywhere in diaspora by closing themselves off in the manner of old Jewish ghettos, diaspora should not prompt the church to be any less missionary—any less intent, that is, on influencing public affairs and institutions for the good.[17] If anything, Christians could now direct their missionary fervor and concern for the common good toward the true tasks of inviting and nurturing authentic faith. Too often the desire of the church or its clergy to influence society through control had simply confirmed to people that they would do better to stay outside of the church.[18] In contrast, a cool and compassionate analysis of life in diaspora should mean the very opposite of defeatism. For ceasing to try to baptize everyone meant that the real adventure of inviting people to believe the Christian Gospel and to grow in its practice could begin; Christians would thus be demanding "less of ourselves, but that less [would be] the right thing."[19]

To embrace life in diaspora is an opportunity rather than a retreat because the tensions of diaspora are such richly creative ones. In diaspora, Christians can willingly embrace the best of the cultures that host them precisely because they enjoy a sense of their own identity, which also gives them the confidence to resist any idolatrous worst. Yet trusting that God the loving Creator of all peoples is at work in all history, and that their blest calling is to be a blessing to all peoples, their very identity simultaneously allows them to risk a life of skirting borders. Learning to live and work along and across borders, in fact, the Christian community paradoxically finds its way back to the heart of its homeland.

Social ethics in an age of globalization

To be sure, in the previous chapter we had to recognize that borders have often been problematic for Christian ethics. As we reminded ourselves, Jesus made quite clear to his disciples that there is nothing particularly remarkable about a love that extends only to our own kind. Ignoring this clarity, though, Christians have not always recognized the problem of borders. Globalization is now making borders problematic for *everyone*, however, and that can prompt Christians to recognize overlooked truths about their faith, their ecclesiology, their ethical practice, and even their liturgical practice that have been there all along. In chapter 6 we will seek to retrieve the long and ancient Christian self-understanding as a diaspora people that always lives in exile. For as St. Cyprian of Carthage noted in the third century, it is precisely because Christians can never be entirely at home in any country that they are at home in every country.

Now, however, *everyone* lives in diaspora, in some way, anyway.[20] Globalization has done this to us. Within some nation-states—thanks to centuries of migration—no single ethnic, racial, religious, or hyphenated national group may be able to claim majority status. And thanks to the interlacing of economic ties, even a population that constitutes a clear majority within one territorial set of borders will necessarily constitute a minority within the borderless global economy. Meanwhile the borders of putatively sovereign nation-states themselves are increasingly porous. Even if nation-states are successful at keeping out invaders or undocumented immigrants, cheaply produced goods from abroad may flood them. And they certainly cannot keep out acid rain or climate change. In this global configuration, nation-states may not disappear entirely, but as they lose confidence that they can enact significant reforms, while subcontracting much of the work that they do still take on, they become—as one commentator has noted—"just one form of governance among many."[21] Sometimes new technologies do give local cultures a new lease on life, thus offsetting relentless pressures to homogenize. Think of local farms and microbreweries that have a chance at solvency, thanks both to new productive efficiencies and internet marketing that extend sales beyond their actual locales. Think of performers in niche musical genres who build a fan base through virtual communities within industrialized countries—or even more tellingly, among migrants around the world who can easily access and thus help sustain the musicians of their home countries. But notice too how many of the dynamics of diaspora a "virtual community" on the internet must take on in order to prove durable. The same is true even for a single entrepreneur whose very work is to link disparate production streams with dispersed markets. For the geographies in which they locate are not so much that of some contiguous territory; rather, their location is some node within a network that crosses yet connects many locales.

Globalization might best be defined as the exponentially increasing interconnection of interconnections.[22] Economic links transform technological links, which transform communication links, which transform economic-technological-communication links, which transform cultural-legal-ideological-religious links, which transform economies and technologies and media and culture and laws and ideologies and religions and on and on.[23] To be sure, links and transformations often bring disruptions as well. But with its relentlessly exponential process, globalization transforms the identity of every strand or node, every individual or community, in its ever-complexifying web.[24] And so we begin to wonder who we are, not just as individuals and families, but as communities. And Christian communities are no exception. The dislocations of globalization alternately tempt us to retrench at the risk of estrangement *from* wider cultures, or to adapt at the risk of complete assimilation *into* wider cultures. What often—in the midst of churchly culture wars—feels like a particular challenge for Catholics or Christians or religious believers is in fact the challenge facing every diaspora community: How to be true to itself in a world that offers all kinds of new tools for renewing our human bonds of communication when those very tools always come with wires attached, which then link us in to the forces of identity-erasing homogenization?

There is opportunity here, though, whatever the challenges. If borders have always been something of a problem for Christians, and properly so, then the way that globalization forces everyone to live in diaspora offers Christians an opportunity to recognize and recover the very social ethic by which God has long been trying to map the life of God's people among the families of the world. But we will not really understand either the challenge or the opportunity unless we carry out that very sort of study that Pope John Paul II called for as he spoke before the United Nations, in which we decouple the concept of "nation" from that of the nation-state,[25] and do so by navigating between what John Paul called the two poles of the human condition:

> The human condition thus finds itself between these two poles—universality and particularity—with a vital tension between them; an inevitable tension, but singularly fruitful if they are lived in a calm and balanced way.[26]

We are not really understanding the challenge of globalization—nor the challenge of being a truly catholic church in solidarity both with one another and with all human beings—unless we can recognize why the drive toward universality can be a mixed blessing. After all, despite everything we have said about how Christlike love of neighbor has been stretching Christians all along and breaking them out of merely proximate loves that so easily translate into tribalism, nationalism, and sectarianism, Christians dare not be smug.

On the one hand, Christians have found all kinds of ways to rationalize away Jesus' teaching to love their enemies in favor of love for their own particular tribe, nation, or kind. Recognizing this temptation and indeed this failure is essential if we are to take up the challenge of becoming a global Catholic peace church. And to do either requires us to take a fresh look at centuries-long Christian debates over war and violence. But on the other hand, Christian universalism has itself offered all kinds of ways to rationalize the homogenization of diverse cultures at best, and imperialism at worst.

Jewish intellectuals Daniel and Jonathan Boyarin have stated the problem succinctly: "The genius of Christianity is its concern for all the peoples of the world; the genius of Judaism is its ability to leave other people alone. And the evils of the two systems are the precise obverse of those genii." As staunch critics of modern Israel's policies toward the Palestinians, the Boyarins are deeply worried about what Israeli power is doing to Judaism. But clear ethnic or religious identities themselves are not the problem, nor is the threat that Christian anti-Semitism long saw in the Jews as an unassimilated people living among them in the West. No, the problem is what power over others does when combined *either* with particularism *or* with universalism. "Particularism plus power yields tribal warfare or fascism. Christianity plus power has also yielded horror. If particularism plus power tends toward fascism, then universalism plus power produces imperialism and cultural annihilation as well as, all too often, actual genocide of those who refuse to conform." The genius of Christianity and the genius of Judaism "all too easily become demons. Christian universalism, even at its most liberal and benevolent, has been a powerful force for coercion discourses of sameness, denying . . . the rights of Jews, women, and others to retain their difference."[27]

Behind the Boyarins' critique is an analysis of Christianity that Christians need to take seriously. As elaborated in Daniel Boyarin's book *A Radical Jew: Paul and the Politics of Identity*,[28] the Jewish rabbi whom Christians know as Saint Paul the apostle certainly deserves credit for universalizing the faith of Abraham and Moses as embodied in the Torah, thus breaking out of Jewish particularism. In Christ, according to the baptismal formula that Paul records in Galatians 3:26-29, there is no Jew or Greek; all are one in Christ Jesus and an allegorical genealogy rather than a literal genealogy links the baptized Christian to the promise God made to all the "seed of Abraham."

Pauline generosity has a potential dark side, however. Yes, it invites anyone and everyone to become a Jewish child of Abraham in an abstract spiritual sense. But those who then stubbornly continue to insist on Jewish identity in any concrete fleshly sense come to signify "unruly difference" and discord. "From this perspective the drive toward sameness was precisely to be understood as the fulfillment of Judaism"—but within the Pauline legacy that then meant actual Jews might actually be false Jews. To be sure, Paul himself was neither anti-Semitic nor anti-Jewish. But the potentially violent logic of Paul's universalizing project not only bore bitter fruit in centuries of anti-Semitism in the Christian West; it continues in post-Christian secular proposals for liberal modern and post-modern community that delegitimize or trivialize the ethnic identities of actual communities. Whatever their good intentions, such proposals not only hurt Jews, they leave the Navajo and the Lakota of North America, the Murdi and the Palawah of Australia, the Berbers and the Oromo of Africa, and five or six thousand other nations with no basis for claiming distinct identities either.[29]

The Boyarins thus see rabbinical Jewish diaspora as an alternative to both tribalism and universalism.[30] Diaspora offers a way of grounding and preserving the distinctive identities, cultures, and polities of nations without their needing to control either territory or the reins of state power.[31] It is not that diaspora communities are powerless. Yes, "the rabbinic answer to Paul's challenge was to renounce any possibility of domination over Others by being perpetually out of power."[32] Yet even while renouncing sovereignty, diaspora carries with it other paradoxical forms of cultural power and social creativity.[33] It is thus no more "sectarian" than it is tribalistic, for it anticipates neither the abolishing of communal frontiers nor their strict identification with territorial borders but rather "the mutual fructification of different life-styles and traditions"[34] who live dispersed—in diaspora—among one another. Indeed, far from addressing strictly Jewish debates, the Boyarins have been at least as concerned to address international politics in ways that offer models for other diaspora communities and benefit other marginalized peoples. (Note that such an interplay is both fitting and necessary for the very methodology they advocate, in which one can *only* address universal human questions from out of particular histories.) They admit to privileging diaspora as a sociopolitical model in many though not all ways.[35] But the point is to break the hold that standard tight associations between ethnicity and political hegemony have upon our imaginations (and likewise, to disarm the need to assimilate all difference for the sake of political hegemony). Far from withdrawing into a new Jewish ghetto, then, they are offering other ethnic, religious, and political communities a path toward peace. The diasporic consciousness of rabbinical Judaism, they argue, offers to

> an already interdependent world . . . some of the pieces to the puzzle of how humanity can survive as another millennium draws to a close with no messiah on the horizon. The renunciation of difference seems both an impoverishment of human life and an inevitable harbinger of oppression. Yet the renunciation of sovereignty . . . combined with a fierce tenacity in holding onto cultural identity, might well have something to offer to a world in which these two forces, together, kill thousands daily.[36]

So if the Boyarins have offered diaspora *both* as a paradigm for communities seeking to guard and celebrate their particular identities amid the homogenizing pressures of globalization *and* as an approach to peaceful international restructuring, then a fresh model for Christian social ethics and peacemaking surely opens up somewhere in between. To heed their corrective critique of Christianity is especially appropriate, given the formative-if-contentious history that Jews and Christians share along with growing recognition of the Jewishness of Jesus. Intuitively, the Second Vatican Council has already embraced this model by underscoring the proper identity of the church as a "pilgrim people," thus suggesting a framework for the continuing development of Catholic social teaching. Chapter 6 will retrieve numerous precedents within the Catholic tradition for a Christian "diasporic consciousness" of our own.

And to all of these pointers we may add the Vatican mandate to learn from the historic peace church theology and experience of Mennonites.[37] In the last century Mennonites have deepened their commitment not only to living peaceably but to building peace and working for justice in the world as acts of Christlike love for neighbor and witness to the shape of God's in-breaking kingdom. Critique from other Christians, however—most pointedly, from the twentieth-century American Protestant theologian Reinhold Niebuhr and those who have carried forward his "Christian Realism"—has pressed

Mennonites to demonstrate how they as Christian pacifists can exercise political and social responsibility if they have renounced participation in the affairs of state, which most social theorists see as depending in the final instance on violent coercion.[38] The twentieth century's most prominent Mennonite theologian and ethicist, John Howard Yoder, returned to this challenge continuously throughout his career.[39] And to do so he increasingly turned to the model and resources of Jewish diaspora, beginning with Jeremiah's guidance to Hebrew exiles in Babylon (Jer 29:1-7ff.). Others have followed his lead.[40]

Diaspora Judaism, argued Yoder, belies the Niebuhrian charge that Christians who embrace the nonviolent ethic of Jesus may get Jesus' teaching right but nonetheless render themselves politically irrelevant and socially irresponsible. What Jeremiah had made clear when he wrote to the first exiles, urging them to seek the peace of the very city that had taken them captive, was that living in exile without political sovereignty was an opportunity for mission and constructive contribution to the good of other cultures. Though countercultural in one sense, it was pro-cultural and "for the nations" in another; Jeremiah's injunction could be translated far more forcefully, according to Yoder: " 'Seek the salvation of the culture to which God has sent you.' "[41] Diaspora Jews down through the centuries may have done this in ways that were sometimes "grudging and clumsy" and sometimes "wholehearted and creative."[42] But doing so had depended on neither their own ability to gain access to reins of power nor their host culture's ability to comprehend on its own terms the *shalom* to which God's people were contributing.[43] Diaspora Jews had contributed more, not less, to Near Eastern and European societies precisely because they repeatedly became fluent in other peoples' cultural "languages" without losing the thought world of their own particular "language" or identity.[44] In other words the social posture of diaspora actually gave them resources to be more, rather than less, socially engaged, responsible, and efficacious.[45]

Other Christians who call themselves pilgrim people, even while seeking the common good they share with the societies and cultures that host them along the way, therefore, should pause to reconsider what Daniel and Jonathan Boyarin have called "the powers of diaspora."

Diaspora and the possibility of a transnational nation (replies to objections)

In the end, we might need to admit that the Christian Church does not live in diaspora quite like other diaspora peoples do. No one ethnicity or culture marks its identity, after all, for that very identity is to be the reconciliation made possible through the peace who is Christ Jesus, in whose flesh the dividing wall between hostile groups breaks down, creating one body through the cross (Eph 2:14-16). For

> he came and proclaimed peace to you who were far off and peace to those who were near; for through him both of us have access in one Spirit to the Father. So then you are no longer strangers and aliens, but you are citizens with the saints and also members of the household of God, built upon the foundation of the apostles and prophets, with Christ Jesus himself as the cornerstone. (Eph 2:17-20)

Such reconciliation in one body should never mean homogenized sameness, of course. Even in the Christian vision of heaven itself the "great multitude that no one could count," having gathered in praise around the throne of the Lamb, remains recognizably comprised of people "from every nation, from all tribes and peoples and languages" (Rev 7:9; also see 5:9).

The name for this multicultural multitude is not simply a "religion." Even though the one around whom they have gathered is a lamb who has reached the throne through the paradoxical victory of having been slain, not by slaying, *these* people (plural) have become *a* people (singular). The descriptors that apply to them are as much political as religious or spiritual, therefore, for the Lamb has "made them to be a kingdom and priests serving our God, and they will reign on earth" (Rev 5:10). Indeed, according to 1 Peter 2:9-10, God has already constituted the people called church as a "nation," now, in this age, long before heaven:

> But you are a chosen race, a royal priesthood, a holy nation, God's own people, in order that you may proclaim the mighty acts of him who called you out of darkness into his marvelous light. Once you were not a people, but now you are God's people;

once you had not received mercy, but now you have received mercy.

However other diasporas may have formed, then, we are going to have to name the diaspora called church a multiethnic ethnicity, a multicultural culture, or indeed, *a transnational nation.*

To name the church a transnational nation may initially seem strange or even threatening. At one level, this is simply another way of saying diaspora, so that it says no more or less than Rahner did when he urged Catholic Christians to begin recognizing it as their reality. To explain the reality of diaspora by speaking of nationhood, however, may begin to make uncomfortably clear that to embrace life in diaspora is to realign our loyalties, our relationship to land and resources, our trust in different kinds of power, and our sense of duty. The shifts required to embrace life in diaspora could be formidable, and objections may nag. We do well, therefore, to attend forthrightly to some of those possible objections.

Objection 1: To call the church a diaspora stretches the term beyond its usefulness, and does so by stealing the experience of dislocation from those who have suffered it most.

On one hand I am making an expansive argument that "we are all in diaspora now" anyway. Yet on the other hand I keep narrowing my scope by turning to Judaism as the privileged precedent for any particularly Christian way of embracing life in diaspora. The astute reader may thus be wondering whether the notion of diaspora is so elastic as to be useless as a guide for Christian social ethics and ecclesiology. One answer is that debates in the field of "Diaspora Studies" concerning the very concept of diaspora are not only not unknown, those debates in fact point to reasons that diaspora offers such a helpful and illuminating conceptual tool for theology.

From its very earliest appearance the Greek term "diaspora" has reflected and held together a number of creative tensions. As the Oxford English Dictionary explains, "The term originated in the Septuagint (Deuteronomy 28:25) in the phrase *esē diaspora en pasais basileias tēs gēs* 'thou shalt be a dispersion in all kingdoms of the earth.'" In context in Deuteronomy 28, to be sure, this dispersal was something unwelcome, for it was part of the judgment God threatened upon Israel if it proved unfaithful. And yet the Septuagint translation of the Hebrew Scriptures into Greek reflects the very cultural creativity that has often been the result of diaspora when Hebrews and Jews have actually been dispersed among other nations. The Jewish scholars who translated the Hebrew Scriptures into Greek beginning in the third century BCE, and thus produced what became known as the Septuagint, were themselves responding to the challenges of diaspora. At least according to legend, they lived not in Palestine but in the great Egyptian intellectual center, Alexandria. To be the scholars they were, they were necessarily "Hellenized" to some extent—influenced, conversant, and acculturated into the Greek (or Hellenic) world. And yet the very act of translating their scriptures into Greek was a strategy for resisting complete assimilation by keeping the deepest core and source of their tradition accessible to younger generations who were no doubt losing fluency in Hebrew language and culture.

For almost two millennia, any reference to *the* diaspora was solely a reference to the *Jewish* Diaspora as a wide geographical dispersal through Northern Africa, Asia, and Europe, necessarily with many local, cultural, and historical iterations.[46] Only rarely did the term apply to any other group, and until the 1950s only to religious groups.[47] As de-colonization and globalization began to pick up momentum in the second half of the twentieth century, however, the term increasingly came to apply to any ethnic or national group living in geographical dispersion in multiple territories and continents. By the time the phenomenon was prominent enough for social scientists, historians, and philosophers to converge in an academic field called "Diaspora Studies," worries were inevitable that the term was suffering from an "inflation" that could include groups with no common place of origin,[48] or that it was becoming "a catch-all phrase . . . for all movements, however privileged, and for all dislocations, even symbolic ones."[49] Attempting to define the term with greater precision produced useful lists of characteristics and yet no group—not even the classic Jewish Diaspora—met every criterion.[50]

The fact that diaspora is not a clean and precise category, however, is actually what makes it so helpful. A pure diaspora would be an oxymoron! "Even the 'pure' forms of diaspora," James Clifford has suggested, "are ambivalent, even embattled, over basic features.

Moreover, at different times in their history, societies may wax and wane in diasporism, depending on changing possibilities—obstacles, openings, antagonisms, and connections—in their host countries and transnationally."[51]

Much of what makes a diasporic community recognizable precisely as a diaspora is this very tensive quality. Individual members of diaspora communities must negotiate hybrid identities. The generational dynamic of diaspora is such that one generation may be seeking to assimilate out of it as quickly as possible, even while their elders seek to preserve—or their children seek to regain!—their primary loyalty and lived connection to an older identity.[52] The geographic dynamic of diaspora is such that communities are at once local and global, for as Stéphane Dufoix has noted, "In creating a geography without physical territory, dispersion is never so unified as when the local is able to give meaning to the global, and vice versa."[53] To be sure, justice requires that when we appropriate the category of diaspora widely, we privilege and ground our conceptualization in the concrete and particular experiences of those refugees, exiles, and dispossessed who have been displaced against their will.[54] Yet to press the realization that "we're all in diaspora now" is to invite those who have long dominated cultural and territorial space to divest themselves of entitlement by making peace with the de-territorialization that is such a central force in the modern world that it is now threatening their privilege too.[55]

Objection 2: Nationhood is a dangerous term to associate with church. This is starting to sound theocratic, as though the church should aspire to control the state.

The anxiety here is quite understandable. People with strong religious affiliations that cross borders can make other people nervous, for their merely contingent loyalty to ruling cultural mores and political authorities makes them suspect. One source of anti-Semitism was precisely this, that century after century the distinct people of Jews—with a transnational network of communal relationships that seemed impenetrable, mysterious, and thus conspiratorial to European Christians—lived unassimilated, "in but not of" society. Today there are Christian conservatives and secular liberals alike who harbor similar anxieties about Muslims in their midst. The sense of solidarity that many Muslims feel for other Muslims in the worldwide *ummah*, or community of those who profess that "there is no God but Allah and Muhammad is his prophet," could well be a model for global Christian solidarity. Those who are anxious about Islam, however, hear in such transnational loyalty the threat of Islamic extremists who dream of establishing a caliphate or Islamic empire. Meanwhile, Christians fear the specter of other Christians too; Protestants in the United States long feared that Catholics in political office would be more loyal to the pope than to America. In fact, among Catholics themselves one name for those whose militant devotion to papal authority above all else makes them embarrassing, if not threatening, is "ultramontane." Ultramontanism has stood for a succession of positions down through the centuries, but the root meaning of the word itself is telling—*across the mountains*—for it bespeaks foreign loyalties that trump local ones in suspect ways.

Perhaps there is a particularly "Abrahamic" prompt for this anxiety insofar as the monotheism that Jews, Christians, and Muslims all trace back to Abraham may indeed place loyalty to the one God above every other human loyalty. My most important reply, however, will actually be to double down. In the following chapter, I will argue that to be the pilgrim people that Vatican II called for, and thus to be more clearly a people of peace, Catholic Christians need to be more Abrahamic not less. For the paradox of a deeply Abrahamic identity—I will argue—is this: A people that recognizes itself as blessed for the purpose of being a blessing (Gen 12:1-3) will actually lose its identity through the defensiveness of siege mentality, whether that means retreating into a cultural ghetto or attempting cultural imperialism. To the contrary, then, the exquisite paradox of salvation history is that God's people finds its most authentic identity precisely by risking it for others. An Abrahamic community cannot keep such an identity to itself nor protect it at the expense of others. It cannot share such an identity with others by insisting that they become exactly like it, but must rather extend its identity through a far more complex process of respectful evangelization and inculturation. All three Abrahamic religions hold up Abraham and Sarah as the archetypes or patron saints of hospitality. Speaking at least for Christians, therefore, I will argue that if we would be faithful to the faith of Abraham and Sarah, then the social posture of our communities—aka our Christian social ethic—must be an ethic of hospitality all the way down.

We're All in Diaspora Now: Being Global Church in an Age of Globalization   111

For the moment, however, let us clear the deck with a much simpler observation.

A large part of the difficulty we have in thinking of the church as a nation is that in the last few hundred years we have come to conflate "nations" almost entirely with nation-states. Ask a classroom or audience how many nations there are in the world and the answer will almost always be "about 200." Trick question. For while the answer would be correct if the question concerned the number of *nation-states* in the world—the sort of political entity that can hold full membership in the United Nations—that was not the question. The answer to the question of how many *nations* there are is in fact in the thousands. How one attempts an exact count depends on how one uses categories of culture, linguistics, and genetic genealogy to define a nation, so estimates vary widely. A cautious way to estimate is to count the number of languages while grouping dialects together; the most authoritative catalog by linguists now lists the world's languages at around 6,900.[56] Using different methodologies, other estimates of the number of nations in the world run as high as 12,000 or more.[57] But even if estimates were to run lower, the order of magnitude would surely remain in the thousands.

But there is simply no way in the world that all of these nations can hold "sovereign" territory. Not in any peaceful world. Not in any possible world. At most only an estimated 800 of these nations, so defined, even aspire to become nation-states—with their intellectual and political leaders dreaming, agitating, and in a few cases fighting for political control of territory—but only a very few of these can ever possibly succeed, and then at great cost.[58] This brute fact will be relevant to any peacebuilding work among the nations: Insofar as the task of such work is sometimes to vindicate the communal rights and preserve the cultural integrity of oppressed populations, one lesson will be that the goal peacebuilding efforts must envision requires political structures that are themselves diasporic. In other words, in our globalized world, the only peace accords that are realistic and sustainable will be ones that set up political frameworks in which territorially overlapping nations can find ways to live together in federated states and international alliances. But for our more immediate and church-related purposes, the lesson is this:

Nothing prevents us from thinking—and indeed much impels us to think—of the church itself as a transnational nation. To recognize the church as a transnational nation will in fact prove necessary for keeping the nationalistic pretensions of nation-states, and the theocratic pretensions of confused believers, in check. When guided by a well-formed Christian love of neighbor, patriotic love toward the land and people with whom one is most proximate can be appropriate. But that patriotism which distinguishes itself as proximate love of neighbor rather than jingoistic and idolatrous nationalism requires a constant reminder: Ultimately, Christians are citizens of a people and a nation called church that demands a far deeper loyalty, and that is in turn subject to a still larger allegiance to God's kingdom under the Lordship of the Lamb That Was Slain. Theirs then is a nation that frankly does transcend all other borders, however nervous this makes some in their host societies. That very transcendence, however, is supposed to make control of geographic borders and the territory inside those borders an alien project for them.

Objection 3: The church cannot constitute a diaspora because it takes in many peoples rather than dispersing one people.

As a diaspora people, what will perhaps make the church different from other diasporas is that its identity as a nation is not only transnational but multinational—a people constituted by the communion of many peoples. And yet even this is not entirely unique.

The influential theorist of globalization, Arjun Appadurai, has noted, after all, that national identities of both colonizers and colonized during the modern era have often resulted from what he calls "the paradox of constructed primordialism."[59] In other words, however strong or weak the commonality of territory or genetics—land or blood—may be, it is actually quite common for nations to strengthen, extend, or even create their sense of identity and nationhood in the first place by *narrating* a story of common origins. Narratives of common origin are hardly unique to diaspora communities. Indeed, they are all the more important for maintaining the cohesion across time (generations) and space (geographic dispersal) that diaspora peoples need in order to be a people at all.

Christians should know this already. The reading and rereading of that eclectic yet somehow cohesive set of ancient texts we call the Bible creates a common narrative of origins. Theological debates over just what is the character of the master story and what makes these texts cohesive are often contentious up close, to be sure. But in the long run the extended debate that constitutes theology is necessary if the Christian community itself is to cohere. Telling the story is not just an intellectual exercise. Even amid conflicts over the meaning of their story, Christians have already begun to enact that story through liturgy and to extend it through prayer. And we cannot tell a truthful story of shared origins at all without attending to Israel and the Jews.

Judaism is the precedent diaspora that should loom largest when Christians think theologically about their ecclesiology as a global catholic people. Judaism is the paradigm from which other diasporas have borrowed the word. But more than that, Gentile (non-Jewish) Christians can only keep their own identity straight if they recognize themselves as mysteriously grafted into Israel (Rom 11). To be sure, Christians historically have too often misunderstood this relationship with Judaism to be one of displacement or "supersessionism." So any corrective must involve Christians learning respectively from Judaism and, if anything, becoming more Jewish in their own character, thought, and sociology.

In any case, ancient Israel itself was formed of many tribes and peoples. The many genealogies of the Torah or Pentateuch (the first five books of the Hebrew Scriptures), which have bored or puzzled Christians as they quickly skim past, but which Jews treasure, served exactly this purpose. Whatever their exact value as historical records, their political and theological value is actually all the greater insofar as they functioned in a quasi-mythical or legendary way to weave disparate tribes, families, and clans together by narrating a shared past, even or especially when groups did *not* initially share bloodlines. This is no less true for contemporary Judaism. As Daniel and Jonathan Boyarin interpret matters, anyway, the deep meaning of male circumcision is precisely that it performs the cultural construction of genealogy—creating a biological status that does not depend altogether on actual direct genealogy. A convert to Judaism, whether male or female, is always named a son or daughter of Abraham: "The convert is adopted into the family and assigned a new 'genealogical' identity, but because Abraham is the first convert in Jewish tradition, converts are his descendants in that sense as well."[60]

If the paradigmatic diaspora of Judaism has formed through the genealogical grafting in of multiple tribes and nations since its ancient biblical beginnings, then again, nothing prevents us from applying the category of diaspora to Christianity. Indeed, because Israel is for Christians a theological precedent and not merely a sociological one, much impels us to do so.

Objection 4: To qualify as a diaspora, a people needs a homeland of origin to which it could at least theoretically return.

That a people has geographically dispersed *from somewhere* would seem to be a necessary implication of "diaspora"—but where would that be for Christians? The Roman Catholic Church has its headquarters on the tiny patch of land that is Vatican City (44 hectares or 110 acres—0.17 square miles!), and it previously controlled a significant swathe of "Papal States" across the middle of the Italian Peninsula. A modern consensus that included Pope John XXIII now considers church control of temporal authority to have been more of an obstacle to Christian faith and faithfulness than an aid.[61] But even when temporal Vatican power was at its apex, no one hoped that all Catholics would one day relocate to the region. And of course Eastern Orthodox and Protestant Christians have an even more tenuous relationship to Rome. If a Christian diaspora requires a Christian homeland, we thus have an obvious conceptual mismatch.

On the other hand, a long Christian tradition with a biblical basis in Philippians 3:20 identifies the Christian homeland as heaven. In Philippians, St. Paul contrasted those "whose minds are set on earthly things" and thus oppose the cross of Christ, with believers whose "citizenship is in heaven," and who thus look to heaven for their Savior, the crucified Lord Jesus Christ. A few centuries later in his book, *City of God*, St. Augustine gave classic expression to the worldview that heavenly citizenship implies by contrasting "the earthly city" with the "heavenly city." One part of the heavenly city is mixed within the earthly city while the other part has already gone on to full communion with God and one another in heaven. When the Second Vatican Council retrieved this theme and used it to underscore the character of the church as a pilgrim people on a journey toward heaven, though, it took pains to clarify that the destination of a heavenly homeland should not diminish earthly engagement:

> In their pilgrimage to the heavenly city Christians are to seek and value the things that are above [Col 3:1-2]; this involves not

less, but greater commitment to working with everyone for the establishment of a more human world. Indeed, the mystery of their faith provides Christians with greater incentive and encouragement to fulfill their role more willingly and to assess the significance of activities capable of assigning to human culture its honored role in the complete vocation of humanity.[62]

Even so, the apparent need to remind certain kinds of pious Christians that their hope in a heavenly homeland dare not express itself in earthly escapism admits in a way to the force of the objection here. The homeland of the Christian diaspora can seem too elusive to qualify.

If a specific land of origin and longed-for return is required to be a diaspora people, however, some others also fail to meet this requirement. The Roma, long known pejoratively as Gypsies, apparently migrated out of Northern India as long as a millennium and a half ago, for example, but carry with them neither a clear memory of departure nor a dream of return. One scholar of diaspora, Avtar Brah, argues in fact that the very concept of diaspora actually "offers a critique of discourses of fixed origins." What characterizes diaspora communities, she has suggested, is "a homing desire, which is not the same thing as desire for a 'homeland.'" To be sure, not every journey or migration is a diaspora, but on the other hand, "not all diasporas sustain an ideology of 'return,'" either.[63]

This is not to say that the longing for land and its return should be of no concern. *How* to live rightly in the land is in a way our very question—whatever that land may be.[64] We turn to the model of diaspora both because Christian traditions, ancient and modern, give us reason to do so, and because globalization has made us all the more aware that to be a people of peace Christians will simply have to live in the land with others. But as I have written elsewhere, "we do no favor to any dispossessed people if we think of land only in a figurative rather than earthy sense."[65] As we follow an "Abrahamic" pattern of recognizing that the very identity Christians consider a blessing from God is inextricable from a vocation of being a blessing to the families of the earth, we dare not efface the close association with specific lands that makes many traditional societies, peoples, and cultures who and what they are. Otherwise we will be a curse to them rather than a blessing. Furthermore, even or especially in the context of modern industrialized societies, Christian social ethics veers dangerously away from its Jewish roots as well as its incarnational center and toward a subtle Gnosticism instead if it fails to attend to the concrete patterns of resource use, economics, and the natural environment that are all quite literally grounded in the land.

Nor is this to weigh in on debates within modern Judaism over the relationship between historical or contemporary Jewish diasporas, the state of Israel, or the land on which it sits. Scholar of modern Judaic studies Peter Ochs has warned against Christian appropriations of Jewish diaspora that oversimplify Jewish relationships to the land. Even Jewish thinkers who refuse to fit into neat categories in favor or in opposition to political Zionism, Ochs has noted, "know that the biblical record ties them to the land of Israel, whether they like or not, in ways that Exilic Judaism never abrogated and in ways with which the disciples of the gospels [Christians] are not burdened."[66] How contemporary Jews might live rightly in the land of Israel / Palestine, whether diaspora Jews who continue to live elsewhere should return, and the shape that any fresh transformative political models for modern Jewish landedness might take—these are questions that Christians cannot decide for them.[67] We are doing Christian theology and social ethics here, not Jewish.

Still, debates within Judaism remain illuminating for Christian theology, and for the question of what it should mean for Christians to identify a heavenly homeland while living dispersed in many earthly lands. Even Daniel and Jonathan Boyarin in their celebration of rabbinical Jewish diaspora and the model it might offer for a transformational international politics continue to identify with the Jewish "sense of being rooted somewhere in the world through twenty centuries of exile from that someplace."[68] This renders it all the more striking when they refuse to ground that rootedness in "autochthony"—the claims of an indigenous people upon a particular land based on belief that they had sprung from that very soil. No, "the biblical story is not one of autochthony but one of always coming from somewhere else."[69] For the Boyarins, ancient Israel's very belief that God had promised and given it the land reflected a struggle of conscience over having displaced others and a "self-critique as well as a critique of identities based on notions of autochthony."[70] Israel's origins are nomadic, after all; "there is a sense in which Israel was born in exile."[71] Later diaspora is thus but a return to the material conditions of nomadic life, and to the radical project of being a nation through genealogical linkage over time more than—and sometimes without—territorial control over space.[72]

In the Boyarins' telling, then, the relationship of rabbinical Judaism to a Jewish homeland turns out to be quite like Christians' relationship to their heavenly homeland, especially when Christians envision it as a new heaven *and a new earth*:[73] "The point is not that the Land was devalued by the rabbis but that they renounced it until the final redemption"; for the time being, therefore, "in an unredeemed world"; no definitive identification between land and people is possible now because until that final redemption, "temporal domination and ethnic particularity are impossibly compromised."[74] If such a conviction is possibly true for Judaism, it surely ought to be true for Christianity.

In any case, what should at least be clear by now is that it is an open question as to whether a geographical homeland of origin and possible return is necessary for a nation to be a people of diaspora.[75] The space that defines a diaspora is arguably of a different sort. It is the tensive cultural, sociological, and moral space that stands between—but then requires negotiation in two directions at once *from in between*—the claims of nation-state and tribe, those of local solidarity and global solidarity, and those of living entangled here while remembering or desiring another place.[76]

Objection 5: It isn't clear: Are you saying that the church is *a diaspora, or that it* should be *a diaspora?*

An earlier objection asked whether the category of diaspora as I have been using it is too elastic to guide theological and social-ethical reflection. This new objection suggests that the category might be too slippery, for I seem to be sliding between "descriptive" claims about what *is* ("we're all in diaspora now") and "normative" claims about what *should* be ("Christians should embrace life as a diaspora people").

Here the reply is to plead "no contest," but to remind the reader of what the structure of my argument has been all along:

> Globalization is merely making obvious something that has always been true of Christ's Church: Namely, we are properly a diaspora people and must embrace this identity in order to

practice Christian love of neighbor through global solidarity in all the ways to which Catholic social teaching has been calling us, thus to become a catholic peace church.[77]

Thus, I certainly believe that my descriptive arguments about the empirical realities of globalization, diaspora communities, and (in a few pages) the southward shift in global Christianity are defensible. Yet I also admit to making these descriptive arguments in the service of normative arguments about what the posture or social ethic of the church in the world *should* be. As with Rahner's argument, so with mine: The descriptive throws the urgency of the normative into relief, therefore, but the normative arguments that I will be extending in coming chapters have an integrity of their own.

Appropriate to its tensive quality, in fact, the concept of diaspora *always* operates at the very hinge between descriptive and normative, for all diaspora peoples. Even if diaspora did not have Jewish roots that ought to prompt Christian theology to pay it special attention, and even if Christians did not have their own diaspora roots to recover (as the following chapters will argue we should), the empirical realities of any diaspora life inevitably pose normative questions for social ethics. As a window into the moral lives of communities and their members, therefore, the structures and challenges of life in diaspora map the basic ethical challenges that face anyone with a modicum of communal sensitivity, but certainly face Christians who seek to follow Christ together with other disciples in the context of Christian community.

Consider how life in diaspora forces moral questions on *anyone*: The empirical truism is that every ethnic or religious diaspora is geographically dispersed into proximity with peoples and cultures other than their own. The cultural life that this situation creates, then, necessarily places them not only at seams between cultures, but at the seam between *what has come to be* (the descriptive or empirical) and *what they should do* (the normative or ethical). How much to assimilate and how much to resist? *How* to assimilate *or* resist? How to train up and form the next generation? What is core to one's cultural, ethnic, or religious identity and what is peripheral? Should they aspire to return to their homeland if they have one? What stories of their homeland are the truest and most instructive ones to pass on? Whose laws and customs—the host society's or the guest community's—apply when and where? All this is the stuff of moral reflection and communal discernment.

After all, each of these questions responds to the de-territorialization, cultural flux, and hybridity that force questions upon a diaspora people they might otherwise have taken for granted. It is thus that the very elasticity of diaspora stretches every particular diaspora community into relationship with other communities and diasporas. In a globalizing world that is overlapping and de-territorializing our identities, the normative questions that diaspora imposes press themselves upon many peoples, perhaps all peoples. And those questions—questions of loyalty or even idolatry, questions of relationality or even love and solidarity, questions of catechesis as well as liturgy, questions that Talmudic rabbis debated in order to adapt faithfully within a Gentile world, and questions that Christian ethicists now debate under the rubric of "Christ and culture"[78]—*these are the questions that Israel and the church were* always *supposed to be facing.*

Christian thinkers have used various typologies in order to make sense of the ways that churches of varied dispositions and traditions have positioned themselves in order to engage the world around them, alternately contributing and resisting, seeking to influence or withdraw from worldly affairs. Drawing on earlier traditions while articulating a formula that other traditions have since picked up on, Protestant Reformer John Calvin believed that Jesus himself had exercised three different offices—prophet, king, and priest—and that his followers may alternately play corresponding roles: proclaiming God's word of challenge, governing according to God's will, and mediating God's mercy.[79] This reflects a continuum from judgment to grace, with "tough love" somewhere in the middle. It also seeks to hold together two opposite tendencies in Christianity that have pulled some Christians toward demanding ethical standards or even to an unbending *rigorism*, while pulling other Christians toward generosity in the face of human fallibility or even to a pliant *laxism*.

A century ago the German church historian Ernst Troeltsch argued that these tendencies had produced two types of Christian community—the independent *sect* that could attempt to practice Jesus' demanding ethic only in relatively small and tightly bound face-to-face communities, and the established *church* that had exchanged rigor for wide influence and the hope of permeating all of society with grace.[80] Influenced by Troeltsch, H. Richard Niebuhr later expanded

Troeltsch's two basic "types" into five different ways that "Christ" (or really, the Christian community) relates to "culture": *against, of, above, in paradox*, and *transforming*.[81] Something of the same polarity between affirming all that is good in human experience and society as an expression of God's own goodness, and critiquing endemic human propensities to twist and fall short of God's goodness, appears in the contrast that Catholic theologian David Tracy has drawn between two basic ways of doing theology—the *analogical* and the *dialectic*.[82] Other Catholic thinkers play out a similar debate by drawing a sharp contrast between "neo-Augustinian" theologians and prelates whose first instinct is to decry the corruptions of our age and withdraw into a countercultural church stance, and "neo-Thomist" theologians and prelates who embrace the opportunities of our age through more optimistic cultural engagement.[83]

Even when these and other Christian thinkers harbor a preference for one or the other of the "types" in their typologies, they usually admit that each of the models they are laying out can sometimes be legitimate. Each—they say—enjoys a biblical basis, has precedents within the Christian tradition, and may be appropriate depending on historical circumstance. If that is so, my argument is that this is because one underlying model holds them together—the supple, flexible, yet consistent pattern of diaspora. A Christian community that knows itself in diaspora, after all, will recognize that it must sometimes be countercultural in order to serve its host culture in a pro-cultural way. And vice versa. For it also knows that it can only challenge society with prophetic imagination or serve it with kingly effectiveness, if it does both as it offers the embrace of priestly mercy. It navigates the complexity of doing all of these simultaneously with a steady conviction: Intrinsic to its very identity is the life it is called to live and to risk for others.

That, anyway, is the normative *should* that the descriptive *is* of diaspora invites us to embrace.

Objection 6: Okay. "Diaspora" may be a useful metaphor, but admit it: that's really all it is, right?

Certainly I would be satisfied to convince my fellow Christian ethicists, to say nothing of the moral teachers of the Roman Catholic Church and other Christian communions, that "diaspora" offers a powerful metaphor for thinking through the challenges we face as we seek to live as a Christian people in the world. At some level, all language is metaphorical, so perhaps that should be enough. But consider, then, a parallel metaphor:

Democracy. Is the United States democratic? Americans have a constitution that sets up a democratic form of government. But how much citizen participation is required to qualify a society as truly democratic? When only roughly half of the population votes, and most of these only vote every four years—when citizens across the political spectrum feel powerless in the fact of monied lobbyists, complex bureaucracies, and corporate manipulation—is this a truly *participatory* democracy? Or is the system democratic only in metaphorical ways? What then happens if we compare the following two statements?

1. "Americans live in a democracy."

2. "Christians live in diaspora."

Arguably the second is at least as empirically descriptive as the first. And when we survey global demographic trends that have tilted the axis of world Christianity to the Global South, away from traditional Christian power centers, and toward the poor and disempowered of the earth, we may well have to conclude that the second is far *more* of an empirical description than the first.

The reality of diaspora then underscores the normativity of diaspora. For if Rahner was right to notice already in 1961 that diaspora is the reality in which Christians increasingly live, we are not just saying that Christian communal life in relationship to wider societies is *like* living in diaspora. We are saying that we *are* a diaspora people. Perhaps we are only beginning to awaken to that fact. Awakening to our reality, however, is itself a moral task.

Becoming Catholic again for the first time: Implications of global Christianity

Looking back on the Second Vatican Council in 1979—nearly fifteen years after its close, and approaching twenty years after his essay on the emerging reality of Christian diaspora—Karl Rahner could now make his essential point in a fresh and different way. The question before him as he worked "Towards a Fundamental Theological

Interpretation of Vatican II" was: What was the "inner, essential connection" that held all of the events and documents of the council together in a coherent way and gave it its continuing significance? His answer: Though only barely beginning to grope for its identity within a new era of Christianity, at Vatican II the Roman Catholic Church had for the first time officially recognized itself as a world church, and in a "rudimentary" way it had begun to act as such.[84]

The church had always been a world church "in potency" but had required a long historical process to begin realizing this potential, and would need generations if not centuries to come to terms fully with its identity as a world church. Surveying church history from the widest, most "macroscopic," perspective possible, Rahner argued that theologically there had really only been three epochs of church history—the first lasting but a few decades, the third and present having barely begun:

> First, the short period of Jewish Christianity. Second, the period of the Church in a distinct cultural region, namely, that of Hellenism and of European culture and civilization. Third, the period in which the sphere of the Church's life is in fact the entire world. These three periods signify three essential and different basic situations for Christianity and its preaching.[85]

As it had made its transition from Jewish to Gentile identity, Christianity *in principle* was already accessible to all cultures, but in fact it had largely identified with the Roman Empire and later with its remnants.[86] Even as missionary efforts were spreading Christianity throughout the world roughly since the year 1500,

> the actual concrete activity of the Church in its relation to the world outside of Europe was in fact (if you will pardon the expression) the activity of an export firm which exported a European religion as a commodity it did not really want to change but sent throughout the world together with the rest of the culture and civilization it considered superior.[87]

To be sure, strictly as a reader of history, Rahner may himself have remained more captive than he recognized to a Roman, Eurocentric perspective that recognized too little of the centuries of continuing vitality of Coptic, Syrian, Ethiopian and other Orthodox churches far to the south and east of Europe.[88] The very epoch he was describing was only beginning to dawn, in his telling, so that even he may only have begun to readjust his perspective. Yet his core theological analysis about the significance of shifts first from Jewish to localized Gentile then Gentile to world Christianity is still illuminating even if those shifts have happened at different times for different traditions. And at the very least both Rahner's theological and historical frameworks are apropos for Roman Catholicism.

Only in the epoch that the Second Vatican Council had now officially opened up, Rahner noted, was the church beginning to exercise a real interdependence in which European and North American churches might themselves hear the Gospel afresh from churches who had inculturated it into their own settings. A "world Church as such begins to act through the reciprocal influence exercised by all its components."[89] A dynamic that we might call the Cornelius Effect—by which Saint Peter once evangelized the Gentile Cornelius, only to find Cornelius evangelizing him—was now playing out on the world stage.

Only now, in other words, was the Roman church becoming a truly catholic Catholic Church.

If the initial epoch-making shift from Jewish to Gentile Christianity had launched an era lasting nearly nineteen centuries, at least for European Christianity, it should be no surprise that the implications of the shift from Eurocentric Gentile Christianity to multicultural world Christianity were but barely beginning to show themselves.[90] Rahner dismissed the temptation to predict the future, but could not entirely resist. He had seen a "reciprocal influence" already developing at Vatican II between different parts of the church and expected it to release creative powers within the church that it had never needed in previous centuries. Certainly Christians would need those powers now. For as the Vatican II era was getting under way, the world church was experiencing cross-cultural differences that felt as deep as the original tensions between Jewish and Gentile Christianity.[91] Christians in other cultures would need to figure out for themselves how to proclaim the Gospel faithfully within their own cultural and historical settings.[92] Roman ecclesial authorities would need to figure out how to embrace an "authentic pluralism" as they relearned their task of maintaining the unity of faith but without assuming "a common Western horizon of understanding."[93] All kinds of pastoral challenges would inevitably arise. Rahner mentioned questions about how best to affirm a plurality of liturgies reflecting local cultures, and how best to apply canon law outside its original European context.[94] But these are only generalizations for the myriad of nitty-gritty challenges that a transnational community with a global structure of accountability is bound to face as it better learns to share and embody the one Gospel of Christ in endlessly variant cultural settings.

Making his "fundamental theological interpretation of Vatican II" in 1979, Rahner was not the first to recognize the fundamental importance of a fast-hastening tilt in Christianity's global axis toward the Southern Hemisphere or Global South, and he certainly has not been the last. In the mid-1970s, at a time when most commentators referred to the Global South as the "Third World," the Swiss theologian and mission thinker Walbert Bühlmann, OFM, had drawn attention to this developing shift in a book on *The Coming of the Third Church*.[95] More recently, historian Philip Jenkins's masterful survey of "the coming of global Christianity," titled *The Next Christendom*, has gone through three editions in less than a decade as Jenkins has sought to keep up with unfolding developments.[96] Bühlmann and especially Jenkins have attended to Christian traditions and movements far beyond Roman Catholicism alone, of course. The fastest growing Christian movement worldwide is Pentecostalism, though its dynamic spills over into Charismatic movements within historic Christian traditions, including Catholicism on the one hand and autonomous grassroots churches such as African Initiated Churches on the other hand.[97] Still, when Vatican correspondent John Allen Jr. did his own survey specifically of Roman Catholicism in *The Future Church: How Ten Trends Are Revolutionizing the Catholic Church*, he began by noting that amid all the trends pulling in different directions and sometimes "work[ing] at cross-purposes," one was driving all the others: "In a sense there's really only one trend here, globalization, which is producing reactions inside the Catholic Church as well as creating a whole new series of challenges outside."[98] Not surprisingly, then, his first chapter surveyed the trend that flows into and shapes all the others; as we should be coming to expect by now, its chapter title is "A World Church."

We're All in Diaspora Now: Being Global Church in an Age of Globalization   125

A 2011 report by the Pew Forum on Religion and Public Life confirmed this overarching narrative in many ways as it compared how the demographics of the world's Christian population had changed between 1910 and 2010.[99] As a portion of the world's population, Christians had constituted roughly a third at both the beginning (35%) and the end (32%) of that century, though of course the total world population had more than tripled.[100] The striking news in the Pew Forum report was not that Christianity had kept pace with population growth, however, but that the geographic distribution of Christians was now so widespread. In 1910, two-thirds of Christians had lived in Europe, 15 percent in North America, with less than 19 percent elsewhere.[101] A century later, only a quarter lived in Europe, an eighth lived in North America, but more than 60 percent lived in the rest of the world—the Global South.[102] Nigeria now had more than double the number of Protestants as Germany, where the Protestant Reformation began; Brazil now had more Catholics than any other country, with more than double the number in Italy, and with more than Italy, France, and Spain combined.[103] So geographically "far-flung" was twenty-first-century Christianity—the Pew Forum's executive summary of its report began—"that no single continent or region can indisputably claim to be the center of global Christianity."[104]

Catholicism has inevitably been very much a part of Christianity's tectonic shift southward. Its 1.1 billion adherents make up more than half of all Christians worldwide;[105] Latin America was already overwhelmingly Catholic in 1910. Even as Christianity had expanded throughout the world, however, a century of population growth in Latin America was expanding its proportion within the worldwide Christian population at a far faster pace than the global average, from less than an eighth of the total in 1910 to nearly a quarter in 2010. The distribution of Catholics within the overall Christian population of Latin America and the Caribbean shifted somewhat, as the Catholic Church lost members to Protestantism between 1910 and 2010. But even so, Catholicism retained 69 percent of the Christian population in Latin America, so that by 2010 Catholics in Latin America and the Caribbean constituted nearly 40 percent of the global Catholic population.[106] Meanwhile, Catholicism was growing at a remarkable pace elsewhere in the Global South as well, so that even if we bracket traditionally Catholic Latin America, by 2010 Catholics in Sub-Saharan Africa and Asia-Pacific combined were nearing parity with

Catholics in Europe and North America combined.[107] And we can expect the trend line to continue; Jenkins has cited projections that by 2025, for example, Africans will comprise one-sixth of all Catholics worldwide.[108]

In any case, the bottom line is this: Already in the early twenty-first century, less than one third of Catholics (31.9%) lived in the Global North, while more than two thirds (68.1%) lived in the Global South. The southward shift in global Catholicism has thus prompted John Allen Jr. to chide American Catholics for their self-centered preoccupations, but his point could apply to many other Catholics throughout the Global North in some way:

> I like to remind American Catholics that we constitute 6 percent of the global Catholic population, which means that 94 percent of the Catholics in the world are not necessarily like us. If anything, the United States probably looms too large already on the global Catholic scene.[109]

Despite conventional assumptions to the contrary Christianity is growing in the Global South because it has an authentic appeal that does not depend on Western imperialism to take root or Western culture to sustain it. Jenkins has stressed this point in his survey of global Christianity: Historically, Christianity has never just been a Western religion, and for more than a millennium was not predominantly Western at all; thus, as it now grows in eastward and southward directions it is actually returning to its non-European roots.[110] Often—perhaps typically—it has flourished as a minority religion without need for the sort of state support that established churches in Europe long thought necessary.[111] Where Christianity *has* in fact spread along with imperialist power and through colonialist alliances, it has only really taken hold when it has begun to mesh with local cultures, often as a counterforce against those very same dominant powers.[112] Generally, its strongest appeal has been to the marginalized.[113] Foreign missionaries themselves have often been the first to recognize the need for Christianity to express itself in local ways, and for churches to gain local leadership.[114] However well or poorly those missionaries have realized that vision through their own efforts, Christian churches have in fact grown all the faster once they have gotten out from the yoke of colonial control and foreign association.[115] This has not only been true for locally founded groups such as African Initiated Churches and for much of Pentecostalism, but also for historic or "mainline" Protestant churches—even for Roman Catholicism with its liturgical standardization and institutional reach.[116] Think about it, Jenkins has urged: Christian churches would have withered after colonialist powers and foreign missionaries departed if Christianity had not developed indigenous flavors and put down local roots; certainly Christian martyrs would have acquiesced in the face of persecution if their conversions had been merely opportunistic or their cause had been Western commerce or political hegemony.[117]

In one way, though, Rahner may admittedly have overstated his case back in 1961 when he remarked that Christianity "is effectually, *in terms of numbers*, a minority everywhere."[118] Precisely because of the growth of world Christianity that he later took stock of in 1979 and that was producing such striking demographics by 2010, the Pew Forum reported in 2011 that actually most Christians "live in countries where Christians are in the majority."[119] Particularly if we are talking about Catholicism and its social teaching, the Pew Forum would remind us: "Most of the countries with the largest Catholic populations have Catholic majorities. . . . There are 67 countries in which Catholics make up a majority of the population."[120] Must we therefore withdraw Rahner's claim that "[t]he mere fact of being a diaspora on this planet has had to be gradually admitted" and that "this signifies, in terms of the history of salvation, a 'must,' from which we may and must draw conclusions about our behavior as Christians"?[121]

Not at all, for at least three reasons: First, diaspora and minority status often coincide but neither is a criterion for the other.[122] If "we are all in diaspora now" that is because globalization has taken us there in *other* ways: Globalizing forces are literally dispersing some ethnic and ecclesial communities across borders. Thus, even if one perceives oneself to be part of a majority in one's immediate territory or country, one is still intermixed, perhaps with some other kind of minority status, within a wider expanse. In the mental map that results, even though Christians are the largest world religion and Catholics constitute the largest church, they are still a dispersed minority of humanity and certainly—in Rahner's words—"a diaspora *on this planet.*" Second, Rahner's point was not just about numbers anyway but about democratization, secularization, and the opportunity that comes as the church focuses not upon baptizing large numbers but upon authentic proclamation of the Gospel in ways that may be countercultural even when Christians engage culture supportively. Thus, even if his remarks about numbers require greater nuance, what he said about political and social influence generally pertains. Latin America may constitute the most Catholic continent on the globe, for example, but political anti-clericalism has constitutionally limited the church's role in a number of countries there, and secularization has effectively limited the church's role even where it retains an official established status.[123] In still other places, given the realities of Christian division, Protestants or Catholics or Pentecostals may all experience themselves as minorities in one another's presence—sometimes in the same country, as regimes come and go.[124] A people can live in diaspora, therefore, even when they enjoy the numbers to constitute a majority.

The ambiguities of Christian leadership and witness here point to a third issue—the number of Christians arguably in name only. A study like that of the Pew Forum is immensely useful for surveying global trends, but can only point vaguely to the actual quality of Christian life in any particular setting.[125] Whatever the percentage of serious Christians who are seeking to respond to the Gospel of Jesus Christ in every area of their lives, therefore, it falls well short of 100 percent, except perhaps where savage persecution has driven all hangers-on out of churches. In his apostolic exhortation on mission and evangelization, *Evangelii Nuntiandi*, Pope Paul VI recognized this reality when he anticipated the way that the living witness of a Christian community would prompt questions from "baptized people who do not practice, or people who live as nominal Christians but according to principles that are in no way Christian."[126] Christians endeavoring to lead lives of discipleship, then, easily experience themselves as a minority and constitute a diaspora even within countries where there is a nominal Christian majority.

Rahner's thesis stands, therefore, and with it my own: Catholic social teaching, Christian social ethics, and the peacebuilding strategies that follow from them simply cannot operate well or realistically when they begin by assuming access to the reins of nation-state power, or insist that gaining such access must be their first goal.

Rushing to underscore a "both/and" theological sensibility that over the long haul has proven quintessential to a Catholic worldview, we must remain clear: This is not an argument for obstinate sectarianism or countercultural intransigence. Rather it is an argument for a social posture with the self-confidence that comes from an identity in Christ and the vocation he has given his church within the drama of salvation history—a posture that then is free alternately to counter or to support wider cultural, social, and political developments as necessary. Living as a diaspora people amid many peoples and times, Christians will find that exceptional opportunities arise when a few have direct access to the inner circles of nation-state power or when democratic processes allow more to influence policymaking. Like the capable young Hebrews in the book of Daniel who became civil servants in Babylon, that possible way of engaging culture for the sake of the common good and the *shalom* of the city is itself part of the diaspora story. But it will always be exceptional. When we stand in solidarity with the many Christians down through the centuries and across the globe who all have been called to practice a peacemaking character that identifies them as children of God (Matt 5:9, 44-45), yet who never have and never will hold reins of power or offices for policymaking, we will recognize what a distortion and a disservice it is to project a Christian social ethic or present Catholic social teaching as though access to societal power can ever be a norm Christians can count on. A possibility, yes. But one we will have a chance to practice faithfully only if we are pivoting from the social posture of diaspora.

Power exercised through social control, technocratic attempts to manage history, and recourse to violence are only one kind of power. We may leave as an open question whether pacifist streams within the Christian tradition have been wrong to reject many or all forms of Christian participation in the exercise of such power. But even if they have been overly suspicious, they have been right to say this much: To focus on the ethics of domineering power will leave Christian theologians speaking only to a tiny elite of Christians. For even if Christians constitute majorities in some places, or are in a position to influence social policies, (1) Christians around the world, when they do enjoy increasing numbers, have often grown first among the dispossessed. (2) Even where a church is established or Christians are culturally dominant, only a few Christians will ever be policymakers, much less rulers. And (3) even in the unlikely event that the dreams of those who wish to restore political Christendom were somehow, somewhere fulfilled, any Catholic leader (at least) who claims to govern in an accountably Christian way will now have to attend to the teaching of the Second Vatican Council on religious liberty, and thus will not in good conscience be able to exercise power or influence in the domineering ways of earlier centuries.

Better then to learn the lessons that the Catholic writer J. R. R. Tolkien wove into his epic trilogy, *The Lord of the Rings*. The epic is filled with captivating battles and political machinations, to be sure. Those who only know the story from the movie series, with all of its stunning computer-generated images, will be all the more distracted by these. Yet distraction was the very ruse that was all that military campaigns could finally accomplish, according to the wise wizard Gandalf,[127]—and many readers have fallen for the very ruse that tricked Sauron the evil one into missing the real plot. In Tolkien's epic, after all, those who bear the real plot of history are not the wizards or the wraiths or their armies, but the hobbits. These are the peace-loving "little people" who are prepared to renounce the seductive ring of domineering power. They are the only ones who can be trusted to bear it to Mount Doom, the place of its forging, in order to cast it away and destroy it. All along their journey they must renounce the temptation to wield the ring, with its alluring promise that some truly great one might master it for good. All others, who think they can use its evil for their just causes, have been and will be destroyed by it. And the lesson within Tolkien's lesson: Unbeknownst even to themselves, hobbits have, with their patient unheralded work of ordinary community life, been bearing the secret of history all along.

PART II

Tent Stakes for a Pilgrim People

The Church is first and foremost a people advancing on its pilgrim way towards God. She is certainly a mystery rooted in the Trinity, yet she exists concretely in history as a people of pilgrims and evangelizers, transcending any institutional expression, however necessary. . . .

The Church is sent by Jesus Christ as the sacrament of the salvation offered by God. Through her evangelizing activity, she cooperates as an instrument of that divine grace which works unceasingly and inscrutably. This principle of the primacy of grace must be a beacon which constantly illuminates our reflections on evangelization. . . .

God has found a way to unite himself to every human being in every age He has chosen to call them together as a people and not as isolated individuals. No one is saved by himself or herself, individually, or by his or her own efforts. God attracts us by taking into account the complex interweaving of personal relationships entailed in the life of a human community. This people which God has chosen and called is the Church. Jesus did not tell the apostles to form an exclusive and elite group. . . .

Being Church means that we are to be God's leaven in the midst of humanity. The Church must be a place of mercy freely given, where everyone can feel welcomed, loved, forgiven and encouraged to live the good life of the Gospel. . . .

—Pope Francis, *Evangelii Gaudium* §§111–15

Chapter 5

Abrahamic Community as the Grammar of Gospel

> Already the final age of the world is with us (see 1 Cor 10:11) and the renewal of the world is irrevocably under way; it is even now anticipated in a certain real way, for the church on earth is endowed already with a sanctity that is real though imperfect. However, until the arrival of the new heavens and the new earth in which justice dwells . . . the pilgrim church, in its sacraments and institutions, which belong to this present age, carries the mark of this world which will pass . . .
>
> —Second Vatican Council, *Lumen Gentium* §48

> I dream of a "missionary option," that is, a missionary impulse capable of transforming everything, so that the Church's customs, ways of doing things, times and schedules, language and structures can be suitably channeled for the evangelization of today's world rather than for her self-preservation. . . . As John Paul II once said to the Bishops of Oceania: "All renewal in the Church must have mission as its goal if it is not to fall prey to a kind of ecclesial introversion." [Jesus] takes us from the midst of his people and he sends us to his people; without this sense of belonging we cannot understand our deepest identity.
>
> —Pope Francis, *Evangelii Gaudium* §§27, 268

The first pontiff from the Global South and the first pope fully of the Vatican II era, Pope Francis had experienced even more personally than his predecessors the globalizing forces that buffet the peoples of the world. Amid the cultural corrosions and economic exploitations that modern life accelerates, Jorge Bergoglio had learned before becoming pope that none can take *peoplehood* itself for granted. But neither—amid the anxiety of some Christians to protect their own group identity—can the church's goal be to protect its own sense of identity as a people by settling down comfortably behind institutional or cultural walls, as though it could complete its pilgrimage through history prematurely, before God draws history to a close.[1]

In writing his first apostolic exhortation eight months after his elevation from cardinal archbishop of Buenos Aires to the papacy in 2013, therefore, Pope Francis reiterated core lessons of Catholic social teaching—that to do the work of justice with special attention to the impact of policies on the poor is integral to peacebuilding, and that peacebuilding is integral to any living proclamation of the Gospel. Christians proclaim a Gospel that concerns the fullness of the kingdom of God and begins to take shape in this life, after all, not simply in personal salvation or individual acts of charity: "To the extent that [God] reigns within us, the life of society will be a setting for universal fraternity, justice, peace and dignity"; necessarily then, Christian preaching and life are both "meant to have an impact on society."[2] Francis's agenda highlighted the inclusion of the poor, peacemaking, and social dialogue both within nations and between faiths. Since peace is not mere pacification or absence of violence, peacemakers must attend to the distribution of wealth, integral human development, and the priority of human rights and dignity for all over the comfort of the privileged.[3]

But that is not all. To summarize his vision, Francis turned to a fresh and suggestive image—that of a polyhedron. Both a sphere and a polyhedron can serve as metaphors for human equality, but one is individualistic and the other is communal. While a sphere seems to offer perfect equidistance from the center, the egalitarian justice of a sphere is deceptive, for its cost is the globalized smoothing out of all cultural differences. A polyhedron, in contrast, offers the image of a richer justice of equality through participation in cultures that have not lost their distinctiveness:

> There is a place for the poor and their culture, their aspirations and their potential. Even people who can be considered dubious on account of their errors have something to offer which must not be overlooked. It is the convergence of peoples who, within

the universal order, maintain their own individuality; it is the sum total of persons within a society which pursues the common good, which truly has a place for everyone.[4]

Almost of necessity and just as strikingly, therefore, Francis framed peacebuilding as more than a specialized kind of policymaking, statecraft, activism, or prophetic Christian advocacy—important as these can be as tools for promoting peace with justice. Rather, the first pope from the Global South framed the work of peacebuilding as the very task of becoming a people of peace whose social posture in the world faces outward toward the common good of all peoples.[5]

And this is hardly the idiosyncratic thought or emphasis of one pope alone.

The grammar of salvation history[6]

Whatever has been fresh and distinctive about Pope Francis, his thought reflects the deep grammar of biblical narrative and church history. Before returning to his thought at the end of this chapter, I wish in the pages that follow to retell this narrative in a way that elucidates that grammar. In the next chapter I will show that grammar at work shaping the self-understanding of the church at key junctures in church history.

A deep "Abrahamic" grammar structures the living proclamation of the Gospel whenever the church allows its Lord to unsettle it into continuing its pilgrimage through history. In order to convey that grammar, then, we can do no better than to retell the biblical story. Though old-school grammarians have sometimes attempted to distill a grammar down into a few constitutive rules, few actually learn the grammar of a living language by rote. Rather we first come to intuit the rules of a grammar through participation in a community that converses widely, debates richly, and tells stories with subtlety, complexity, and nuance. The richness of the biblical story invites preachers and homilists to tell and retell it with endless variation, of course, in order to highlight the themes and lessons most apropos for the place and moment in which the gathered faithful find themselves on pilgrimage. If my own retelling succeeds at something more ambitious than this, it will be because the goal is to discern the big picture, the overarching plot to the story, and thus the deep continuities that hold the biblical drama together "grammatically."[7]

Since God's call to Abraham, Sarah, and their children in Genesis 12:1-3, the vocation of turning the identity that God's blessing gives to us—whoever we may be—into a blessing for others has been the deep grammar of salvation history, the underlying pattern of God's work. Individuals find protection, meaning, and identity as they are blessed within particular families, tribes, and communities—and woe to social groups or leaders who lose sight of their calling by sacrificing the God-given dignity of any member in the name of group preservation. And yet no group, especially if it identifies with the biblical tradition, will fulfill God's calling or even thrive over time if it only faces inward and not outward. Its interior-facing work is to protect the life and dignity of each member within. But each has an exterior-facing work as well. Like a series of nested Russian dolls, each person, then community, then people, then solidarity-of-peoples is also called to be a blessing to still-larger wholes. Just as God's love necessarily stretches beyond borders,[8] that blessing can finally stop nowhere short of the common good of "all the families of the earth" (Gen 12:3). To recognize the church as the sacrament of salvation and human unity and to recover its identity as a "pilgrim people," as did the Second Vatican Council, is simply to choose fresh words and images according to the same grammar. It should hardly surprise us to find Pope Francis having done the same.

What dare we hope?[9]

Any broad vision of peace or "reconciled diversity"[10] will sometimes prompt worries that the vision is unrealistic. Pope Francis's image of a polyhedron of equality between peoples that does not entail the smoothing out of all differences into a homogenized sphere is one such vision. Presented with such a picture, even allies may hang back. Perhaps they themselves have once been full of hope at the prospect of a better world, but faced setbacks and grew discouraged. At the very least, they may fairly ask, *So how do we get there from here?*

Our world easily discourages us. Climate change. Injustice. Sexual exploitation. Racism. Indifference to the lives of the unborn and those whose handicap or age renders them "unproductive." Deforestation and soil erosion. National and international debt. Corrupt officials.

Cynical citizens. Nuclear arms. Military dictatorships. War. Torture. Terrorism. And always more mouths to feed, more sick to treat.

However difficult for us to imagine a fresh, clean, creation "like new," that is exactly what the Hebrew and Christian Scriptures promise. The biblical promise is that God's saving work will bring forth nothing short of a "new creation," a "new heaven and a new earth." In the old earth in which we live, few may expect justice for anyone but themselves, and that only with a fight, leading at best to a standoff or a balance of power. Peace is elusive and hunger rampant. So perhaps it should not surprise us that so many Christians communicate despair even when they preach, "For God so loved the world" (John 3:16). In both Catholic and Protestant versions, the only hope that many Christians offer to the needy, after all, has sometimes been beatific vision or heavenly bliss for their souls after death.[11] If we do promise hope for this life, in these bodies, the best we sometimes offer is a tiny sphere of personal peace, or perhaps family prosperity. To the world that "God so loved," Christians have often offered judgment and damnation, while expecting the church to escape like the Ark of Noah, floating above the waters of destruction. In other words, we have given up on God's creation! And that is a word of surrender. It is a word of despair.

But we are not the first Christians to grow discouraged. The message of Jesus was that the kingdom of God was "at hand." In other words, *it was right at the door, knocking hard, even breaking in!* The picture Jesus painted was not one of ceaseless heavenly bliss for our souls. Rather, Jesus gave a word picture of a banquet table with ample food for the hungry and full human fellowship together with the Lord of the banquet (Luke 13:29; 14:15ff.). Another picture placed the disciples next to Jesus in the ongoing work of bringing justice to the nations (Luke 22:28-29). A banquet of food means a bodily existence. Justice implies a social existence. This adds up to a new society where God's will is "done on earth as it is in heaven." Sure enough, Jesus spoke of the in-breaking kingdom as a new society. Here the favored ones would be—no, already were!—the hungry, the sorrowful, the downtrodden, the merciful, the peacemakers, the persecuted (Matt 5:3-11; 11:2-6; Luke 6:20-26; 7:18-23). In turn, various New Testament writers spoke of our ultimate destiny as a whole new world, "new heavens and a new earth" (2 Pet 3:13; Rev 3:12; 14:3; 21:1-2; see also: Isa 65:17; 66:22; Rom 8:19-23; Heb 11:10, 16). Of course, to those facing death they also offered this assurance: we will be with Christ until this present age gives way to the fullness of the age to come (Luke 16:23; 23:43; Phil 1:23).

When Jesus did not return as quickly as the first Christians expected, however, some grew understandably discouraged. Their hope shifted. Already by the end of the century in which Christ lived many seem *only* to have been hoping that after death their souls would enjoy a heavenly existence. By the fourth century, Western Christians had a growing stake in the Roman Empire. Perhaps that is why few saw God to be actively challenging the established earthly order with a radically new one. Even so, the Apostles' Creed had by now cemented the most audacious of hopes into the Christian faith and tradition: "I believe in . . . the resurrection of the body" not just the immortal soul (cf. Rom 8:11; 1 Cor 15).

To be sure, the early Christians did not think they could build God's kingdom by their own strength. Nor should we. Human projects promising to create a utopia on earth usually rely on violence and often end up in tyranny. That is true for godless ideologies *and* for crusades in God's name. As we will discuss further, at the core of Christian faith is the conviction that God has come to us as a suffering servant; this challenges Christian efforts as well as secular efforts that would pretend to forcibly usher in any kingdom, to say nothing of God's! But God's saving goal is no less to re-create a whole new world—not just rescue our souls from the world. That should have a profound influence on the church's ministry. In word and deed, liturgy and outreach, we are joyfully to speak, be, and live *good news for whole people*. This is *evangelii gaudium*—the joy of the Gospel that Pope Francis has proclaimed anew.

From deep within, human beings long for meaning—yes, for something that will satisfy our souls forever. But when God's healing, forgiving, and reassuring work touches our souls indeed, we cannot stop caring about this world. If anything, freed from the need to grasp desperately onto this life and its goods, it is now that we can at last rightly value our food, our families, our tribes, our neighborhoods, our forests and fields and work, our music and customs and art—as God's gifts. In other words, if a God-given hope is deep within our souls, we will love God's world and its cultures all the more. We will groan together with the Holy Spirit and with creation itself as we yearn for the fullness of salvation (Rom 8:18-27).

The Catholic understanding of sacrament should help us get this right. As we will discuss further in the next chapter, at the Second Vatican Council the church described itself as the "sacrament of salvation" and the "sacrament of human unity."[12] Pope John Paul II elaborated further by speaking of the church as the sacrament of the world's peace.[13] With these rich concepts the Second Vatican Council has invited us to let Catholic sacramentality widely orient our social ethics. One standard definition of a sacrament is that it is the visible sign of an invisible reality or grace. Rightly understood, God's work is not anti-material or anti-worldly at all, for God's grace comes to us precisely through the materiality of water, wine, bread, oil, marital union, and well-ordered service to others in this world. Yet these always point beyond themselves to God's vibrant though hidden work. To call the church itself a sacrament, then, is to name its distinctive and indispensable role within God's saving work in history, even while insisting that the church can never limit God's work to itself, precisely because *its* work is to point beyond itself.

Obviously there is a tension here. In some ways, the kingdom is *already* among us. In other ways, it has *not yet* come. In its very human life in this world, the church itself often makes not-yet realities all *too* visible! To relieve the tension between the "already" and the "not yet," Christians do various things. Some are tempted to think they can force the kingdom to come through violence, or at least through frenzied activism. Others are tempted simply to wait passively for God alone to bring the kingdom. But if we recover the early Christian hope in a *bodily* resurrection, while fathoming the Vatican II understanding of the church as sacrament and sign, then we may do better at keeping things straight. For the new heavens and earth, where we will experience a bodily resurrection, promises to be much like Jesus' resurrected body.

In the weeks between the resurrection and the ascension of Jesus, the disciples witnessed a reality that was both like and unlike any bodily existence they knew. Jesus appeared among them when they had locked the doors in fear (John 20:19). He vanished after breaking bread (Luke 24:30-31). Obviously, this is not like our bodies. Yet Jesus was not a ghost or a hallucination either. His body was enough like it had been that the disciples could touch his wounds and serve him fish, which he ate (Luke 24:39-43).

In the same way, God's new heaven and earth will be different from anything we have known. Yet it will be easier to recognize than we may think—especially if we have imagined playing harps on clouds or blissfully floating around as spirits or angels in heaven. According to the Hebrew prophet Isaiah, life in the new world will still involve houses and vineyards and agriculture (65:17-25). According to the authors of Hebrews and Revelation, the new order will come as a city (Heb 11:16; 12:22; Rev 3:12; 21:2). A city (*polis* in Greek) means a social, even a political existence.

So the new world that God is bringing will be something like the resurrected body of Jesus. What then of our present service, peacebuilding, and work for social justice? These are more like the resurrected body of Lazarus. John 11 tells of the last great sign that Jesus performed before his crucifixion, raising his friend Lazarus from the dead. Lazarus still had the same body, though, and surely he had to die again. Yet his very existence was such a powerful and threatening sign that the religious authorities plotted to kill him along with Jesus (John 12:10-11). Our work in the world for the peace and common good of all humanity and indeed all of the planet's creatures is like this. It depends on an infusion of God's grace and Jesus' servanthood power. Even so, our own best achievements will pass away. Yet when infused by grace, they are no less worthwhile. They still prolong life. And they always point toward the fullness of God's kingdom.

God's social change strategy[14]

It would seem that God once grew discouraged too. At least that is the way it looks if we read the first eleven chapters of the Bible strictly as literature, dispensing with every pious need to soften the story or provide a spoiler from later in the biblical narrative. In the opening eleven chapters of the Bible, in the book of Genesis, humanity's rebellion against God and fratricide toward one another quickly began to mar the goodness of God's first, fresh, new creation. God's first efforts to check the human spiral of violence, then wipe the world clean with a flood, then disempower human pride by decentralizing it away from Babel, all had two things in common. One, God was attempting to work with humanity as a whole, all at once. Two, the results were inconclusive, time and again.

The opening chapters leave no doubt of God's loving concern for all the families of the earth. The writers of Genesis signaled this with those repeated genealogies that many modern readers skip over, for it was important to them to list all the human families they knew. Yet the destruction of the tower of Babel and the dispersal of all those families left God's redemptive work apparently stymied. Unlike the happy conclusion to the story of Noah and the flood, a question, not a rainbow, hung in the air as humanity spread out from Babel. God had promised to save and care for all. Yet strikingly—in what should constitute a warning to reformers, prelates, and ethicists who imagine the success of top-down, macro solutions to social problems that do not involve the participation of grassroots—even God's own providence had apparently been of little avail. "Providence" refers to God's overarching management of history and humanity as a whole, but that strategy seemed to require regular rebooting.

At the close of Genesis, chapter 11 and the beginning of 12, however, God made a strategic pivot. First, there was a rustling in history, a sifting among the world's families. The tribes of Shem, son of Noah, now called for special attention. Among them, one clan was restless. Terah was on the move, though uncertain of his destination. But Terah had a son and a daughter-in-law, Abram and Sarai—later to be renamed Abraham and Sarah. As we read the narrative our eyes now focus in on them, still wondering, still awaiting a word of hope. Suddenly, from out of all the families of the earth, Yahweh the Sovereign LORD chooses to address one family.

> Now the LORD said to Abram: "Go from your country and your kindred and your father's house to the land that I will show you. And I will make of you a great nation, and I will bless you, and make your name great, so that you will be a blessing. I will bless those who bless you, and him who curses you I will curse; and by you all the families of the earth shall bless themselves." So Abram went, as the LORD had told him; and Lot went with him (Gen 12:1-4).[15]

Those of us who are long-familiar with biblical stories may easily miss how much changes as the page turns from the eleventh to the twelfth chapter of Genesis. God's strategy itself changes! The shift is momentous enough that biblical scholars sometimes refer to this, rather than anything in the previous chapters, as the beginning of salvation history. God's sphere of action was still all the families of the earth. God still longed to restore all relationships to the potential they had at creation. But to reach that constant and unchanging goal, God suddenly narrowed the focus of action. God called and created a distinct people. This people was to serve God by living in a way that was a service to all other peoples. This people would not live for themselves alone. God was not calling Abraham *out of the world* as God had called Noah. God was calling Abraham *for the world*.

Now, to understand God's social change strategy we must hold together what it means *to be blessed* and *to bless others*. The Judeo-Christian doctrine of election has been the source of much confusion—not least among the "elect"! The temptation to hoard God's blessings and to see them as a mandate for ruling over others tempts all who consider themselves God's chosen people. Meanwhile, for many the claim that the God of the universe reveals God's self through a single family or person seems a great scandal. For them it is reason enough to reject the faith of Abraham and Jesus.

Make no mistake. Abraham needed to experience the blessing of God to become a blessing. God wanted Abraham to offer something new, fresh, and life-giving to all history and peoples. God achieved this by creating, through Abraham, a distinct people with a new and different kind of history. This people had to know God's love and care amid all kinds of trials to offer love and compassion to suffering humanity. Blessing meant access to land (Gen 12:1). It meant descendants (Gen 15; 17; 18:9f.; 21:1-7). It meant new names, a new identity from God (Gen 12:2; 17:5, 15). Above all, it meant a covenant relationship with God. In this covenant, God's demands on Abraham were small in comparison with God's promise to Abraham.

Even so, *the blessing is never an end in itself*. As the fate of the ungodly cities of Sodom and Gomorrah, which were not even fulfilling the ancient Middle Eastern code of hospitality toward strangers, hung in the balance, God in the form of three mysterious guests took Abraham into God's own counsel:

> Shall I hide from Abraham what I am about to do, seeing that Abraham shall become a great and mighty nation, and all the nations of the earth shall be blessed in him? No, for I have chosen him, that he may charge his children and his household after

him to keep the way of the LORD by doing righteousness and justice. (Gen 18:17-19)

The "way of the LORD" meant Abraham and his family would take part in God's justice. So God even allowed Abraham to question the justice of God's own plan to destroy the two cities (Gen 18:23-25). In other words, "the blessing of the nations" and the "way of the LORD" meant an earnest longing for the good of others. Abraham interceded with God for the kind of justice that sought mercy, not punishment. Yes, the culture before him was corrupt. Yet as long as there was hope that some good could come from it, Abraham sought to preserve and nurture the best that remained in the wicked cities.

Already in the first four generations of the Abrahamic community, then, models of blessing to other nations or families of the earth emerged. Not only did the Abrahamic people-for-other-peoples intercede with God even on behalf of cities infamous for their corruption. The community was ready to resolve conflicts peacefully so that neighboring peoples might share access to natural resources (Gen 26), and perhaps even more challenging, it resolved at least some of its own potentially fratricidal conflicts (Gen 27–33; 35:29). It shared economic aid and technical knowledge (Gen 30:27). It managed resources wisely in time of scarcity, even though that meant working with the empire that would eventually turn around and oppress the descendants of Abraham (Gen 41–50).

None of this is to say that the full meaning of God's covenant was clear to Abraham, Isaac, Jacob, or Joseph, or that they always followed "the way of the LORD." Abraham himself blundered mightily, as Genesis 12 records it, immediately after hearing God's great call. His first descendants' warts and worse appear in the narrative right alongside their witness. How to be a blessing to other families without simply assimilating would be a constant tension that they were sometimes tempted to relieve with premature solutions, as when Abraham's great-grandsons slaughtered the clan of Shechem in vengeance for his rape of their sister Dinah, despite their willingness to join their families together not only through marriage but by accepting circumcision (Gen 34). Later descendants struggled generation after generation, through crisis after crisis, to learn the meaning of the call that had founded their peoplehood.

Such questions especially came to a head once the people asked God for a king. They wanted to "be like other nations," with a king who would "govern us and go out before us and fight our battles" (1 Sam 8:20). Other nations fought and oppressed in order to secure their own self-interests at the expense of others. But was this the "way of the LORD"? How could blessing fit such a foreign policy? And what sort of blessing would they have to offer if they simply became like other nations? To adopt the policy of defending themselves against others through military dominance was actually—paradoxically—to assimilate.

Biblical scholars believe that it was in precisely this context that the writers of Genesis gathered the stories that they had inherited through oral tradition. What they saw in the first generations of Abraham, Sarah, and their descendants was an underlying pattern of blessing and service to other nations, not domination or oppression. As they compiled those stories, they tweaked them in order to bring that pattern to the foreground and challenge the narrow-visioned and self-interested nationalism of their own day.[16]

For if anything, to come into possession of the land through territorial control and kingship rather than through nomadic negotiation and hospitality actually constituted the greatest occasion for temptation, according to warnings in Deuteronomy 8–9.[17] As a nation, Israel's constant temptation was to celebrate identity in Abraham, liberation at Exodus, and a "land flowing with milk and honey"— while forgetting to welcome the stranger, free the slaves, and remember the oppressed, the widow, the orphan, and the immigrant. It is not always easy, after all, to hungrily welcome God's blessing without hoarding it. It is rarely easy to bless others if that means risking one's own well-being. It can be hard to remember God's deliverance from slavery in Egypt without thinking God has now given us the right to dominate others. It is certainly hard to gain our life by losing it.

Yet faithful service to God and others always requires that we do two sets of things simultaneously. We must ever celebrate God's blessing even as we give God's blessings up to others. The path of faithfulness lies between twin temptations: easy *assimilation* and harsh *exclusivity*. In the face of the temptation of easy assimilation, the people of God must live boldly in the world without spreading themselves so thinly that they no longer have anything distinct to offer. Meanwhile, in the face of the temptation of harsh exclusivity, we must not maintain our distinction by barricading ourselves against the challenges, needs, and needy ones for whom God has called us together. For just here, this paradoxical yet creative tension defines the core logic of the deep Abrahamic grammar of the gospel: With Abraham, God's people have an identity they actually lose by hoarding. With Jesus, God's people live a life they gain only by risking its loss for his sake. The path to cross and resurrection begins where Abram began his pilgrimage, in Ur.

Given this pattern, it is not surprising that both Jews and Christians see God's initiative being reborn and purposes clarified precisely in exile. However much the glories of David's reign seemed to represent the fulfillment of God's promises to Abraham and Sarah, they soon gave way to infighting and bloodletting within David's dynasty, as well as oppression not just of David's imperial subjects but of the children of Israel themselves. This was just as the prophet Samuel, who reluctantly anointed Israel's first kings, had warned (1 Sam 8:10-18). Israel's prophets held up "the way of the LORD" with all the more clarity as the prospect of a faithful people seemed to fade, even as they warned that God's faithfulness would not exempt God's people from judgment and disaster. The prophets also widened the international horizon of God's purposes as they did so.

When empires to the east first undermined the political independence of Israel and Judah in the eighth to sixth centuries BCE, then invaded and took captive the best and brightest of the Hebrews in 597 BCE, many wondered whether God had abandoned God's people and belied their covenant identity. Yet as the Hebrews found themselves in Babylonian exile back in the region of Abraham's origin, Judaism as we now know it began to emerge. Precisely in exile, amid all the creative tensions of life as resident aliens, Jewish scholars began the definitive compilation of the Hebrew Scriptures and launched rabbinic traditions of commentary on the Torah. At the same time, it was the very prophetic vision that emerged in this historical juncture that would do most to shape Jesus' own self-identity.

In Jerusalem, as disaster had loomed, the prophet Jeremiah had been as blunt about the self-righteous complacency of Judah's ruling elites as any, with a personal despair to match. Yet once King Nebuchadnezzar of Babylon had destroyed what remained of Judah's political independence and carried off those elites to serve him there, it was Jeremiah who encouraged them with a way forward. His letter to the exiles appears in Jeremiah 29. Do not be afraid to carry on with life, he told them in effect. "Build houses and live in them; plant gardens and eat their produce. Take wives and have sons and daughters; take wives for your sons, and give your daughters in marriage, that they may bear sons and daughters; multiply there, and do not decrease" (Jer 29:5-6). You should expect to reside in Babylon for a few generations at least, he told them. Far from wallowing in resentment toward the empire that had taken them captive,[18] they should work for its good, the common good that the exiles shared with it: "But seek the welfare"—the *shalom*, the prosperity, the peace—"of the city where I have sent you into exile, and pray to the LORD on its behalf, for in its welfare you will find your welfare" (Jer 29:7-8).

Of course, the tensions that needed navigation for faithful life in exile never promised to be simple or free of suffering. Though the book of Daniel bears some of the qualities of legend, it gives us a window into those tensions and in any case seems written to offer lessons in just how to navigate the shoals of exile and diaspora. Daniel and the other young men whose challenges the book recounts had apparently heeded Jeremiah's exhortation to settle down and seek the peace of the city. Far from remaining resentfully disengaged from their host culture, after all, they were civil servants in the highest levels of Babylonian government, known for their integrity and promoted for their wisdom. Yet they could only do this well if they were clear that their primary identity was a response to the *Shema*, the call to faith in the one God and fidelity to God's Law or Torah that is at the core of Judaism:

> Hear, O Israel: The LORD is our God, the LORD alone. You shall love the LORD your God with all your heart, and with all your soul, and with all your might. Keep these words that I am commanding you today in your heart. Recite them to your children and talk about them when you are at home and when you are away, when you lie down and when you rise. Bind them as a sign on your hand, fix them as an emblem on your forehead, and write them on the doorposts of your house and on your gates. (Deut 6:4-9[19])

The priority of their identity as people of the covenant required an ability to recognize when their *yes* to the *shalom*, peace, and welfare of their host culture also required a *no* to its rulers' pretensions and idolatry. Facing worst-case scenarios of death in a fiery furnace or den of lions, some no doubt preferred to fade into Babylonian society through assimilation, leaving little trace except perhaps for a story that ten entire tribes of Israel had been lost there. Even for those who found faithful ways to keep their loyalty to God primary while seeking the *shalom* of the city, creative tensions could be acute enough that their experience of exile prompted them to describe their community as a desolate "remnant."

Indeed, the other most formative prophetic vision to emerge from this period of life in exile poignantly held together both acute suffering and expansive hope. This was the prophetic tradition associated with Isaiah, and it seems especially to have shaped the consciousness of Jesus of Nazareth six centuries later, then to permeate the Christian Scriptures.[20] The visionary named Isaiah whose words we know from the first thirty-nine chapters of the book with that title had been among the most prominent and eloquent of the prophets in the years prior to the fall of Jerusalem and the exile of its leaders. Biblical scholars believe, however, that his legacy continued into exile in Babylon through a circle of disciples, one or two of whom gave us chapters 40–66 of the book of Isaiah. The first prophet, Isaiah, speaking amid the gloom of gathering disaster prior to Judah's collapse and exile, had anticipated the experience of diminished hopes in which only a remnant would remain faithful.[21] Yet even as the actual experience of exile prompted some of the Bible's most hauntingly eloquent poetry of suffering, that same experience also evoked one of its widest visions of hope. Perhaps this is simply paradoxical. But perhaps it reflects that very creativity in the creative tensions of exile and diaspora. In their very faithfulness, the remnant-like circle of Isaiah's disciples simply could not hunker down under siege, fatalistic about their prospects for wide engagement with God's purposes among the families of the earth.

Simply for the exiles to find that they could still practice the faith of Abraham, Sarah, and Moses in another land, away from homeland and without access to temple, must itself have been revelatory. If God heard their prayers even here, then truly God was Lord of all the earth. The exiles still longed to return to their homeland. But their loss had meaning, their desolation came with opportunity. Emerging to name this hope were a series of songs about a "Servant of the LORD" who would finally be faithful to God's purposes even through suffering. The examples of both Jeremiah or Isaiah no doubt inspired the remnant. They had suffered much yet persisted when the nation rejected their warnings, and on the other side of their suffering they had found fresh hope.

The "Songs of the Servant" appear in Isaiah 42:1-9; 49:1-6; 50:4-11; 52:13–53:12.[22] Sometimes these songs seem to refer to a dynamic prophet among the exiled disciples of Isaiah. Sometimes it seems that a remnant of Israel itself would become the Servant by learning the lessons of captivity and faithfully adhering to the just ways of the LORD (see Isa 41:8-10 and 51:1-2). And sometimes the songs hint at an altogether faithful Servant-Messiah still to come. But since God had called *all* Abraham's children to be a blessing, we really need not choose among these multiple layers of meaning. All apply.

The Abrahamic pattern of communities-within-peoples-within-peoples in fact shows why. The whole people was to be the Lord's Servant. But if Israel faltered, a single Servant, faithful despite suffering, might simultaneously call them back even while standing in their place. Such a figure would serve all peoples as the whole people of God was meant to do. At the same time, neither his own work nor his outreach could displace the people already called. For God's Abrahamic strategy (picture nested Russian dolls again) is always that creative minorities serve the good of larger wholes, not delegitimize them, even when that means forming within them a new community to live as a people-for-other-peoples.[23]

From the first "Here is my servant" onward, then, the Songs of the Servant bear a twin focus that faithfully corresponds to the call of Abraham. The Spirit of God would anoint the Servant to free the Israelite exiles, open their eyes to God's continuing care for them, and lead them home in a new exodus. This certainly meant renewed blessing for the children of Abraham. Yet simultaneously, the Servant would "not grow faint or be crushed until he has established justice in the earth." After all, even the farthest "coastlands wait for his teaching" (Isa 42:1-9). In other words, the Servant would bless all peoples; the Servant's mission would be global. "It is too light a thing that you should be my servant to raise up the tribes of Jacob and restore the survivors of Israel; I will give you as a light to the nations, that my salvation may reach to the ends of the earth" (Isa 49:6).

The Servant would establish justice, witness, and give light—though at great cost. The Servant would be despised. His own people would reject him (49:7; 53:2-3). The nations would misunderstand him (52:15). And this was only the beginning. The Servant faced blows, insults, spitting, and death. Yet he did not rebel against God's way of working justice and liberation through servanthood. Rather, he trusted that God would vindicate him (49:7; 50:4-7; 53:4-10). Ultimately the Servant would prosper, "be exalted and lifted up . . . very high" (52:13). Yet any such way of achieving justice and liberation for the nations is difficult for all people in all times to understand—or if we do understand, to embrace. What is clear is that this Servant is one who lives and dies for others—including us ourselves who trust that God has called us to be God's people yet continue to misunderstand and misappropriate God's ways. He lives and dies for the very nations who are astonished at his ugliness and offended at his apparent weakness (52:14-15). In response, the kings of the nations are startled and tight-lipped. Dimly they perceive what they never expected to see—that the way of suffering service, not domination, is ultimately most powerful.

The one-for-others and a people-for-all peoples

The songs and prophecies of the disciples of Isaiah gave many exiles courage to return to their now-scorched homeland and razed cities in what the book of Isaiah portrays as a kind of new exodus. But after exile, the community of Israel did not quite seem to have known what to do with the larger vision of the Suffering Servant of the LORD. What nation can be restored to prosperity yet remain a suffering servant of other nations?

In centuries following the return from exile, therefore, new questions arose. Did a renewed exodus require a restored state and a sovereign territory for them to be a people? The Maccabees and Zealots who revolted against foreign domination of Palestine insisted that God's people needed their own state. But Jews who remained in Babylon together with new Jewish communities dispersed through the Mediterranean—what we have come to call *the* "Diaspora" in the original, classical, Jewish meaning of the word—showed they could remain a distinct people even amid other peoples. Was there not, however, a danger of mixing *too* freely with other races and cultures?

Ezra and Nehemiah insisted on strict separation and refused to tolerate any intermarriage. But the writer of Jonah called for greater, more loving openness. After all, even the Assyrian Nineveh of Jonah's story and other centers of political power that Israelites resented might repent.

It was into this crucible of questions and debates that Jesus of Nazareth entered.

When Jesus inaugurated his ministry in his home synagogue, he read from Isaiah and at least by implication identified himself with Isaiah's Servant of the LORD. God's Spirit was upon him, he said, to bring good news to the poor, proclaim release for prisoners, give sight to the blind, free the oppressed, and announce a new beginning of justice and economic redistribution. The project that Jesus announced was so radical he nearly got himself stoned even before his ministry had really begun (Luke 4:16-30). Yet it was not necessarily Jesus' identification with the Servant of the LORD that provoked his fellow citizens. They were glad to welcome God's blessings. But nationalistically, they wanted those blessings primarily for themselves. Jesus reminded them therefore that God often chose to work through and to bless people of other nations as well. *That* is when a lynch mob formed in Nazareth. Had Jesus chosen to be a messiah who saved and served Israel at the expense of other peoples, he might never have been executed. He rejected the main political options of his day not because they were political, but because they were all nationalistic.

When Jesus made the entire Servant vision of Isaiah his own, that included its international, intercultural scope. Yet he continued to work at it according to the Abrahamic strategy we saw as the page turned from chapter 11 to chapter 12 of Genesis. Recall that there, at what theologians and biblical scholars consider the launching of "salvation history," God pivoted from an undifferentiated providential strategy to the formation of a community that would be a pilot project, embodied witness, and creative minority whose very existence was to be a blessing to all those other families, communities, and peoples that a loving Creator could never abandon. The motley band of disciples whom Jesus first called to follow him in Galilee was no mere happenstance. It recapitulated a deliberate Abrahamic strategy to communicate the gospel message not primarily as teaching or *gnosis* (Greek for knowledge, often understood as secret saving

Abrahamic Community as the Grammar of Gospel 151

knowledge) but embodied in a people. Hence the community, the people, we call church.

The first Christians immediately recognized and proclaimed Jesus as the Servant of the LORD whom Isaiah had described (see Acts 3:13-26; 4:27-30; 8:26-35). In an early hymn, which Paul quoted in Philippians 2:6-11, they expressed their conviction that servanthood was at the heart of who Jesus was. To become like human beings in every way, Jesus had given up "equality with God, . . . emptied himself," and taken "the form of a slave" (or servant). And the identity of Jesus also had immediate consequences for the new community of disciples who followed him. The "mind of Christ" that motivated his servanthood was to be their own. Jesus had insisted that a servant is never greater than the master (John 13:16; 15:20). As Jesus washed the feet of other people, so must they. As he suffered and even died, so might they. To achieve God's purposes, they too should use power different from the world's (Mark 10:41-45).

To live lives of servanthood and blessing to others, then, was not to be so much a command as a character trait or virtue. It was not an optional vocation for a specially called few. It was not an extra "way of perfection" or "evangelical counsel" for those Christians who are particularly serious about faith. All believers were to be servants from the moment they began life "in Christ" (see Gal 3:27; Eph 4:23-24; Col 3:9b-15). And as they formed a community of servant-believers who embodied Christ for the world, it had to be international and intercultural. Putting on Christ's "new person" did not simply mean that individual believers took on a new Christlike character. Rather, it meant forming a new collective entity where old barriers of race, class, and gender broke down (Gal 3:28; Eph 2:13-18; Col 3:11).

To be sure, the early church still needed to work out much about how to be a servant people, a blessing to all nations. The book of Acts and the letters of St. Paul reveal a community struggling with many practical and theological issues as Jew and Gentile began relating to one another in one body. Remember the twin temptations of assimilation and exclusivity? Hebrew Christians had reason to fear assimilation. Gentile Christians had reason to feel excluded or at least marginalized as second-class citizens.

The apostle Paul strove mightily to lay out a path through the twin challenges of assimilation and exclusion. We know him as the apostle to the Gentiles. We read in Acts and Galatians how he boldly defended the right of Gentile churches to welcome and apply the Gospel in ways appropriate to their own cultures. Paul wanted to spread the Gospel widely, to take its blessing to all nations. But this same Paul also worked vigorously to keep the Gospel from mixing uncritically with Gentile ways. With its distinct identity and lifestyle, it was to be just as "transformed" and "nonconformed," as those who received the teaching of Moses at Sinai were to be holy and set apart among the nations (Rom 12:1-2). The letters of Paul thus show many efforts to deal with problems that disorderly, once-lawless Gentiles had in living the Christian life (Eph 2:1-3, 11-12). The Jesus story dare not become one more "mystery religion" current in the Mediterranean world, offering cosmic escape from the world. Rather, it was to change that world (Acts 17:6).

The very existence of a reconciled, servanthood community in the midst of the nations was a culture-building service, not just a countercultural challenge. Yes, it defied the wisdom of all the world's ruling powers. But God had a different wisdom. If bitter enemies like Jew and Gentile and even "barbarian" could live for one another, what else might start to change? In Christ and through the church, God was working "to reconcile to himself all things, whether on earth or in heaven, by making peace through the blood of his cross" (Eph 1:15–2:22; Col 1:15-29). A community where rich and poor, Jew and Gentile, simple and cultured, all loved each other and served others challenged the current order. It set an example that many in power found dangerous. Its very existence publicly showed that the injustice, violence, and prejudice of the current order were false, failed, and fading. These were not the inevitable fate of humanity after all. They were not and are not "just the way things are" (Col 2:15).

Violent domination is the very opposite of servanthood. Many, however, either believe that servanthood is equivalent to subservience, or believe that violence is necessary to hold together a social order, or both. But no, affirmed Paul, it is Christ who holds all things together—the very Jesus whom the so-called powerful had crucified. Together with his church, Jesus had begun transforming the present order of things (Eph 1:19-23; Col 1:17-18). Though cosmic in scope (Rom 8), Christ's great transforming work always begins with simple, almost mundane acts of hospitality, encouragement, and blessing (Rom 12)—what Catholics have come to call the "works of mercy."

And not just toward fellow Christians. "Give the same consideration to all others alike," urged Paul. "Pay no regard to social standing, but meet humble people on their own terms. . . . As much as possible, and to the utmost of your ability, be at peace with everyone" (Rom 12:16-18, New Jerusalem Bible). "God's holy people" are never the exclusive object of Abrahamic blessing or Christian servanthood. Even persecutors are to benefit. When God's people are faithful they will joyfully celebrate God's blessing, yet find themselves unable to hold that blessing tightly to themselves alone.

This is the underlying grammar of Gospel. This is the consistent pattern running through salvation history since the call of Abraham. But it must be embodied in the life of a people. To summarize, such a people is an "Abrahamic community" insofar as it celebrates the calling and grace that has shaped its identity, yet knows instinctively that it cannot hoard this "blessing" for itself without losing that identity. God calls it to be a people-for-others as its Lord was the person-for-others, after all. It thus negotiates the path of faithfulness between the twin temptations of exclusivity and assimilation. It must engage boldly in the world by *inculturating* the gospel message, without *acculturating* so indiscriminately that it no longer has anything distinct to offer. Yet it must not maintain its distinctiveness by barricading itself against the challenges, needs, and needy ones for whom God has called it together. Ultimately it finds and sustains its identity by "dying to itself," by putting its very identity at risk through its service to other communities.[24]

Peacebuilding principles: people-building principles

An intriguing passage of Pope Francis's apostolic exhortation *Evangelii Gaudium* (The Joy of the Gospel) lays out four essential principles for peacebuilding. None stands in isolation from the others, nor could they. Together they require embodiment. Hence, peacebuilding for Francis is necessarily the building of peoples. For Christians to work for peace within and among the nations, they must ever seek to live out their own vocational identity as a people, a pilgrim people—sacrament of human salvation, and indeed, sacrament of unity and peaceable peoplehood among all the families of the earth.

It would of course be disingenuous of me to suggest that Francis was anticipating exactly the theology of peace that I have been developing here. Where I have been speaking of Abrahamic community, *Evangelii Gaudium* speaks of a "community of missionary disciples,"[25] in which "being Church means being God's people" even as God's "great plan" for this very people is that it be "God's leaven in the midst of humanity."[26] Yet here is the Abrahamic grammar; here are those nested Russian dolls again. For Francis, the community's inward-looking work and the identity it rightly seeks to preserve are lost unless it looks outward and gives its gift away with a paradoxical risk to that very identity.[27] Thus Francis has warned that church renewal must have mission and evangelization as its goal if renewal is to be more than what John Paul II had called "'ecclesial introversion'"; thus he has dreamed of an outward orientation or "missionary impulse capable of transforming everything, so that the church's customs, ways of doing things, times and schedules, language and structures can be suitably channeled for the evangelization of today's world rather than for her self-preservation."[28] (And remember: in Catholic thought, *evangelization* is a much richer notion than simply personal *evangelism*, for it incorporates all work for the peace and common good of humanity according to gospel values.) An invitation to savor being a people in Jesus Christ with a deep sense of belonging thus appears in *Evangelii Gaudium* in immediate proximity to a reminder that this belonging means that Christ both "takes us from the midst of his people and he sends us to his people."[29]

My contention then is this: Only by living out, by whatever name, the pattern of social life that I am identifying as "Abrahamic community" can the Catholic Church be a catholic peace church that integrates and embodies Francis's four principles of peacebuilding in its very life:

1. "Time is greater than space."[30]

However urgently we sense the world's needs, our first and most basic task as Christians is not to seize power in our desperation but to generate processes of people-building—not to hold territory but to be patient with history: "One of the faults which we occasionally observe in sociopolitical activity is that spaces and power are preferred to time and processes," Francis observed. "Giving priority to space means madly attempting to keep everything together in the present, trying to possess all the spaces of power and of self-assertion." To instead give priority to time puts spaces (and by implication the material resources that exist within spaces) in their proper perspective. "What we need, then, is to give priority to actions which generate new processes in society and engage other persons and groups who can develop them to the point where they bear fruit in significant historical events. Without anxiety, but with clear convictions and tenacity."[31]

The Christian horizon of action, after all, is not geographical but eschatological; the most important location we live within is not a space we can pretend to possess but a time given to us as a gift. For us this is the time between the *already* of God's promised future that Francis called "the final cause which draws us to itself" and the *not yet* of our limited human condition. To be sure, life in this in-between time presents a "constant tension." But recognizing that "time is greater than space" gives us "a first principle for progress in building a people." We can live in that "constant tension [that] exists between fullness and limitation" and "work slowly but surely, without being obsessed with immediate results."

By implication, one may add, here in the principle that time is greater than space we find solid philosophical grounding for a social ethic of diaspora: The constant that orients our lives and defines our peoplehood must be a journey through time and history. Such a pilgrimage must always journey through geographical space and territory, of course. But this is secondary, for no one space defines the pilgrimage and in fact to identify definitively with one territory or nation-state is to abort the pilgrimage. The pilgrim people of God must travel through many spaces, dwelling lightly in many territories but settling permanently in none.

2. "Unity prevails over conflict."[32]

In introducing his four peacebuilding principles, Francis had joined with earlier popes and the Second Vatican Council itself in reminding us that peace is not the mere absence of violence or warfare. That is especially true whenever what has wrought a false and "transient peace for a contented minority" is in fact the domination by the affluent in a way that silences the poor and suppresses their rights and dignity in the name of a false "consensus on paper."[33] The implication as Francis moved from his first to his second principle was that conflict can in fact be a "link in the chain of a new process" of people-building, but only if it is "faced" rather than "ignored or concealed."

Facing conflict frankly, with a willingness to work for resolution "head on," in fact makes it "possible to build communion amid disagreement," according to Francis. Such honest confrontation opens a "third way" between callous evasion of conflictual realities and resentful entrapment within conflicts. To instead enter conflict frankly but nonviolently first requires a living hope that beyond our differences and underneath our conflicts lies a more profound unity that allows us to build friendship in society and act in solidarity. After all, the peace toward which the Gospel of Jesus Christ calls us is neither the syncretism of an easy but superficial tolerance nor the homogenization that absorbs one into the other, nor even a mere "negotiated settlement." Rather it is a " 'reconciled diversity' " within a "life-giving unity."

3. "Realities are more important than ideas."[34]

Cardinal Jorge Bergoglio, SJ, had only been Pope Francis for a few weeks when—to the consternation of some and the comforting of many—he began to signal his intention to realign the priorities of the Roman Catholic Church. Too many Catholics had been obsessing over abortion, contraception, and homosexuality in a disjointed way to the exclusion of other issues, he would soon explain; the church's doctrine and moral teaching can only be intelligible within a context where people know that ministers of the Gospel are accompanying them with mercy, healing, and clear recognition of their dignity as persons.[35]

Francis's third peacebuilding principle no doubt reflected this emphasis. But here in his apostolic exhortation he spoke explicitly not only of faith but of politics. And in the context of peacebuilding that carries additional lessons.

Whether coming from reformers or fundamentalists, Francis noted, ideas that are "detached from realities" and "dwell in the realm of words alone, of images and rhetoric," are "dangerous."[36] Though he did not explicitly connect his point with his larger theme of "building a people" just here, surely this is why peacebuilding for him was first of all about people-building. One of Mahatma Gandhi's most famous aphorisms, we might once again recall, was to "be the change you seek in the world." Likewise, Francis insisted that Christian peacebuilding must be incarnate. What we propose to the world cannot be mere policy proposals, therefore; it must be embodied in the life of the people called church.

To collaborate for peace among all the families and peoples of the world, the church itself must become a people of peace. Learning to talk constructively in our parishes about effective responses to poverty, about what will really discourage abortions, about how to welcome immigrants, about when to resist unjust wars, and for that matter about how to negotiate our liturgy wars—all of this contributes to world peace as surely as does Vatican diplomacy. In the context of a discussion earlier in the document concerning war, violence, individualism, and divisive conflict, Francis had thus made a point of lamenting and then requesting: "How many wars take place within the people of God and in our different communities! . . . I especially ask Christians in communities throughout the world to offer a radiant and attractive witness of fraternal communion."[37]

4. "The whole is greater than the part."[38]

Just as Pope John Paul had insisted in his address to the United Nations in 1975 that the family of peoples on earth must pay attention to the fruitful tension between the two poles of universality and particularity in order to build a civilization of love,[39] Pope Francis now turned to the "innate tension" that "exists between globalization and localization. We need to pay attention to the global so as to avoid narrowness and banality," he urged. "Yet we also need to look to the local, which keeps our feet on the ground."[40] Inversely, we should neither allow the glitter of global culture to seduce us, nor encase local cultures unchangeably in museums of folklore. No, the relationship between the local and the global, the particular and the universal, is too dynamic for that: "The whole is greater than the part, but it is also greater than the sum of its parts."[41]

Our challenge is to broaden our horizons even while putting deep roots down into our native places. Again, to work right where we are for strong families, vibrant but hospitable neighborhoods, and racial justice across urban/suburban divides is as crucial to people-building and thus peacebuilding as international diplomacy, policymaking in national capitals, or mediation in war zones. "We can work on a small scale, in our own neighbourhood, but with a larger perspective. . . . The global need not stifle, nor the particular prove barren."[42]

Here then is where Francis presented his many-faced "polyhedron" as a model of global reconciled unity, not a smoothly undifferentiated sphere. According to such a model, "There is a place for the poor and their culture, their aspirations and their potential." Even those whom we are tempted to dismiss as "dubious on account of their errors have something to offer" that we dare not overlook.[43] The whole that Francis envisioned as a polyhedron, therefore, "is the convergence of peoples who, within the universal order, maintain their own individuality; it is the sum total of persons within a society which pursues the common good, which truly has a place for everyone."

To be sure, some "principle of totality" must be intrinsic to the very Gospel that Christians proclaim, since the scope of that Gospel surely embraces all people universally. But the Gospel does so in a way that affirms every personal vocation and channels the cultural genius of every people, leaving no lost sheep behind. "Pastoral and political activity alike seek to gather in this polyhedron the best of each."[44]

Also, it works

To imagine and flesh out an "Abrahamic" strategy of social change through a church with a diaspora ecclesiology is not mere idealism. Why? Number one, we have found reason to believe that God's project all along has been to form a people blessed with that paradoxical Abrahamic identity, which they only preserve by putting it at risk as they seek to bless all the families of the earth. And number two, because it is effective. A brief turn from theology to political science will show why.

One of the biggest stories of the twenty-first century is that despite the assumption that religion would recede to strictly private spaces if not die out entirely in modernity, it is resurgent both in domestic and global politics. For many this is a fearful thing, especially because the attacks of September 11, 2001, are what jolted them into noticing.

Already before 9/11 but with new urgency afterward, a team of scholars—Monica Duffy Toft, Daniel Philpott, and Timothy Samuel Shah—launched a project "to show not only that religion matters but also to show how it matters."[45] Using the tools of political science they sought to move beyond simplistic arguments about whether religion is a positive or negative force in global politics. Instead they did a more finely grained analysis of the factors that lead some religiously inspired actors not only to fight civil wars or engage in terrorism in the name of religion, but lead others to promote democratization and peacebuilding.

What they found after examining the political processes in countries around the world, and the role of actors from various religions, was that two variables were key—the political theology or "set of ideas that a religious community holds about political authority and justice" and "the mutual independence of religious authority and political authority."[46] When political theologies envisioned the tight integration of religious and political authorities, or historic relations between them had institutionalized dependency, the results were either authoritarian regimes or bitter civil wars to overthrow them, using terroristic tactics in the most dramatic cases.[47] Religion was most likely to inspire violence when used to justify an integrationist status quo or to try to create some new one. In contrast, in country after country where religious actors were effective either as contributors or key players in processes of democratization or of transitioning from war to just peace, they had *both* a clear political theology envisioning participatory democracy or social reconciliation to guide them, *and* a sense of independence resulting from rootedness in their own religious tradition.[48] In other words, they had a clear sense of their own identity and higher loyalty without being sectarian. But that very identity was one that required social and political engagement, in a way that took them beyond captivity to narrow interests, either tribalistic or nationalistic.

This is God's "Abrahamic" strategy of social change. This is what a diaspora ecclesiology gives us.

Conclusion

Early in his papacy, church and world alike welcomed Francis preeminently as a pastor. Yet by introducing his four principles for peacebuilding through people-building into Catholic social teaching, the pope from Argentina demonstrated his depth as a theologian and philosopher as well. True to the Vatican II principle of *ressourcement*—going forward in history by reaching back to ancient Christian sources of wisdom—Pope Francis extended the church's theology, in this case its theology of peace, precisely by tapping into ancient traditions in order to call the church to a pattern of life that I have called Abrahamic community. According to this pattern it is the very *evangelii gaudium* or joy of the Gospel to celebrate God's blessing upon our own family of faith or people of God in a way that necessarily orients our life outward toward the blessing of all the families of the earth. As we have traced out those ancient traditions biblically in this chapter, we will continue into post-biblical church traditions in the next chapter.

In their understandable yet limiting impatience, of course, Christians have sometimes obscured this pattern by treating space as greater than time, the opposite of Pope Francis's first principle of peacebuilding. Thus have they—have we—sometimes obscured the Abrahamic pattern by seeking, as Francis put it, to obtain "immediate results which yield easy, quick short-term political gains, but do not enhance human fullness."[49] Even so, the deep Abrahamic pattern of the Gospel has been at work, such that "grammatical" errors nag at us even if we cannot quite explain why. Recognizing the underlying unity of that pattern, however, will allow us to practice Francis's four principles of peace- and people-building simultaneously. It will allow us to turn fruitful and creative the necessary tensions

- between our limitations within time and the fullness of God's time,
- between conflicted difference and deeper unity,
- between reality and ideas—both ideas about doctrine and political ideals—, and
- between local particularities and larger ultimately global wholes.

Recognizing the Abrahamic grammar of the Christian Gospel will help to reenter the story of God's pilgrim people of peace whose very life is a sacrament, given within the world to the world and its family of peoples.

Chapter 6

The Church as Sacrament of Human Salvation

> Lord God,
> your pilgrim Church,
> which you ever sanctify in the blood of your Son,
> counts among her children in every age
> members whose holiness shines brightly forth
> and members whose disobedience to you
> contradicts the faith we profess and the Holy Gospel.
> You, who remain ever faithful,
> even when we are unfaithful,
> forgive our sins
> and grant that we may bear true witness to you
> before all men and women.
> We ask this through Christ our Lord.
>
> —Pope John Paul II, Jubilee 2000[1]

At the deepest and widest substratum of the Christian tradition is God's ever-yearning work through salvation history to form an Abrahamic people-for-all-peoples. We have seen how that claim applies to Scripture, but it also applies to continuing church tradition. In its earliest centuries Christianity spread through the existing social networks of the Jewish Diaspora, thus retaining the character, social ethic, and often the self-understanding of a diaspora people despite the tragedy of growing alienation with rabbinical Judaism. Even when Christianity won tolerance from the Roman Empire and began to settle into centuries of European Christendom, no less towering a figure than St. Augustine left room for reassessment of those very moves. A diaspora people could not really abandon its pilgrimage, after all, and Augustine made clear that the church should continue to make Jeremiah's Babylonian exiles the normative model for its ecclesiology, cultural engagement, and social ethics. Such then are the resources to which the Second Vatican Council could return for retrieval ("*ressourcement*") as it spoke of the church as a "pilgrim people" and as the sacrament of human salvation and unity.

Formed as a transnational nation

The patristic substratum of the church's first centuries of theological reflection reveals a continuing pattern of diaspora, in which Christians were to recognize themselves as resident aliens, often negotiating dual identities as a nation among nations. The more willing we are to abandon the Jewish-Christian polemics that have skewed both theological and historical interpretation for centuries, the less surprised we will be to find evidence of just how long the growth of early Christianity tracked with the Jewish Diaspora itself. Indeed, patristic textual evidence offers numerous motifs—exile, a heavenly homeland, identification with a worldwide commonwealth, Christians constituting a "third race" that was both and neither Jewish nor Gentile—that all reflect a diaspora sensibility.

A Christian resident alien in the second century

Self-recognition as resident aliens goes to the existential heart of what it means to embrace life in diaspora. But as with "diaspora," so too with the status of "resident aliens": we do well to avoid prejudgments formed amid contemporary debates in which the term sometimes serves as a code word for countercultural impulses so reflexive as to seem sectarian.[2] Our discussion so far should have made clear that to embrace diaspora as a social stance does not always and necessarily have to be countercultural—though of course it is not so unquestioningly pro-cultural as to allow for easy assimilationism either. Rather, diaspora offers a supple enough stance that it allows for both cultural affirmation and cultural resistance, according to circumstances. Think again of that prototypical example from the

Hebrew Scriptures or Old Testament—Daniel and his Hebrew colleagues in Babylon. In the book of Daniel, the heroes of the story were in a position to counter the idolatrous pretensions of the emperor precisely because they had also embraced their life in exile and were willing to "seek the peace of the city" (Jer 29:7), as valued civil servants within the pagan order no less! As we move into the Christian era, we should likewise allow the lived experience of early Christians who actually lived as resident aliens to define the term and demonstrate its creative possibilities before we rule out the approach.

A strange but winsome account of a second-century Roman Christian, titled *The Shepherd of Hermas*, allows us to do so. The document is an idiosyncratic mix of genres from the apocalyptic to the hortatory.[3] Yet it conveys the struggles of someone whom one scholar has called "the most 'average' Roman Christian to leave behind a body of writing" that we have.[4] Hermas was a freedman or former slave, perhaps a Jewish Christian, who had been brought from the east as a young man. Upon gaining his freedom he had gone into business with some success but then suffered a setback. Meanwhile, following classic sociological patterns that kick in once religious movements move beyond the first generation of convert zeal, Hermas's children were less committed to the faith than he, and leaders of the Christian community themselves sometimes seemed more interested in luxury and prestige than faithfulness. In other words, the standard challenges for Christians of the next nineteen centuries were already starting to converge. Now that Jesus did not seem about to return in the way that many first-century Christians expected, how should church and Christians settle in for the long haul without becoming tangled in church conflict, detoured by upward mobility, or unduly distracted amid family life? Encoded in a recurring warning to Hermas against double-mindedness was one key part of the answer: Keep your primary loyalty to Christ primary indeed, not as a way to dismiss other responsibilities and loyalties but to guide your responses to them with single-minded orientation to the Gospel.

Neither the challenge that Hermas faced nor the recommendation that his angelic shepherd gave him were merely psychological, however. Double-mindedness was not just an issue of moral, spiritual, or mental resolution, after all. It was every bit as much about sociology, or perhaps even citizenship.

Both as a bicultural émigré and as a businessman who must cultivate contacts beyond the Christian community,[5] Hermas knew the pressure to assimilate and the tension that comes from moving between overlapping yet competing communities of loyalty. "Resident alien" may or may not have been his actual legal status; unlike other early Christian writers he did not explicitly employ the term.[6] But the tensions that come with hybrid identities of many kinds surface throughout *The Shepherd of Hermas*. And in the first of a series of parables (or in some translations "similitudes"), the resident alien experience itself becomes the guide for living faithfully amid all the others. In the voice of his angelic guide, Hermas's cultural, if not legal identity as a resident alien, was hardly something to discard as soon as possible. Rather he should welcome it as a map to navigate his moral challenges:

> He [the shepherd] said to me: "You know . . . that you who are servants of God are living in a foreign country, for your city is far from this city. If, therefore, you know . . . your city in which you are destined to live, why do you prepare fields and expensive possessions and buildings and useless rooms here? The one who prepares these things for this [host] city, therefore, does not plan to return to his own city. Foolish and doubleminded and miserable man, don't you realize that all these things are foreign to you, and under someone else's authority? For the lord of this [host] city [has every right to] say, 'I don't want you to live in my city; instead, leave this city, because you do not conform to my laws.' So, you who have fields and dwellings and many other possessions, what will you do with your field and your house and all the other things you have prepared for yourself when you are expelled by him? . . ."[7]

Christians like Hermas, in other words, responded to two sets of "laws" or ethics or customs and expectations at once. They were subject to the society, culture, and civil authorities that hosted them, even while bound to the moral law, relationships, and customs of another culture, another people, spread beyond their immediate locale through links to another city or homeland. The challenge they faced was very much the one that any immigrant community faces, that of respecting their host culture and its expectations while remaining true to their own cultural identity and sacred ways. As ordinary concerns of life surface throughout *The Shepherd of Hermas*, it becomes amply clear that Hermas had no choice but to engage the host society if he was to make a living and guide his family. But if he put his roots down too deeply in the land of his residence, or tied his heart too firmly to the goods it offered, he might never be able to return home to his true and ultimate homeland if expelled, and would then be homeless indeed—a "foolish, and unstable, and miserable man."

To navigate the demands of multiple, overlapping communities well, therefore, Hermas must keep his primary loyalty, his formative community, and his ultimate ground of trust clear:

> So take care; as one living in a foreign land, do not prepare for yourself one thing more than is necessary to be self-sufficient, and be prepared so that whenever the master of this [host] city wants to expel you because of your opposition to his law, you can leave his city and come to your own city, and joyfully conform to your law, free from all insult. Take care, therefore, that you serve God and have him in your heart; work God's works, remembering his commands and the promises that he made, and trust him to keep [those promises], if his commandments are kept.[8]

Such a recollection did not require divestment or disengagement from the surrounding host culture, but rather a kind of reinvestment. It was not of necessity sectarian or separationist. Rather it required the arguably deeper engagement in society that would come by investing not in material goods, but in relationships above all with the needy. For this kind of investment was not only true to the "laws" of a Christian's homeland but it strengthened the network that sustained ties back to there:

> So, instead of fields buy souls that are in distress, as anyone is able, and visit widows and orphans, and do not neglect them; and spend your wealth and all your possessions, which you received from God, on fields and houses of this kind. For this is why the Master made you rich, so that you might perform these ministries for him. It is much better to purchase fields and possessions and houses of this kind, which you will find in your

own city when you go home to it. This lavish expenditure is
beautiful and joyous; it does not bring grief or fear, but joy. . . .[9]

No church without diaspora

As a text *The Shepherd of Hermas* may be idiosyncratic, but the experience of Hermas was not. When Rodney Stark took his tools as a sociologist of religion back into the historical record in order to ask how Christianity arose and grew in its formative centuries, the social dynamics of diaspora proved a critical factor. Between the year 30 CE and the year 300, the Christian community grew from the 120 believers who regrouped in the wake of Jesus' departure (Acts 1:14-15) to an estimated six million, or 10 percent of the population of the Roman Empire. That would require 40 percent growth per decade, and based on his study of contemporary religious moments, Stark knew this to be eminently possible.[10] But how? Modern churches may attempt to evangelize through electronic media, revival meetings in tents or stadiums, and door-to-door witnessing. But as an illegal and intermittently persecuted group, believers in the first centuries of the Christian movement could not have counted on equivalently public strategies or depended on mass conversions. It turns out, however, that even now, with modern technology available, contemporary religious movements gain the majority of their converts through personal contacts embedded in social and familial networks.[11] Stark called this "a *structure of direct and intimate interpersonal attachments*" and explained: "Successful movements discover techniques for remaining open networks, able to reach out and into new adjacent social networks. And herein lies the capacity of movements to sustain exponential rates of growth over a long period of time."[12]

To be sure, Stark's book on *The Rise of Christianity* examines additional phenomena that reinforced interpersonal ones, but social networking was basic to these as well. Willingness to care for the sick amid epidemics, when anyone with resources usually tried to flee, looked convincingly miraculous to observers but also built relationships with grateful survivors.[13] Women found a dignity in Christian circles that ancient patriarchy denied them, but their marriages and their households then became critical nodes in the spreading movement.[14] Even if persecution was more intermittent than Christian hagiography would have it, "the blood of the martyrs" certainly was *one* "seed of the church" if not *the* only one, as Tertullian famously described it. Part of this dynamic was that observers were so impressed with the courage and confidence in an afterlife they saw in the martyrs that they wanted whatever it was that Christians had— but observers had to be up close to see and report these qualities.[15]

If social networks wove together all of these dynamics, however, one network was especially critical for spreading the Christian movement—the Jewish Diaspora—and Stark became convinced that it played a role far longer than historians have assumed. In the face of "received wisdom" that Christianity grew despite the failure of the apostles' initial "mission to the Jews," Stark devoted a chapter to "why it probably succeeded." Finding surprisingly little evidence for an alleged failure, and applying sociological hypotheses that shift the burden of proof, Stark found ample evidence for a counterclaim: "Jewish Christianity played a central role until much later in the rise of Christianity [than we have thought]." For "not only was it the Jews of the diaspora who provided the initial basis for church growth during the first and early second centuries, [they] continued as a significant source of Christian converts until at least as late as the fourth century," if not the fifth.[16]

Given the critical role that friends and family play in the growth of successful religious movements, what would be surprising would be for Christianity to have grown apart from existing social networks like the Jewish Diaspora. The psychology of bicultural hybrid identity offers further reason to expect this. Hellenized Jews, like other culturally "marginal" people,[17] needed ways to sustain continuity with their past and its resources while loosening the demands of ethnicity and explaining themselves to the dominant culture. Far more Jews lived in the Diaspora than in Palestine already by the first century[18] often experiencing just these pressures.[19] Christianity offered Hellenized Jews a way "to retain much of the religious content of *both* cultures and to resolve the contradictions between them."[20] Strong, intact Jewish communities certainly persisted, of course, leaving archaeological evidence of impressive synagogues, and more importantly forging the legacy of rabbinical Judaism. But the fact that most Jews did not become Christian does not lessen the role of those who did, nor require the cutting of social ties between the two communities. Yes, mutual polemics between Christian and Jewish leaders grew increasingly bitter in the third and fourth centuries. But rather than providing evidence of a total Jewish-Christian schism, that acrimony more credibly suggests a continuing sociological entanglement that both rabbis and bishops found frustrating to the point of threat.[21]

Stark may be a sociologist first and a revisionist surely, but evidence from more conventional historians bears him out. Evidence from the earliest phase of growth from the New Testament itself has always been obvious and never contested. Even with Jesus' sharp warnings against putting loyalty to family above loyalty to him and his movement, family ties run through his movement: John the Baptist was his own cousin; two pairs of siblings are among his twelve disciples; the house of Simon is the place for prominent healings that launch Jesus' ministry in the Gospel of Mark; Simon's mother-in-law is among those healed there; the sibling household of Martha, Mary, and Lazarus plays a key role in the gospel drama; and so on. The apostle Paul regularly began his preaching in new locales by visiting synagogues, and later greeted households in his letters to young churches. In an exhaustive study of the church in Rome in its first two centuries, early-church historian Peter Lampe thus found ample confirmation that "earliest Christianity spread along the routes that Judaism had already followed."[22]

As Stark recognized, of course, "virtually all New Testament historians agree" that the first Christian missionaries concentrated on Hellenized Jews, "but *only* in the beginning;[23] the question is how long the pattern continued. Complaints by the second-century pagan critic Celsus that Christians were spreading their message nefariously by inviting women and children to meet in the backrooms of unlearned wool workers and cobblers certainly align with Stark's general expectations about growth through interpersonal social networking.[24] Meanwhile the interest of Gentile "god-fearers" generally and Christian "Judaizers" particularly attests to continuing contact and exchange between communities in what the editors of a study of *The Jews Among Pagans and Christians in the Roman Empire* have insisted was a complex "marketplace" of religious ideas.[25] Lampe thus found that Jewish Christians exercised an "astonishing influence on the formation of theology in urban Roman Christianity in the first century" such that even when they were a minority they left a strong imprint well into the second century.²⁶ As an outsider, Cassius Dio, third-century historian of Rome, could thus be forgiven for continuing to designate Christians as Jews.²⁷ And when fourth-century church fathers such as John Chrysostom inadvertently attested to the abiding attraction of Judaism among Christians by railing against it, they felt a need to do so because synagogues and now-public churches were sometimes on the same block. Indeed, one synagogue in fourth-century Rome was operating a lending library that seems to have served as a center for intellectual dialogue with Christians.²⁸

Contemporary Evangelical missiologists Chandler H. Im and Tereso Casiño are on to something when they declare their faith that

> God is the master conductor of the global diasporas. God has devised and orchestrated the scattering and gathering of individuals and people groups since the creation of the progenitor of the human family. . . . Global diasporas . . . have played a major role in Christian history, [and now] are contributing to the shifting of the centers of Christianity from European and North American cities to other Majority World metropolises."²⁹

As Christianity spread in its first centuries, after all, Christian Diaspora had tracked with, overlaid, and continued to entwine with the Jewish Diaspora.

At home nowhere, yet anywhere

Such is the historical and sociological basis for speaking of the church as a diaspora people, a transnational nation. This identity was more than an accident of history or a transitory phase of historical development. Precisely as a *self*-identity the status of resident aliens who were networked together in diaspora was integral to that theological and communal self-understanding we call ecclesiology. A number of motifs in patristic thought—the theology of leading Christian thinkers or "church fathers" in the first formative centuries of Christianity, that is—not only reflect diaspora life but make it theologically normative. As such they address Christians of other centuries and geographies with a continuing call to embrace life in diaspora. As such they also reflect the social patterns by which "the people of God" as a visible historical reality permeates the world as a blessing to all peoples with the invisible reality of that sacramental grace to which the Second Vatican Council pointed when it called the church the sacrament of human salvation.

More resident aliens and exiles. The descriptive fact of Christian dispersion began to take on normative implications already in the New Testament itself. The author of 1 Peter opened his letter addressing "the exiles of the Dispersion in Pontus, Galatia, Cappadocia, Asia, and Bithynia" but soon urged them precisely "as aliens and exiles" (*hōs paroikous kai parepidēmous*) to live holy lives that will convince Gentiles who malign them to reconsider (1 Pet 1:1; 2:11-12[30]). The majestic eleventh chapter of Hebrews calls on readers to place themselves in the trajectory of faith that took its definitive direction when Abraham obeyed in faith and "set out for a place that he was to receive as an inheritance; and he set out, not knowing where he was going" and had to live in the very land God had promised "as in a foreign land, living in tents" (11:8-9). Abraham looked for a homeland, of course, "to the city that has foundations, whose architect and builder is God" (11:10). But he and his descendants could only see that homeland by faith from a distance: "They confessed that they were strangers and foreigners on the earth, for people who speak in this way make it clear that they are seeking a homeland" (11:13-14). Christians could hardly expect a quick and secure arrival at that homeland either, for Jesus himself "also suffered outside the city gate in order to sanctify the people by his own blood" (Heb 13:12). Identification with Jesus thus required that they too "go to him outside the camp and bear the abuse he endured. For here we have no lasting city, but we are looking for the city that is to come" (Heb 13:13-14).

The Christian apologist who wrote *The Epistle to Diognetus* sometime between the late second and early fourth centuries (though probably on the early end of that range) elaborated on how Christians, at least at their best, were retaining their identification with another city while in fact living embedded in other cities and lands.[31] *Diognetus*, like *The Shepherd of Hermas*, uses the realities of life as a resident alien to map the normative path of Christian life, but does so more systematically. "Christians are not distinguished from the rest of humanity by country, language, or custom. For nowhere do they live in cities of their own, nor do they speak some unusual dialect, nor do they practice an eccentric life-style" (5.1-2). Every land is both native and strange to them. For while following "local customs in dress and food and other aspects of life," their actual citizenship is "remarkable and admittedly unusual [in] character" (5.4):

> They live in their own countries, but only as resident aliens [*paroikoi*]; they participate in everything as citizens [*politai*], and endure everything as foreigners [*xenoi*]. Every foreign country [*xenē*] is their homeland, and every homeland is foreign. . . . They live on earth but their citizenship [*politeuontai*] is in heaven. (5.5,9)

If not distinguished according to the ordinary markers of language, territory, or custom, there were still notable aspects of their lifestyle that set them off.[32] Misunderstood, reviled, and persecuted, they nonetheless demonstrated love toward all. Poor, they nonetheless made many rich. Condemned and cursed by those who really did not know them, they nonetheless blessed. Thus, summarized the apologist, "what the soul is to the body, Christians are to the world"—dispersed, invisible in one way, yet loving the body that too often hates and mistreats it (6.1-9). The apologist's purpose here was not to reinforce an ancient body/soul dualism, but simply to use a standard assumption among ancient philosophers to make other points.[33] "The soul is enclosed in the body, but it holds the body together; and though Christians are detained in the world as in a prison, they in fact hold the world together" (6.7). Reinforced by the writer's language of love and the soul's immortality, as well as the ancients' very conceptualization of the soul, *Diognetus*'s vision is one of Christians animating and giving life to the world. *Nota bene*: This is exactly how Catholics understand a sacrament to work, as the "invisible sign of an invisible reality," the grace that gives life by way of material realities. Thus we tap into a vein of *ressourcement* for the Second Vatican Council's affirmation of the church as sacrament of the salvation and unity of all humanity.

Almost in passing, the *Epistle to Diognetus* briefly notes two distinguishing elements—or perhaps just one—in the culture of these resident aliens called Christians: "They marry like everyone else, and have children, but they do not expose their offspring. They set a common table, but not a common bed" (5.6-7). If anything, the rejection of infanticide stands out as the single most specific marker on the apologist's list.[34] But the practices of disciplined hospitality that immediately follow are not an altogether separate item. Rejection of violence and respect for life, especially of the most vulnerable, reflect a recurring argument in the writings of other Christian apologists in the church's first three centuries. For a number of them, strong evidence for the truthfulness of Christianity came in the way that once-warring ethnic groups and nationalities were now welcoming one another and being reconciled in the same body. In its very composition, they argued, the church was thus fulfilling the prophesies of Isaiah 2 and Micah 4—beating the swords by which they once fought each other into plowshares.[35]

Still, if Christians who recognized themselves as resident aliens were not quite at home in any land or nation short of their ultimate homeland, paradoxically they might thereby be at home in any. Under threat of exile, two of the most important figures in third- and fourth-century Christianity witnessed to exactly this. During a wave of persecution in mid-third-century North Africa, Cyprian, bishop of Carthage, first suffered banishment and later martyrdom. His attitude under interrogation inspired his biographer, Pontius the Deacon, to affirm the place of Christians both anywhere and nowhere:

> To [others], it is a severe punishment to live outside their own city; to the Christian, the whole of this world is one home. Wherefore, though he were banished into a hidden and secret place, yet, associated with the affairs of his God, he cannot regard it as an exile. In addition, while honestly serving God, he is a stranger even in his own city.[36]

Likewise, Gregory Nazianzen recounted the testimony of his close associate Basil the Great in fourth-century Cappadocia in Asia Minor under interrogation by the Roman prefect Modestus. Frustrated that Basil seemed to have no fear of his authority, the prefect reminded the bishop that he had recourse to confiscation, banishment, torture, and even death. Basil replied that he did not own enough for confiscation to be a threat, that his body was too frail for torture to be very effective, that death would simply return him more quickly to God. And exile? It was a moot point, not even relevant:

Banishment is impossible for me, who am confined by no limit of place, counting my own neither the land where I now dwell, nor all [of the places] into which I may be hurled; or, rather, counting it all God's, whose guest and dependent I am.[37]

Pilgrimage journey, to another homeland. If pressed to name their ultimate homeland, Christians in most centuries and certainly in the patristic period would no doubt have said heaven. That conviction and theme extends from the matter-of-fact remark by the apostle Paul in Philippians 3:20 that "our citizenship [*politouma*] is in heaven" to the massive exploration by Augustine of how the *City of God* is a "pilgrim city" journeying through history and intermixed in society—the earthly city—as it travels toward its destination of heaven, where some have already arrived. Thus we have already encountered the assumption in the *Epistle to Diognetus* 5.9, echoing Paul that for those resident aliens called Christians, "their citizenship is in heaven." Such convictions constitute the background for the Second Vatican Council's reemphasis on the church's identity as a "pilgrim people" that has not yet finished its journey through history.

Students of diasporas both ancient and contemporary often note a certain elasticity in the conception that a scattered people has of its homeland.[38] Sometimes the homeland is an actual ancestral home, and sometimes an "imaginary." Sometimes, the longing for an actual homeland comes with debate and flexibility about where actually to land. Through the centuries that has even—perhaps especially—been the case for Judaism, for neither the biblical promises of land nor the modern state of Israel have ever settled the matter; other creative centers of Jewish life have sometimes seemed the places for return and one leading argument is that the matter cannot be settled until the messianic age.[39] As a sociologist, Avtar Brah has argued that an actual homeland is less constitutive of a diaspora identity than is a "homing desire."[40] As a church historian and missiologist proposing a theology of migration, Dale Irvin has likewise emphasized "homegoing" in hope of "homecoming" over any one memory of home.[41]

In hindsight, then, it is not surprising so much as telling that *The Shepherd of Hermas* never exactly specified the city or homeland to which Hermas must retain his primary loyalty. Heaven was most likely the ultimate homeland to which Hermas's angelic shepherd alluded when he spoke of another land, city, and law. But to be one of those who remembered this ultimate place of return was to have a home among God's scattered people already in time. Having another homeland to complicate one's residence with a sense of overlapping obligations offered moral guidance either way, and both ways.

Writing toward the end of the second century, Clement of Alexandria indicated how this works. For his learned readers to become Christian was to make a deliberate choice of citizenship. Just as Athenians, Argives, and Spartans were to live in accordance with the laws of their respective cities, if the non-Christian reader to whom he was appealing would "enroll yourself as one of God's people, heaven is your country and God your lawgiver."[42] Heaven came later but enrollment embedded the Christian in a people and a way of life now. Hope of heaven had practical implications because a Christian was on a journey: "He makes preparation for a self-sufficing mode of life, for simplicity, and for girding up our loins, and for free and unimpeded readiness of our journey; in order to the attainment of an eternity of beatitude, teaching each one of us to be his own storehouse."[43] And intrinsic to this way of life, learning to live in peace was not to be deferred: "For it is not in war, but in peace, that we are trained. War needs great preparation, and luxury craves profusion; but peace and love, simple and quiet sisters, require no arms nor excessive preparation. The Word is their sustenance."[44]

A third race? Lest there be any doubt about how fundamentally this enrollment was to transform identity, Clement of Alexandria turned to one other phrase that had begun to circulate about the transnational nation that was the Christian people. In relation to Greeks or Gentiles and Jews, "we, who worship Him in a new way, in the third form [*genos*], are Christians"; whether formed in Greek ways or Jewish law, Christians "gathered into the one race [*genos*] of the saved people those who accept faith."[45] Already in the New Testament, the author of 1 Peter could address Christians as "aliens and exiles" (2:11) precisely because God had called and formed them into "a chosen race, a royal priesthood, a holy nation, God's own people" (2:9). Strange as it may seem to moderns—particularly since nineteenth-century pseudoscience has so badly skewed our language and assumptions about race—Clement was hardly the only early Christian thinker to speak of race or ethnicity as an identity into which one could deliberately enter. "Why this new race [*genos*] or way of life?" was in fact one of the questions that also prompted the author of *The Epistle to Diognetus* to write his apology.[46] What Clement called enrollment into that third *genos* or race of Christians was potentially transformative in part because it offered a particular identity *and yet* was potentially universal; these were not antithetical.[47] If anything, Christian identity was particular precisely in its capacity to universally welcome identities that would not simply find that reconciliation erased their own particularities.

Precisely because this is such a key to a peaceful and hospitable Christian social ethic, it can also be hard to get right. In a masterful study exhibiting a care and nuance that I can only begin to convey, Denise Kimber Buell has examined more widely what she calls "ethnic reasoning" in early Christianity and antiquity. Buell brought to her book, *Why This New Race: Ethnic Reasoning in Early Christianity*, both a solidarity with anti-racist struggles today and a concern that Christians reject ideologies that have underwritten anti-Judaism historically. Although Christian universalism might seem unreservedly to encourage human equality and thus critique racism, Buell also noted its dangerous underside—the way that universalizing claims can delegitimize the very existence of groups that stubbornly retain their particular identities, archetypically the Jews.[48] Thus she was predisposed to take a fresh look at the ways that early Christians appealed to categories of group identity—"ethnicity," "lineage," "kind," "peoplehood," as well as race, and to religion itself as a racial/ethnic marker—in order to argue for their own truth claims, orthodoxy, and very legitimacy.[49]

Buell did not say whether she actually wanted to *retrieve* this "ethnic reasoning" as a resource for social and racial justice today. But she was certainly convinced that modern Christians do not need to downplay the record of such language either out of embarrassment or to emphasize biblical and early Christian practices that provide a precedent for transcending racial and ethnic differences instead. Race and identity, as ancients understood the categories, were not immutably fixed—as nineteenth-century pseudoscience taught moderns to assume—but could somehow be both fixed and fluid. That was true enough among the many cultures of the Roman Empire, but was especially true for a people whose faith turned an otherwise biological necessity into a possible choice by offering "rebirth."[50] Christians could thus use universalizing claims in the way that other minority groups used them—to resist and negotiate relations with imperial power structures by marking out their own identity even while claiming a moral high ground.[51] To be sure, once Christians gained access to majority power this simultaneous "rhetoric of openness and restrictiveness" might turn "double-edged" and serve oppressive uses.[52] But as long as Christians saw themselves as resident aliens who properly embrace life in diaspora, their fixed-yet-fluid identity could indeed prove invitational—not only by welcoming others in hospitality but by requiring reconciliation of themselves across national, ethnic, and tribal divisions.

I have lingered over the fraught designation of Christians as a "third race" because it does at least underscore the early Christian sense that they belonged to a multicultural people, a transnational nation. As I have been arguing, that sense should be integral to the very ecclesiology or theological self-understanding of Christians in the church today.

Still, if contemporary Christians are anxious about "ethnic reasoning" and rightly hesitate to call themselves a "third race" in our own settings, it may be reassuring to know that some theologians in the patristic period also hesitated. While adding to evidence for its usage, Tertullian saw it as pejorative, assumed that critics of Christianity had coined it, and thus protested: "We are indeed said to be the 'third race' of men. What, a dog-faced race? Or broadly shadow-footed? Or some subterranean Antipodes? If you attach any meaning to these names, pray tell us what are the first and the second race, that so we may know something of this 'third.'" If indeed the term had any meaning or use, he continued, that could only be because it admitted that Christians spanned national boundaries: "Take care, however, lest those whom you call the third race should obtain the first rank, since there is no nation indeed which is not Christian"—in other words, which has not come to include Christians."[53]

Unable to know the geography of the entire planet, Tertullian's rhetorical flourish was objectively wrong at the time, but theologically right. And today, another correction might be in order. Perhaps it is nationalistic Christians who have forgotten that they are a pilgrim people, wrongly identify God's cause with their own, and are thus the ones who should "take care."

In the commonwealth of humanity. Tertullian's chafing at the "third race" moniker is all the more striking because his reputation as something of a separationist might suggest that he would welcome a clear identity marker. He was the early-church thinker who asked the famous rhetorical question, "What does Athens have to do with Jerusalem?" He also gravitated toward the ascetic and prophecy-oriented Christian group known as Montanists. And yet, concern for Christian particularity is only antithetical to universal human concern if we forget that the particular calling of all who claim Abraham and Sarah as their parents is to receive that blessing while accepting the Abrahamic calling to be a blessing to all the families of the earth. In contrast, to identify primarily with a nation-state or even an empire is what may be truly sectarian and no less so because the group in question is large. After all, size and domineering power easily allow a given culture or powerful nation to blind itself to its own parochialism.

So even though other Christian thinkers embraced the term, what is striking about Tertullian's objection to "third race" is that his particularly Christian commitment actually required the widest possible embrace of humanity. Writing in his own *Apology*, Tertullian sought to answer the charge that Christians were being disloyal or even a threat to public order because they refused to participate in civic events. He acknowledged to the critics whom he hoped would read his manifest that "we have no pressing inducement to take part in your public meetings; nor is there aught more entirely foreign to us than affairs of state." One reason was that in Christians "all ardour in the pursuit of glory and honour is dead," especially when glory came through public spectacles of arena, circus, or theater, and honor was falsely associated with violence and atrocity. But another was that the political entity with which Christians *could* identify with was: "We acknowledge one all-embracing commonwealth—the world."[54]

So too with Christianity's great third-century theologian, Origen.[55] In his lengthy rebuttal of accusations from the pagan philosopher Celsus, Origen took on the claim that Christians were anti-civil or even misanthropic because they refused military service and declined to hold public office. No, rejoined Origen, Christians do take on public duties and the ordering of social life: They have leaders who rule the church, after all, but these leaders are to rule according to the logic of divine commands that enjoin modesty, service, and true piety, not the misleading logic of worldly policy. This body, governed according to the Word of God and through the very power of persuasive words, was indeed "a divine nation." Thus do Christians "recognise in each state the existence of another national organization."[56]

How Origen understood that Christians would work out the competing demands that come with what we can identify as the creative tensions of life in Christian Diaspora is not without ambiguity. Part of Origen's purpose in writing was an assimilationist project of gaining greater acceptance from the larger body politic. Thus he assured the authorities that Christians had more not less to offer to the social order and even to the armies of the emperor (at least insofar as the emperor fought righteously for a truly righteous cause). That contribution was their prayer, fasting, spiritual warfare, and asceticism, all of which came with all-the-greater power insofar as they abstained from bloodshed.[57]

Summary. The claim here is not that the tensions of life in diaspora are ones that Christians have always gotten right, however. Through the centuries, some have probably been too reticent to involve themselves in the exercise of civil authority, while others (or, as with Origen, even the same ones!) have certainly been too ready to bless the armies of emperors. No, the point is simply that the question of how to navigate the sometimes coinciding, sometimes competing, always simultaneous demands that come with life in overlapping moral communities is the right debate to have, the right discernment to do—but that we will not do it well or at all unless we embrace the creative tension of diaspora by which we keep our primary loyalty to that transnational nation called church above nationalistic loyalty to the nations that host us.

What Benjamin Dunning has said of *The Epistle to Diognetus* can thus apply to all those Christians who have embraced life in diaspora as exiles or resident aliens: It is altogether misleading to peg them neatly as either countercultural or pro-cultural, as either uncooperative or assimilationist. Yes, there was a "tension between radical outsider identity and Roman cultural norms" or any dominant cultural norms, and it was implicit already in the New Testament book of

Hebrews, noted Dunning. As the author of *Diognetus* attempted to work out this relationship more carefully, "The result is a vision of identity in which Christians are socially integrated (and indeed exemplary) members of Roman society." After all, "their alien status is actually a function of the degree to which they outstrip the Romans in their ability to fulfill Roman norms," or at least their best and highest ones. Yet such a stance has no less capacity for that proper resistance to injustice and risk-taking for peace that is actually pro-cultural insofar as it engages society and contributes to the common good: "[T]he implications of this position are not serenely assimilationist. Rather, *Diognetus*'s stance is an agonistic one, appealing to Roman ethical and cultural ideals as a platform upon which to valorize Christian alien identity and thus oppose its relegation to a site of reproach among the hierarchies of status and power that structure Roman society."[58]

The point of seeing ourselves as resident aliens and exiles, then, is not standoffishness but freedom for authentic Christian service to *all* the lands and neighbors in which Christians find themselves. As the Second Vatican Council insisted,

> In their pilgrimage to the heavenly city Christians are to seek and value the things that are above; this involves not less, but greater commitment to working with everyone for the establishment of a more human world. Indeed, the mystery of their faith provides Christians with greater incentive and encouragement to fulfill their role more willingly and to assess the significance of activities capable of assigning to human culture its honored role in the complete vocation of humanity.[59]

The point of letting a global nation called the church define our primary citizenship is international Christian solidarity in the service of a still-wider human solidarity. To orient our lives accordingly is to enter the long arc of a story that stretches all the way from Abraham and Sarah through the continuing struggle of the contemporary church to come to terms with the Second Vatican Council. But before we turn to the council, we must confirm whether the diaspora ecclesiology of the church's first three centuries was merely transitory, preparatory but thus anomalous, or is theologically normative indeed.

Seeking the peace of the city

And so we come to Saint Augustine.

Trained to practice rhetoric and thus to serve in roles roughly equivalent to that of a lawyer and civic spokesperson today, Augustine of Hippo became a Christian, then priest, then bishop, in the final two decades of the fourth century. These were the same decades in which the emperor Theodosius was promulgating a series of laws that made Christianity the official religion of the Roman Empire. Combining a brilliant mind, a penetrating vision of the restless soul longing for God but tragically settling for less, and a dogged yet eloquent penchant for argumentation, Augustine became the greatest and most systematic of theologians in Christianity for centuries, at least in the Latin-speaking world. By leaving such a legacy at such a momentous juncture, Augustine has alternately drawn praise and blame, century after century, for the treasures and burdens that Western Christianity has borne. That includes the intellectual architecture he is said to have forged for the cooperative relationship between church and state that was essential to medieval Christendom. And a cornerstone of that architecture was his Christianizing of Roman thought about how wars might be just, thus reassuring Christian magistrates and soldiers who were by now joining in the exercise of potentially lethal force in the practice of governance. How one stands in continuing debates over Christianity's uneasy relationship to war often tracks with one's relationship with Augustine.

Why Augustine

Any sustained treatment of Catholic peacebuilding must somehow take account of Augustine, therefore—but how? For many Catholic peace activists, Augustine and his launching of a Christian just-war theory are *the* definitive problem—the tragic misstep that has allowed Christians to dismiss the plainly nonviolent teachings of Jesus for centuries, to bless war after war, and to blunt the truly transformative power of the Gospel.[60] Readers such as these will wonder why we lingered over his theory of love for God, neighbor, self, temporal goods—but what about Christlike love of enemies?—in chapter 3. Some will wonder why we will even consider him, too, as source for *ressourcement* in the coming pages, rather than strive to discredit and thus discard his thought entirely. A methodological aside is thus in order.

One reason is the very lesson that emerged in chapter 3: Augustine's legacy is not univocal. After all, in some important ways that legacy is the set of critical questions that he put to later centuries, which rival Christian traditions have had to regularly revisit. A controversialist throughout his life, who thought through his positions via debate, Augustine was at his best when he held together paradoxes and creative tensions.[61] Arguably, he has been influential for later theology primarily because he so eloquently posed abiding questions in Christianity (if not the human condition itself), not because he promulgated definitive doctrine.[62] Thus Augustine has left the church with unfinished business. Even later traditions that think they are discarding his answers still find themselves grappling with the questions he posed and the paradoxes he held taut as he sought to answer them. Exactly *how* to journey on pilgrimage as the still-earthbound portion of the one heavenly city of God that for now is intermixed within the earthly city was—from the beginning and by definition—a *necessarily* unfinished question.

Having grappled with Augustine for decades, I have concluded that we do not have to dispense with him anyway. A second reason for turning to him as one resource for becoming a Catholic peace church will emerge in the coming pages as we examine what his final answer actually was in his portrayal of the church in his massive work *City of God*. And then, if my argument there is at all convincing, an additional though more tactical reason for coming to terms with Augustine will have presented itself. Let me put it this way:

A longstanding dictum of political life is to "keep your friends close and your 'enemies' closer." Given Augustine's influence on centuries of Christian thought, with most major traditions in Western Christianity claiming him as an authority in some way, he will serve as an ally for reclaiming Catholic traditions of peacebuilding if we can at least keep him in proximity. *My* goal, at least, is to offer a vision of how the Roman Catholic Church can fulfill the Vatican II call to make "a completely fresh reappraisal of war" and thus become a truly Catholic peace church *by doing precisely what the council did*—reforming by returning to ancient sources, changing through continuity, critiqu-

The Church as Sacrament of Human Salvation 183

ing within communion. To follow through on the Vatican II mandate, Catholic peacebuilders and theologians alike must "think with the church" in exactly this way. We must make our arguments from within the tradition even when we critique some of our church's *traditions*. None of this dare come by distorting or denying the historical record, to be sure. But precisely because history—even church history as it examines great saints and learns from the doctors of the church—means studying the messy complexity of past lives and movements. Sometimes that allows us to identify roads not taken, where we then discover treasures long, too long, abandoned.

Still Jeremiah's exiles[63]

St. Augustine has exercised such an abiding influence upon political thought in the West for a curious reason: intrinsic to his vision of human society is the insight that we can never quite set our affairs in order and never quite get our politics right. The world's best possible peace is a shadowy one; its most stable order is a tenuous one; its fullest possible justice is always only somewhat more just than current arrangements. In fact, the very effort to forge a definitive political order lies at the root of many of humanity's gravest injustices, disorders, and conflicts. For when the earthly city imagines itself to be too like the heavenly city—eternal and approaching the glory that is proper only to God—it intensifies the very conditions of human fallenness and thus invites its own falling. Inevitably if not explicitly, therefore, politics according to Augustine must always be temporal, tentative, and revisable. This leaves every generation with a remainder to rework. And that makes Augustinian political thought itself into an ongoing debate that no age, system, or ideology can definitively capture. Paradoxically, it thrives upon the recognition of human limitations—but that must also include the limits of any particular "political Augustinianism."[64]

If the politics Augustine charted for the earthly city is *necessarily* and *rightly* incomplete, however, the same cannot be said of Augustine's ecclesiology. Given the rigor of Augustine's critique of the Roman Empire in *City of God*, and the depth of political insight that his critique occasioned, one might have expected from him an ecclesiology at least as thorough as his political theory. If an adequate account of the life of the church must include not just a theological metaphysic but a practicable sociology, however, Augustine's ecclesiology is elusive and suggestive at best.[65]

In a strictly theological sense, no doubt, Augustine's ecclesiology is immensely rich. For Augustine, the church is nothing short of shared participation in God's own trinitarian life of mutual love.[66] Such communion is possible insofar as the earthy, bloody incarnation of God in Christ, together with the outpouring of love into our hearts by the Holy Spirit, heals both our divided wills and our disordered relationships. If the church remains a hospital for convalescents, and the mystery of healing renders an invisible quality to the final identities of the church's members, that is because the church lives in an eschatological tension between already-in-communion and not-yet-fully-transformed. In short, Augustine's ecclesiology is seamlessly integrated with his trinitarian theology, which in turn is seamlessly integrated with his doctrine of love and with his eschatology.

In fact, Augustine's vision of the church was not devoid of practical, sociological, or political specification either. Virtually all of Augustine's writings were "occasional" in some way, insofar as they responded to specific controversies, accusations, or pastoral challenges. Whatever else *City of God* became through its twenty-two lengthy "books," therefore, it began as a response to an accusation.[67] Roman aristocrats were saying that the reason their city had been sacked in 410 was that Christianity had weakened its citizens' virtue and diverted their devotion away from the gods. So when Augustine countered that Rome (the most immediate instantiation of "the earthly city") had slipped because it had risen too high, had deteriorated because it had overextended itself, was humbled because it had grown through imperial pride,[68] his critique came with lessons for that other society that was making its way through the earthly city. The pilgrim heavenly city that is the church must thrive by humbling itself and glorifying God not self, nor the collective self of a worldly nation; its love cannot be for domination, but for God, neighbor, and even enemy. And though no one may mistake Augustine for a pacifist, he certainly recognized that the church had in fact extended itself through the faithfulness of the martyrs and the witness of a people who, like the Hebrews, "was gathered into one republic, as it were, to enact [the] mystery" of God's revelation through "signs and symbols appropriate to the times."⁶⁹ This witnessing presence in the world hints at the affirmation of the Second Vatican Council that the church itself is the sacrament of the world's salvation. It also hints at the truthful power of what historic-peace-church-theologian John Howard Yoder called the creative minority whose presence is the "original revolution" in the world.⁷⁰

But by now we are *only* talking about hints. What Augustine's ecclesiology lacks is a politics or sociology to chart out how Christians are to live simultaneously in the earthly and heavenly cities, without confusing their loyalties or conflating their duties. To be sure, just as no politics for the earthly city can be definitive—given the eschatological tension of the age—likewise any polity for the heavenly city that is intermixed within the earthly must have a certain open-ended quality. After all, Christians must not only anticipate variations according to culture, history, and circumstances, but must remember precisely that they *are* on pilgrimage, never fully settled but intermixed within the earthly city, and thus still being perfected.

What we may rightly wish of Augustine, however, is that he had at least been clearer about whether and when his political commentary on the earthly city applied normatively to Christians.

A passage often assumed to settle the case may illustrate. How are we to interpret book 19 of the *City of God* in general, and the identity of the wise man who is the reluctant judge of *City of God* 19.6 in particular? The chapter begins with recognition that even in human cities that are relatively at peace, some must pass judgments upon others. For those judgments to be just, Roman jurisprudence could not imagine the interrogation of suspects without recourse to torture. But anyone informed by the best wisdom of human philosophy (the subject of his previous chapters) would recognize how imperfect was the juridical process. Torturing suspects to extract the truth might prompt the innocent to lie—though less so if they too heeded the philosophers, who counseled courage to welcome death and escape the miseries of this life! Doing one's duty to preserve justice in the earthly city thus necessitated an array of tragic choices: release the innocent only after undeserved torture, execute the innocent upon false confession, or execute an actual criminal without certainty of the grounds. Because Augustine's wise man recognized "these dark shadows of the social life" without flinching, he would accept its claims, do his duty, and sit on the bench without shirking. "All this certainly shows, therefore the human misery of which I am speaking," wrote Augustine. And if the wise man was not to be called wicked, that was only because he hated the very "necessities" of his own actions, was learning a further wisdom from devotion to God, and cried out for deliverance from his necessities.

To most interpreters, unfortunately, the lesson we should take from Augustine has seemed so obvious that it did not require interrogation. In the following chapter, *City of God* 19.7, the "wise man" turned "wise judge" serves as template for explaining why even the best and wisest philosopher-officials will not only punish wrongdoers but wage wars, though they will wage even just wars reluctantly. But although that much is straightforward in the text, the standard interpretation goes further than the text itself warrants. For when it makes the wise man into the exemplar for any politician informed by Augustinian sensibilities—and thus for any politically involved Christian—it assumes that Augustine's purpose was to provide a normative argument rather than a description of the human predicament apart from God.

Most of *City of God* 19 is about indictment, not guidance. It is one of Augustine's many and characteristic endeavors to drive his readers nearly to despair precisely in order that they, like he, will look elsewhere for hope, recognize their need for God, and cry out for deliverance.[71] The first chapters of *City of God* 19 constitute the climax to a long series of similarly structured indictments that build upon each other and thus reiterate the master argument of Augustine's tome: The Roman aristocrats who accuse Christianity of weakening Roman virtue are the ones who have weakened the empire by failing to match the virtues of the old Romans.[72] But the virtues of the old and founding Romans in fact had rested on vices—love of glory, praise, domination, and self—so that whatever glories they had in fact achieved in this world, "they have received their reward" and could look forward to nothing eternal (Matt 6:2, 5, 16).[73] Ancient philosophers offered somewhat better counsel about where to lodge one's hope and how to pursue the human good; of all the various philosophical sects Platonism came closest to an answer—Augustine believed—by recognizing that we must look beyond this life for life's happiness.[74] But even they fell short by seeking their good through pride in their own efforts, rather than faith in God.[75] And if the one thing the philosophers all agreed upon was that the human good must be social, the best that human society actually had to offer amid all its ills, enmity, and tragic choices was the shadowy pretense of peace—a peace that was merely the "clever disguise" of allies who might yet turn and betray.[76] Such is the panorama of misery Augustine has just finished presenting in *City of God* 19.5.

The wise man of 19.6, then, was the one who had learned all these lessons—the best that Roman civic culture and antique philosophical eclecticism had to offer. He was Stoic in composure, Platonic in aspiration, and perhaps somewhere upon the threshold of Christian devotion to God, but no more than that was certain. What he should do next in his official capacity simply was not the driving point of Augustine's argument.

Augustine knew and counseled many such men, of course. Aspiring, he had once been one of them. Though he had then understood himself to be renouncing public life when he became a Christian, he later found himself reimmersed in it as a bishop. The *City of God* itself he directed to Marcellinus, a genuinely pious Christian and a Roman official in North Africa. When another such leader, Count Boniface, was considering the monastery—wishing deliverance from his necessities, perhaps—Augustine urged him to stay in the military, only to see his moral stature deteriorate in the following years.[77]

Such pastoral counsel often responded as much to Augustine's pragmatism as to his principle, however.[78] Disjunctures between his systematic reflection and his occasional letters are as much a sign that he himself was unsettled about what the wise man and judge should do next, once devoted to God, as they are an authoritative template for Christian political engagement. To Boniface he wrote famously, for example, that his only objective in war should be peace, not vengeance. Yet Augustine's more systematic reflections in *City of God* 19.12 demonstrate that all creatures, even monsters, seek peace as their ultimate end anyway. So only that "only" in Augustine's counsel to Boniface is normative, and then at risk of devolving into a mere platitude. Further, even that "only" is problematic, for of all the church fathers, Augustine knew better than any that no one can really know one's own intentions, leaving no way to verify when one is acting justly in war.[79]

The normative guidance that Augustine did offer to worldly wise Christians in *City of God* 19, was that they look to God for hope, look to the heavenly city for citizenship, and look at the earthly city as little better than a captivity.[80] They should not cease to be a society of resident aliens drawn from many languages and cultures—not abandon therefore the status that Christians had embraced prior to Constantine and Theodosius.[81] The inadequate, shadowy peace of the earthly city surely had value insofar as it gave the church time and space to grow in the worship of God, but Christians should merely *use* this earthly peace, not rest in it or identify with it as their own.[82]

To "seek the peace of the city," the earthly city, was in fact an obligation for members of the pilgriming heavenly city, but they should do so precisely as did the captive exiles to whom Jeremiah once wrote.[83] If Jeremiah's exiles were the template for Christian political engagement (and assuming that the young Jewish men in the Babylon of the book of Daniel have a historical basis), then yes, one way to seek the peace of the city might be to work as civil servants. But unlike the Roman officials with whom Augustine corresponded, Diaspora Jews had had far less trouble remembering themselves to be captives. Their memory of violent uprooting was fresh. They dare not forgot that they *were* in Babylon, that resistance to imperial idolatry could never cease to be an option, and that they belonged first to God and God's people.

For all practical purposes, Jeremiah's final exhortation was Augustine's last word on politics and Christian engagement in *City of God*. It does not solve but rather leaves hanging the fruitful question of *how* exactly Christians are to seek the peace of the earthly city. To take the practices of Augustine's wise but more-Stoic-than-Christian judge as our final answer to the question of how to seek the peace of the city is to misread his larger argument, to ignore his rhetorical practices, and above all to beg the question Augustine left hanging. The wise man of *City of God* 19 then serves as a blank for later interpreters to fill in with whatever they have already decided to be the best wisdom of their age; his "necessities" become whatever they think they must do when they "do what they have to do" on other grounds. And if Augustine himself could only barely imagine a Christian politics that helped answer the wise man's cry for deliverance—if he himself assumed that the best his Christian friends in high places could do was act like the wise man and carry out their "necessities" with purer intentions and authentic grief in their hearts—that only means that he too was begging the question that Jeremiah put to *him*, even as he posed it definitively for later Christian traditions.

The new status that Christianity now enjoyed in the Roman Empire would become its status in a long succession of kingdoms, principalities, and nation-states down through the centuries. But if anything, that made it all the more crucial that Christians recognize themselves as pilgrims, exiles like those to whom Jeremiah had written, resident aliens like Hermas and the writer of *Diognetus*. Just because the fourth century was a watershed does not mean that Augustine changed this. Rather, he reiterated it. If centuries of interpreters have read him otherwise, that may simply be a sign of the very captivity Augustine inevitably expected pilgrim people to travel through—but hoped they would see through.

A sacrament for the world[84]

The power of the church's formative self-understanding as a pilgrim people, living in exile as resident aliens amid the many cultures and nations whose good they seek, is evident as it not only survives by vestiges in the thought of St. Augustine but if anything comes to maturity. That self-understanding is what provides the very architecture for his theology of history in the *City of God*. Legal status under Constantine and official status under Theodosius did not render it obsolete; rather it made identification with diaspora more urgent. At the climax of Augustine's long march through biblical theology and Roman history, he seems to have become one of T. S. Eliot's returning explorers: "We will arrive where we started and know the place for the first time." For at the climax of *City of God* 19—which is really the climax of Augustine's entire twenty-two-book march through history and beyond—we return to Jeremiah exhorting the exiles to seek the peace of the earthly city precisely as those who remember their exile and thus their higher loyalty. Augustine might seem to have helped ally Christianity with the Roman Empire, but in the end he confirmed that the church can never settle there. Indeed, the pilgrim people could only return to Jerusalem by way of imperial Rome if it recognized Rome as Babylon and its residence there as a continuing exilic diaspora.

The Second Vatican Council has now retraced Augustine's own Eliot-like steps. For it is these patterns and motifs from ancient Christian life in diaspora that the council followed when it reaffirmed the church's identity as a "pilgrim people," and as the sacrament of salvation and unity for the whole human family. A prominent and standard interpretation of Vatican II is that the Catholic Church, as gathered through its bishops, was making peace with the modern world. And this is not wrong. But what kind of peace for what kind of church in what kind of world?

By its very composition as it brought bishops of many colors and continents together, and then through its work, the Second Vatican Council stood for what had now become a truly global church of all continents and myriad cultures in a fast-globalizing world. In convoking the council, Pope John XXIII wanted to speed but also guide the church's transition away from the defensive posture that had tended to characterize it since the sixteenth-century struggle with the Protestant Reformation, which had climaxed in the Council of Trent. But more than that, he hoped this transition would leave behind the centuries of entanglements with civil authorities that had begun with Constantine. Even when the "princes of this world, indeed, sometimes in all sincerity, intended thus to protect the Church," observed the pope in his opening address to the council, "more frequently this [has brought] spiritual damage and danger, since their interest therein was guided by the views of a selfish and perilous policy."[85] His hope was that releasing the church from such entanglements would free it to receive from the Holy Spirit a "new Pentecost" and with it "a new phase of witness and proclamation."[86] But while the council indeed initiated this as the first church council of a truly world church—as Karl Rahner analyzed it, looking back in 1979[87]— that process was only beginning and could only continue as Catholic Christians accepted that they were a diaspora church more obviously than ever,[88] thus living indeed as the pilgrim people that the council proclaimed they are.

Admittedly, the Second Vatican Council did not work out fully the meaning or implications of "pilgrim people" but only sketched out a pointer.[89] Still, an unmistakable line of continuity runs through

Vatican II documents. That line joins the long arc of salvation history that we have seen marked by Abraham, Jeremiah, Jesus, his first apostles as they took the Gospel into and through the Jewish Diaspora, and the church fathers who then had to discern how to live it out in Christian Diaspora. What it points to is that the church does not simply administer the sacraments. It must be and *is by its very nature* the sacrament of the world's salvation, "a sign and instrument, that is, of communion with God and of the unity of the entire human race."[90]

Thus opens *Lumen Gentium*, the Dogmatic Constitution of the Church; but a sign and instrument requires a purpose. The opening paragraph goes on to identify the church's purpose as larger than itself: The "present situation lends greater urgency" to the church's duty by underscoring that its "universal mission" is unfinished agenda. Despite the ever-greater "social, technical and cultural bonds" linking people together, humanity is hardly living out the unity that Christ has offered. *Lumen Gentium* §48 elaborates on the role of the church in the world:

> Already the final age of the world is with us (see 1 Cor 10:11) and the renewal of the world is irrevocably under way; it is even now anticipated in a certain real way, for the church on earth is endowed already with a sanctity that is real though imperfect. However, until the arrival of the new heavens and the new earth in which justice dwells (see 2 Pet 3:13) the pilgrim church, in its sacraments and institutions, which belong to this present age, carries the mark of this world which will pass, and it takes its place among the creatures which groan and suffer and await the revelation of the children of God (see Rom 8:19-22).

The church lives in and with the world, that is, in the overlap of an eschatological in-between. The renewal of the world may be irrevocable, but it is also painfully unfinished or "not yet." In the meantime, the very process of renewal requires that the church, however imperfectly, embody an eschatological "already." Pilgrim and sacramental identities come together here because both characterize the life of a church that finds in that very meantime its vocation.

The final document of the council, *Gaudium et Spes*, The Pastoral Constitution on the Church in the Modern World, thus continues this thread as it further elaborates on the larger purpose of the church and again unites its pilgrim and sacramental identities:

> Whether it aids the world or whether it benefits from it, the church has but one sole purpose—that the kingdom of God may come and the salvation of the human race may be accomplished. Every benefit the people of God can confer on humanity during its earthly pilgrimage is rooted in the church's being "the universal sacrament of salvation," at once manifesting and actualizing the mystery of God's love for humanity.[91]

Of course, the pilgrimage will only be complete in the heavenly city, notes *Gaudium et Spes* a few sections later. But any particular graces that come through a confident faith that a transcendent homeland awaits are to be plowed back into other-oriented service, not defended with a smug or otherworldly triumphalism:

> In their pilgrimage to the heavenly city Christians are to seek and value the things that are above; this involves not less, but greater commitment to working with everyone for the establishment of a more human world. Indeed, the mystery of their faith provides Christians with greater incentive and encouragement to fulfil their role more willingly and to assess the significance of activites capable of assigning to human culture its honored role in the complete vocation of humanity.[92]

The pilgrim people of God may be earthbound for now, therefore, but its citizens are not bound strictly to any one culture or nation. For as *Gaudium et Spes* soon picks up the thread,

> There are many links between the message of salvation and culture. In his self-revelation to his people, fully manifesting himself in his incarnate Son, God spoke in the context of the culture proper to each age. Similarly the church has existed through the centuries in varying circumstances and has utilized the resources of different cultures to spread and explain the message of Christ in its preaching, to examine and understand it more deeply, and to express it more perfectly in the liturgy and in the life of the multiform community of the faithful.

Nevertheless, the church has been sent to all ages and nations and, therefore, is not tied exclusively and indissolubly to any race or nation, to any one particular way of life, or to any set of customs, ancient or modern. The church . . . can, then, enter into communion with different forms of culture, thereby enriching both itself and the cultures themselves.[93]

So while salvation finds its ultimate realization through eternal communion with God, it begins to take shape now already as a first fruit of unity within the whole human family. Precisely as sacramental "sign and instrument" the church is to be the "real presence" of what God seeks for the whole world, a visible sign of the invisible reality of God's transforming work in the world.

Thus we may now recognize the pattern all the more clearly: Blessed—to be a blessing. Pilgrims—who remain engaged in service to the lands of their sojourn. Exiles—who still seek the peace of the city in which they find themselves. A sacrament—which is an instrument making present in the world that very reality toward which it points as a sign. In other words, a consistent pattern has been at work throughout the Christian tradition. In every case, we see patterns of cultural transformation, something like those nested Russian dolls we envisioned in the last chapter. As with the pattern of Abrahamic community we discerned in Scripture and the imprint of that pattern on the diaspora ecclesiology of the church's first centuries, so too in these cornerstones of Vatican II ecclesiology: Communities embedded within communities, people embedded within peoples, each with a distinct identity yet called to serve the common good of larger wholes. The peace to which the church is to point, according to Vatican II, is of course incomplete. Indeed the peacebuilding skills and habits by which the church is to be an instrument of peace remain underdeveloped. But that is how sacraments work: The visible sign of a still-not-altogether-visible reality is not ethereal. If the largest of those nested Russian dolls remains unpainted, one should be able to find the pattern on a smaller one inside. And if an intermediate doll remains unpainted, one must go deeper into one's locale or diocese or parish or ecclesial movement or base community and keep sketching.

Surveying the map

The technical word for the study of the church and its nature is "ecclesiology," and it is a huge topic. Much ink and not a little blood have been spilled over how to recognize *the* true church, what are the "marks" of the church, how it should be governed, and so on. This is not the place to arbitrate all those disputes, but we should notice one thing: Catholics use the word *catholic*, Protestants use the word *ecumenical*, and Evangelicals cite Christ's Great Commission to go into all the *world*. And so they all acknowledge, implicitly agree upon, but often ignore one key point of consensus concerning the nature of Christ's church: It is *katholou*—throughout the whole. It is gathered and spread throughout *hē oikoumēnē*, the whole inhabited world. And now more clearly than ever. For despite whatever faults, the modern missionary movement has reinforced ancient and contemporary Christian migrations to give us a church that geographically is truly global.[94]

What does this have to do with war, peace, and what it means to be a peace church? In a word: citizenship.

When ordinary Christians go to war, most often it is not because they have seriously examined the tradition of Christian pacifism or the efficacy of active nonviolence and found them wanting. Nor, most often, is it because they have used the just-war theory and found that a given war fulfills all the criteria for a justifiable war. No doubt some Christians have exercised their consciences in these ways, and for doing so they deserve the highest respect even if prudential judgments differ about given wars. But when ordinary Christians go to war, most often it is because national loyalty trumps Christian loyalty—because love of country trumps love of neighbor, at least as Jesus understood such love.

As launched by St. Augustine, even the just-war tradition has at least attempted to insist that in fighting to defend the innocent neighbor one must still endeavor to extend Christian love of neighbor to the enemy. Christian pacifists are not alone in doubting, of course, that it is really possible to love the enemy one is attempting to kill, as Augustine apparently believed.[95] But let us stipulate for a moment that this might somehow be possible and give the tradition its due. However dubious may be the just-war commitment to loving one's enemies even in war, after all, it does represent an acknowledgment that Christian love of neighbor is to be qualitatively different from pagan love of neighbor. "For if you love those who love you, what reward do you have? Do not even the tax collectors do the same? And if you greet only your brothers and sisters, what more are you doing than others? Do not even the Gentiles do the same?" (Matt 5:46–47). The honest answer to Jesus' question here is that of course they do the same, and so do we. All too often we let some other loyalty and some other love define our stance toward those who threaten us; we then make enemies of many more, and easily assume that all who are not with us and *our* kind are against us. Then and thus, ordinary Christians go off not to arguably just wars but to wars of national self-interest or even crusades—where "necessity," honor, or the righteousness of "our side" seem so clear that the morality of our actions needs little examination.[96]

Love of country is a tricky thing for Christians. At one level, it is surely not wrong. As someone who holds a U.S. passport, I for one love the grandeur of America's land, the energy of its people, the wisdom embedded in its constitution. I love its baseball, its jazz and blues, its diners and bowling clubs and skylines. I love my revitalized multicultural neighborhood of Hmong, African-American, Somali, Hispanic, and Anglo, literally in the shadow of our stately Minnesota capitol. Amid everything I have just said to distinguish Christian love of neighbor from pagan love of neighbor, I would certainly acknowledge that Christian love *includes* our geographical neighbors even if it does not *confine* itself to them. Social activists who do not share a deep love for the society they claim to want to better easily become hypocrites, ideologues, or simply doomed to foolish ineffectuality.

But in the end we still must ask: What really is a Christian's true country or nation or homeland? The Second Vatican Council helped to recover the ancient Christian answer to that question by speaking of the church as a "pilgrim church" that will continue on its "earthly pilgrimage" "to the heavenly city" "until there be realized new heavens and a new earth in which justice dwells."[97] Though some might interpret this to endorse an otherworldly piety that sees a Christian's home in heaven alone, note that what the council here endorses is a thoroughly biblical hope that does not expect either God or God's people to rest in heaven until the earth as well as the heavens are made new. This is a hope that the Old and New Testaments share.[98] It is the hope of St. Paul[99] and the Apostles' Creed in a resurrection not just of our souls or spirits but somehow our bodies. It is the hope assuring St. Augustine that the communion characterizing the heavenly city is already stretching to include among its citizens those of us who are still making our way through the earthly city.

The practical down-to-earth implication of this vision is that the nation with which Christians should identify their primary citizenship is that transnational people called church. Thus to identify ourselves is to embrace life in diaspora. Thus to identify ourselves is essential to becoming a catholic peace church.

PART III

Maps for Peacebuilding by a Pilgrim People

This Sunday's Gospel contains some of the most typical and forceful words of Jesus' preaching: "Love your enemies" (Lk 6: 27). . . .
This Gospel passage is rightly considered the *magna carta* of Christian non-violence. It does not consist in succumbing to evil, as a false interpretation of "turning the other cheek" (cf. Lk 6: 29) claims, but in responding to evil with good (cf. Rom 12: 17-21) and thereby breaking the chain of injustice.

One then understands that for Christians, non-violence is not merely tactical behaviour but a person's way of being, the attitude of one who is so convinced of God's love and power that he is not afraid to tackle evil with the weapons of love and truth alone.

Love of one's enemy constitutes the nucleus of the "Christian revolution," a revolution not based on strategies of economic, political or media power: the revolution of love, a love that does not rely ultimately on human resources but is a gift of God which is obtained by trusting solely and unreservedly in his merciful goodness. Here is the newness of the Gospel which silently changes the world! Here is the heroism of the "lowly" who believe in God's love and spread it, even at the cost of their lives.

—Pope Benedict XVI
February 18, 2007, *Angelus*, St. Peter's Square

Chapter 7

Guesthood and the Politics of Hospitality

> It is essential to draw near to new forms of poverty and vulnerability, in which we are called to recognize the suffering Christ, even if this appears to bring us no tangible and immediate benefits. I think of the homeless, the addicted, refugees, indigenous peoples, the elderly who are increasingly isolated and abandoned, and many others. Migrants present a particular challenge for me, since I am the pastor of a Church without *fronteras* [Spanish for borders], a Church which considers herself mother to all. For this reason, I exhort all countries to a generous openness which, rather than fearing the loss of local identity, will prove capable of creating new forms of cultural synthesis.
>
> —Pope Francis, *Evangelii Gaudium*, §210

Shaping this book has been a guiding assumption that however urgent the tasks of peacebuilding may be, we will only get our *doing* of peace right if we first attend to what God calls us to *become* and to *be* as a people of peace in the world. Still, eventually we must also attend to our doing too, of course. Fortunately, all the work we have done to embrace Christian life in diaspora turns out to have a practical payoff. Not only does it allow the pilgrim church to return like T. S. Eliot's explorers to see again for the first time that it has always meant to be a global, catholic church—ecclesiology; it also offers maps to guide our action—ethics. Life in diaspora, after all, always requires codes and practices of hospitality and of guesthood.

Hospitality is not just about being good hosts; it is also about being good guests. And there is the rub. For many reasons, Christian thinkers and activists alike have been paying increasing attention in recent decades to the biblical call, ancient traditions, and saintly models of hospitality toward strangers, refugees, the poor, and other "others." All this is surely welcome. Yet whenever theological and philosophical work on hospitality focuses mainly on the responsibilities of hosts, it continues to assume a position of power.[1] And that actually hints at the deepest taproot of nationalism, fear-goaded violence, and ultimately war—indeed it might even reinforce it. Namely, we may not really want to be guests.

By now, the reader may be wondering how to flesh out life in diaspora anyway. The promise all along has been that a diaspora ecclesiology would help us find ways to navigate the "tension between the particular and the universal" that Pope John Paul II recognized as intrinsic to human nature. The motive for peacebuilding may be a universal regard for all human beings—perhaps prompted among Christians by Jesus' reminder in Matthew 5:43-48 that to take on the character of their heavenly Father, their love must extend far beyond their own kind. But that very regard must simultaneously respect the human rights and synchronize the just claims of particular peoples, persons, communities, nations, and cultures.[2]

The promise is this: Precisely as it guides the life of that *transnational* nation called church, a diaspora ecclesiology will refuse to mark Christians off in any kind of sectarian enclave. A diaspora ecclesiology frankly celebrates and preserves the particular communal identity into which Christians have been baptized. It names that identity as nothing short of citizenship within the transnational *nation* called church, which is to supersede all other tribal and national identities. Yet the Gospel itself simultaneously requires an inculturation that embraces, redeems, and offers Christian suffering service to those same particularities of human identities in tribe, nation, and culture.[3] The very identity of this people is to be a gift to the nations and a source of fresh and life-giving cultural creativity, after all. Like Jeremiah's exiles who became the Babylonian civil servants in the book of Daniel, Christians living out a diaspora ecclesiology by means of a diaspora social ethic will contribute all the more to the common good of their host cultures because they know who they are and refuse to bow down to any proud and idolatrous pretensions of their hosts. A diaspora ecclesiology, in other words, promises to show Christians how to participate widely in public policy debates and work for the common good even when they cannot assume control. Which actually is always.

An ethic of guesthood

For an Iraqi man, the anniversary was a bittersweet one at best. The U.S. journalist interviewing him on the occasion was not a soldier, but to the Iraqi man he nonetheless represented the nation that had invaded his country in March 2003, and remained an occupying force. The man was glad that Iraq's longtime dictator Saddam Hussein was gone, but he did not want to live under foreign occupation forces. "Go home," he said to the journalist who to him stood for all Americans, "and then come back as my guest, so that I can be your host."[4]

Hospitality is always an elaborate but delicate dance. Hosts must welcome others into their cultural spaces. Guests may transform those spaces. Gracious hosts may invite guests to help prepare or serve a meal, thus allowing guests to join them in hosting. Guests may sometimes prove such engaging conversationalists that they become honorary hosts. And yet "guests" who take over other people's spaces violate implicit codes of hospitality; they become intruders, invaders, or occupying forces instead. True guests, after all, do not relocate the furniture, or revise the menu, or occupy a bedroom uninvited, or overstay their welcome. As warmly as a host may welcome a guest, invisible boundaries and norms remain. In Latin America, *"esta es su casa"* or "this is your house" is a common welcome, but a guest would be boorish to take that greeting literally. Any "radical hospitality" that discredits all boundaries and disparages all such norms in the name of totally unfettered "inclusivity" will thus breed resentment as quickly as a bumbling but imperious foreigner who somehow expected the standard Latin American welcome to bring with it a legal title to the *casa*.

Any actual, functioning, life-giving ethic of hospitality, in other words, must come with a corresponding ethic of guesthood. Heir to codes of ancient Middle-Eastern hospitality that have endured for millennia, the Iraqi man in the interview was signaling this. He wanted to offer the rich and elaborate practices of hospitality that his culture shares with many—indeed most—ancient and indigenous cultures. But a boorish guest will strain if not break the code of hospitality. Indeed, it is doubtful that anyone can be a very good host who has not first learned to be a very flexible and generous guest. For, if anything, the capacity for guesthood is basic to a capacity to host.

Hospitality rediscovered

Even before refugees and immigrants became one of the most prominent and divisive political topics in Europe, the United States, and elsewhere in the early twenty-first century, Christian theologians had begun recovering the neglected theme of hospitality in Hebrew, early Christian, and ongoing church tradition. Hospitality speaks directly to a wide range of situations, after all, from parish life and outreach, to public policy at national and international levels. It names a Christian community's basic stance not just toward migrants but toward the poor, the marginalized, and those long despised. It invites a transformation of relationships with "bothersome" homeless people, long-suppressed sexual minorities, other races, and strange or apparently threatening religions. And the transformation it invites is happily entry-level. A parish cautious about being so unpatriotic as to challenge its nation's foreign policy might still feel called to sponsor a refugee family. A congregation divided about the role of government in alleviating poverty might still agree to open its own doors and pantries to struggling families in its neighborhood. Critics might rightly worry that such simple acts of charity will prove paternalistic; they may insist that much more is needed to counter the injustices and alter the systems that are the source of poverty, marginalization, and displacement. Yet those same critics often owe that very analysis to biographies in which simple acts of hospitality, whether given or received, initially broke them out of their own enclaves; entry-level hospitality is often what led to new relationships that transformed their own worldviews and prompted their now-trenchant analysis and persistent advocacy. Even as Pope Paul VI promoted the need for human development, economic justice, and structural change on nothing short of a global scale, therefore, his 1967 encyclical, *Populorum Progressio*, underscored this: "We cannot insist too much on the duty of welcoming others—a duty springing from human solidarity and Christian charity—which is incumbent both on the families and the cultural organizations of the host countries."[5]

Examples, models, and calls to hospitality abound in both the Hebrew and Christian Scriptures. Abraham, the archetype of faith for Judaism, Christianity, and Islam, has also been the archetype of hospitality in the lore of all three traditions since he and Sarah welcomed three mysterious visitors in Genesis 18.[6] Indeed, the faith and the hospitality of Abraham are arguably inseparable. Joshua Jipp has emphasized that "at least some early Christians thought Abraham was justified by his faith *and hospitality to strangers.*"[7]

For Christians the supreme model and source of hospitality is of course Jesus himself. The great christological text of John, chapter 1, is more than an announcement of a new metaphysical formula for understanding how the Word became flesh; the Incarnation had become known to us through the narrative of Jesus coming to us as "the heavenly stranger" who had made his home or "tent" with us (1:14, *eskēnosēn*) despite our unwarm welcome (1:11), thus mediating God's own hospitality.[8] As Jesus then inaugurated his ministry according to Luke 4, hospitality was the very core and character of that ministry as he proclaimed what is sometimes translated as "the year of the Lord's *welcome.*" As Jipp has explained, "The programmatic function of Jesus's Nazareth sermon [in Luke 4] invites the reader to pay attention to the way in which the entirety of Jesus's ministry *and particularly his meals with strangers* enact divine hospitality to the poor, the captives, the blind, and the oppressed."[9] Encounters in which Jesus was guest, yet also proved to be the true host, ran throughout his ministry—as many have noted—along with sayings and teachings in which table sharing is prominent.[10] Jesus' climactic self-disclosure at the table in which he had just washed his disciples' feet in welcome, and then offered them his very body and blood in the form of bread and wine, thus became the preeminent place by which Christians through the centuries believe themselves to be encountering the real presence of the risen Christ in the Eucharist.

The gospel writers were not simply chroniclers, though; they always highlighted themes such as Jesus' hospitality with a view to the life of the early church.[11] Luke's vision is especially apparent because he carried his narrative forward into the Acts of the Apostles, where, as John Koenig has put it, he "pictures the first church in

Jerusalem as a banquet community and documents its expanding mission to the Roman world with a long string of narratives about guests and hosts."[12] Paul, both as portrayed in Acts and by his own account in 1 Corinthians 9, carefully navigated the codes of hospitality he found in each cultural setting—alternately accepting hospitality as a guest, paying his own expenses, and taking up communal leadership as host himself—in order to do whatever would advance the gospel message and build up the fledgling Christian communities in each locale.[13] And by all accounts, the message and the practice of hospitality took root. As Christine Pohl has summarized,

> The richness of the story of hospitality continues beyond the many biblical texts. Early Christian writers claimed that transcending social and ethnic differences by sharing meals, homes, and worship with persons of different backgrounds was a proof of the truth of the Christian faith. In the fourth century, church leaders warned clergy—who might be tempted to use hospitality to gain favor with the powerful—to welcome instead the poorest people to their tables. In doing so, they would have Christ as their guest.[14]

Biblical hospitality is not simply a matter of individual or familial acts of charity, however, nor merely a missionary technique that young churches found useful for recruiting new members. The *Torah* or Law of Moses had encoded hospitality toward strangers and foreigners into legal protections and rights that were akin to those of citizens. Having been slaves in Egypt, Israel was to do justice to resident aliens or other vulnerable groups (Deut 24:17-18; 27:19). Agricultural profits were not to be maximized, precisely so that resident aliens, widows, and orphans could glean from fields of harvest, olive groves, and vineyards (Deut 24:19-24; cf. Ruth 2). In Leviticus 25:23, the entire premise of Jubilee provisions for the redistribution of land every fifty years was that Israelites and the resident aliens among them had virtually the same status.[15] While the *Torah* certainly made careful distinctions among the rights of resident aliens,[16] and while those who were merely passing through enjoyed the fewest privileges, citizenship was very much a continuum; the foreigner whom Exodus 23:43-49 initially seemed to exclude entirely from the identity-marking meal of Passover was to be "regarded as a native of the land" once male family members were circumcised.[17] Exodus 23:49 underscored the essential principle: "There shall be one law for the native and for the alien who resides among you."

Although Jesus neither found nor placed himself in a position to promulgate new laws,[18] he clearly promised in Matthew 25:31-46 that God would judge the nations according to whether they treat the hungry, the thirsty, the stranger, the naked, the sick, and the prisoner in ways that we may quite fairly describe as alternately hospitable or inhospitable. Many ancient peoples had considered hospitality to be one of their most basic moral expectations, given the vulnerability of travelers in pre-modern times and the desire for reciprocal protection.[19] But Christian communities in the church's first centuries went noticeably further, as the Gospel stretched ancient codes of hospitality to include those who had often been ignored or feared. Pohl has underscored this distinction. Hospitality in all cultures,

> because it was such a fundamental human practice, always included family, friends, and influential contacts. The distinctive Christian contribution was the emphasis on including the poor and neediest, the ones who could not return the favor. This focus did not diminish the value of hospitality to family and friends; rather, it broadened the practice so that the close relations formed by table fellowship and conversation could be extended to the most vulnerable.[20]

Lucien Richard has thus gone so far as to propose that we think of "hospitality to the stranger" as "a shortcut formula expressing the core of the Christian vision."[21]

The metaphysics of guesthood

Indeed, the ground of all human hospitality turns out, upon on fuller reflection, to be God's own. Human hospitality is ultimately but a response to God's hospitality. In the gift of creation, God first set the table. In the exodus, God dramatically acted to rescue enslaved Israel and lead the people into a land of milk and honey where they were never to forget that they had been strangers and aliens themselves. For Christians, as we have noted, the Incarnation itself is nothing less than Jesus "the heavenly stranger" coming to sojourn among alienated human beings, "enabling them to partake of the hospitality of God."[22] In his life and ministry, then, Jesus is "the divine host who extends God's hospitality to sinners, outcasts, and strangers and thereby draws them—and us—into friendship with God;" it is in response that "our friendship with God [becomes] the foundation of and cause for our friendship with one another."[23]

But there is another implication. Preaching on the duty of hospitality, Augustine put it this way:

> You receive a stranger, whose companion you yourself also are on the road, because we are all foreign visitors [or resident aliens]. Those people are the real Christians who realize that both in their own homes and their own country they are foreign visitors. Our native country is up above, there we shall not be strangers. I mean here each one of us, even in his own home, is a stranger. If you are not a stranger, you don't move on from here; if you are going to move on, you are a stranger. Don't kid yourself, you're a stranger.[24]

After all, as Pope Francis much more recently has reminded us: "We are not God. The earth was here before us and it has been given to us."[25] Citing Leviticus 25:23 on the Jubilee, and speaking to the care of the earth in his encyclical *Laudato Si'*, the blunt lesson that Francis drew from this also has far-reaching implications for how we think about borders and the spaces into which we either invite others, or exclude them, or enter as guests. As Francis continued: "God rejects every claim to absolute ownership."

It is not that no claim to ownership or private property *whatsoever* is legitimate; Francis's reminder concerned *absolute* ownership. As we will explore later in this chapter, ownership and thus inevitable boundaries of some kind are in fact a necessary condition for hospitality. Yet we will only negotiate ways to own and host and share and live at peace with one another if we first recognize that fact of our existence that should be most obvious, but that we in our fear of mortality are so prone to suppress: Namely, human beings are first of all—ontologically, metaphysically, ever and always fundamentally —guests.

We think we can control. We desperately want to control. For we want to survive. But we will not survive—not forever, anyway, except

Guesthood and the Politics of Hospitality 207

as God gives us the *gift* of eternal life and *welcomes us* into that new heaven and new earth to live as a city of communion in which God is all in all.²⁶ To deny our status as guests is thus to deny our very creaturehood. As Lucien Richard put it on his way to explaining why "'hospitality to the stranger' is a shortcut formula expressing the core of the Christian vision,"

> The refusal of creaturehood involves the refusal to be interdependent, the avoidance of the limiting conditions of relationship; it denies the possibility of being shaped by something other than our own choice; it is the refusal of indebtedness. Creatureliness, and therefore contingency, historicity, and finitude characterize human existence. . . . While for-otherness is constitutive of personhood, so is from-otherness. That we derive from others, that we live from others, is fundamental. It is through being loved that we learn to love; we have to receive in order to be able to give.²⁷

Absolute ownership and control themselves, in other words, are not simply wrong, they are illusory. Ownership is only ever temporary. It is really but a mortgage or a lease, not a permanent holding. At best we secure it through peaceable negotiation embedded in trusting relationship.

Even when Israel came into "possession" of the land, God's people were to remember this reality in order to stay in right relationship to God, other inhabitants, and the land itself. In a succinct yet thorough article titled "The Alien According to the Torah," Georges Chawkat Moucarry has traced a thread of reminders in the Hebrew Scriptures that suggest that even when God fulfilled the promise of land to Abraham, Sarah, and their descendants, "possession" was never absolute because they themselves were to live as resident aliens and guests of God.²⁸ Readers easily assume that the opening move in salvation history by which God called Abraham into exile from his native land (Gen 12:1-3) was only stage-setting—a necessary prelude to owning the real estate that God promised only a few verses later (Gen 12:7). Yet when Abraham began taking up residence he did so by way of peace treaties that acknowledged his status as a resident alien (Gen 21:22-34), and when he actually negotiated the purchase of his first parcel of land in order to bury Sarah his wife, he reiterated his status as a guest (Gen 23:4).[29] Both Isaac and Jacob continued their migrations even before famine forced the family of Israel-née-Jacob to flee to Egypt. "Twice an alien or immigrant" and counting—as Moucarry put it—Moses later recognized this identity during his refuge in Midian by naming his son Gershom, meaning "I have become an alien in a foreign land."[30]

Of course, the obvious question is whether all this changed with the conquest of the Promised Land, so that the land became theirs, simply and unequivocally. Not according to the law of Jubilee, which insisted: "The land shall not be sold in perpetuity, for the land is mine; with me you are but aliens and tenants" (Lev 25:23). "In other words," Moucarry observed, Jubilee provisions were "given to remind the Israelites that their conquest of the Promised Land did not make them its owners, but rather its caretakers. . . . With one stroke, the law placed the Israelites in a right perspective of their relationship to God."[31] Even when the kingship of David seemed to be allowing Israel to settle fully in the land and secure the nation's tenure through political domination of the region, David himself insisted upon a spirituality of guesthood:

> And now, our God, we give thanks to you and praise your glorious name. But who am I, and what is my people, that we should be able to make this freewill offering? For all things come from you, and of your own have we given you. For we are aliens and transients before you, as were all our ancestors; our days on the earth are like a shadow, and there is no hope.[32]

Right relationship with God in turn required right relationship with other immigrants dwelling in the land; hospitality included the extension of legal minimums aiming to prevent their exploitation and abuse. Moucarry listed at least sixteen examples of laws that extended to them in some way, together showing "that aliens living in Israel were closely associated with and even integrated into the national life."[33] When the *Torah* did make distinctions in the status and treatment of resident aliens, the intent was not so much to exclude them as to protect them in light of their vulnerability. Hence the constant reminders that the Israelites had been aliens in Egypt and should thus treat strangers in their midst in ways corresponding to God's gracious liberation of them.[34] As Leviticus 19:34 made clear, "The alien who resides with you shall be to you as the citizen among you; you shall love the alien as yourself, for you were aliens in the land of Egypt: I am the LORD your God."

We should not have needed phenomena like globalization to recognize these biblical and theological truths. But now we have no excuse. As the Vietnamese-born theologian Fr. Peter C. Phan has put it, "We all are migrants, or better, co-migrants now," and the very distinction between natives and migrants has become "otiose," for "we are all pilgrims, not back to where we came from (the countries of origin) nor to the foreign lands (the countries of destination) because neither is our true home."[35] What Jipp has said of the apostle Paul applies also to us: If we, like Paul, seek truly to evangelize, we must do so by "embodying and extending God's hospitality" to others—but for that we must actually begin not by hosting but by "intentionally [entering] into the role of the guest."[36]

If we too are guests

So we too are guests. This simple recognition offers a key for unlocking a number of puzzles of peacebuilding as a people of peace. Our friend the stymied Iraqi host hints at why. He could not offer his culture's rich tradition of hospitality so long as his potential guests were occupiers instead. Motivating the U.S. occupation were a stew of potentially noble, frankly economic, and crassly nationalistic intentions, such that even if the stated desire to liberate Iraq from a repressive regime was authentic on the part of some American leaders and ground troops alike, he had ample reason to suspect otherwise. He was not saying that outsiders had nothing to contribute; nor should we conclude that solidarity across borders always has ulterior motives. But outsiders who know themselves to be guests will be in a far better position to offer "help" that is truly helpful. And those who recognize themselves as guests even in their own lands will have been developing the capacity for cross-cultural relationships that propose without imposing—to cite Pope Paul VI.[37] They will better know how to celebrate the gifts of their own cultural identities without the jingoism that prevents them from exchanging gifts with other peoples.

Recall Pope John Paul II's reminder in his address to the United Nations in 1995: "The human condition . . . finds itself between these two poles—universality and particularity—with a vital tension between them." That tension is "immanent" in all human beings, he noted, for we simultaneously recognize ourselves as "members of one great family" yet are "necessarily bound in a *more intense* way to particular human groups." This, he insisted, is "an inevitable tension, but singularly fruitful if [the contrasting poles] are lived in a calm and balanced way." Indeed, recognition of this tension is the "anthropological foundation" upon which to build "a just world order" by synchronizing the proper rights of peoples, nations, and cultures all the way down to "the specific level of community life."[38]

The reasons for careful attention to the inevitable but fruitful tension between universality and particularity is one that we should be even more prepared to recognize now than at the time of Pope John Paul II's address to the United Nations. Three decades after the end of the Cold War upon which he was reflecting, his words apply also to the globalized twenty-first century world that may be further than ever from a "calm and balanced way" of distinguishing legitimate aspirations for national and cultural integrity from nativist nationalism on the one hand. Nor are we doing well at instituting a universal regime of human rights without imposing a homogenizing culture of consumer capitalism and technological control on the other hand.[39] Indeed his prescient 1995 diagnosis seems more accurate than ever:

> Today the problem of nationalities forms part of a new world horizon marked by a great "mobility" that has blurred the ethnic and cultural frontiers of the different peoples, as a result of a variety of processes such as migrations, mass-media and the globalization of the economy. And yet, precisely against this horizon of universality we see the powerful re-emergence of a certain ethnic and cultural consciousness, as it were an explosive need for identity and survival, a sort of counterweight to the tendency toward uniformity. This is a phenomenon that must not be underestimated or regarded as a simple left-over of the past. It demands serious interpretation, and a closer examination on the levels of anthropology, ethics and law.[40]

The challenge is this: People of generosity may find themselves resisting the very need to preserve particular cultural identities when that impulse rears its head as nativism, vehement forms of nationalism, religious triumphalism, and ultimately war, for then "the need for identity and survival" seems explosive indeed. But ignoring or suppressing that need will only make it more explosive. What David Hollenbach, SJ, once said of religious convictions applies to any strong and formative claims on human or personal identity: they are even more "potentially explosive when confined to small spaces."[41] And yet, as soon as we appeal to principles of universal regard in order to counter uglier forms of particularism, we may find ourselves defending the rights and claims of still other particular cultures.

The goal cannot be to suppress particular identities, even "tribal" ones—as Enlightenment dreams of a universal culture based on reason alone apart from any tradition has sometimes aspired to do. It must be something richer and more complex. When I watch the news and see white nationalists marching with torches on the stately campus founded by Thomas Jefferson in Charlottesville, Virginia, I may be tempted to see strong demands to preserve an identity as the very problem. But then I travel to the highlands of Guatemala for a research project among my Mayan Indian friends, and celebrate their historic resistance to conquest and repression, while worrying that the forces of globalization might do them in at last. From a greater distance, over decades, I have watched Poland—the homeland of Pope John Paul II, née Karol Wojtyła—proudly reasserting its identity after centuries of foreign domination, but then barring refugees from war-torn Syria lest Muslims among them threaten that identity. Likewise, post-apartheid South Africa has struggled to define its immigration policy toward refugees from neighboring African countries as black South Africans recover their own rights of ownership after centuries being treated as aliens in their own land. And for that matter but closer to home, my own university, like many institutions of Christian higher education, often seems a laboratory for living out tensions between particularity and universality: Can we preserve a vibrant Catholic identity while practicing hospitality and a widening inclusivity toward others? An ethic of hospitality may prompt us to welcome others warmly into our space—but what if guests do start to move the furniture? Guests have responsibilities and hosts may need to set limits. But have I actually set up another "we / them" relationship and confirmed a second-class status in the community for some? Maybe guesthood is not such a welcome concept, one wonders! Clearly John Paul II was right to call the polarity between particularity and universality an "inevitable tension" in the human condition, but how can we ensure that it is indeed a "singularly fruitful" one, as he hoped, and fruitful for more than academic study?

One obvious way to distinguish between rightful efforts to preserve a collective identity, and problematic ones, is to note power differentials. Struggling to preserve Polish identity over against German then Soviet domination is one thing. Doing so at the expense of destitute and traumatized Syrian refugees is another. Speaking up for poor and working-class white folks who get labeled "white trash" or "trailer trash" is one thing. Chanting "Jews will not replace us" and attacking black counterprotesters in Charlottesville because U.S. society is haltingly attempting to create a more even playing field for previously disadvantaged minorities—such that a privileged white male is no longer guaranteed the career track he thinks he deserves—is another. Historically privileged colonial powers are one thing; vulnerable indigenous cultures are another.

The problem for peacebuilders, though, is that *saying* this much does not really *resolve* very much. Even when we have accurately analyzed power differentials, how do we go about distributing power—to say nothing of *re*-distributing power—justly and effectively? Justice may well be on my side; opponents may well be holding and wielding their power unjustly even as they wrongly believe themselves to be the ones who are victims under siege. But if I attempt to force them to become generous and hospitable I will only confirm their perception that I, or the vulnerable ones for whom I am advocating, are not even guests but intruders. Because identity is so powerful, it can finally only be complicated and thus transformed, not forcibly imposed through frontal attacks.

So many of the debates that embroil social change movements spring from this reality, and the dilemmas it entails. A certain amount of power, privilege, or recognition is required even to be a guest, after all. Marginalized persons and groups may have no way to assert their dignity and win recognition of their just claims other than to intrude quite impolitely with their demands.[42] That is why strategic nonviolence cannot depend on converting oppressors, even as practitioners issue invitations and keep open routes by which their opponents might yet do so. Thus, social movements that renounce violent means must exercise alternative forms of possibly coercive social power in order to remove support for unjust policies and oppressive regimes. For that, though, the power they most need is not the power that some might dream of taking over from the oppressor, but other forms of relational power that they discover as they build coalitions of mutual support and shift the societal balance of power by winning support from previously complacent or fearful sectors that have been passively supporting their opponents.[43]

Precisely here we see why practices of guesthood and hospitality do not cease to be relevant and indeed powerful even for those whose long marginalization has forced them to be quite unruly guests. Even when they wield tactics of social coercion accompanied by loud cries of protest, movements practicing strategic nonviolence cannot abandon all hope of a reconciled transformation that embraces opponents, nor thus, some transformed version of their opponents' closely held senses of identity. Otherwise advocates and activists for social change are reducing social process to pure power play in which violence may after all be inevitable. Unless we can hold out hope for reconciliation and transformation, in other words, then strangely and covertly we are dreaming of incongruous solutions akin to ethnic cleansing, in which we imagine that our opponents somehow just go away and their cultural identities altogether disappear. That is why the answer cannot be to suppress identity but to complicate it.

My proposal is this: We should start by recognizing that we are always in some sense guests who must continually learn to make our homes in shared spaces over which we have only limited control. In doing so, we will actually be better positioned, and likely become more skillful, both at preserving our own identities and defending the vulnerable identities of others—even among unwelcoming hosts who are desperate to preserve their own dubious identities and the power they believe is rightly theirs. Embracing the vulnerability of life in diaspora, in other words, brings its own power.

The politics of hospitality

The church does not depend—and individual Christians should not depend—on the political system in which they live to practice hospitality, but it may help. Likewise, a people that recognizes itself as living in diaspora among many peoples cannot wait to do so until other nations recognize that we are all living in diaspora anyway or begin to organize the international system accordingly as a thoroughgoing federation of nations, though this would be welcome.[44] It is of a piece with the diaspora social ethics of a pilgrim people, after all, that they work diligently for greater justice in the earthly city even if they can only expect a succession of interim improvements that fall short of the Reign of God yet point to its promise as signs. In an Abrahamic model of social change that lives out God's blessing even while hoping to bless other families of the earth, our first task is to "be the change we seek in the world" precisely as we do that seeking. Those who know themselves to be guests should thus be able to advocate for wider politics of hospitality in the societies that host them. But how?

Too often the operative assumption of Christians working in politics or policymaking is that the *sine qua non* of political effectiveness is that they get themselves "in the room where it happens"—to quote the musical *Hamilton*—and then stay in the loop at all costs.[45] Perhaps this is the lesson they thought they were supposed to learn from the twentieth-century Protestant ethicist Reinhold Niebuhr and his call for a "Christian Realism" that is unapologetic about exercising worldly power while dismissing those with more scruples than he as politically irrelevant or even irresponsible.[46] Among American Catholics whose parents or grandparents were themselves immigrants, memories of exclusion sometimes add another set of pressures not only to assimilate but to "make it" into power and, once there, hold on to the status and influence it affords. In either case, what one certainly does not want to be accused of is the theological s-word, "sectarianism." But as we have seen, a diaspora social ethic seeks neither to be assimilationist nor sectarian. It expects that—on the model of Jeremiah's exiles and Daniel's colleagues in the Babylonian civil service—faithful Christians may indeed find themselves serving God and the common good of the nations while "in the room where it happens." But it also counsels that they will need to be morally agile enough in their faithfulness that they anticipate when to draw the line and refuse to bow down to idolatrous demands.

We will do better at discerning such liminal moments if we do not fear what is on the other side of the line, but instead recognize that there are possibilities for political effectiveness on the far side of that threshold too. This is where, in other words, we are not "in the room where it happens"—unless perhaps as guests—much less in control. In the remainder of this chapter I thus hope to do two things. First, I hope to demonstrate the fruitfulness of a diaspora ecclesiology and the social ethic it implies by applying it to the obvious and necessary case study of immigration policy. People who recognize themselves as resident aliens even when they hold passports from the same country that hosts them will find themselves in a complicated role; whether as resident aliens or as dual citizens, they will have to attend to the claims of at least two moral communities, even while advocating for still others. But if this is possible, then a second lesson will be that a strong, radical, and sometimes countercultural witness for peace through principled nonviolence does not preclude responsible public advocacy and involvement either.

The link between those two points is this: It turns out that Catholic advocacy on behalf of immigrants already works a lot more like historic peace church advocacy than one might think. Catholics do not have to hold back from a more robust peace witness because their best efforts at an immigration witness already show them how. Indeed, their work both for peace and for hospitality toward migrants would be more coherent—and thus clearer and more effective—if they recognized this affinity.

National immigration policy: Translators needed

The result of a case study on immigration illuminates concerns that involve more than ecclesiology and social ethics. Although neither my own expertise nor the scope of the present book will allow us to extend this question all the way out into a proposal for reconceiving the international system, a political theory does start to appear on the horizon. How might a people living in diaspora help its host societies build and strengthen a polity whereby overlapping communities live in peace without losing their particular identities? Anyone who advocates along the lines of Catholic social teaching for a hospitable immigration policy, aiming at something more generous than begrudging assimilation, is beginning to translate the dynamics of diaspora into a polity of communal and cultural federation. That very advocacy will have to find a way to work faithfully from one set of moral convictions within the very context of other ethical communities that do not share all of one's own convictions—even if one believes that because God's will is one, they ultimately should. In order to avoid either relativism or unprincipled compromises while working for the common good, one will have to learn to be savvy to the realities of stark moral disagreement yet somehow learn to translate across moral languages.

In the context of immigration policy, the reality of moral disagreement is stark indeed: Almost all of the deepest and most foundational principles of Catholic social teaching point toward an argument for open borders—but in many societies this will obviously be a tough sell. Even before a rising tide of anti-immigration sentiment and border protectionism began to sweep Europe, the United States, and other countries in the early decades of the twenty-first century, many would simply have dismissed any hint of "open borders" as unrealistic. In order to convince skeptics that they are not being unreasonable, therefore, Catholic moral theologians and bishops regularly add one more principle to their discourse. Whatever else church leaders might have to say about the human rights of migrants, eventually they also concede that according to natural law, nations have a right to defend and regulate their borders. The problem is not that borders have no place at all within either an ethic or a politics of hospitality, but that dropping a free-standing natural right to defend borders into an argument on behalf of migrant rights tends to trump every other moral claim. Skeptics in the audience will then conclude readily that "we knew you didn't really mean it." Migrants themselves will thus continue to remain in limbo.

If migrants are to enjoy effective protection, yet borders do also enjoy some proper moral meaning, advocates will have to do better. We must translate more carefully between the ethical system of the body politic that the nation-state claims to represent, and the church's own moral convictions. Yes, to posit a notion of the natural law that God has woven into the very fabric of reality may well offer confidence that translation is possible. But that confidence does not relieve us from the hard work of actually translating. My proposal is that Catholic policy advocacy will be more effective if, instead of appealing to natural law as though everyone already spoke Esperanto or

Latin, we should recognize—as people living in diaspora must do—that gaps in meaning, assumptions, and thus understanding indeed exist between the ethical languages of nation-states and the transnational nation called church.

Historic peace churches like the Mennonites have had to recognize that as long as they hold to Christian pacifism they will effectively be guests, who have no choice but to become multilingual. At least if they hope to respond to the Gospel not only by being formed into a peaceable people, but also by becoming active peacemakers,[47] they will need to be conversant within the discourses of the dominant culture without simply being dominated into silence or assimilation. This requires a far more nuanced role than standard accounts generally allow them. Ethical and ecclesiological typologies easily miss this nuance when they peg historic peace churches as "sects" that are "withdrawn" or "separationist." At best such characterization is what sociologists call an *ideal type*,[48] but at worst is a lazy stereotype.[49] By the second half of the twentieth century, many Mennonites were deeply engaged with "culture" in the very sense that H. Richard Niebuhr used the term in his famous book *Christ and Culture*, referring to the sum total of human social activity in the world.[50] But they did not merely constitute a position of "Christ against culture," to use the phrase that Niebuhr pegged them with. Yes, in the face of the nuclear arms race and proxy wars in Indochina and other places in the so-called "Third World," some Mennonites took a new look at their belief that peace and the healing of broken relationships is integral to the Gospel itself, and became more active antiwar activists in the process. But many others were "against" a militaristic culture too; this was actually a form of cultural engagement. And in any case, not all Mennonite activism was oppositional. As Duane Friesen noted when he explained the need for fresh ethical guidance from Mennonite peace theology concerning issues of security and public order, "In North America, Mennonites' work is . . . shaped by changes in our communities. Mennonites are increasingly serving in public office, working as civil servants, and entering into professions such as criminal justice, law, and social work that regularly engage issues of public order."[51]

If they were going to be faithful to Christ in the diverse roles that by now we recognize as befitting a diasporic social stance, Mennonites and indeed all Christians must learn to speak at least *five* languages, Friesen suggested. Most basic is the language that shapes Christian identity itself: "Our primary confessional language is the narrative that shapes our identity as Christians, the story of the people of God from Abraham through Pentecost and beyond. The language of scripture and liturgy, hymn and sacrament, creeds and confessions of faith must nourish any genuine understanding of security" along with virtues and ethical practices that encourage hospitality, forgiveness, and mutual aid as fitting to the Body of Christ. If "we learn our own language well," however, Christian churches can and should be "help[ing] members discern when, where, and how to use . . . other languages in ways that are consistent with their primary identity as followers of Jesus Christ."[52]

The other four languages that Christians need in order to witness and work within the larger social order are these, according to Friesen: (1) *"Prophetic witness"* recognizes appropriate times and places to unmask unjust powers and name evil. However difficult it may be to dislodge social illusions or the propaganda that peddles false values, prophetic voices find creative ways to speak truth, and do so with the credentials that come with a willingness to suffer for the truth.[53] (2) *"Christian vocation"* is the language Christians need in order "to engage the professional worlds beyond the church" while placing their "practices and disciplines within a theological context." Instead of uncritically accepting a profession's own ways of thinking or acting as though it were autonomous, the language of a calling (Latin: *vocatio*) narrates lines of accountability back to a Christian's "primary vocation, that of living lives that witness to the way of Christ."[54] Still more widely, (3) a language of *"the common good within the discourse of democracy"* is appropriate as Christians enter into the public sphere. It should not require Christians to "leave behind [their] convictions as Christians and accept a neutral, secular discourse" or renounce any specifically Christian theological reason-giving. But it does require that they "account [for their] convictions by giving reasons and empirical evidence for why we believe policies that flow from our convictions will contribute to the common good." After all, since "our conversation partners represent a plurality of points of view, we appropriately speak differently than we do when we speak to fellow believers, just to be understood."[55]

Guesthood and the Politics of Hospitality   219

Note that so far, the moral languages that Friesen has identified could often enough be dialects of the same language, or closely related languages such as Spanish and Italian, or more distant languages that nonetheless offer numerous cognates that make translation easier. But sometimes one must learn to speak another language altogether, and for this Mennonites such as Friesen have turned to the notion of (4) *middle axioms*.[56] A middle axiom calls other people or institutions to live up to their own stated moral principles, highest ideals, or long-term enlightened self-interests without endorsing all of the assumptions behind others' ethical systems. (A simple example would be the reminder to heroin addicts that they at least use clean needles—without in any way approving of their lifestyle and while in fact looking for opportunities to help them move into a healthier one.)

A challenge is obvious, after all, when Christian pacifists try to engage in faith-based advocacy against wars, militarism, and foreign policies that they believe are distorted by shortsighted national self-interest. Such Christians will have to be realistic: Very few nation-states have dismantled their militaries and none are altogether pacifist.[57] Any effective advocacy must therefore account for a gap between the moral logic of a minority peace church and the moral logic of a worldly state, yet do so without simply allowing the nation-state to claim moral autonomy outside of God's ultimate will, as epitomized in Jesus' proclamation of the in-breaking Reign of God.[58] Middle axioms are a way of addressing officials in "a government that is not committed to principled nonviolence [but] may nevertheless be held accountable to do everything in its power to seek a just peace without violence." After all, wrote Friesen, "When it does resort to force, pacifists can hold it accountable to principles of just-war theory. Likewise, they can hold a police force accountable to serve the community welfare by employing the least amount of force and use force only as a last resort.[59] Yet by being clear when one is speaking the language of others, Christians committed to a gospel-based ethic of peacemaking will be able to gradate their collaboration with other social movements, with government initiatives, and within the international system, as they distinguish between what Friesen called "shalom practices" that clearly accord with the teachings of Jesus, and more problematic yet relatively less violent "practices that presuppose the language of middle axioms."[60]

The larger point, however, is this: The challenge that Catholics face as they advocate for less xenophobic and more humane immigration policies is structurally equivalent to what Mennonites and other historic peace churches do when they advocate for less militaristic and more peaceful solutions to international conflicts. Indeed, when we look at the actual practice of Catholic political advocacy in a case such as immigration, it already looks more like the "multilingual" advocacy that Mennonite ethicist Friesen has charted than we might have expected. Arguably, it would be even more effective if it recognized this affinity.

Rough translations, at best

In some ways, Catholic advocacy on behalf of the rights of migrants and refugees is simply an extension of its bedrock affirmation of human rights generally, grounded *both* in a biblical vision of God's loving care for all creatures but especially those made in God's image, *and* in philosophical—natural law—arguments concerning human dignity and equality. In the wake of two world wars and the Holocaust, and in the face of totalitarian objectification of human beings, Catholic social teaching has been translating its own natural-law tradition of respect for the dignity of every person into modern human rights discourse for many decades.[61] Since the vulnerable and their protection are priorities in either case, and since all those who for any reason must seek a new home are clearly vulnerable, the human rights of migrants and refugees is an obvious concern.

Meanwhile, the pastoral responsibility that the church bears for all members of its flock does much, in practice, to keep its commitment to migrants and refugees a priority.[62] As the pontifical council that is charged with migrant and refugee concerns noted in 1992, Christians at every level of the church are called to put aside fear and act with solidarity toward "new arrivals":

> The first place for the Church's attention to refugees remains the parish community, which has the task of sensitizing its members to the plight of refugees, exhorting them to welcome as Jesus taught: "I was a stranger and you welcomed me" (Mt 25:35). It should not view the new arrivals as a threat to its cultural identity

and well-being, but as an incentive to walk together with these new brothers and sisters who are themselves rich in particular gifts, in an ever-new process of forming a people capable of celebrating its unity in diversity. . . . The Christian community must overcome fear and suspicion toward refugees, and be able to see in them the Savior's face.[63]

Even in a time and place of growing suspicion toward immigrants of all types, bishops in the United States have thus been willing to challenge U.S. immigration policy. Both the historic experience of so many Catholic immigrant communities, and the growing presence of recent immigrants within the current Catholic population, have encouraged this stance. After all, priests, other pastoral personnel, church-related service agencies, and bishops themselves often must respond daily to the social and economic needs of migrants, adapt liturgies and pastoral practices to ensure that they are culturally appropriate, and integrate new immigrant communities into historic ones. Here the uneasy relationship that Catholics have with their own immigrant pasts in a place like the United States can help reinforce empathy, prompt a deep sense of fairness, and forge a goal of *integrating* migrants that honors the particularity of their cultures rather than only begrudgingly *assimilating* them, if not barring them outright.

And yet when the church moves from pastoral care to advocacy, something easily gets lost in translation. Translation is surely necessary either as we move between the church's own natural-law discourse and secular human-rights discourse, or as either one of these moves into policy application. But what may be lost is the very humanity of migrants. However comprehensive the church's insistence that the dignity of the human person stems from their status as creatures made in the image and likeness of God, and however "universal" the United Nations' 1948 declaration of human rights, the standard mechanism that most quickly recognizes a legal standing worthy of protection is not human rights but *citizen* rights. But that is precisely what is in flux (or worse) for migrants and refugees. As Hannah Arendt so aptly described the plight of stateless persons, they are those who have lost "the right to have rights."[64] Tisha Rajendra has elaborated in her masterful book, *Migrants and Citizens: Justice and Responsibility in the Ethics of Immigration*, that even the best statements from Catholic bishops, aiming to inspire and guide advocacy on behalf of migrants, tend to leave this "moral distinction between migrants and citizens" intact; migrants thus remain objects of charity or "supererogatory benevolence," not those to whom we owe justice.[65] Practically, it then is rarely clear who has a binding obligation to defend them in any way.

One would think that Catholic advocacy on behalf of migrants would be able to find firmer footing. To make their human rights contingent on citizenship rights is especially incongruous because in so many other ways, Catholic social and political theory sees the state and its civil authority as derivative. In other words, other rights and realities are supposed to have lexical priority in Catholic thought, especially those of the family. Launching as he did the modern tradition of Catholic social teaching in 1891 with his encyclical *Rerum Novarum*, Pope Leo XIII was clear to the point of trenchancy as he insisted on the point. So long as a family is pursuing its rightful purposes, it "has at least equal rights with the State in the choice and pursuit of the things needful to its preservation and its just liberty"—which surely includes all that migrants and refugees are seeking when they cross borders in order to feed, house, and educate their families. Clearly worried that to concede even this much to the state was risky, however, Leo elaborated:

> We say, "at least equal rights"; for, inasmuch as the domestic household is antecedent, as well in idea as in fact, to the gathering of men into a community, the family must necessarily have rights and duties which are prior to those of the community, and founded more immediately in nature. If the citizens, if the families on entering into association and fellowship, were to experience hindrance in a commonwealth instead of help, and were to find their rights attacked instead of being upheld, society would rightly be an object of detestation rather than of desire.[66]

Catholics across the political spectrum thus have had good reason to insist on the "family values" by which a society creates and preserves conditions in which families can thrive. But if families are prior to the state, then logically, nothing in Leo's formulation gives standing to the state to mark a definitive border between the basic human rights of some families over others.[67]

The moral meaning of borders is problematic, therefore.⁶⁸ Indeed, the very *reality* of borders is far more ambiguous than we tend to assume.⁶⁹ Geographic features such as rivers, mountain ranges, and ravines may sometimes help to define political boundaries—but only sometimes and never decisively. The decision is always human, always a social construction. In other words, borders are never real in a strictly material sense but only become real in provisional ways through the collective minds and relational practices of human beings. (I think of this whenever I fish on a favorite lake that straddles the U.S.–Canada border in the Boundary Waters Canoe Area Wilderness of northern Minnesota and Quetico Provincial Park in Ontario. Although there are metal stakes on either shore identifying each "sovereign" territory, to recognize the actual border transecting the lake requires all the human ingenuity built into my GPS device and the system of satellites overhead.) Borders are only real insofar as human beings enforce them through technology and the threat of violence. Historically, tight border control as an expression of national sovereignty is barely a century old.⁷⁰ Even today, the global marketplace requires more transnational exchange than nation-state regulatory regimes can keep up with, even as "transnational security, health issues, and environmental threats transgress borders."⁷¹ This can sometimes make border zones themselves into places of creativity and resilience for the stateless, but also makes them particularly dangerous.⁷² Yet as Marianne Heimbach-Steins has put it, despite efforts to seal them, "Borders do not and cannot keep out unwanted and possibly disturbing influences from a certain territory or society. . . . Thus, in a particular nonidealistic way a *future without borders* seems to have already come into existence."⁷³

Despite all the reasons that Catholic leaders have to advocate for open borders, though, they regularly add a concessionary "yes, but" clause in the end. And the reason for *that* is not hard to infer. In the public square or the offices of policymakers it is not enough to say, "You should welcome strangers—because the Bible says so." This is exactly why the church has adopted human rights discourse in the modern era as a *lingua franca* for communicating its moral concerns in a way that it hopes will be accessible to those with other worldviews, whether religious or secular. But then, to converse in good faith one will also need to listen to their messages. The hope or need or right to defend one's borders (whether those of a literal territory or a cultural identity) is an objection one must expect to hear. Indeed, precisely because Christians always live hyphenated lives as dual citizens who should constantly be subjecting their loyalties to scrutiny—but may or may not be doing so well—church members themselves may demand to defend borders and identities other than the complex Abrahamic one that they have inherited in Christ. One way or another, therefore, effective advocates on behalf of migrants feel they must provide some kind of reassurance that they are also listening to the concerns of policymakers and those they believe themselves to represent.

Here, though, is where translation most easily gets muddled. Notice what happens in a pivotable paragraph in the 2001 pastoral statement from the United States Conference of Catholic Bishops, *Welcoming the Stranger among Us*:

> *Without condoning undocumented migration*, the Church supports the human rights of all people and offers them pastoral care, education, and social services, no matter what the circumstances of entry into this country, and it works for the respect of the human dignity of all—especially those who find themselves in desperate circumstances. *We recognize that nations have the right to control their borders*. We also recognize and strongly assert that all human persons, created as they are in the image of God, possess a fundamental dignity that gives rise to *a more compelling claim* to the conditions worthy of human life. Accordingly, the Church also advocates legalization opportunities for the maximum number of undocumented persons, particularly those who have built equities and otherwise contributed to their communities.[74]

However judiciously balanced this statement may be, it gives no specific guidance as to how to adjudicate between the rights it enumerates. No doubt the bishops hoped that the "more compelling claim" of migrants to humane living conditions would tip the balance just enough to inspire generosity on the part of the American body politic. Yet migrants and their advocates are left with nothing to do except wait for the receiving nation to somehow become charitable enough that it deigns to offer legal status. Logically, undocumented migration might actually have been "condoned" as an act of civil disobedience and self-defense on the part of desperate people with a legitimate claim on "last resort"—a phrase that bishops have been quite ready to apply in other attempts at careful casuistry. Instead, the right to self-defense lands solely on the side of the nation-state. By explicitly delegitimizing undocumented migration while explicitly recognizing the right of nations to border control, the rhetorical effect of the document is to supply ample rationalization for turning back the rightful claims of migrants in the end.[75]

Occasionally Catholic moral theologians try to clarify the message of Catholic social teaching by offering reassurance that instead of favoring "open borders" it favors "permeable" or "porous borders" in which "a person's right to change nationality for social and economic as well as political reasons" enjoys legal recognition but also some degree of regulation.[76] Something like this has to be the goal of immigration advocates, and certainly porousness could be an apt way to describe a vision of federated overlap between communities with strong identities that live respectfully together in mutual diaspora within a geographic territory. So long as nation-states continue to claim "sovereignty" over such territories however, the metaphor of a porous or permeable border will falter. Applied to contested external borders, the notion clarifies little except perhaps the need for better translation skills, for it leaves all crucial policy questions unresolved. To those who want to limit migration severely, a "porous border" is still a dangerously open border, after all. Meanwhile, for migrants themselves or those defending their dignity, a border that works like a membrane in which they must elude authorities in a desperate search for tiny openings is if anything all the more dangerous!

What those who speak of "porous borders" probably intend to advocate for external borders is *well-oiled gates*—reliable mechanisms that may close when necessary but also swing wide open to welcome new immigrants, asylum seekers, and refugees into deepening relationship. The oil that makes well-oiled gates work well would not be legal changes alone—though finding a political consensus to forge humane and enforceable legislation might create the tool needed to remove years of corrosion and release the locks and hinges of the gates. Rather, the oil needed to improve immigration policy would be means of communication that confirm and deepen the relationships that already exist across borders, applied through institutions by which communities offer hospitality to migrants so that they may then go on to set up their own homes. As Rajendra has argued, justice requires more than abstract principles or well-crafted laws; it requires responsibility to relationships, and that in turn requires us to understand "the particularities of the relationships binding people across borders," already, in all their messiness.[77] Citizens of the United States, for example, have particular responsibilities to peoples south of their border. Illuminating those responsibilities are the narratives of family ties, of previous guest-worker programs, of some people benefiting more than others from free-trade regimes, and yes, of past political domination and economic exploitation. Likewise, citizens of France or the United Kingdom have particular responsibilities as former colonial powers. It is the role of solidarity to continue recounting these narratives, correcting past wrongs, acknowledging historical responsibility, and cultivating ongoing relationships.[78]

Reentering the public square—as guests

Still, this is a vision and an agenda that is easier to articulate using the church's own narrative language than the body politic's language of national self-interest. So we still need to do some further translating. If I have summarized current Catholic advocacy on behalf of migrants fairly, we can affirm the important translation work it has done even while noting that its translations have often remained too rough to reach a reliable consensus, much less supply the sort of precision that policymakers and legislators demand. The problem is not the Catholic Church's long tradition of appealing to natural law, per se. The problem is that because the tradition of natural law works more like a language than an already agreed-upon consensus—much less an established body of laws—it is under-determinative at best. At worst it short-circuits policymaking because people operating from different first languages sometimes take different meanings from the same words.[79] The "right to defend" oneself or one's borders is one of those terms, for it can mean one thing within a Christian ethic of hospitality, something cognate within a cosmopolitan ethos of *human* security, but something quite different within the nation-state's ethos of *national* security.[80]

A Christian sense of our own guesthood and solidarity as a diaspora people will help preserve the accent on *human* security in our discourse, even in the public square and in conversation with officials charged with protecting *national* security. To be sure, if the conversation is truly two-way, immigration advocates will still have to address the moral status of borders and the anxieties of those who favor strong borders with smaller gates that are harder to unlock. We also cannot rule out entirely the possibility that translation will prove impossible; linguists and philosophers alike recognize that some concepts and terms are so dependent on the cultures and worldviews in which they arise as to be "incommensurable" and untranslatable. But we will only find out by trying, case-by-case.

What then would Catholic Christian advocacy on behalf of immigrants look like if we were more realistic and self-conscious about the translational character of the task? Catholics certainly do not have to start over from scratch. Yet much that we are already doing would be more coherent and likely more effective if we were to frame it precisely as translation across multiple moral languages. This will of course come more easily if we also recognize that we are already a multilingual diaspora people. Continuing to use immigration policy to illustrate, let me propose at least five practices that such a people can use effectively even when they enter the public square as guests:

1. As Duane Friesen has suggested, *Christians should always begin by being sure that they speak their own narrative language well*. In the case of immigration policy, this means that they will be most articulate and least likely to invite misunderstanding concerning the moral status of borders if they first name the place of borders within the dynamics of biblically inspired hospitality itself. It turns out that living out a Christian commitment to hospitality seriously, over time, in all its gritty reality, gives its own reasons to recognize the need for boundaries or borders, but also helps ensure that we will articulate those reasons with a particularly Christian accent.[81]

Having founded "houses of hospitality" on both sides of the Atlantic and made homes with the homeless for decades, the Catholic lay theologian Rosemary Haughton has brought care and credibility to the question of borders. Guided by and embodying the long biblical and church traditions of hospitality that we examined in the first half of this chapter, Haughton derived the place for ownership, and thus the borders that implicitly mark its purview, from out of Christian practices of hospitality—not in contradistinction to them. To be sure, borders did not have a self-evident, intrinsic, moral status for her, independent of their service to other goods.[82] If anything was intrinsic it was that hospitality itself, "even in its most restricted sense, is about breaking down barriers." After all, "To invite another person into the space I regard as my own is, at least temporarily, to give up a measure of privacy. It is already to make a breach in the division between the public and the private to create the common—and it happens in the space called home."[83]

Hospitality itself requires ownership, however, which means taking more responsibility for some things and spaces than others, and which in turn implies some kinds of borders to mark the difference.[84] Even when hosts are creating a communal space in which barriers are dissolving and guests share a growing measure of ownership, those hosts cannot do so without material capacity: "At its simplest," noted Haughton,

> I can't give a dinner party unless I can be sure that the means to cook it and the dishes to eat it off and the place where it is to be eaten are certain to be available to me. If I don't actually "own" them, then whoever does own them must make them available to me. Whether ownership be private or communal, the possibility of hospitality . . . depends on the continuity of control and availability which we ensure under the heading of ownership.[85]

What keeps "the very dangerous concept of ownership" from devolving into fearful expressions of what Haughton called "the Scrooge syndrome" is clarity as to the purpose or *telos* of ownership. "Without ownership there cannot be hospitality; but ownership becomes something different—legally, emotionally, morally—when it is governed by a question: ownership for what? And the answer is itself hospitality, of space, of ideas, of creativity."[86] Ownership is a condition for the possibility of making a home. "But the impregnable home where the only comers are clones of the hosts becomes not a home but a fortress and a prison combined."[87]

2. *Use the language of natural law to translate in* both *directions.* Haughton's analysis of the phenomenology of hospitality and owner-

ship is itself a form of natural-law discourse insofar as it attends not to revelation but to the basic structures and conditions of human life. Any such practice must certainly welcome messages from the data of wider human experience *into* a Christian worldview. Yet Haughton demonstrates that the exchange can and must also allow messages *from out of* a Christian worldview if it is truly to translate Christian moral commitments, not drown them out. Being fluent in the Catholic tradition of natural-law discourse actually allows us to give voice to some surprisingly radical insights from unexpected places. To wit, Haughton's conclusion that ownership must fulfill its purpose through a hospitality that opens common spaces for host and stranger alike in fact reiterates what Thomas Aquinas said of private property in his *Summa theologiae* (II-II.66).

Even while explaining the proper role of private property, Aquinas accepted as an opening premise that the goods of creation are common to all, given by God that human beings may sustain themselves and thrive together in community.[88] Private ownership is justified but derivative and conditional, not absolute. It is a stewardship that certainly does not transfer ultimate ownership away from the one of whom the Psalmist says, "The earth is the Lord's."[89] The justification for private property is simply that it is the best way to manage and care for what all hold in common as a gift.[90] Some may properly own more than others, but those who are wealthier may not forget either that they received their goods from God, or that God's purpose is precisely that they manage those goods in a way that serves the common good, and that they share with the poor.[91] Private property thus begins to lose its very justification when the wealthy obstruct the purpose of the created goods they own by hoarding rather than sharing. Indeed, privately held property reverts to the status of property-held-in-common in cases of "extreme" or "manifest and urgent" need, such that an apparent act of "theft" is no longer a sin, because it is not even an act that constitutes theft.[92]

The insights of Aquinas (and Haughton) help us begin to adjudicate the conflicting claims to rights that converge in border zones, because they finally allow us to narrate more carefully the moral status of borders. Although the borders of a nation-state do not in the first instance demark *private* property, they do stake a claim as to who "owns" and has responsibility for that *national* property that we more commonly speak of as "sovereign territory." Thus, everything in Haughton's phenomenology of ownership and in Aquinas's casuistry of private property and "theft" corresponds quite precisely to the purpose—but also to the contingency—of borders. If borders are not serving the shared good of humanity, they are not what is sacred; human lives are what is sacred. We may still have to determine precisely what qualifies as "extreme" or "manifest and urgent" need. But when those who are truly seeking political asylum out of fear for their lives—or even when those whose economic motives are desperate enough that they are willing to risk grave dangers in order to free their families from poverty—legal definitions should adjust to their need, not grind away their hope.

Until then, a church that follows Aquinas's natural-law reasoning may need to positively "condone" their undocumented migration after all. In other words, civil disobedience may well be required as a last resort, not only by migrants but by Christians in solidarity with them. Still, further efforts at translation may be required before we reach that point of last resort.

3. *Listen to the concerns, fears, and interests of opponents, out of a love of neighbor that extends even to "enemies," in a continuing posture of guesthood.* A consistent ethic of hospitality will reach a crucial juncture and may even miscarry when former strangers to us have so become friends that *their* "others" become *our* own others. Unless we are very mindful, we may then fail to offer appropriate forms of welcome to those we thought we once knew—those fellow citizens with whom we continue in many ways to be identified, but whose unreceptive, intransigent treatment of the former strangers-then-guests who have become our friends is now estranging us from *them*. Though Haughton did not take up this challenge directly, she clearly sensed it. Her narration of the process by which hospitality creates true homes (not fortresses), in which host and guest share a space that blurs distinctions, anticipates with great sensitivity the danger that still others then may sense:

> The history of humankind is horribly also the history of the lengths to which groups of people will go to protect the bit of ground they call home, or to regain it if it has been conquered. . . . When nations, as well as individual homeowners,

practice hospitality, they take great credit for it and also surround it with safeguards, as I have suggested, and they do this because home is about identity. Home is the place where I belong, and that belongs to me. It defines who I am. . . . Hospitality is difficult and dangerous because it threatens to weaken that sense of identity that home gives us . . .[93]

Besides, those others-of-our-formerly-other may wield power on behalf of the very xenophobia that we are trying to counter as we advocate for more hospitable policies on the part of the nation-state. Even though I hold a United States passport, if I want Americans to be more hospitable I will in some way have to be willing to recognize myself as a guest in less-than-hospitable offices and regions of "red-state America." To work from a posture of guesthood is not to cede the struggle for recognition of the dignity of migrants, however, but to work all the more effectively precisely by recognizing reality: Even when I enjoy a degree of privilege I am never fully in control; the most crucial forms of power that I exercise will have to come from somewhere else. Trying to *make* someone be hospitable will not work anyway, because then I am acting as an intruder, not a guest. And the fact that I may wish I might somehow force others to be hospitable on behalf of those with even less power or privilege than I enjoy does not mean that the just intent of my strategy will make it work. I have to offer basic human hospitality even to those with whom I profoundly disagree—listening to their concerns, fears, and other interests even as I counter their positions.[94] To do so is the very art of strategic nonviolence of the sort that Jesus taught in his Sermon on the Mount, which gives the apparently "powerless" ways to resist evil even on the part of true enemies, without resisting in kind and thus perpetuating cycles of violence and dehumanization (much more on this in the following chapter).

Pope Francis's advocacy on behalf of migrants seems to follow exactly this strategy. When he dedicated his 2018 World Day of Peace to "Migrants and Refugees" and celebrated them as "Men and Women in Search of Peace," he did not cite a stand-alone right on the part of nation-states to defend their borders. Yet he did recognize that "[l]eaders have a clear responsibility towards their own communities, whose legitimate rights and harmonious development they must ensure, lest they become like the rash builder who miscalculated and failed to complete the tower he had begun to construct."[95] By making his warning against miscalculation, Francis attended to the legitimate concerns of current citizens in receiving countries, yet did so in a way that simultaneously bent back to embrace migrants themselves.

4. *Appeal to the highest principles and most enlightened self-interests of policymakers and opponents.* Now is when the creative use of "middle axioms" becomes especially appropriate. The creativity required here must be as artistic as it is tactical and well-informed because the interests and principles that others claim will inevitably vary according to audience and constituency:

- To politicians who have staked their careers on preserving family values, one may point to the love of family that has motivated so many migrants, documented or otherwise.

- Where constituents are proud of their own immigrant pasts (as is true of many in the United States), one may point to their loftiest self-image as "a nation of immigrants," which claims to welcome "your tired, your poor, your huddled masses yearning to breathe free."

- In European countries, one may appeal to the desire of many to undo or not repeat past persecutions, or to recapitulate the heroism of those who did harbor persecuted Jews and others in World War II. In South Africa, one may likewise appeal to pan-African solidarity, or in parts of the Middle East to pan-Arab solidarity.

- In countries with aging demographics, one may appeal to the need to replenish the tax base of the safety nets that sustain retirees with medical and pension benefits.

- For those anxious to protect the jobs of current citizens, one may point to all of the ways that immigrants of all classes create new jobs, whether through fresh entrepreneurship or simple consumer demand.

None of these arguments are particularly original on my part; the point is simply to situate them. They may not constitute an advocate's own reasons for promoting more generous immigration policies or more stable regulation (that well-oiled gate). But that does not mean one is compromising one's principles or sullying one's own motivations when one appeals to middle axioms. Indeed, even if one does not entirely share all of the assumptions at work, say, in some rhetorics of "family values,"[96] these may be the points of contact available in the language of one's interlocutors, so that appealing to them may make a real difference for migrants in limbo. One's own principles are still operative in the effort to gain at least some greater measure of justice in the lives of the vulnerable.

And then, if one does achieve policy "wins," framing the entire effort as translation should help keep us grounded in our own Christian narrative at those crucial junctures in which we are invited to help implement the changes we have been calling for.[97] Those junctures are particularly pivotal, morally, because they bring all the opportunities and dangers that face a diaspora people when some among them begin to move from the margins into a posture of "working within the system" and its power centers. Here it is that they will require all of the nuance and mindfulness of Jeremiah's exiles and Daniel's companions, called as they are to remember their primary loyalty even—especially—while working as peacemakers in Babylon. After all, they may need to resist idolatry yet again.

5. *Be honest about the gaps between worldviews and anticipate the need for strategic nonviolence should one's best efforts to translate across those gaps fail.* What is increasingly clear for Catholic social teaching becomes all the clearer when we recognize it as a diaspora social ethic for a people whose "catholic" identity has always crossed borders and spanned cultures. Namely, we should be just as prepared to affirm the good of human society as to strive to correct the evils that mar it. We should look charitably on the work of those who must make imperfect decisions in order to serve the common good through vocations of governance, but be no less prepared to challenge them prophetically as we maintain a "preferential option for the poor and vulnerable" who are so often invisible inside the offices where decision makers decide. We should be just as prepared to resist what Pope John Paul II called "cultures of death" and what Pope Francis has called "the throwaway culture" as we are to befriend new cultures in accord with the commitments of the Second Vatican Council. Indeed, we should find inspiration in the very genius of the council,

which was to hold together a warm invitation to the modern world with tough love, as is necessary in any true friendship. Thus we should avoid the temptation to despair—either for theological reasons or simple cynicism—that institutions or governments might better embody God's justice, since they too share in the goodness of God's creation. But we should also avoid being lulled into assuming that they are already doing fine, especially when either we as individuals or the church as an institution have come to share in the privileges of the status quo.

As New Testament scholar Walter Wink summarized so well, the powers that be (1) are good, (2) are fallen, and (3) must be redeemed.[98] Without ever demonizing or giving up on those who do not yet profess faith in Jesus Christ, or who do profess Christ but fail to recognize the shape of the Reign of God he came proclaiming, we must be realistic. Good-faith efforts to translate Christian moral commitments into other ethical systems and narratives will sometimes fail; we should hardly be shocked. Instead, we should be prepared for civil disobedience, other forms of nonviolent action, and a full range of just-peacemaking practices. Developing such a repertoire will allow the church to work more effectively from outside "the system," or from its margins, as well as from the inside. We might even think of this full and agile range of practices as the diplomatic tools by which the church as a transnational nation conducts its foreign policy—except that living in diaspora among the nations makes it the church's domestic policy as well.

Conclusions

The five practices I have listed for translating the moral commitments of that pilgrim people called church into public policies—using immigration as an especially salient case study—are certainly not an exhaustive list. Toward the end of the following chapter we will in fact pick up where we have just left off and lay out ten normative practices of just-peacemaking theory at greater length. What is certain is that the methodology evident here is not a one-size-fits-all formula or an abstract set of norms so much as a habit of deep engagement with others, by which well-formed peacemakers seek both to form the whole church to be a pilgrim people of peace, and, from out of that blessing, to bless all the families of the earth.

A formula would be impersonal, but Cardinal Peter Turkson, president of the Vatican's Dicastery for the Promotion of Integral Human Development, has defined justice as requiring something more, for it means "to respect the demands of the relationships in which we live."[99] Rajendra has applied the relational anthropology that grows from this biblical understanding of justice to the issue of migration, precisely because any adequate ethic of migration "must be able to respond to the complex and messy relational reality that characterizes migration."[100] All this is true of all Christian peacemaking, however. Christians have a long tradition to rediscover in order to train ourselves more fully to live in diaspora. But as a pilgrim people, we are already there. What is true of nomads, exiles, guests, pilgrims, and resident aliens alike is thus true for the church: Peace, safety, and security come through the strength of those relationships by which we perpetually negotiate and renegotiate the management of goods—not the strength of our weapons or the height of our walls.

Chapter 8

Escaping Our Vicious Cycles[1]

> Peacebuilding through active nonviolence is the natural and necessary complement to the Church's continuing efforts to limit the use of force by the application of moral norms; she does so by her participation in the work of international institutions and through the competent contribution made by so many Christians to the drafting of legislation at all levels. Jesus himself offers a "manual" for this strategy of peacemaking in the Sermon on the Mount. . . .
>
> This is also a programme and a challenge for political and religious leaders, the heads of international institutions, and business and media executives: to apply the Beatitudes in the exercise of their respective responsibilities. It is a challenge to build up society, communities and businesses by acting as peacemakers. . . . Certainly differences can cause frictions. But let us face them constructively and non-violently, so that "tensions and oppositions can achieve a diversified and life-giving unity," preserving "what is valid and useful on both sides."
>
> I pledge the assistance of the Church in every effort to build peace through active and creative nonviolence. . . .
>
> —Pope Francis, World Day of Peace 2017, §6

The fresh reappraisal of war in the modern world that the Second Vatican Council called for is well underway. In his 2017 World Day of Peace message, Pope Francis continued that process of churchwide discernment as he built on the work of predecessors and responded to Catholic peacebuilders and activists,[2] while recognizing the role of policymakers and diplomats even as he urged that "active and creative nonviolence" become our "style of politics for peace." Consistent with Pope John Paul II's insistence that peacemaking is essential to the vocations of all the faithful,[3] Francis not only identified "peacebuilding through nonviolence" as "a programme and a challenge for political and religious leaders," but he even included "the heads of international institutions, and business and media executives" in that calling. The qualities in Jesus' Beatitudes of meekness, mercy, peacemaking, purity of heart, and hunger and thirst for justice that open the Sermon on the Mount (Matt 5–7) must in all cases characterize "the exercise of their respective responsibilities." After all—posited Francis in a theological move at once stunning and subtle—the "manual" that Jesus has given the church to guide its strategy of peacebuilding at every level is the Sermon on the Mount itself.[4]

Against the backdrop of what Francis called a "horrifying *world war fought piecemeal*" across the globe, the pope insisted that violence cannot be a "cure for our broken world."[5] After all, it inevitably perpetuates cycles of suffering and retaliation even when used "at best" to counter other violence. In contrast, "When victims of violence are able to resist the temptation to retaliate, they become the most credible promoters of nonviolent peacemaking." This is the courageous, life-giving, and creative nonviolence that Jesus lived and taught as the way to break free from chains of injustice. This active kind of nonviolence is not simply for some simpler first-century setting, for "Jesus himself lived in violent times." Nor should it be falsely confused with "surrender, lack of involvement and passivity," but is instead a "radically positive approach." To illustrate, Francis cited examples of how the "decisive and consistent practice of nonviolence has produced effective results" in campaigns by the Hindu Mahatma Gandhi, the Muslim Khan Abdul Ghaffar Khan, the Christian Dr. Martin Luther King Jr., Liberian women led by Leymah Gbowee, and in the fall of Communist regimes in 1989 Europe, where Pope John Paul II himself played a role. Citing his predecessor, Pope Benedict XVI, Francis especially reminded Christian readers that for them, "nonviolence is not merely tactical behaviour." It responds with a person's entire "way of being" to God's love as it reciprocates by extending such love even to enemies. As Benedict went on to say and Francis now underscored, Christlike love of one's enemies "constitutes the nucleus of the 'Christian revolution.'" As such, and on the world's stage, not just in Christian hearts, nonviolence is "more powerful than violence."[6]

Highlighting the power of gospel nonviolence in this way indicated how far the Catholic Church had come in its reappraisal of war, yet Francis also pointed toward a continuing area for discernment as he affirmed a complementarity in the church's work for peace:

> Peacebuilding through active nonviolence is the natural and necessary complement to the Church's continuing efforts to limit the use of force by the application of moral norms; she does so by her participation in the work of international institutions and through the competent contribution made by so many Christians to the drafting of legislation at all levels.[7]

Now, anyone who reads Catholic Church documents learns to recognize a certain kind of savvy rhetorical strategy. The Vatican's carefully finessed language may sometimes be frustrating in its nuance, but can also serve to balance considerations and forge consensus in a complex global community. Pope Francis was thus exercising an appropriate Vatican savvy by alluding here to the possible use of "just-war" criteria, yet he left the theory unnamed—for the moment, neither rejected outright nor defended. What Francis did name instead is the space that the Vatican and Catholic moral traditions have hoped the "just-war" theory would fill. Yes, "just-war" theory has long provided the framework for those efforts of the church to "limit the use of force by the application of moral norms." Indeed the just-war framework has helped build the architecture for international law along the way. Francis's sentence might thus seem to validate its continued use. And yet the papal restraint that left "just-war" theory here unnamed also recalls the unease that once prompted Cardinal Joseph Ratzinger—later Pope Benedict XVI—to wonder out loud whether "today we should be asking ourselves if it is still licit to admit the very existence of a 'just war.'"[8] After all, Francis was not done here.

While affirming that the space for church engagement in international diplomacy and public policy work stands in a mutually supportive relationship with active nonviolence, what Pope Francis did next in his World Day of Peace message is breathtaking. For it is precisely here where he insisted that "Jesus himself offers a 'manual' for this [integrated] strategy of peacemaking in the Sermon on the Mount." The full weight of the message's title thus bears down: gospel nonviolence guided by the Sermon on the Mount is supposed to be a "style of *politics* for peace." It is not just for the personal lives of particularly saintly Christians, but is intended to guide the vocations of politicians, business and media executives, and heads of international institutions. It applies to the public realm.

Further still, Francis's very choice of the word "manual" is a most intriguing one. "Manualism" was the neo-scholastic mode of Catholic moral deliberation ascendant from the seventeenth century until the Second Vatican Council. Drawing on St. Thomas Aquinas's carefully reasoned reflection on the natural law, the manualist mode sought to rival Enlightenment rationalism. Whatever its virtues, it tended therefore to de-emphasize biblical sources and thus offered a comfortable home for "just-war" casuistry.[9] To now, instead, call the Sermon on the Mount the church's manual for peacemaking hardly seems an accident.

Can the gospel really be our "manual"?

One could trace centuries of ethical debate among Christian thinkers by following a thick central thread of contention over whether Jesus' Sermon on the Mount can be such a straightforward manual for *any* tough moral issue. Among all such issues, the justifiability of killing and the possibility of enemy love has often been paradigmatic. Christians appealing to an alternative authority in order to give reasons why they might legitimately override the words and example of Jesus have most often appealed to some version of "natural law" or a theological account of what is "realistic." At its best the impulse for this move has been a desire to name shared moral norms that might be accessible to those in positions of public responsibility. In order to reappropriate Jesus' teachings and live out the virtues he held up in his Beatitudes—even while "thinking with the church" as it draws on centuries of experience facing difficult moral challenges—we need therefore to accept that challenge and explore how Jesus' radical call to a distinct way of being in the world might actually be *realistic*.

Historically, the Catholic Church may never have *explicitly* denied the applicability of Jesus' teachings to public affairs.[10] It has not officially endorsed a view like that of the leading 20th-century Protestant thinker Reinhold Niebuhr. Niebuhr bluntly argued that while human beings might *barely* be able to practice Jesus' ethic or "law of love" in a small face-to-face community or *Gemeinde*, Jesus' teachings could never apply to complex, modern, industrial societies—much less the international arena where the rough justice of a balance of power and national self-interest is the best we can hope for.[11] And yet, the working Catholic tradition has in effect taught exactly that for centuries, by drawing almost entirely on natural-law categories to address public affairs, and by sometimes relegating Jesus' "hard sayings" to "evangelical counsels" for those with special vocations calling them to holiness.

With a "universal call to holiness" by the Second Vatican Council, this started to change. That call came in the context of related developments. In the twentieth century, first among theologians, then with the endorsement of the council, and then among the faithful, Catholics have been rediscovering Scripture. In moral theology, that has not only meant taking a fresh look at the relevance of biblical sources rather than natural law alone, but it has meant supplementing abstract principles with a fuller account of how Christians grow in virtue as they let the narrative shape of Jesus' life and the lives of the saints shape the pattern of their own lives. With its universal call to holiness, then, the council implicitly abandoned longstanding Catholic tendencies to assume that different vocations for laypeople and clergy or others in consecrated religious life implied that only some Christians are expected to follow Jesus as disciples through those "evangelical counsels."

But then, one way or another, the church's teachings on war and peace would also have to begin changing. One could thus draw a direct line from the council's call to holiness in its 1964 dogmatic constitution *Lumen Gentium*,[12] to the council's praise in *Gaudium et Spes* a year later for those who renounce using violence to vindicate their own rights in an act of personal holiness,[13] to the growing recognition of active nonviolence in public affairs since John Paul II's *Centesimus Annus*,[14] to Francis calling the Sermon on the Mount the church's manual for peacemaking. The council's universal call to holiness was a massive tectonic shift, a slow-moving earthquake, and Catholic moral theology as well as pastoral practice are still trying to recover their footing. Francis's calling the Sermon on the Mount our manual for all peacemaking was one more tremor.

The clue for recognizing this move as more than mere idealism, and the mandate for drawing upon a fresh way of interpreting and receiving Jesus' words, is the attention Francis gave in his World Day of Peace message to *vicious cycles*. What he calls the "horrifying world war [being] fought piecemeal" in the twenty-first century results from "countering violence with violence," over and over. The pope certainly did not deny that war may sometimes respond to injustice and attempt to counter it. Yet, he asked, "Where does this lead? Does violence achieve any goal of lasting value?" No, it leads "to retaliation and a cycle of deadly conflict" rather than any "cure for our broken world." That is why "the force of arms is deceptive." Gospel nonviolence is the truly revolutionary alternative, therefore, because "responding to evil with good" rather than "succumbing to evil" by responding in kind means "thereby breaking the chain of injustice."[15]

Christians long locked into the standard impasse between pacifism and just-war theory have begun to find common ground in recognizing that even putatively just wars plant the seeds for new wars. Meanwhile, groundbreaking literary analysis of the Sermon on the Mount demonstrates that Jesus was not simply giving his disciples idealistic "hard sayings" either to stretch them to do at least a little better morally, or to convict them of sin that they might turn to God in forgiveness. Rather, in teaching after teaching, he provided realistic and practicable guidance for escaping vicious cycles. In this context, even the difficult challenge of loving our enemies turns out to be relevant—politically relevant.

This, I will argue, is the way to receive Francis's stunning claim that the Sermon on the Mount is the church's very "manual" for peacebuilding. By attending to vicious cycles of violence and what it takes to escape them, Christians may also be able to escape the standoff over war that has left them vacillating between "idealism" and "realism"—between the church's call to holiness and growth in virtue, and effective action in our complicated and often unforgiving world. That standoff would not have long endured if both sides in the centuries-long debate between Christian pacifist and just-war thinkers did not have strong arguments, so we cannot expect to escape it if we do not learn from what we hope to transcend.

The theological case for principled nonviolence

The case for thoroughgoing, principled, Christian nonviolence is not based on Jesus' teachings alone, much less the Sermon on the Mount alone. It is not—in other words—simply the result of quasi-fundamentalist "proof-texting" of the sort that first reads the Bible literalistically and then applies it legalistically. A stronger case for Christian nonviolence lies in the entire trajectory of life and ministry that gave Jesus' words their context and meaning. In the life, death, and resurrection of this obscure rabbi from Nazareth, Jesus' followers would come to find a cipher revealing the very character of God and thus the deepest reality of the cosmos. If anything, the doctrines of Incarnation and the Trinity that they formulated in subsequent centuries in order to name that reality constitute the strongest case of all for the power and principle of nonviolence—though the grammatically negative term *"non*violence" cannot do justice to its dynamic. It is, after all, completely of a piece with the entirely orthodox Christian conviction that God's strength reveals itself most fully in *apparent* weakness.[16] According to this conviction, the hope of Israel and the Savior of the world has come to us in the very vulnerability of human flesh, then suffered the most gruesome and humiliating of deaths. In the cross and resurrection Christians believe they recognize God's victorious power over evil. The "lamb that was slain" was the one who unlocked the scroll of history (Rev 5:1-10); the faithful themselves were participating in this victory "by the blood of the Lamb and by the word of their testimony," even at risk of death (Rev 12:10-11).

In the church's very first proclamation on the day of Pentecost, what Peter most needed to explain was God's totally unexpected vindication of a totally unexpected way of messianic liberation.[17] You encountered Jesus of Nazareth for yourself, Peter reminded his listeners. Nazareth was a backwater town in an outlying province, an unlikely source of greatness. Yet God had "attested" to him with "deeds of power, wonders, and signs." Jesus' deeds of power— Peter's listeners would have recalled—were acts of healing and feeding and compassion for outcasts, not military prowess. Even so, his ministry and teaching were threatening enough that Jewish and Roman authorities had conspired to end it with the exclamation point of crucifixion.[18] "But God raised him up, having freed him from death, because it was impossible for him to be held in its power" (Acts 2:24). Turning to texts from the Hebrew Scriptures, Peter argued that for this Jesus to turn out to be the messiah should not have been altogether surprising. Of course, Peter himself had required the vindication of resurrection and illumination by the Holy Spirit to fully comprehend Jesus' identity.[19] Now, however, "[t]his Jesus God raised up, and of that all of us are witnesses" (Acts 2:32). The message of God's act of vindication was that God was showing "this Jesus" who had been crucified to be "both Lord and Messiah" (Acts 2:36).

Kyrios Christos—Jesus Christ is Lord. This basic confession recurs at the core of other earliest proclamations and hymns embedded in New Testament texts. Its simple formula may even constitute the earliest Christian creed. In any case, it is prominent among a cluster of confessional affirmations that filled it out and gave it its intelligibility. Centuries of repetition have now turned "Lord" into what might merely seem an honorific title, so that we easily miss its revolutionary claim. In the Septuagint, the Jewish translation of the Hebrew Scriptures into Greek, *Kyrios* was the word that ancient Jewish scholars had used for *Elohim*. *Elohim* in turn was the word that pious Jews spoke in place of the holy revealed name for God, *YHWH*. Applied to Jesus, the unmistakable resonance of the title *Kyrios* bespoke the ground-spring of what soon became orthodox Christian creedal affirmation—that Jesus is not just from God but *is* God incarnate, the Word of God made flesh, Second Person of the Trinity.

For to say—as Peter reportedly did on the day of Pentecost—that God was acting in history to reveal Jesus of Nazareth as "both Lord and Messiah" (Acts 2:36) was to make an extraordinarily powerful claim not only in its Jewish context but in its Roman setting as well: To proclaim that "Jesus Christ is Lord" meant that *this* one—crucified according to the most gruesome and humiliating of deaths, a death reserved for traitors and thus fraught with political overtones, but then vindicated by resurrection—this one is (of all people!) the true *Kyrios*. It was to say that the idolatrous Roman emperor whom his subjects called *Kyrios*, or Caesar, decidedly was not. To be sure, many

Jews had been longing for God's Messiah to displace the Roman overlord, not to demonstrate a new and paradoxically non-domineering form of lordship. So to say that *this* one was the Messiah or Christ was to say that God was fulfilling the hopes and longings of the Jewish people in a way that initially dismayed even Jesus' closest disciples. None less than Peter himself, after all, had tried to dissuade Jesus when he began to warn his disciples of his impending death; Peter and other disciples too were looking for a military uprising that would install the Messiah Jesus as a conventional ruler—with them as his lieutenants![20] For these Jewish disciples of Jesus to turn around, post-Pentecost, and proclaim the crucified Jesus as *Kyrios* was to critique the covert idolatry of their earlier nationalism, which might have relished the sacrifice of their enemies' lives in a military victory exalting their own national and ethic identity over all Gentiles. The resurrection and outpouring of the Holy Spirit had opened their eyes; Christianity now moved out into the Gentile world offering God's faithfulness toward the children of Abraham to all nations. As they did so, their very use of the confession "Jesus is Lord" in turn became an affront to idolatrous Roman claims on behalf of the emperor who also called himself *Kyrios*.

To argue, then, that the strongest case for Christian pacifism begins in the core theological convictions of orthodox Christianity is not to dismiss other arguments for the thoroughgoing renunciation of violence, but to locate them properly. Aided by the politically savvy development of Gandhian nonviolence in the twentieth century among social scientists such as Gene Sharp, Erica Chenoweth, and Maria Stephan,[21] advocates for nonviolence have strong arguments to make about which strategies of social change, peacebuilding, and security are most effective. But these are secondary supporting considerations, for Christian pacifism does not finally rest on utilitarian arguments about "what works." Staking its ultimate claim on the character and ways of God, whose power and wisdom the apostle Paul identified precisely with the cross that seems so foolish to human beings (1 Cor 1:18-25), Christian pacifism can also go on to make a kind of natural law argument about ways in which "people who bear crosses are working with the grain of the universe."[22] Yet Christian pacifism is amenable to "natural law" argumentation only if Christians take care to integrate "nature" and "reality" in the light of Jesus rather than subjecting Jesus to preexisting categories of the natural that we have developed autonomously, apart from Jesus.

Certainly, anyone who cares about victims of violence and oppression must care about effectiveness in the pursuit of concrete results. According to Luke 4, Jesus inaugurated his ministry in his hometown synagogue at Nazareth by identifying himself with God's promise in Isaiah 61 that the anointed one would bring a message of truly "good news to the poor," would "proclaim release to the captives and recovery of sight to the blind, to let the oppressed go free, to proclaim the year of the Lord's favor." Such goals had their spiritual and transhistorical dimensions, yet were not *merely* other-worldly. How then to achieve them in history?

Jesus did not even announce the goals of his ministry in Luke 4 until he had first faced and rejected three temptations in the wilderness that upon close examination turn out to coincide with the ordinary stuff of politics in its standard forms.[23] Luke and the other gospels make clear that Jesus' encounter in the wilderness was only a preview of the very real political options that would tempt Jesus throughout his ministry—when he miraculously fed the people and they wanted to make him into their own kind of king; when he dramatically entered Jerusalem to cleanse the temple but did so on a humble donkey rather than a war horse. Above all, right when his closest associates expected him at last to marshal a violent insurrection, he refused to kill for the justice of his cause, dying for it instead.[24] The reason is not that his ministry was apolitical or unmoved by cries for justice and liberation, but that Jesus was opting for a qualitatively different kind of politics. His would be a truly original revolution because it broke with the cycles of violence by which one regime after another throughout history has promised justice but recapitulated patterns of unjust domination as they sought their ends through violent means.[25]

But what if you win?

The problem that Christians faced in subsequent centuries was not that gospel nonviolence proved ineffective and failed, but that it succeeded.[26] The challenge is comparable to that of social-change movements today. The more that social-justice advocacy succeeds, the more it invites a reciprocal invitation to participate first in policymaking and then in governance. And in every human community I have ever encountered, governing requires some kind of enforcement, coercion, or policing, even if it is nonlethal policing through social sanctions. One option for avoiding the dilemma has been principled anarchism, which seems to offer a way to impact the larger society perpetually from the margins, through perpetual prophetic critique and small-scale local alternative patterns of life. But this only defers rather than avoids the challenge. For one must either abandon all hope that anyone else will actually listen or else must anticipate the question, "So will you help us do what you've been calling us to do?"

As I have observed or participated in various social movements over four decades—reformist and revolutionary, violent and nonviolent, Christian and secular—neglect for this question has often been the great lacuna that has tripped them up. Working from the margins and struggling against hopelessness, they often have reason to be cynical about established institutions. For those absorbed in the urgent tasks of resisting unjust powers that be, the task of specifying how they would actually exercise power in order to enact the changes they are calling for often feels like more of a luxury than it is. Along the way, an oppositional or "prophetic" stance may become so much a part of their identity that it serves as the only psychological home in which they feel comfortable, and the "compromises" they might have to make in order to actually run things all come to feel like selling out.

Scholars have explained the changes that Christianity underwent as it moved from a motley gathering of fearful disciples in an upper room in Jerusalem to a movement whose growing numbers and influence forced the Roman Empire to accommodate it in a number of ways. Those who question the decision of fourth-century church leaders to accept not only legal toleration but imperial patronage and eventually the status of official religion believe Christians were slowly seduced by power and lost the nerve they needed to challenge imperial violence and oppression. Those who are grateful for recognition and cooperation with civil authorities, then and now, point to the delay in Jesus' promised return (or *Parousia*), which required Christians to settle back into ordinary life in the world and take up responsibilities for which Jesus seems to have given them little ethical guidance.[27] But all such explanations are plausible, and actually more so, if we recognize an overarching dynamic and the issues it poses.

Every social movement comes to a watershed if it actually wins, and its leaders must decide whether and how to govern the changes for which they have been calling. Christianity came to such a watershed in its fourth century. Though the tributaries flowing through that watershed were complex, the name of a single historical figure often marks the entire era. When the Roman Emperor Constantine legalized Christianity in 313, inserted himself in church affairs, and accepted baptism shortly before his death in 337, his policies required Christian bishops and theologians to rethink both their relationship to state power and the question of whether Christians may properly wield its sometimes violent tools. Constantine himself may have delayed baptism in part because he continued to recognize the sword-bearing responsibilities of an emperor as incompatible with Christian faith and life.[28] Yet Christian leaders were soon saying otherwise—celebrating the ascendancy of Christians into the ranks of civil authority and rationalizing Christian participation in the military.

Christian thought has divided ever since over whether the Constantinian settlement constituted a victory or a betrayal. In Eastern Christianity, Constantine is a saint, and though the Roman Church has never canonized him, a feast day on the church calendar celebrates the basilica in Rome that he offered to the church. Pacifist Christian traditions, however, often use the term "Constantinianism" as a pejorative for the close cooperation of church and state that they consider a centuries-long mistake, if not an outright betrayal resulting in "the fall of the church." If a consensus exists, it is that Christianity was in fact steadily winning over the Roman Empire and defeating the pagan religious ideology that undergirded it; the open question for debate, then, becomes what to do next at such a juncture.

The conscientious case for just-war exceptions

Rules are certainly valuable. To be sure, what should ultimately shape the moral coherence of any Christian community, or animate any life of discipleship within it, is encounter with the person of Jesus Christ as known through the rich narrative of God's revelation within history and his re-presentation in the sacraments. But on any given day, amid any stressful situation, it is helpful to have encapsulated key implications of this encounter into simple guiding maxims. For example, I do not need to rehearse all my reasons for seeking to live a life of integrity every time I need to act if I am remembering certain basic rules: "don't cheat" the wait staff in a restaurant; "don't lie" to my colleagues by taking undeserved credit for a project. Likewise, while my marriage vow was to a person not an idea, it entailed a commitment of faithfulness that is partially summarized in the commandment, "Thou shalt not commit adultery." Internalizing that rule strengthens my relationship with the person and may do more in a moment of temptation to reinforce my resolve than recalling a lecture on sexual ethics (even if I was the lecturer). In just this way, it has not only been understandable but valuable that many Christians committed to following Jesus have sought to preempt any option for violence by encapsulating the lessons of his life and teaching into a succinct and absolute prohibition against the shedding of blood. In this sense it has been fair though potentially misleading for some moral theologians and philosophers to characterize Christian pacifism according to just such an absolute rule.

When gospel nonviolence as embodied in Jesus' entire life trajectory is seen mainly as a teaching or rule, however, puzzles ensue—and then the working out of puzzles invites the making of exceptions. The classical puzzle goes like this: As a follower of Christ I should be committed to love my neighbor with a self-sacrificial preference for his or her needs that both imitates Jesus and rules out violence. Should that neighbor turn against me, become my enemy, and attack, he or she remains God's beloved whom I am still called to love, and thus return good for evil, as Matthew 5:38-48 and Romans 12:14-21 remind me. But what if I have two such neighbors, and one of them is attacking the other? Even if I not only know in principle that I should love my neighbor's enemy, but actually feel that love deeply, should love for the one not compel me to do all I can to protect the vulnerable one from the violent one? True, "do all I can" may first include risking my own body by interposing it between the two, looking for ways to deflect and defuse the aggression, and so on—nonviolently. But it is not indisputably obvious that physical threat, coercion, and counterattack might not be required to stop the aggressor in the end. Hence the puzzle.

And hence, faithfulness to the command of love does not preclude the challenge of justice, but invites it, as one discerns how to respond to many neighbors at once, prioritizing their needs and ordering our responses. In chapter 3 we encountered Augustine's influential framework for analyzing all relationships and hence all moral decisions according to four kinds of love—for God, for temporal goods, for neighbor, and for self. Neither his claim nor mine was that one could simply plug a pending decision into this framework and watch it fall like a marble in an antique marble roller into an unambiguous slot. Indeed, the lesson in chapter 3 was that even as Augustine demonstrated that Christlike love must stretch beyond the proximate love of family, tribe, local community, or land and thus elicit solidarity with distant neighbors, Augustine remained both unsettled and unsettling concerning those neighbors who are distanced through enmity—adversaries and enemies. We thus see his critical role in the Christian development of just-war theory emerging as he worked out a version of the classical puzzle about how a Christian can love multiple neighbors when some of them are also enemies.

Strikingly, Augustine remained as skeptical of violent acts of *personal* self-defense as any early Christian.[29] Prominent Christian thinkers would later treat the right of personal self-defense as a given, at least after Thomas Aquinas explicitly broke with Augustine.[30] But Augustine's position was bluntly opposed: "I do not approve of . . . killing human beings for fear that one might be killed by them," he wrote to Publicola in 398, "unless one is perhaps a soldier or is obligated by public office so that he does this, not for himself, but for others or for the city where he himself also lives, after he has received lawful authority, it is appropriate to his person."[31] While Augustine had jumped here from the simple case of one person defending one neighbor from a third, to the still more complex situation in which one person is charged with protecting the common good of many neighbors, his underlying principle is clear: lethal force is not permissible for oneself but may be, in some conditions, on behalf of others.

The just-war theory was a way to enumerate those conditions in greater and greater detail. Moral theologian David Hollenbach, SJ, has thus characterized Christian just-war thinking as "a theory of *exceptions*" to the "general obligation of nonviolence.[32] Depending on the Roman Stoic thinker Cicero for systematic enumeration,[33] the details of Augustine's own guidance tended to emerge piecemeal in pastoral contexts as he corresponded with Christian leaders in positions of civil and military authority—sometimes reassuring them of their vocations,[34] sometimes helping them synchronize their duties with biblical injunctions,[35] and sometimes pleading for leniency toward those in their power.[36] Detailed elaboration by Christian thinkers would come with Thomas Aquinas in the eleventh century,[37] and would begin to shape modern international law as Francisco de Vitoria used just-war criteria to critique the Spanish conquest of the Americas in the sixteenth century,[38] for example, or as the Calvinist Hugo Grotius sought a framework to avoid wars of religion in the seventeenth.[39] Augustine did however lay the basis for a Christian just-war tradition as he named overall requirements like just cause, legitimate authority, and the right intention to achieve peace and security for a community.[40]

Today the criteria for determining whether a war or military operation is justifiable are organized into two or three groups,[41] with Latin phrases serving to name them.[42] When is it just to go to war? These are *jus ad bellum* considerations. How is war to be waged justly? These are *jus in bello* considerations. How must warriors and their leaders plan for restoring peaceful relationships and rebuilding from the outset? These are *jus post bellum* considerations that scholars have been developing and debating in recent decades in recognition of the failure to plan well for actual peacemaking in the aftermath, especially of the United States' war in Iraq.[43] This third category is still being standardized, but a pastoral letter from U.S. Catholic bishops, *The Harvest of Justice Is Sown in Peace*, tabulates the first two with both brevity and thoroughness:

First, whether lethal force may be used is governed by the following criteria:

- *Just Cause*: force may be used only to correct a grave, public evil (i.e., aggression or massive violation of the basic rights of whole populations);

- *Comparative Justice*: while there may be rights and wrongs on all sides of a conflict, to override the presumption against the use of force the injustice suffered by one party must significantly outweigh that suffered by the other;

- *Legitimate Authority*: only duly constituted public authorities may use deadly force or wage war;

- *Right Intention*: force may be used only in a truly just cause and solely for that purpose;

- *Probability of Success*: arms may not be used in a futile cause or in a case where disproportionate measures are required to achieve success;

- *Proportionality*: the overall destruction expected from the use of force must be outweighed by the good to be achieved;

- *Last Resort*: force may be used only after all peaceful alternatives have been seriously tried and exhausted.

These criteria (*jus ad bellum*), taken as a whole, must be satisfied in order to override the strong presumption against the use of force.

Second, the just-war tradition seeks also to curb the violence of war through restraint on armed combat between the contending parties by imposing the following moral standards (*jus in bello*) for the conduct of armed conflict:

- *Noncombatant Immunity*: civilians may not be the object of direct attack, and military personnel must take due care to avoid and minimize indirect harm to civilians;

- *Proportionality*: in the conduct of hostilities, efforts must be made to attain military objectives with no more force than is militarily necessary and to avoid disproportionate collateral damage to civilian life and property;

- *Right Intention*: even in the midst of conflict, the aim of political and military leaders must be peace with justice, so that acts of vengeance and indiscriminate violence, whether by individuals, military units, or governments, are forbidden.

For all the value of careful deliberation, what too easily gets lost as criteria allowing policymakers to "override the strong presumption against the use of force" receive more and more detailed exposition is the impulse that requires that care—the forest that the study of trees may actually obscure. What Augustine did to launch the Christian development of just-war thought was to make this critical move: Love for one neighbor might require an exception from the usual way that one respects the dignity even of an enemy. But any such exception would have to be truly exceptional because Augustine still recognized the enemy as a neighbor whose treatment constituted the ultimate test of neighbor-love.[44]

Indeed, the continuing pull of Jesus' teaching to love our enemies is a far more persistent theme in Augustine's reflections than his later reputation might have it.[45] Some blame Augustine's Platonism for distorting his theology and biblical interpretation, but in key ways, his philosophical orientation also buttressed his biblical commitments. Platonic teaching concerning a cosmic hierarchy of goods led to the conclusion that bodily preservation was not an ultimate value, and it warned him against grasping after temporal goods.[46] This in turn meant that "in no way at all can your raving enemy do more harm than you do to yourself, if you don't love your enemy" and by such a failure of love "do damage to your soul."[47] Besides, the enemy might turn out to be a future brother and fellow citizen in the heavenly city, for whom the Christian should be prepared to undergo all kinds of suffering.[48] In the hope of such conversion, Augustine even seems to have intuited some of the power of nonviolent suffering to evangelize and transform enemies while thwarting cycles of violence: "Every righteous and pious person, then, ought to be ready to endure with patience evils from those whom he wants to become good in order that the number of the good may rather increase and that he may not add himself by an equal sinfulness to the number of the evil."[49]

Learning to think like Jesus[50]

If the Sermon on the Mount has *not* served as our "manual" for peacemaking, that is arguably because of a widespread, longstanding, understandable, yet no less misleading approach to its interpretation. *We have read it in twos, not threes*—as a series of stark binaries, dyads, or antitheses rather than as triads. Admittedly, a drumbeat of contrasts does set the pace in Matthew 5: "You have heard it said . . . but I say unto you. . . ." Six times. The ready impression is that Jesus' goal was to set a really high bar with a series of nearly impossible ideals: don't even be angry, don't even lust, don't take any oaths, don't even resist an evildoer, love even your enemies and persecutors without discrimination, thus be as perfect as your Father in heaven. Jesus must have thought that these high bars would at least make us jump a little higher, we conclude—before we despair. To be a manual for politics, business, and peacemaking at every level, the Sermon on the Mount must be practical, and all this sounds noble but it isn't very realistic, we say. Practical morality must look instead to common sense, or natural law, or the utilitarian necessity wherein "you do what you gotta do" and ask forgiveness later. So goes the standard interpretation of the Sermon on the Mount as it vacillates between idealistic rigorism and a moral despair that calls itself realism.

In a widely accepted exegesis of the Sermon on the Mount, the late Christian ethicist Glen Stassen has demonstrated otherwise.[51] It is no accident that Stassen was also the force of nature who led a group of Christian ethicists and political scientists from both historically pacifist and historically just-war churches in developing and advocating for "just-peacemaking theory."[52] The project reflected wider efforts to reframe Christian ethics in response to war and violence in some kind of "just-peace" or "just-peacemaking" framework,[53] and has become one of the most influential. Biblical exegesis and efforts to forge a new ecumenical consensus emerged side-by-side in his original 1992 book on just peacemaking.[54] In the wake of the Cold War, he then drew other scholars into a wider just-peacemaking project that seized on the opportunity to identify how, realistically and empirically, an unexpected measure of peace had broken out. Key both to the practicability of the Sermon on the Mount and to contemporary just-peacemaking practices are the power of *transforming initiatives* that break us out of *vicious cycles* of violence and sin in ways that the *traditional righteousness* "you have heard it said" cannot do.

Notice the triad I have just named. This threefold pattern of teaching is most identifiable in Matthew 5, but Stassen convincingly showed it to structure Matthew 6 and 7 as well, in a series of fourteen triads. With only slight and explainable variations that are the exceptions which prove the rule, Jesus *first* named the *traditional righteousness* that his Jewish listeners had heard either from rabbis or popular morality, *then* diagnosed the *vicious cycles* from which traditional righteousness could not escape, *and then* offered realistic, practicable *transforming initiatives* to escape those vicious cycles at last. Sometimes the triads are more obvious than other times; sometimes they come with anomalies that turn out to be revealing in themselves. But ultimately the pattern holds with remarkable consistency and an ability to resolve long-standing interpretive puzzles. Yes, they had heard it said, and yes, Jesus now said unto them. But what Jesus then said unto them in his own distinct teachings came in a second, then third, part. And—how did we miss this for centuries?—in Greek his imperatives consistently came not in what we hear as hard sayings but in that third part, the transforming initiative. This is where the accent was to be for his disciples. This is where the accent should be for the church, in all its teaching and programming.

The first of the fourteen triads that Stassen identified in the Sermon on the Mount illustrates well both the triadic literary pattern and its practical ethical import. The Matthew 5:21-26 passage is the first of the fourteen teachings that constitute the long central portion of the Sermon, and it demonstrates the issues and pattern most transparently. If we see in the 5:21-26 passage a *two*-part teaching that places Old Testament teachings against murder on one side of Jesus' "but I say to you," and then places a radically interiorized prohibition against anger on the other side, many standard difficulties in interpreting and applying Jesus' teachings surface immediately. It is a sign of these problems that when editors of modern translations want to add non-canonical subtitles, they do not even know how to label this passage. Is it about murder? That is what verse 21 seems to announce. Then Jesus shifts our attention to anger and name-calling, and we hear Jesus saying never to be angry at all. But then we start to protest: *That's impossible! In fact, Jesus himself got angry.* The gospels themselves report this.[55] So what is the paragraph really about? Such difficulties are only the beginning.[56]

We are starting to dismiss Jesus' teaching before we have even gotten through half of the first triad! If we do continue reading, a dyadic interpretation will have to assume that the latter half of the passage about promptly seeking reconciliation is some kind of illustration, rather than the point of the whole teaching. In fact, if we were not so hasty we would notice that Jesus never actually gave the imperative, "don't ever get angry." Nor did he threaten hell fire upon those who fail. Rather, his phrase was, "if you are angry." *If* you are angry, judgmental, and insulting, certain things will logically follow. You are setting up a standard of judgment to which you yourself will be liable. By implication, so too will those who judge you. Unchecked, the ensuing cycle will spiral from an interpersonal "calling out," to a community council, to the ultimate judgment you are inviting from God. This is not a threat. It is simply a description of how things work, a diagnosis of a vicious cycle. There is certainly nothing wrong with the ancient injunction against murder. But in and of itself that traditional righteousness "said to those of ancient times" does not come with guidance about how to avoid the conditions that lead to temptation, hypocrisy, and recrimination, much less an ultimate breakdown of human relations through fratricide.[57]

If our habit were to expect a climactic third element in the outline of Jesus' teachings we would anticipate his gracious guidance. Giving that practical guidance is Jesus' primary concern, and a triadic exegesis puts the accent back where his intention lay: *Take the initiative to seek out the one whom you have offended. Don't wait! Leave the altar itself if necessary! Get going, and don't drag your feet.* The imperatives—six of them—now come quickly, "staccato-like."[58] In other words, take the initiative—the initiative that will free you from vicious cycles of resentment, anger, counterjudgment, and potential violence—that will transform your relationship through reconciling practice. In teaching "as one having authority" (Matt 7:29), Jesus has placed the accent here.

Practical grace

Turning to the two triads at the end of chapter 5 that also relate to violence and enmity, we find the Hebrews' functional precedent for Christian "just-war" attempts to regulate and delimit warfare encapsulated in "an eye for an eye and a tooth for a tooth," the so-called *lex talionis*. This expression of traditional righteousness was certainly an improvement over the code of Lamech that promised a seventy-sevenfold retaliation against any threat, exponentially upping Cain's promise of a sevenfold retaliation (Gen 4:15, 23-24). Likewise, in "Love your neighbor, hate your enemy," we have traditional background assumptions at work when any tribe or nation prioritizes self-defense over everyone else's good. As crassly tribalistic as that formula sounds, we can recognize that it too is an obvious improvement over Cain's fratricide of his own brother, Abel (Gen 4:1-16). But an eye for an eye for an eye and a tooth for a tooth for a tooth still perpetuate the cycle of violence.

The vicious cycle that Jesus diagnoses is implicit not only in the eyes and teeth but in Jesus' alternative response: *mē antistēnai tō ponērō*. The famous phrase in Matthew 5:39 about how to respond in the face of evil has often been translated in a way that is easily dismissible as totally passive nonresistance: "Do not resist evil," or a little better, "Do not resist the evil one." But a far better translation recognizes the dative Greek word behind our English word "evil" not as substantive but as instrumental, and renders the phrase: "Do not resist *in an evil way*."[59] In other words, do not respond *in kind*. Cycles of reciprocal retaliation were also implicit in Paul's take on Jesus' teaching in Romans 12: "Do not repay anyone evil for evil. . . . Do not be overcome by evil but overcome evil with good." Older than the Gospel of Matthew, Paul's letter to the Romans is probably citing the oral tradition that initially conveyed Jesus' teaching, and in any case fits the context of the Sermon on the Mount perfectly: Jesus diagnoses the vicious cycles from which traditional righteousness will not extricate us. An eye for an eye, after all, can easily issue in an endless cycle of retaliation, or more likely escalate, despite the best efforts of those who apply the *lex talionis* in hope of checking violence with mathematical equity.

So how to escape? After naming the traditional righteousness of the *lex talionis* and underscoring its limits, Matthew 5:38-42 concludes with Jesus' three famous teachings to turn the other cheek, go the second mile, and give freely. Stassen has hardly been alone among recent interpreters who see those three practices not as passive nonresistance but as prototypical examples of active nonviolence that transform conflict by humanizing oppressor and oppressed alike.[60] Examined closely in their first-century social context, offering the left cheek specifically in order to stand as an equal, giving up one's cloak in order to shame a loan shark in what was probably a debtor's court, or going a second mile when a Roman soldier pressed a subject under occupation into service, were all ways to transform the power dynamics of oppression through social creativity. Jesus was actually giving the oppressed ways to resist but not in kind, not violently, not hatefully.⁶¹ For Jesus' immediate audience these were potent, recognizable examples of those trickster smarts that the folktales of oppressed peoples of many cultures celebrate: Anansi the spider in West Africa, Br'er Rabbit in Afro-Caribbean and African-American cultures, Loki in Scandinavia, and Jacob for the ancient Hebrews. Like those of classic tricksters, Jesus' tactics evened the power without giving the oppressor excuses to smash them. For us they are prototypes for the creative strategies of nonviolent action we have to invent for our own historical junctures.⁶²

In Matthew 5:43-48 on love of enemy, one anomaly is that the order of the last two elements of the triad is reversed. Stassen speculated that Matthew placed the transforming initiative of love for enemy ahead of the vicious cycle in this triad in order to signal the climax of the subsection of the Sermon that contains its first six triadic teachings. And this makes sense. Emphasizing Jesus' call to transcend the vicious cycle by which we tend merely to love those who love us in return highlights precisely the way in which Jesus has fulfilled, and would have his disciples fulfill, the Law and the Prophets (Matt 5:17-20). Traditional righteousness as passed down and developed since Moses is wise and good and affirmed so far as it goes, but Jesus has prompted us to empathize more widely and imagine more creatively.

Another *possible* anomaly is that when Jesus names the relevant item of traditional righteousness—"You shall love your neighbor and hate your enemy"—the latter half of this saying seems not to come from Hebrew Scriptures at all but from the Essene community of Qumran, and perhaps from popular Judaism as well. And, of course, the teaching on love of enemies that Jesus is introducing would seem to rule out any hatred of enemies whatsoever. Still, to honestly study the Scriptures as authoritative means to grapple with uncomfortable texts and allow our study to lead us where we might not wish to go. The basic principle of interpreting texts in context places a very heavy burden of proof upon us if we wish to claim that the Matthean Jesus was building affirmatively upon traditional righteousness each of fourteen times—except one. Furthermore, we are ignoring evidence if we try. Although the phrase "hate your enemies" does not appear in the Hebrew Scriptures per se, the sentiment surely does.⁶³ It is not just that the imprecatory psalms, for example, serve a cathartic function by letting the faithful get out of their system a desire to cast their captors' babies against the rocks (Ps 137:8-9). It is that hatred of enemies is held up as a positive sign of pious identification with God's justice and God's cause, as for example in Psalm 139:19-22.

Such sentiments do not have the last word, of course. But we ought at least to ask whether hatred of enemies, too, might in some way do the usual work of traditional righteousness in the Sermon on the Mount, by laying groundwork for liberation from vicious cycles, through transforming initiatives. We should not confuse Jesus' call to love our enemies with a naive sentimentality that suggests a faithful Christian disciple will never have any enemies in the first place. The best way to destroy one's enemies may well be to make them our friends. But a friendly disposition still has to do the hard, honest, and sometimes confrontational work of transforming the actual reality of enmity. It is in this sense that anger, revulsion, and repudiation of everything associated with an evil—including evildoers themselves, at some transitory psychological level—arguably should function as traditional righteousness even for Christian pacifists and other practitioners of active nonviolence. At the very least, even if *we* are seeking to respond in our own lives to Jesus' call to transcend every such elemental, unloving, and less-than-compassionate response to evildoers, Christian peacebuilders are coming to recognize that they dare not shut down such responses in *others* prematurely. Forgiving dare not mean forgetting, and truth-telling is a condition for reconciliation. The survivors of genocide and human rights abuse who most need to voice the truth about how they have been violated, after all, may initially do so with deep tones of hatred. We may long, pray, and gently work for the day when grace breaks through and survivors are able to disassociate evildoer from evil. But other tasks often come before such reconciliation that may only be eschatologically possible anyway.[64]

If Stassen's exegesis required him to account for a few anomalies and do some reading between the lines, commending it is a capacity to solve far more irregularities and long-standing interpretive puzzles.[65] Thanks to its explanatory power, Stassen's exegesis of the Sermon on the Mount has been quite well received among biblical scholars.[66] His exegesis also points toward ways of solving some of the most abiding puzzles in the field of Christian ethics. His exegesis rescues Jesus' teaching from the idealism that so often gets it dismissed as impracticable, unrealistic, or simply a series of hard sayings that serve to set up some other theological point. As we will see, it offers a way to reintegrate the Catholic Church's call to grow in holiness through the practice of biblically inspired virtues with its tradition of reflection on natural law. Stassen's triadic exegesis may initially have looked like a technical matter of literary analysis, but by showing that Jesus was placing the accent of his teachings on transforming initiatives, Stassen has done nothing less than point us back to the seamless unity in Jesus' teachings. The gracious deliverance without which there can be no proclamation of good news must be God's initiative and ultimate doing alone; this is not about "works-righteousness." Yet Jesus' ethical teachings, in fulfillment of Torah, are no less integral to God's deliverance. And so too are the practices of discipleship by which Christians participate in God's salvation.

The political relevance of enemy love

"Love your enemies" (Matt 5:44) is not simply a high-minded principle, then. Jesus has fleshed it out with practical guidance that offers us transforming initiatives and the promise of real-world deliverance from cycles of retribution. The overarching pattern helps explain what is going on when *any* just-peacemaking practice takes risks, but thus takes the initiative, in ways that break out of vicious cycles. To recognize the power and priority of transformative initiatives, we need to recognize the power of all kinds of cycles of social reciprocity both to capture us through vicious cycles and to liberate us through virtuous cycles—which is precisely what transforming initiatives aim to initiate.

Catholic social thought works from a core assumption about what makes us human: The human person is constituted through relationship. Certainly the dignity of every individual human being is bedrock to Catholic social teaching, as Pope John XXIII insisted in his 1961 encyclical, *Mater et Magistra*: "This teaching rests on one basic principle: individual human beings are the foundation, the cause and the end of every social institution."[67] And yet those individual persons are never atomized in an "individualistic" sense. For as Pope John immediately continued, all humans "are by nature social beings," and necessarily so.[68] A few years later the Second Vatican Council reaffirmed this core assumption: "Human dignity rests above all on the fact that humanity is called to communion with God."[69] God has in turn imprinted that call to "communion between persons" onto humanity, which was created in relationship from the very beginning, as reflected in the archetype by which "'male and female he created them' (Gen 1:27)."[70] Thus, an "individual" can never really be simply *individual* for—as Pope John Paul II constantly quoted the council— human beings "can fully discover their true selves only in sincere self-giving."[71] After all, "[l]ife in society is not something accessory to man himself" but rather is intrinsic, such that persons can only thrive "through mutual service, and through fraternal dialogue."[72] As Francis has more recently noted, "The very mystery of the Trinity reminds us that we have been created in the image of that divine communion, and so we cannot achieve fulfilment or salvation purely by our own efforts."[73] Indeed, there can be no more profound grounding for this core assumption than Christian trinitarian theology, for if God has from all eternity been a community of three persons in subsistent relationship, and humans are created in God's image, we are not human beings before we enter into relationship, but are human beings because relationships have made us so.[74]

Mimesis has made us human (for better and worse)

Reciprocity, in other words, is formative; virtuous and vicious cycles together have made us who we are. But one hardly needs to rely on theological assertion alone to affirm this. A foundational school of thought within classical social psychology, lately receiving fresh confirmation through the emerging field of neuroanthropology, helps explain why. If the social theorist George Herbert Mead was on to something roughly a century ago,[75] that is, or the neuroscientist Merlin Donald[76] and the sociologist Robert Bellah[77] have accurately been filling out details in the last few decades, then the reciprocal processes of social mirroring known as *mimesis* not only generated language and culture among early human ancestors, but mind and self-consciousness themselves.[78]

According to these theorists, self-consciousness began in a "conversation of gestures."[79] Though only instinctively at first, our hominid ancestors recognized danger in some other creatures, and comfort or collaboration in others. It was not that the dog or the chimp or the early human *decided* upon flight or fight, much less determined to glare or snarl in response. Yet at some point, as brains evolved in size and complexity, our ancestors surely noticed that the gesture might substitute for the act. Threatening gestures had always been more efficient than actual aggression; coos might reassure an infant from a distance. To notice that one's own growl was similar to the other's growl opened the possibility of self-consciousness. To notice that one's cowering in response to the threatening growl of an enemy resembled the cowering one hoped to elicit in that enemy further deepened self-consciousness. To then anticipate and choose such gestures deliberately rather than instinctively was to begin to *signify*— to create and project intended meaning through kinetic action and raw vocalization. Such signification was a long way from language, to be sure, and whether language emerged early or late in the process remains a matter of dispute.[80] But to deliberately signify at all, even if purely through gestures, required one to see oneself being seen, or hear oneself being heard. As we began to become objects to ourselves, self-consciousness and indeed *self* were emerging.[81]

Sociality and culture were thus constitutively prior to self or self-consciousness.[82] Cognitive reflexivity, after all, required a social matrix within which the self could recognize itself. As Mead explained, while the subject "I" is certainly more than the object "me"—insofar as emerging consciousness creates a center of deliberative reflection and action that is more than simply the totality of roles that one's social group expects of the "me"—nonetheless the "I" can only emerge through the "me," by becoming aware of itself as perceived by others.[83] Notice, though, that every time we speak of a conversation of gestures, or reflexive self-recognition, or mimetic action, or even simply "meaning," we are naming or at least alluding to a cycle of human interaction, whether vicious or virtuous.[84]

While vicious cycles can ultimately prove destructive, they nonetheless played a powerful role in the building of civilization and the deepening of culture. To be sure, not all formative mimetic action would have been aggressive. If our hominid ancestors were like modern primates, they spent far more time in reciprocal grooming and interactive childcare than they did fending off predators or fighting with rivals. Toolmaking was undoubtedly a group project; passing on the sophisticated art of chipping the proper stones at the best angle for producing sharp edges required mimetic pedagogy down through the generations, over many millennia. (While much neuroanthropologic theory must necessarily proceed by speculative theorizing, prehistoric stonecutting is one practice that has left behind hard evidence. Anthropologists attempting to replicate the art have largely failed at reproducing tools and weapons of equal quality, but thus succeeded at demonstrating the skill required.[85]) Still, it is striking how often scholars find in the aggressive mimesis of predators and rivals their paradigm case for explaining human origins.[86]

Indeed the ancients did so themselves, in their own more mythological way. Coming from the very era when nomadic culture was giving way to settled civilization through agriculture and hierarchical divisions of labor in Mesopotamia four millennia ago, the Sumerian Gilgamesh Epic may well be the world's oldest surviving work of literature.[87] In its first story cycle, Gilgamesh the semi-divine king of Uruk does battle with his opposite, Enkidu the wild animal-man. Nearly fighting to a draw, Gilgamesh wins but knows he has met his equal. Having come to respect one another, he and Enkidu become fast friends. In the process, both, in differing ways, are humanized. Through friendship with an equal, Gilgamesh finds relief from his solitude and becomes less tyrannical, while Enkidu learns to shave, wash, and eat cooked food.[88] As a modern rendering puts it, once the two are exhausted as competitors, each is able see himself in the other.[89]

Yet now that they are equals and friends, Gilgamesh and Enkidu seem to need some new enemy in order to cement their friendship. They determine to do battle against Humbaba, whom they describe as evil but whom the gods favored as protector of sacred groves of trees. When the elders of Uruk counsel that it is imprudent to transgress sacred boundaries, Gilgamesh insists that he must prove his strength and win an enduring name for himself. When Gilgamesh actually encounters Humbaba for the first time he seems to recognize that the gods are using the monster as a slave for their own purposes. Gilgamesh must thus resist the temptation to pity and spare him, for his goal is now clear—to make the servants of the divine serve humanity instead, in order to build towns from the sacred![90] And so he does, and yet the tragic poignancy of the trade-off is evident as the

Escaping Our Vicious Cycles 263

elders' warning is eventually fulfilled. When Gilgamesh continues to defy the gods, they send the Bull of Heaven against Gilgamesh. In the ensuing battle, his comrade Enkidu is killed. The remaining story cycles play out the sense of tragedy as a grieving Gilgamesh quests in vain for secret life-giving means to restore his friend to life.

In other words, the identification or even the outright creation of enemies offers a certain reprieve from in-group violence, which often passes for peace, as mimetic rivalry within one community vents itself and seals camaraderie through fear of some outsider—then another—always another. René Girard's further insight was that often these outsiders are actually insiders made into scapegoats, and likely they are innocent scapegoats besides.[91] In any case, whatever actual or manufactured threat that enemies pose, they have consistently provided the occasion for human beings to build up civilization through vicious cycles of oppositional bonding. Yet vicious cycles vitiate even otherwise virtuous cycles of friendship. Such a peace is always fragile at best. And this is not simply the inevitable fragility of mortality and vulnerability. It is a fragility we build into our cultures and social systems, at some level knowingly, as the tragic poignancy of the ancient Sumerian myth challenges us to admit to ourselves.

The possibility of social creativity

Still, and more hopefully, mimetic theory also demonstrates why social creativity, too, is possible. Mimesis is not simple imitation; it does not leave us locked into endless replication of inherited patterns. Against more deterministic schools of thought, the theorists I am citing not only allow for but expect that mimesis will issue in innovation. Even among pre-linguistic early humans, Donald has noted, "a purely mimetic culture can evolve. Mimetic acts are expressive and thus inherently inventive and creative."[92] Paradoxically, doing the expected more self-consciously under-determines the expected. As Mead explained: "The very taking of . . . expected steps puts [a person] in a certain situation which has a slightly different aspect from what is expected, which is in a certain sense novel. . . . Now, the attitudes he is taking toward [others] are present in his own experience, but his response to them will contain a novel element."[93]

This process is especially obvious in the great change agents of history—Mead named Jesus, the Buddha, and Socrates as examples.[94] These are "geniuses" of mind and character not simply in terms of brainpower, but insofar as they take in the attitudes of their society so deeply that they are able both to embody the whole of the community and to envision, then demonstrate, how it could transform. "These are the conditions," noted Mead, "under which that seeming paradox arises, [in which] the individual sacrifices himself for the whole which makes his own life as a self possible."[95] *All* conscious minds live "at the cognitive cutting edge of culture," Donald has clarified; "[t]his is true of everyone, not only of geniuses." But those who most clearly represent "the strange phenomenon we call 'genius'" demonstrate both what makes them notable and why they must always be part of a larger social movement in order to have their effect:

> Geniuses travel inside the same knowledge vortex as everyone else, and the current state of that vortex may fix the possibilities available to each generation, but only geniuses can realize those possibilities. Under the right circumstances, the cognitive resources of an entire culture can become concentrated inside a single mind, and this can bring about an awesome concatenation of forces, like those giant hurricanes observed over the Caribbean that focus huge energies on a tiny geographic point.[96]

Recognizing the dynamics of mimetic processes, then, allows us to recognize why the Niebuhrian commonplace—that those who would seek to follow Jesus' teachings by loving their enemies must thereby render themselves politically irrelevant—seems both so obvious *and is so misleading*. To love a community's enemy will never enjoy broad political support; this is nearly a truism. And yet in times of crisis, creative initiatives that embody enemy love may be precisely what the social order needs in order to become more fully itself according to its best emerging values, to discover win-win solutions, or even to survive. Loving *sentiments* toward enemies may be quite optional here. What matters is to break out of vicious cycles of regard merely for one's own kind, through precisely the salvation-historical transforming initiative that Jesus introduced when he taught "love your enemies" in Matthew 5:43-48, doing so according to practical strategies drawn from the paradigmatic transforming initiatives of Matthew 5:38-42.

Love of enemies may seem like the most unattainable of the virtues to which Jesus pointed in Matthew 5—even more difficult than the Beatitudes. Yet it is also the most powerful and fundamental, for it breaks the deep and ancient vicious cycle that the Gilgamesh Epic so poignantly represents, by which rivals within one community forge friendship, camaraderie, and a measure of social peace only by uniting against outsiders whom they join in fearing. Lest "love your enemies" simply comes to us as a "hard saying," Jesus has bent the arc of history and civilization by stretching our imaginations with four simple rhetorical, yet revolutionary, questions:

> For if you love those who love you, what reward do you have? Do not even the tax collectors do the same? And if you greet only your brothers and sisters, what more are you doing than others? Do not even the Gentiles do the same? (Matt 5:46-47)

Meanwhile Jesus has also flustered the casuist by upending the very definition of neighbor and making an outcast Samaritan the model for imitation if one wants to claim to be following the God-given moral code of any people that believes itself chosen. Within its setting, the so-called Parable of the Good Samaritan (Luke 10:25-37) offers a *virtuous* cycle of reciprocity aiming to break out of a *vicious* cycle. The distress of the wounded man on the road to Jericho calls out the empathy of the Samaritan. Jesus then holds up the Samaritan's example in order to evoke the empathy and neighborliness of the lawyer who had come to question him. The closed vicious cycle of only recognizing dignity or need among one's own kind thus spirals out into virtuous cycles of potential solidarity within wider circles of human community—at least in the centuries of retelling, whether or not for the lawyer who initially interrogated him.[97]

To practice love for aggressive, hateful, life-threatening enemies is obviously harder indeed, yet, if anything, all the *more* politically creative. The Israeli martyr for peace Prime Minister Yitzhak Rabin once stated what should be obvious: "You don't make peace with friends; you make it with very unsavory enemies." On the really tough issues where one's society most needs to escape its vicious cycles, *only* those who practice unsentimental love of enemies may be the relevant, socially responsible ones. And by offering us concrete, prototypical, transforming initiatives, Jesus has freed us from sentimentality. As Martin Luther King Jr. said of his nemesis, "Bull" Connor—the infamous police commissioner in Birmingham, Alabama, who turned police dogs and fire hoses on civil rights protesters, including children—one did not have to like him to love him as a misguided child of God.

Nor is the power of transforming initiatives only evident in heroes of Christian nonviolence such as King, or in local, face-to-face settings. While the prototypes we find in the Sermon on the Mount inevitably come from first-century Palestine, once we begin to discern their dynamic, we will recognize their power at work even at the highest level of international affairs. Whether Nixon subjectively loved Mao Zedong is as immaterial as it is doubtful; the phrase "Nixon-to-China" and the dynamic it represents has found a place even in popular culture.[98] Egyptian President Anwar Sadat likewise launched the Egyptian-Israeli peace process by announcing he would visit Jerusalem. Nelson Mandela won the grudging respect of white South Africans and averted the bloodbath that most expected would come in the wake of apartheid by mastering the art of the unexpected gesture; among the most vivid was his appearance at the 1995 Rugby World Cup finals, during a critical phase of the political transition, wearing the jersey of the white South African team despite its long association with apartheid.[99]

The manual for peacemaking that is the Sermon on the Mount is accessible and translatable even in geopolitics, then. For when a movement or figure we least expect does the unexpected, the mimesis that sets up vicious cycles starts to spiral off into a virtuous cycle instead.[100] More often the unexpected comes not from leaders on the world stage but from the apparently powerless, who as Francis noted, "resist the temptation to retaliate, [and thus] become the most credible promotors of nonviolent peacemaking."[101] Yet this power is not inaccessible anywhere on the sociopolitical map. A Christian may narrate it as the power of the Gospel at work in a world that only dimly acknowledges the Gospel at best. Whatever domestic and geopolitical reasons Nixon might have had for tapping unwittingly into that power, the church has more and better reasons for nurturing the creativity and imagination needed to recognize openings for transforming initiatives sooner and more consistently. That nurturing—that stepping into the breach—is where the church should be investing its resources and taking its own risks.

Just-peacemaking practices

The weight of this book has been on ecclesiology and the formation of Christians as a people of peace. One reason is that it may often be less urgent to identify actions, tactics, strategies, and policies to counter injustice, defuse violence, or nurture peace than it is to find peacemakers who have been formed in the virtues that prepare them to practice peacemaking. And yet the question of *what to be* can never ignore the question of *what to do*.

If we survey the ten "normative practices" that Glen Stassen and his colleagues have commended in their "just-peacemaking theory" for their empirically demonstrable, realistic track records, we may discern the role of modern transforming initiatives in all of them. While their project has been a translation into practices and policies that are accessible in the public square without constant reference to biblical sources, Stassen's exegesis of the Sermon on the Mount is always visible just under the surface as the conceptual foundation for that project of translation, and on at least one occasion, he made the cross-references explicit.[102]

1. *Support nonviolent direct action.* (Cf. Matt 5:38-43.[103]) Strategic nonviolence appears first on the list of just-peacemaking practices for good reason. Done well, boycotts, strikes, marches, civil disobedience, public disclosure of wrongs, accompaniment of the politically vulnerable, and the creation of safe spaces are not simply pressure tactics.[104] Echoing Jesus, they are ways to resist evil but not in kind. They are fresh and creative ways to redirect the social forces at work in one's historical moment (what nonviolence strategist Gene Sharp called "political jiu-jitsu") in order to expose injustice for what it is and turn the violence of the opponent into reasons for more and more erstwhile bystanders to withdraw their consent and shift their support.

2. *Take independent initiatives to reduce threat.* (Cf. Matt 5:38-43.[105]) This just-peacemaking practice demonstrates the power of Jesus' transformative initiatives even for those with no particular commitment to principled nonviolence, even in the sphere of geopolitics. Nixon going to China is but one example. Trust-building gestures to suspend nuclear testing or the production of certain classes of weapons were the key to unlocking arms reduction talks between the United States and the Soviet Union at various junctures. Prisoner releases and partial withdrawals from occupied territory have likewise brought adversaries to the table in regional conflicts.[106]

3. *Use cooperative conflict resolution.* (Cf. Matt 5:21-26.[107]) When parties are locked in conflict, their relationship may not be particularly "cooperative," much less enemy-loving. The art of back-channel negotiators who get them to the table, and the skill of mediators who lead them toward win-win solutions, is to initiate a transformation from limited self-interest to mutual recognition of shared interests. With or without sentiment, this is love of enemy at work in a way that we may not immediately recognize, but only because it is so concrete, so nuts-and-bolts.

4. *Acknowledge responsibility for conflict and injustice and seek repentance and forgiveness.* (Cf. Matt 7:1-5.[108]) Nothing sustains complex historical conflicts so much as mutual recrimination. After decades if not centuries of violent self-defense, all parties to a conflict are likely to have committed injustices or crimes, and all adversaries will thus have reasons to blame the other. As hard as it is for individuals to confess sins and ask forgiveness, it is harder still for groups and nations. Yet doing so, whether publicly or in behind-the-scenes negotiations, has sometimes been the key move that has led to historic peace accords, as when Germany's Chancellor Willy Brandt knelt silently at the Warsaw Ghetto Memorial in 1970 in repentance for Nazi crimes against the Polish people,[109] or Guatemalan insurgent and military representatives rescued failing talks in Norway in 1990 by beginning to admit their mistakes.[110]

These first four just-peacemaking practices demonstrate the character of Christian peacemaking by means of transforming initiatives especially clearly. The dynamics are proactive, as practitioners do their part without letting other parties' blame excuse them. They recognize the dignity and legitimate interests of enemies without approval for dysfunctional positions and wrongful acts. They confront in a way that is invitational rather than destructive, thus strengthening relationships and drawing into community. And as a full reading of *Just Peacemaking: The New Paradigm for the Ethics of Peace and War* would confirm, they are all historically based and empirically validated.[111] But though the role of transforming initiatives may be subtler in the remaining just-peacemaking practices, similar dynamics are crucial nonetheless:

5. *Advance democracy, human rights, and interdependence.* (Cf. Matt 6:19-34.[112]) Jonathan Schell has described the liberal democratic state as a systemization of nonviolence, as people resolve to arbitrate their disputes through politics rather than warfare.[113] Note that such a resolution requires a prior commitment to recognizing others as legitimate claimants whose good is interdependent with those of oneself and one's own kind. A darker take on democracy may well be that it is war by other means—a barely civilized struggle for power in which the only outcome approaching peace will at best be a crass balance of power. Yet a minimal step beyond the clannishness by which "the Gentiles" do no more than "greet only [their] brothers and sisters" is necessary even so. To haltingly begin to respect enemies rather than merely "love those who love you" will bring the "reward" of more robust democratic norms of mutual benefit to all.

6. *Foster just and sustainable economic development.* (Cf. Matt 6:19-34.[114]) Attention to human-oriented markets and poverty alleviation within environmentally sustainable economies belong in any just-peace moral framework as basic to the social conditions that make for peace. But a transforming initiative is at work here too insofar as economic development necessarily encourages virtuous cycles of win-win exchange. Greater recognition of the interconnection between human ecologies and the natural world, as Pope Francis called for in his encyclical *Laudato Si'*, can itself be transformative. Taking the long view about the social and environmental conditions that make for peace—we might add—may well be how the meek inherit the earth.

7. *Work with emerging cooperative forces in the international system.*[115] Globalization, almost by definition, is the most complex human process ever. So while many of its dimensions have been inequitable and culture-eroding, it also carries with it technologies allowing for greater cooperation and, through them, webs of solidarity. Any effort to reinforce the positive dimensions of globalization over the negative ones is an opportunity to extend our circles of moral regard beyond our own kind. As Christians heed Jesus' provocative initiative calling his followers to do more than "even the Gentiles" do, they should welcome and support every sign that the "Gentiles" themselves are doing more, with deepening respect for one another, to institutionalize just and peaceable human relationships.

8. *Strengthen the United Nations and international efforts for cooperation and human rights.*[116] If work for just and peaceful social change is to be sustainable, practitioners must welcome rather than begrudge the need eventually to institutionalize the changes they have been calling for. We saw earlier that Christian pacifism is most vulnerable insofar as pacifists have often been reticent to accept the challenge of just governance at precisely the juncture in which they win, thus requiring themselves to perpetually celebrate prophetic marginality that, in isolation from governance, risks incoherence. Of course, the just-war tradition has too often devolved into crude forms of governance that lose sight of other forms of power and neglect any social conditions necessary for peace other than physical security. Just-peacemaking theory and other just-peace frameworks demonstrate their potential to transcend both respective limitations by anticipating the challenge of just governance. To continue strengthening international institutions is to draw upon the first four transforming initiatives, and to draw together the fifth, sixth, and seventh.

9. *Reduce offensive weapons and weapons trade.* (Matt 26:51-52.[117]) Much national and international institutionalization—however necessary or even welcome for the basic infrastructure it now provides to the benefit of human thriving—has nonetheless emerged through vicious cycles like that of Gilgamesh and Enkidu, who formed their bonds of civilization through battles that required the identification of enemies and the manufacture of scapegoats. We do not have to deny the limited truth that political "Realists" voice when they point

to ways that the threat of mutually assured destruction or combustible balances of power on regional scales bring a measure of "peace." This is the precarious and shadowy imitation of peace that Augustine said was the best that the "earthly city" has to offer. When the risks inherent if such vicious cycles spin out of control have become as risky as they are in the modern world, to risk the transforming initiative of arms reduction alone may not bring the peace of the heavenly city—but will nonetheless be a service that helps the earthly city at least to save itself from itself.

10. *Encourage grassroots peacemaking groups and voluntary associations.* For any of these just-peacemaking practices to take shape in history, we need the most basic transforming initiative of all—the formation of people who will "be the change they seek in the world." This foundational work of formation is essential to fulfilling the mandate of recent popes for all the Catholic faithful to confirm their vocation as peacemakers and builders of justice, in collaboration with other Christians and all people of good will.[118] Grassroots peacemaking-as-*people*-building is always more than "community organizing" alone. Done in faith, hope, and love, it participates in God's own great transforming initiative, launched through Abraham, as God blesses one particular people but always with a view toward how they are to become a blessing to all nations. As Archbishop Hélder Câmara of Brazil used to preach so energetically, beyond any mere coalition is the

> greater and no less indispensable alliance being forged between those minorities that I call "Abrahamic." They already exist; it is not necessary to create them. The Spirit of God raises them up deep within every race, in every religion, every nation, every human group. Who belongs to these Abrahamic minorities? All those who, like Abraham, hope against hope and decide to work to the point of sacrifice for a more just and humane world.[119]

Even Augustine, who did so much to bring Roman just-war theory into the Christian tradition, had to acknowledge the power of nonviolence done in faithfulness to Jesus' teachings. Writing to his friend the Roman tribune Marcellinus no less, and having just discussed Matthew 5:38-48, Augustine concluded: "Every righteous and pious person, then, ought to be ready to endure with patience evils from those whom he wants to become good in order that the number of the good may rather increase and that he may not add himself by an equal sinfulness to the number of the evil."[120] The power of gospel nonviolence lies precisely in its capacity to change the social dynamic between adversaries through virtues that were more valuable than anything the enemy might seize. So too with every transforming initiative to escape our vicious cycles.

An afterword on natural law

To identify the Sermon on the Mount as the church's "manual" for peacemaking at every level should not require Catholic thinkers to abandon their tradition of reflection on the natural law. But it does require them to look deeper into the natural law through a Christic lens. Since the natural law is supposed to be accessible to all people of good will through reliance on reason alone, without reference to the data of revelation, such an effort may seem self-contradictory. But any such objection confuses the act of discovering what is already present in reality or nature with the discipline-bound experiences and presuppositions that allow the perceiver to perceive what others might miss.

At its *best*, the natural-law tradition as Catholics have practiced it has instantiated a commitment to finding common arenas of discourse with other worldviews. Differing religions, cultures, and philosophies may have distinct reasons for articulating common principles that they trust are written into realities that were true before anyone knew them, except—arguably—God. The object of our knowing is set in stone, so to speak, but our knowing must be subject to refinement, correction, and extension through time and history. To read the natural law through a Christic lens is simply to be honest about the Christian conviction that humanity's encounter with God through the person of Jesus Christ is the very hinge of history. But to posit a natural law should mean that humbly we also invite a feedback loop that allows the best data and wisdom of human experience back into a Christian theology or worldview itself.

To state matters in reverse, the natural-law tradition at its *worst* begins with triumphalist certainty about where common ground with other worldviews will be found, *a priori*, without actually exploring the terrain in dialogue with others. And the first whom triumphalism may exclude is our ultimate Other, the divine outsider incarnate who has intruded on the space that human beings have been so intent on controlling for themselves. Claims to a self-evident and natural right of self-defense will then serve to defend ourselves against *Him*. In other words, claims to know the natural law already, apart from Jesus of Nazareth, may backfire not only by allowing "natural law" to trump his claims, but by disqualifying the disconcerting claims of still others out of hand, apart from the discomforts of dialogue. To recognize "the Godhead grown weak by sharing our garments of skin"—in Augustine's extraordinary words from *Confessions* 7.18.24— "heals [the] swollen pride and nourishes [the] love" of those "humble enough to grasp the humble Jesus." Without vulnerability to the nonviolent Jesus, in other words, we may thus preempt adequate discernment of the natural law.

At minimum, the natural law should not be conceived of statically. New findings from social science, neuroscience, and in our case neuroanthropology, should allow us to discern new dimensions of natural law, to gain fresh insight into Scripture, and to draw the two into a lively and mutually illuminating conversation that is welcoming to still others. If such an encounter also enriches Christian praxis, well, by now we are allowed to hope for virtuous cycles.

Chapter 9

Normative Nonviolence and the Unity of the Church

> We agree that the Gospel's vision of peace includes active non-violence for the defence of human life and human rights, for the promotion of economic justice for the poor, and in the interest of fostering solidarity among peoples. . . .
> We hold the conviction in common that reconciliation, nonviolence, and active peacemaking belong to the heart of the Gospel. Christian peacemaking embraces active nonviolence in the resolution of conflict both in domestic disputes and in international ones, and for resolving conflict situations. We believe that the availability of such practices to individual groups and governments reduces the temptation to turn to arms, even as a last resort.
> [We] agree that discipleship, understood as following Christ in life in accordance with the teaching and example of Jesus, is basic to the Christian life. . . . Christian communities have the responsibility to discern the signs of the times and to respond to developments and events with appropriate peace initiatives based on the life and teaching of Jesus. . . .
>
> —*Called Together to Be Peacemakers:*
> *Report of the International Dialogue between the Catholic Church*
> *and Mennonite World Conference*, §§178–81

Our calling and our tasks are really quite clear.
Catholic social teaching throughout the Vatican-II era concerning war and peace has insisted with growing clarity that active nonviolence is normative for all Christians. Normative nonviolence requires

that the focus for Christian discernment and action must be first and ever foremost on the steady and proactive "just peace" or "just-peacemaking" practices that create conditions for peace. It means that we dare not even begin to imagine justifying wars as a last resort unless our churches, communities, and indeed our nations have developed capacities that make strategic nonviolence our first, second, tenth, twentieth resort—as logically was supposed to be true in the classical just-war tradition anyway. It means that if military action actually is justifiable in truly exceptional cases—and I am only stipulating here, because I remain skeptical[1]—just-war deliberation and action will look more like just-policing than warfare.[2] But all this then means that what churches have most to do is catechesis and the formation of peacemakers.

For if Catholic social teaching and peace theology is increasingly clear, and if leading representatives of Christian pacifist and just-war traditions share an unprecedented level of historical consensus concerning the peacebuilding practices that are normative for both, then our task shifts back away from the formulation of peace theory, just-policy, or just-peacemaking strategies by specialists. As important as those tasks will always be, as we get better at them our primary task reverts more and more to a basic pastoral one—to render peacemaking "churchwide and parish deep." Our task is to form ourselves more and more as a catholic people of peace, who identify our primary citizenship within that transnational nation called church. This is a people living in diaspora among many nations, in service to the common good of all other families of the earth, precisely to the degree that our first loyalty is to the Christ who calls us to solidarity with one another and to the love of neighbor that extends beyond every tribalism and nationalism, even to enemies.

Even so, one lingering doubt will surely remain. Because it is a doubt that could have snagged us yet again in the centuries-long impasse between just-war and pacifist Christians over whether killing other human beings is ever justifiable, it is a doubt that I have deferred. For some it remains a necessary question, however, which we cannot defer indefinitely. Namely, can Christians who are prepared to kill or support killing—even if only exceptionally—and those who like the second-century Christian apologist Tertullian believe that "the Lord in disarming Peter unbelted every soldier," recognize one another as fellow Christians?³ By affirming the complementary legitimacy of Christian traditions of active nonviolence and just war, Catholic bishops, as well as official representatives of other Christian traditions, have said yes. But what biblical or theological basis allows the magisterium to affirm both? The abiding issues come into focus when we look at them not only from the Catholic side, but from the side of historic peace churches who refuse to resolve them with a facile both/and formulation.

The challenge and promise of Christian unity

The question here is especially important if one recognizes that the process of working for greater unity among Christians through ecumenical dialogue is itself a mode of peacemaking. The reason is certainly not that peacebuilders must all be believers, or all of exactly one mind, before they can engage in cooperative action. Social movements generally, and mobilization for peace particularly, almost always require that we build coalitions of people who act from different motives, ideologies, and faiths. So if Christian peacemakers can collaborate with people of no explicitly religious faith or of other faiths, then Christians who are principled pacifists and Christians who are conscientious practitioners of just-war theory can surely collaborate according to the shared practices of just-peacemaking theory.

And yet, too often, division in the body of Christ has itself been an obstacle to peace. The scandal of divided witness on pressing contemporary questions—to say nothing of Christians killing others or even one another in the name of Christ—undermines the hope and proclamation that human beings generally can learn that penultimate earthly peace by which we conflict well, humanely, nonviolently, and respectfully. The question of what allows just-war and pacifist Christians to be in full communion with one another must sooner or later matter, therefore, especially among those very Christians who are most concerned that together we become what we claim to be, and thus offer the world the witness and work of a catholic peace church.

Roman Catholics historically have used various formulas to explain how unity-through-diversity and diversity-within-unity are possible. Some have described themselves as a "big tent." Culturally if not always theologically, others have allowed a range of moral standards by rejecting "rigorism" and allowing for pastoral accommodation so that ordinary believers can grow into greater holiness over time through lifetime conversion. With renewed vigor since Pope Francis, they have stressed the priority of mercy and described the church as a field hospital for wounded sinners, not just heroic saints. Thus, when the Second Vatican Council recognized the right of conscientious objection to the military, it followed the pattern of holding them up as saintly examples *worthy* of emulation, without quite *expecting* everyone else to emulate them.[4] Even when U.S. bishops, with Vatican approval, later explained the role that pacifists could play in actively resisting injustice through strategic nonviolence,[5] what they still expected of most Catholics was that they use just-war deliberation as their guide.

For other Christians from historic peace churches, however, as well as Catholic pacifists, the priority of mercy can go another direction, and require mercy not so much toward those with the power to wield violent force, however legitimately, as to those who may suffer at their hands. Instead of explaining why we should be generous toward Christians who have not yet found the courage to renounce recourse to violence in pursuit of self-defense, the priority of mercy can actually press the question of whether any form of homicide is ever justifiable. After all, for those who follow a Lord who taught love of enemy, and took the logic of that love to its ultimate consequence by dying for us when we ourselves were yet enemies of God (Rom 5:1-11), receiving God's mercy requires a mercy toward others that can hardly be compatible with killing them, even for a just cause.

In any case, since the Vatican has given an unmistakable mandate to attend to the ecumenical witness of historic peace churches such as the Mennonites,[6] ecumenical honesty requires listening not only to their perspectives but also to their critiques—and indeed to their very ways of framing those issues that have long been "church-dividing." To use the terminology of ecumenists, principled nonviolence is for historic peace churches a "confessional" issue[7]—something so integral to the Gospel of Jesus Christ that to deny its bindingness upon all Christians is to risk undermining one's very identity as a church or as a Christian.[8] From the historic peace church side of the dialogue, then, the recognition of pacifism and active nonviolence as legitimate options by churches such as the Catholic Church only goes so far. Logically, just-war thought has always required nonviolence as a first resort, after all. For just-war thinkers and practitioners to recognize the power of strategic nonviolence and other strategies that avoid resort to lethal violence is to make the just-war tradition more rather than less credible. In contrast, a rigorous pacifist may not be able to allow for even the most exceptional resort to warfare without ceasing to be a pacifist. To do so would simply mean signing on to just-war theory—a stringent version to be sure, but still the just-war theory. So however glad they might be for that ecumenical generosity by which churches in the just-war tradition have come to recognize the ethics and practices of historic peace churches, a serious asymmetry remains, and it is not obvious how those churches might reciprocate in kind.

Catholic pacifists bring some of this same tension with them, even if they are willing to become or remain Catholic. The combination by which someone like Dorothy Day exercised prophetic critique toward historical Catholic support of war, even while demonstrating patient loyalty to the church, has pastoral implications and arguably has implications for ecclesiology as well.[9] A willingness to work hopefully and persistently within a tradition whose history includes dubious if not deplorable compromises with violence and domineering power may be nothing short of exemplary. But the basis for their cooperation cannot simply be a loose moral relativism, which popes of recent decades have famously condemned. What then is the ecclesiology, to say nothing of the hope, that animates their continuing communion with just-war Christians?

Any credible answer to this question will require a framework for affirming some role for both just-war and pacifist ethics that goes deeper than polite conflict avoidance. On the one hand, such a framework will have to do more than strike the sort of compromise in church politics that the leading Protestant ethicist Paul Ramsey saw in affirmations of both just war and pacifism by Catholics and Methodists in the 1980s.[10] On the other hand, to be acceptable for Christian pacifists both within and beyond the historic peace churches, such a framework will require a firm foothold in the ethical teachings of Jesus, especially the Sermon on the Mount. Fortunately, the same ecumenical collaboration that we surveyed in the previous chapter—the development of just-peacemaking theory—has not only created a framework for practical collaboration; it has opened up a biblical and theological framework for the mutual embrace of full communion as well.

When Glen Stassen developed his breakthrough exegesis of the Sermon on the Mount that we surveyed in the previous chapter,[11] he not only contributed to just-peacemaking theory, but he stumbled upon a framework for mutual recognition and communion among Christians from divergent traditions concerning war—though apparently without noticing. Certainly the ecumenical potential of just-peacemaking theory was on the minds of all who participated in its development. Key to that development was a recognition that just-war and pacifist Christians alike could affirm ten key peacemaking practices as "normative practices" even if they did so for somewhat different reasons, based on starting principles that they do not altogether share. Such collaboration was more a matter of coalition-building than communion, however, more pragmatic than biblical or theological. Stassen himself was often content to advocate for just-peacemaking theory within the both/and, choose-your-tradition, approach that allows a place for both pacifism and just war in the Christian tradition and in our churches.[12] That still left Christians with our long-continuing impasse on the core church-dividing issue about the exceptional permissibility of killing human beings. The ecumenical potential that Stassen's *textual* analysis of the Sermon on the Mount itself might offer as a *conceptual* basis for mutual recognition initially went unnoticed.

To be sure, Christians may indeed continue to disagree for a very long time on whether the killing of human beings is ever permissible as an exception. What Stassen stumbled upon without noticing, however, is a way to disagree so precisely *as* Christians—Christians who fully embrace one another as such, without logically or implicitly excommunicating each other even if we are now polite enough to avoid the polemics of previous centuries. For if Stassen has read the Sermon on the Mount discerningly, then the Matthean Jesus himself has given us a way to transcend or at least to map our impasse by reconceiving the relationship between just war and pacifism in a fresh and eminently biblical way.

Historic strides, historical impasse

Thanks to statements like those of Catholic and Methodist bishops in the 1980s, formulas affirming just war and pacifism or active nonviolence as either parallel or complementary styles of Christian response to war have become commonplace. Coming with broad assurances that mainstream churches have much to learn from the witness of historic peace churches, these both/and formulas extend a hand of authentic ecumenical generosity.

Indeed, such formulas represent hard and serious ecumenical work, which has helped divided Christians make impressive strides in the last century toward a shared ethic of peace and peacemaking. *In the 1930s*, at an ecumenical gathering in Oxford that turned out to be a precursor to the World Council of Churches, representatives of mainstream churches first recognized pacifism as a position "sincerely and conscientiously held by Christians."[13] *In the 1950s*, Mennonite relief workers in war-torn Europe were beginning to earn their tradition new respect, first through their work and then through their representation of peace-church theology in World Council of Churches (WCC) circles.[14] *In the 1960s*, as we have seen, the Second Vatican Council was on its way to calling for a reappraisal of church teaching on war in light of the devastation of modern warfare, and would soon recognize principled renunciation of violent self-defense as a legitimate if heroic position for Christians to take.[15] *In the 1970s*, peace activists from pacifist churches and selective conscientious objectors or "modern-war pacifists" from just-war churches were enjoying a heady period of mutual discovery as they joined forces to oppose the war in Vietnam, the nuclear arms race, and Cold-War proxy wars aligning Western powers with military dictatorships throughout the so-called Third World. *In 1983*, U.S. Catholic bishops, writing their pastoral letter on *The Challenge of Peace*, affirmed both just war and active nonviolence as distinct yet "complementary" moral responses to aggression in pursuit of the common good,[16] and Methodist bishops in the United States echoed this judgment three years later.[17] *In the early 1990s*, just-war and pacifist scholars in the Society of Christian Ethics were meeting together to assess what they might learn from the unexpected end to the Cold War, and would soon identify the positive preventive practices we now know as just-peacemaking theory.[18] *In the early 2000s*, a first-ever five-year bilateral dialogue between Mennonite World Conference and the Pontifical Council for Promoting Christian Unity was coming to a mutual understanding whose final report would bear a title that even the most hopeful Catholic and Mennonite thinkers might have found unimaginable only a few years before: "Called Together to Be Peacemakers."[19]

And in 2007—in a wholly unprecedented development—representatives of those same Mennonite and Catholic bodies followed up with a joint statement contributing to the WCC's Decade to Overcome Violence (DOV) project. The statement offered "theological reflections that Mennonites and Catholics, committed to overcoming violence, may affirm together as a witness to peace in the ecumenical context."[20] The pedestrian character of that sentence obscures its moment. The WCC study process eventually received contributions from various academic institutions and peace networks. But the joint statement by Mennonites and Catholics is all the more remarkable because their "confessional bodies" turned out to be the only worldwide communions to contribute as such. And they did so by melding centuries of divergent moral reflection concerning war in order to do so "together."

For all these developments, any Christian who sees a connection between peacemaking and Christian unity must give thanks. Surely a *divided* church can only offer a fractured and ineffectual peace witness to the world. As one ecumenical consultation lamented in 1995, "The divisions in the Body of Christ in the world are a counter witness to the peace sought and proclaimed by the church as the follower of the Prince of Peace who prayed that his disciples might be one."[21] That conviction in turn must render the work of Christian reconciliation itself a foremost priority for Christian peace activists.

Yet for all of *that*, we must also be honest. For if one reads the fine print in any of the documents that mark the story of Christian convergence on war and peace in the last century, a nagging and apparently intractable gap always remains. The consensus among the scholars who forged the ten "normative practices" of just-peacemaking theory, for example, proved weakest when they had to decide whether to include humanitarian military interventions for the purpose of halting egregious human rights abuses.[22] Likewise, *Called Together to Be Peacemakers* provided what was the strongest statement to date from official Vatican representatives endorsing active nonviolence as normative, which "ought to be implemented in public policies and through public institutions as well as in personal and church practice."[23] But that alone does not rule out the exceptional resort to warfare, and so "nonviolence and just war" remained on the document's list of "divergences."[24] Yes, Mennonite and Catholic peace theology would soon merge even more seamlessly in their joint contribution of 2007 to the World Council of Churches' Decade to Overcome Violence. But how to move beyond historically divergent theories of just war, pacifism, and active nonviolence in order to forge an "ecumenical consensus" around alternatives "to replace violence as a means to resolve serious conflict in society"? Even here, the matter again remained an area for continuing study.[25]

When the WCC's Decade to Overcome concluded its process in 2011, results were yet again inconclusive. The final message of the decade's International Ecumenical Peace Convocation in Kingston in May 2011 marks how much, but also how little, has changed. On the one hand, the convocation readily acknowledged the contributions of pacifist churches: "History, especially in the witness of the historic peace churches, reminds us of the fact that violence is contrary to the will of God and can never resolve conflicts. It is for this reason that we are moving beyond the doctrine of just war towards a commitment to Just Peace." Yet "many practical aspects of the concept of Just Peace [continued to] require discussion, discernment and elaboration." Above all:

> We continue to struggle with how innocent people can be protected from injustice, war and violence. In this light, we struggle with the concept of the "responsibility to protect" and its possible misuse. We urgently request that the WCC and related bodies further clarify their positions regarding this policy.[26]

As John Howard Yoder had pointed out already in 1978, to acknowledge and thank peace churches, then call for further study, has been the pattern for the ecumenical movement at least since 1937.[27] Certainly it is no small thing to agree on a broad—perhaps even a vast—array of practical measures wherein just-war and pacifist Christians can cooperate in peacebuilding. Yet as long as some Christians believe that killing other human beings may sometimes (however exceptionally) contribute to the limited measure of peace that is possible in a fallen world, while others believe that any Christian participation in homicide betrays the Gospel of Jesus Christ, the horizon of Christian unity itself will continue to recede.

Hence, it *seems*, our impasse. As one of my own critics put it when I made a small contribution to recent developments with my first essay on how attention to "just policing" might help just-war and pacifist Christians continue converging to the point that war could possibly cease to be a church dividing issue:[28] sorry, "war remains church dividing."[29]

Unexpected help from the Matthean Jesus

Glen Stassen's exegesis of Jesus' Sermon on the Mount opens up an unexpected path out of this impasse, however. *His* claim, we may recall from the previous chapter, is that Matthew organized the sermon around a consistent succession of triads by which Jesus first named "traditional righteousness," then diagnosed a "vicious cycle," then presented a "transforming initiative" for escaping that cycle. *My* claim is that if he is right, we are in a position to reconceive the relationship between just war and pacifism in entirely fresh ways.[30]

To review the argument by Stassen that we laid out earlier, threefold or triadic outlines structure the fourteen teachings at the heart of Jesus' Sermon on the Mount in Matthew 5–7, and this finding has surprisingly revolutionary implications. Although Christians have long taken it as obvious that the Sermon on the Mount presents a series of antitheses or "dyads" by which Jesus taught "you have heard it said . . . but I say unto you," in fact he consistently proceeded to add a third element according to a structure not of dyads but of triads. Jesus' pattern was to first name what either the Hebrew Scriptures or common sense had traditionally identified as righteousness, then to diagnose why this traditional righteousness only went so far in delivering human beings from vicious cycles of sin and violence, *and then* to present a transforming initiative that promised to break such cycles. Though this triadic literary structure may at first have seemed merely a technical matter, it moves the accent in Jesus' teachings. That accent is on empowering ways to break out of vicious cycles, rather than on difficult prohibitions. As we saw in the last chapter, this has far-reaching implications for rescuing Jesus' ethic from the charge of idealism and demonstrating a practicable realism that offers us fresh insights into both the dynamics of social transformation and "natural law."

The implications for ecclesiology and ecumenism are also profound. For Stassen may have given us nothing less than a window into the way that Jesus himself thought about ethical issues—or at least Jesus according to the Gospel of Matthew. And if that is the case, then Christian pacifists may be able to recognize non-pacifist Christians as true members of the same body without renouncing their confessional claims. The reasons to do so, after all, would derive from nothing less than the very biblical passage that is the wellspring of Christian pacifism.

For, arguably, over the centuries just-war theory has become *our* traditional righteousness—but we can say that without settling there. Some may wish the theory had not come to play this role; some may be grateful. But even those who believe Christians made a huge mistake in the fourth/fifth centuries often find themselves appealing to just-war criteria in order to urge policymakers to do better even if they cannot do the best—to live up to their own highest stated principles even if they cannot see their way politically to courageous and creatively nonviolent strategies. Just-war theory has gotten written into international law in ways that human rights advocates depend upon. It is often the *lingua franca* for debating matters of war in the public square, even for those with another first language. In the very way that Jesus built upon *traditional righteousness*, therefore, peace churches themselves often confirm a limited role for just-war principles by building upon them rather than distancing themselves through strict antithesis.

Traditional righteousness alone never delivers us from *vicious cycles* in Jesus' teaching, however; thus, in the very way that Jesus diagnosed vicious cycles, just-war churches increasingly recognize that even putatively just wars often create conditions for further war. It is in the diagnosis of vicious cycles, then, that the church has already found consensus on the need for "a fresh reappraisal of war" in the modern world. It is here that we continue to build consensus despite lingering uncertainty as to whether and how to use just-war categories to "limit the use of force by the application of moral norms."[31] We have seen the result of totalitarian claims that war might issue in some thousand-year *Reich* of peace or create a socialist new man. No one seriously justifies any war as an opportunity to end all wars, in the way Woodrow Wilson famously did. The best and most conscientious just-war thinkers are attending to the non-military *jus postbellum* actions required for what they hope will achieve a longer-lasting peace. At *most* they argue that the danger of Mutually Assured Destruction has cemented in place a sort of static vicious cycle. But since nuclear deterrence requires the threat to break all norms of just-war theory, the Roman Catholic Church only endorsed deterrence doctrine reluctantly and provisionally, hopefully on the way to disarmament—and now has said in effect that the clock has run out.[32] A close reading of Francis's 2017 World Day of Peace message on nonviolence as a style of politics reveals multiple references to chains or cycles of violence—and thus the need to counter injustice and defend just causes *without* perpetuating violence.

Therefore, the accent in Jesus' teaching on that third element, *transforming initiatives*, ought to translate into our own emphasis on just-peacemaking and active nonviolence. While the prototypes we find in the Sermon on the Mount inevitably come from first-century Palestine, once we began to recognize their dynamic in the previous chapter, we were able to see their power at work even at the highest level of international affairs. Within such a triadic framework in which the accent is on transforming initiatives, historic peace churches as well as pacifists within the Catholic Church and mainline Protestant churches can thus uphold the confessional status of Christian nonviolence as integral to the Gospel—while also recognizing a limited and transitory role for just-war thinking based not merely on political pragmatism but on the structure of Jesus' teaching. And all the more because the basis for such recognition is evident in the text at the very core of Christian pacifism—the Sermon on the Mount.

Critical to this argument is the claim that just-war teaching has now become *our* "traditional righteousness." Unfortunately, Stassen did not provide a biblically derived baseline that summarizes the abiding role traditional righteousness plays for the Matthean Jesus across all fourteen triads.[33] This is not surprising, however, nor is it a criticism. Intrinsically, items of traditional righteousness in the

Sermon on the Mount are always something to fill out, transcend, and move beyond at least in terms of focus and emphasis. In turn, Stassen's contemporary burden was to highlight the theological, practical, and moral importance of diagnosing vicious cycles and calling us into the creative search for transforming initiatives.

Still, once we have absorbed Stassen's interpretive grid, it is not too difficult to recognize the positive and abiding role that traditional righteousness played for Jesus, even as he taught "as one with authority" about how to fulfill the intended meaning of the Law and the Prophets through transforming initiatives. Each of the fourteen items of traditional righteousness in the Sermon on the Mount is a building block, a reference point. Each names the rough consensus to which Jesus could appeal as he called his original Jewish listeners to lives that welcomed the in-breaking kingdom of God. Though not the fullness of God's Reign, each traditional teaching had played a crucial role in salvation history by forming them through the grace of Torah into a people. Among Jesus' listeners, perhaps only a few were learned in the Torah, while a few more were Jesus' own neophyte learners or disciples on the way. Partially formed in the faith of Abraham and the Law of Moses, they might not know how to do rabbinical casuistry in a complicated divorce case, but they knew adultery was wrong and that unchecked lusts can destroy the fabric of communal relationships in village or clan. They might secretly wish to dash the babies of Roman oppressors onto rocks (as in Ps 137:8-9), but would have sensed that retaliation could do little more than take them into the unbridled world of Lamech, where Rome, not they, held the power to clamp down with a seventy-sevenfold power differential (Gen 4:24). Whether their now-common-sense morality derived from what we would today call natural law or from the ways that God had been forming a people in history does not matter here; Jesus could build on what they had "heard that it was said."

The fact that Jesus never rejected traditional righteousness as far as it went is the crucial data point for Christian pacifists as we transpose the triadic pattern into contemporary ecumenical dialogue in hope of church unity. For it provides nothing less than a biblical basis for recognizing a measure of value in the just-war tradition from no less foundational a text for them than the Sermon on the Mount. In fact, I do not need to *propose* that Christian pacifists use just-war teachings in this way; they have been doing so for quite some time. The very structure of John Howard Yoder's 1971 book, *Nevertheless: The Varieties and Shortcomings of Religious Pacifism*, acknowledges a moral continuum in which thoroughgoing biblical pacifism is best, but Christian internationalism and just-war casuistry are good enough to serve as starting points. The latter was what Yoder called "the pacifism of the honest study of cases." Yoder critiqued what he saw as its internal weaknesses, of course, but then continued:

> *Nevertheless*, this position is more honest than any of the alternatives available to those who do not reject all war. It rejects the crusade which blesses war, and the fascism which makes the state an autonomous value subject to no criteria of judgment. Saying yes to war subject to some stated conditions is morally more responsible than saying yes with no limits. Applying the conditions seriously to modern war and actually coming up with a negative answer, is more honest than saying that there are limits but never reaching them.
> This theory recognizes a criterion of moral judgment superior to the state. It recognizes that the instruments of the state must be used only for modest and finite values. . . . [T]he language of the just-war theory is one of the most appropriate ways to communicate a Christian peace concern to Christians or to others who claim to be honest politicians. Outside the historic peace churches, the language of the just-war theory is a most appropriate vehicle for communication since it is the historic position held at least in theory by all the major Christian bodies. . . .
> It might further be pointed out that this pacifism of borderline casuistry is very logically the first step which an individual takes along the path to a more consistent pacifism. One must first get accustomed to the idea that one might ever say no, and that one might ever apply critical moral criteria to the claims of the government, before one can even conceive of a more radical moral independence.[34]

By way of analogy, the very characteristics we have identified in Jesus' use of traditional righteousness in the Sermon on the Mount are all here. Just-war teaching serves as a starting point for conversation and coalition-building with non-pacifist peacemakers, especially other Christians, and then for advocacy vis-à-vis policymakers in the public square.[35] It puts moral limits on warfare, thus constraining modern-day Lamechs and crusaders. It prepares us to receive a fuller and more radical gospel.

Not all thinkers who identify with the just-war tradition have been convinced that it shares with Christian pacifism a presumption against war or violence.[36] Pacifists such as Yoder, however, have been glad to build on that thesis for the purposes both of activist coalition-building and ecumenical bridge-building.[37] Here, within the presumption-against-war framework, is one place where historic peace church thinkers have indeed been willing to reciprocate ecumenical generosity. So long as Yoder could state his terms carefully and neither assume a polite but sloppy relativism nor whitewash the historical record, he was prepared to explore a certain complementarity between just-war theory and pacifism.[38] Few just-war theorists and no mainstream church bodies really ever convinced him that they were applying just-war analysis with the accountability, church discipline, and "honesty" required for it to "bite" in a way that might consistently restrain rather than rationalize warfare.[39] Yet Yoder's recognition of its potential to do so—if only it were stringently applied—remained magnanimous. Even in an essay grappling with the danger that good-faith dialogue with just-war thinkers would end up legitimizing the rationalization of war, Yoder offered this hope:

> If a handful of responsible actors in the realm of politics and war would refrain from abuse and would authentically respect the restraints they claim to honor, that would probably do more to save lives and reduce conflicts than all of my own renunciation of personal responsibility for violence. Indeed, it would perhaps decrease killing more than all of the individuals whom my testimony might convince that all war is wrong.[40]

In fact, the potential of the "just-war inheritance" to mobilize opposition to warfare was not merely hypothetical for Yoder, but had a certain empirical basis in the Vietnam experience. Catholic bishops who came to oppose the war did so under little if any influence from Quakers and Mennonites, he noted.[41] Some combination of rediscovered just-war analysis and common-sense morality among those who had inherited the just-war tradition had done more to stop the War in Vietnam than the witness of peace churches.[42]

Just-war thinking could even play a salvation-historical role in forming God's people and drawing them closer to kingdom practices, akin to what the traditional righteousness Jesus cited in the Sermon on the Mount had done. Yoder himself made the comparison by moving back and forth between discussions of the role that *lex talionis* constraints had played for Israel and the role of just-war constraints in more recent history.[43] Though just-war teaching was not the Gospel, Yoder was ready to see it as able to prepare the way for the Gospel. Catholic antiwar leaders in the Vietnam era, such as Daniel and Phillip Berrigan or Thomas Merton, provided cases in point, after all. They had not started as systematic pacifists. But as they began to apply just-war categories to critique the war they found to be such an atrocity, it radicalized them:

> As they got drawn into the movement, they began to see that atrocity is normal for the military system, and that they needed to engage in a deeper critique of the system itself. . . . The vast majority of Catholic pacifists began with just war reflexes and with a tender capacity to see how bad the Vietnam conflict was. Only gradually did they work themselves into a pacifist position.[44]

If the crucial step for Christian pacifists engaged in ecumenical dialogue regarding the long church-dividing issue of war matches Jesus' first step of triadic moral analysis—the recognition and use of traditional righteousness, which just-war theory has become for us—then the crucial data point that Christian just-war thinkers must recognize is Jesus' second step: However worthy traditional righteousness may be, in Jesus' diagnosis, it will fail to break human social dynamics out of their vicious cycles.

But again, I do not need to propose that just-war thinkers recognize this. Whether or not they find their way to the pacifism that peace churches historically have understood to be a "confessional" matter intrinsic to the Gospel, their circumspection in the face of the realities of modern warfare conforms to the triadic pattern Stassen has identified in the Sermon on the Mount, in precisely this way. Namely, many of those very theologians, prelates, and policymakers who continue to hold to the tragic necessity of war have increasingly recognized that even justifiable wars can never free us from vicious cycles but instead invite new ones.

This is what even the very traditionalist Cardinal Alfredo Ottaviani, head of the Holy Office and successor to the Inquisition, had intuitively recognized in the wake of World War II. Touring southern Italy, Ottaviani saw the devastation that had made an already impoverished region virtually destitute. According to an account by Tom Cornell of the backstory that led the cardinal to support the Second Vatican Council's call for "a completely fresh reappraisal of war"[45] in a surprising speech to the assembled bishops that met with sustained and thunderous applause, Ottaviani recognized that seeking justice through warfare inevitably created new injustices:

> Ottaviani saw the ruin brought upon already impoverished, innocent, and uncomprehending people by the war, and came to the conclusion that justice could no longer be served by war because of the massive injustices it generates, and because of who pays for it—always the poor. "*Bellum omnino interdicendum*," he wrote in a monograph from the Holy Office, "War is to be altogether forbidden."[46]

Ottaviani's ultraconservative respect for the authority not only of church but of state made it difficult to take that pronouncement to a logically pacifist conclusion, but his recognition that even a war that most have come to see as just issued in new injustices left him unsettled in a way that was akin to Jesus' diagnoses of vicious cycles. The statement came to the attention of Jean Goss, a French Catholic who had undergone his own conversion to nonviolence while a soldier during the war. Goss saw an opening, and once he got past initial rebuffs and Swiss Guards, first an audience and then fifteen years of friendship and conversation ensued, soon drawing in Jean's wife, Hildegard Goss-Mayr, as well.[47] During the Second Vatican Council, the cardinal introduced the couple, along with other prominent Catholic peace activists such as Dorothy Day and James Douglass, to bishops who were drafting what would eventually become the groundbreaking statement on war in *Gaudium et Spes*, the Pastoral

Constitution for the Church in the Modern World.[48] Since the earliest pages of this book we have highlighted the importance of the council's condemnation of total war, its doubts about modern war generally, its fresh respect for conscientious objection to military participation, and its resulting call for reappraisal of the church's response to war in light of twentieth-century firepower and death tolls.

Together with other historical developments such as selective conscientious objection, "nuclear" or "modern war pacifism," and the search for ways to transcend the impasse of just-war-versus-pacifism through some new framework of "just peace" or "just peacemaking," therefore, the experience of Cardinal Ottaviani in particular, and of the bishops assembled for the Second Vatican Council generally, all conform strikingly to the triadic method of the Matthean Jesus. When those who start with traditional righteousness honestly diagnose the vicious cycles in which they remain, they are being prepared to welcome transforming initiatives that have potential to deliver us from those cycles and initiate us into kingdom ways. No more than any other form of traditional righteousness does just-war teaching yet free us from vicious cycles of violence. But so far as it goes, it is good and deserves a guarded affirmation.

On one hand, this means that pacifists do not need to separate themselves or exclude conscientious practitioners of just-war teaching from communion in the one body of Christ. On the other hand, pacifists and just-war practitioners alike share all the more responsibility to demonstrate to the world in fact and not just in theory the viability of normative nonviolence and practices of just peacemaking. But at least then any continuing debate between just-war and pacifist positions can be a matter of mutual exhortation as we call one another to the fullness of trust in the Gospel and faithfulness to kingdom ways. War need not be a church-dividing issue.

More important still, peacemaking might be a church-transforming issue. Admittedly, if historic peace churches wish to continue moving toward greater church unity, reconceiving the relationship between just-war and pacifist teaching along "triadic" lines will not just require the continued development of Christian peace theology and social ethics—it might require a somewhat different ecclesiology. Indeed, it might require a different soteriology too, or at least a clarified soteriology. But hopefully this consideration will actually commend the ecumenical proposal that grows from Stassen's exegesis. Theologically, Mennonites and some other historic peace churches have long struggled to maintain a robust peace ethic without implying some kind of Pelagian assumption that we are saved through works-righteousness. Missionally they have struggled with how to welcome new believers into their faith and their communities while giving them time to deepen their commitment to thoroughgoing nonviolence. Pastorally, they have struggled to uphold pacifism without resort to forms of church discipline that their own members have often experienced as unsustainably harsh and inconsistently rigorist.[49]

So yes, thorough reflection on the implications of Stassen's triadic exegesis of the Sermon on the Mount may reveal still further theological implications. But this may very well prove to offer an eminently biblical invitation to cease "putting God to the test by placing on the neck of the disciples a yoke that neither our ancestors nor we have been able to bear" (Acts 15:10). For if Stassen's exegesis is right, Jesus himself called his hearers into deeper lives of discipleship according to the ways of the kingdom not by demanding of them stark and antithetical choices, so much as by working with the good that was their moral and cultural inheritance so far, by inviting them to recognize the incompleteness of their inheritance inasmuch as it kept them enmeshed in vicious cycles, and then by offering alternative ways of living, less by way of critique than by enlivening their imaginations with the good news of God's deliverance.

This is not to say that transformation will only be required from the historic peace church side if Christ's church is to more fully become a catholic peace church. But of this I need say no more. After all, laying out the shape of those transformations by which the Roman Catholic Church might play a leading role as it rediscovers its own diaspora ecclesiology and becomes a Catholic peace church has been the burden of this entire book.

Conclusion

To reiterate, everything I have said with guarded affirmation concerning the just-war tradition is a secondary argument. The direction and emphasis of Jesus' teaching obviously was not on the abiding role of *traditional righteousness* but rather on the gracious deliverance by which the Reign of God breaks into the reality of our lives already in history as we escape our *vicious cycles* through participation in God's *transforming initiatives*. Thus, neither historic peace churches nor pacifists in other traditions need in any way to abandon their confessional claim upon all other Christians that active nonviolence or Christian pacifism is intrinsic to the Gospel of Jesus Christ and places the greater claim upon Christian vocation. Nor, in their collaborative coalitions with non-pacifist Christians, should they focus anywhere other than on learning, practicing, and promoting contemporary transforming initiatives such as those identified in just-peacemaking theory, which actively nurture the just and peaceable social conditions that avoid war.

Nonetheless, it is also intrinsic to Jesus' teaching and Jesus' way that he never renounces, denounces, or otherwise abandons *traditional righteousness*—so far as it goes. An ethic concerning violence that limits retribution to "an eye for an eye" may thus play a transitional role in salvation history even though it will never be transformative and redemptive per se. For insofar as it does anything at all to tame the Lamechs of our world and prevent them from a seventy-sevenfold escalation of violence and arrogance besides (Gen 4:23-24), we can be grateful. Just ask the seventy-six, or seventy, or thirty-five people one can still *look* in the eye at all because Lamech has not blinded or murdered them. In the light of God's inbreaking kingdom, the moral wisdom of "an eye for an eye" will never go far enough, nor free us from our vicious cycles, yet its contribution to human civilization deserves a certain kind of welcome.

Still, even if Jesus' triadic way of thinking allows for some limited-use just-war categories in order to dissuade the Cains and Lamechs of the world, just-war theory cannot be the church's overarching moral framework. If we use it at all, we might better call it "just-policing"[50] or speak of "violence-reduction criteria."[51] For as the church seeks to apply moral norms to international affairs, we must remember that what the world needs most are transforming initiatives to build just peace. Above all, then, this is where the church should focus and invest. We can continue to affirm those whose vocations lead them into public positions where their political options too often seem limited to what currently accepted traditional righteousness allows. But the church will only offer such Christians the good and foresighted pastoral guidance they need to make their hard choices and to find unexpected openings for transforming initiatives amid those hard choices if the weight of Catholic teaching is on diagnosing vicious cycles in search of transforming initiatives. Forming people with the skills, dispositions, and imaginations to find the nonviolent initiatives that will transform their historical situations must be the unmistakable focus of church teaching and the overwhelming priority in church programming.

To any remaining skeptics I would only ask this: Would Jesus really have us excommunicated or live in schism with those who have not yet seen their way beyond traditional righteousness? No more, I suspect, than he would have wanted his first disciples to "think that I have come to abolish the law or the prophets" (Matt 5:17). No more than he wished them to provoke the "Jewish-Christian schism" that later centuries tragically brought.[52] Our most important collaboration across the just-war/pacifist impasse certainly remains the work that we have already been learning we can do together to prevent war in the first place, by creating more just and humane social conditions through practices of just peacemaking. But let us recognize that we do so, and *can* do so, precisely as fellow believers in Christ's church, not simply as begrudging coalition partners. Let us recognize the work of nurturing greater church unity, and with it a common witness in the world, as essential to the peacemaking ministry of reconciliation that none other than God has given us (2 Cor 5:18).

Notes

Acknowledgments—pages ix–xvi

1. See p. 290 in chapter 9.
2. Philip McManus and Gerald Schlabach, eds., *Relentless Persistence: Nonviolent Action in Latin America*, foreword by Leonardo Boff (Philadelphia: New Society Publishers, 1991).
3. See pp. 181–83 in chapter 6 for a methodological aside explaining this engagement.
4. See the introduction to Gerald W. Schlabach, *Unlearning Protestantism: Sustaining Christian Community in an Unstable Age* (Grand Rapids, MI: Brazos Press, 2010), as well as my articles: "You Converted to What? One Mennonite's Journey," *Commonweal* 134, no. 11 (1 June 2007): 14–17; "Catholic and Mennonite: A Journey of Healing," in *Sharing Peace: Mennonites and Catholics in Conversation*, eds. Gerald W. Schlabach and Margaret Pfeil, foreword by Msgr. John A. Radano (Collegeville, MN: Liturgical Press, 2013), 159–78; and "Capitalizing Church: On Finding Catholicism Inevitable," *Conrad Grebel Review* 34, no. 3 (Fall 2016): 284–302.
5. The most significant product of this collaboration was the book that Friesen and I coedited, *At Peace and Unafraid: Public Order, Security and the Wisdom of the Cross* (Scottdale, PA: Herald Press, 2005), which drew together the results of a two-year project of the MCC Peace Committee.
6. At the time its name carried the same acronym, AMBS, but was the Associated Mennonite Biblical Seminaries.
7. Rachel Waltner Goossen, "'Defanging the Beast': Mennonite Responses to John Howard Yoder's Sexual Abuse," *Mennonite Quarterly Review* 89, no. 1 (January 2015): 7–80.
8. My suspicions are reflected in chapter 2 of Schlabach, *Unlearning Protestantism*, or the journal article upon which it largely drew, "Continuity and Sacrament, or Not: Hauerwas, Yoder, and Their Deep Difference," *Journal of the Society of Christian Ethics* 27, no. 2 (Fall-Winter 2007): 171–207.
9. Gerald W. Schlabach, "Deuteronomic or Constantinian: What Is the Most Basic Problem for Christian Social Ethics?," in *The Wisdom of the Cross:*

Essays in Honor of John Howard Yoder, ed. Stanley Hauerwas et al. (Grand Rapids, MI: Eerdmans, 1999), 449-71.

10. Gerald W. Schlabach, "Only Those We Need Can Betray Us: My Relationship with John Howard Yoder and His Legacy," interviewed by Paul Martens and Jonathan Tran (2014), http://www.geraldschlabach.net/2014/07/10/only-those-we-need-can-betray-us-my-relationship-with-john-howard-yoder-and-his-legacy/.

Chapter 1—pages 1-27

1. See Schlabach, *Unlearning Protestantism*.
2. Michel Andraos, "Becoming a Christian, Becoming a Peacemaker," *New Theology Review*, no. 3, (August 2005): 32-40.
3. Pope John Paul II, "Peace on Earth to Those Whom God Loves!," Message for the World Day of Peace (January 1, 2000), §90. Also see John Paul II, "An Ever-Timely Commitment: Teaching Peace," Message for the World Day of Peace (January 1, 2004), §3; Pope Francis, *Evangelii Gaudium* [The Joy of the Gospel], apostolic exhortation (November 24, 2013), §187-90; and note the United States Conference of Catholic Bishops, *The Harvest of Justice Is Sown in Peace* (Washington, DC: USCCB, 1993), on the vocation of peacemaking:

> Part of the legacy of [our previous pastoral letter on] *The Challenge of Peace* is the call to strengthen peacemaking as an essential dimension of our faith, reminding us that Jesus called us to be peacemakers. Our biblical heritage and our body of tradition make the vocation of peacemaking mandatory. Authentic prayer, worship and sacramental life challenge us to conversion of our hearts and summon us to works of peace. These concerns are obviously not ours [as bishops] alone, but are the work of the entire community of faith and of all people of good will.

4. Gerald W. Schlabach, ed. and lead author, *Just Policing, Not War: An Alternative Response to World Violence*, with Drew Christiansen, SJ, et al. (Collegeville, MN: Liturgical Press, 2007), 101.
5. Pope Paul VI, *Populorum Progressio*, Encyclical on the Development of Peoples (March 26, 1967), §76-77; Francis, *Evangelii Gaudium*, §187-90.
6. Pope Paul VI, "If You Want Peace, Work for Justice," Message for the Celebration of the Day of Peace" (January 1, 1972).
7. Pope John Paul II, "No Peace without Justice; No Justice without Forgiveness," Message for the World Day of Peace (January 1, 2002), §15.
8. Second Vatican Council, *Gaudium et Spes*, Pastoral Constitution on the Church in the Modern World (March 26, 1965), §78. (Quotations of Vatican II documents are taken from Austin Flannery, ed., *Vatican Council II: Constitutions, Decrees, Declarations; The Basic Sixteen Documents* [Collegeville, MN: Liturgical Press, 2014].) Cf. Paul VI, *Populorum Progressio*, §76; Pope John

Paul II, *Centesimus Annus*, Encyclical on the Hundredth Anniversary of *Rerum Novarum* (May 1, 1991), §18; Francis, *Evangelii Gaudium*, §218; as well as National Conference of Catholic Bishops (NCCB), *The Challenge of Peace: God's Promise and Our Response* (Washington, DC: United States Catholic Conference, 1983), §68–70, 234.

9. Second Vatican Council, *Gaudium et Spes*, §78.

10. A fascinating recent book by John E. Thiel would suggest that even in heaven, conflict of a sort may continue to be present, even if sinning does not continue, insofar as "the blessed dead are preoccupied with the business of reconciliation." Reconciliation requires direct objects, after all. While that would obviously include the memory of past sins, one might also expect non-sinful differences to be present as part of the ongoing agenda for reconciliation. Certainly the kind of continual building up of peace of which the council spoke is implied when Thiel argues that "to be a disciple of Jesus means that, even in the afterlife, the bonds of reconciliation that unite the communion of the saints must be forged in the work of forgiveness, made and remade in acts of love that grace those who forgive as much as those who are forgiven." See John E. Thiel, *Icons of Hope: The "Last Things" in Catholic Imagination* (Notre Dame, IN: University of Notre Dame Press, 2013), especially pp. 48–57, 172–78, 182–83. Quotations are from pp. 57 and 52, respectively.

11. Nonviolent vulnerability means little if one cannot imagine changing one's mind, even about possible legitimate use of violence. See Farah Godrej, "Nonviolence and Gandhi's Truth: A Method for Moral and Political Arbitration," *The Review of Politics* 68, no. 2 (Spring 2006): 287–317. One might also wish to consult Erik H. Erikson, *Gandhi's Truth: On the Origins of Militant Nonviolence* (New York: W. W. Norton, 1969), 412–14. In a specifically Christian context I have written of the disposition here as "nonviolence toward the truth" (see Gerald W. Schlabach, "Augustine's Hermeneutic of Humility: An Alternative to Moral Imperialism and Moral Relativism," *Journal of Religious Ethics* 22, no. 2 [Fall 1994]: 302, 320, 322–27). Behind this notion lies the thought of John Howard Yoder. Chris K. Huebner has systematically teased out Yoder's pacifist epistemology in section two of his book, *A Precarious Peace: Yoderian Explorations on Theology, Knowledge, and Identity* (Waterloo, ON: Herald Press, 2006). Also see Schlabach, "Anthology in Lieu of System: John H. Yoder's Ecumenical Conversations as Systematic Theology," review essay on *The Royal Priesthood: Essays Ecclesiological and Ecumenical* by John Howard Yoder and Michael G. Cartwright (ed.), *Mennonite Quarterly Review* 71, no. 2 (April 1997): 305–9.

12. Gerald W. Schlabach, "Just Policing: How War Could Cease to Be a Church-Dividing Issue," *Journal of Ecumenical Studies* 41, no. 3–4 (Summer–Fall 2004): 409–30; Schlabach, *Just Policing, Not War*; Gerald W. Schlabach, "Must Christian Pacifists Reject Police Force?," chap. 5 in *A Faith Not Worth*

Fighting For: Addressing Commonly Asked Questions about Christian Nonviolence, ed. Tripp York and Justin Bronson Barringer, The Peaceable Kingdom Series, no. 1 (Eugene, OR: Cascade Books, 2012), 60–84.

13. For my own part, at a personal level, my ground-level understanding of *peace* as a dynamic social process, not a perfect stasis of harmony, also brings implications for what it must mean to be a peace *church*, and why it has not only become possible for me as a Christian pacifist to enter into communion with the Roman Catholic Church, but in some ways is necessary. To engage in continuing, creative, conflict transformation requires embedding oneself in conflict, within, not over or against, one's people. One's preferred resolution of a conflict cannot be a non-negotiable precondition for peaceful relationship. And a commitment to being the change one seeks for Christ's church must make the breaking of communion or the sustaining of schism harder not easier. Helping me to remain in relationship with the Mennonite community that formed me is the recognition that schism may very well have become a tragic necessity at some historical junctures, when the larger church has suppressed prophetic communities in its midst and driven them out; I continue to believe that the sixteenth-century Anabaptist forebears of Mennonites, Amish, and Hutterites were just such communities. But helping me to become a Roman Catholic has been the conviction that if such a community is to claim an identity as a people of peace and reconciliation, it cannot simultaneously claim schism as a hardened identity. Its very desire to faithfully be a peace church should entail active working for the full healing of memory and relationship with the larger church it believes once drove it out. When and how full communion may come is a matter that those within historic peace churches will conscientiously need to decide. I do not believe it is mine to press them to "return" to the Catholic "fold." But I do insist that to live out their peacemaking vocations they must at least be willing to imagine such a possibility and ready themselves to welcome it. The very fact that they are holding in their hands a book about how the Catholic Church can continue to become a catholic peace church is evidence that this possibility is closer than they once imagined.

14. Theron F. Schlabach and Richard T. Hughes, eds., *Proclaim Peace: Christian Pacifism from Unexpected Quarters* (Urbana: University of Illinois Press, 1997); Paul Alexander, *Peace to War: Shifting Allegiances in the Assemblies of God*, The C. Henry Smith Series, vol. 9 (Telford, PA: Cascadia; Scottdale, PA: Herald Press, 2009).

15. Drew Christiansen, SJ, "The Ethics of Peacemaking: The Genesis of *Called Together to Be Peacemakers, Report of the International Mennonite-Catholic Dialogue (2004),*" *Journal of Ecumenical Studies* 45, no. 3 (Summer 2010): 396–97; Gerald W. Schlabach, "Meeting in Exile: Historic Peace Churches and the Emerging Peace Church Catholic," *Journal of Religion, Conflict, and Peace* 1, no. 1 (Fall 2007), https://www.manchester.edu/docs/default-source

/academics/by-major/philosophy-and-religious-studies/journal/volume-1-issue-1-fall-2007/meeting-in-exile.pdf?sfvrsn=4f5b8962_2.

16. See pp. 58–63 and following.

17. Mennonite World Conference and Pontifical Council for Promoting Church Unity, "Called Together to Be Peacemakers: Report of the International Dialogue Between the Catholic Church and Mennonite World Conference, 1998–2003," *Information Service* 2003-II/III, no. 113 (2004): 111–48. The document is also available as Appendix A in Gerald W. Schlabach and Margaret Pfeil, eds., *Sharing Peace: Mennonites and Catholics in Conversation*, foreword by Msgr. John A. Radano (Collegeville, MN: Liturgical Press, 2013), 189–259, and is available in multiple languages at http://www.bridgefolk.net/theology/dialogue.

18. Section 90 provides a summary answer to this question, and sections 162–171 provide an extensive answer to this question, but strictly from the Mennonite side of the dialogue. My commentary is limited to sections of the final report that explicitly record "convergences" or "divergences."

19. See especially "Called Together to Be Peacemakers," §§177–85. Though I do not cite it here, a follow-up document prepared jointly by Vatican and Mennonite World Conference representatives as a contribution to the World Council of Churches' Decade to Overcome Violence presents an even more seamless Catholic and Mennonite theology of peace: Mennonite World Conference and Pontifical Council for Promoting Church Unity, "A Mennonite and Catholic Contribution to the World Council of Churches' *Decade to Overcome Violence*," Report from Mennonite–Catholic Conference, Rome, October 23–25, 2007, http://www.overcomingviolence.org/fileadmin/dov/files/iepc/Mennonite_and_Catholic_contribution_to_DOV.pdf.

20. For a list of ways that Catholics in different roles should be working at this, see Schlabach, *Just Policing, Not War*, 101–6.

21. John Paul II, *Evangelium Vitae* [Gospel of Life], encyclical (March 25, 1995), §56.

22. Linda Bordoni, "Pope Francis: 'Death Penalty Inadmissible,'" *Vatican News Service*, August 2, 2018, https://www.vaticannews.va/en/pope/news/2018-08/pope-francis-cdf-ccc-death-penalty-revision-ladaria.html.

23. ZENIT, "Cardinal Ratzinger on the Abridged Version of Catechism Compendium Expected Out in 2 Years," *ZENIT News Agency*, May 2, 2003, https://zenit.org/articles/cardinal-ratzinger-on-the-abridged-version-of-catechism/. Also see *La Civiltà Cattolica*, "Modern War and the Christian Conscience," editorial, trans. William Shannon, *Origins* 21, no. 28 (December 19, 1992): 450–55.

24. See especially Reinhold Niebuhr, *Moral Man and Immoral Society*, reprint ed., The Scribner Lyceum Editions Library (New York: Scribner's, 1960); Reinhold Niebuhr, "Why the Christian Church Is Not Pacifist," in *Christianity and Power Politics* (New York: Charles Scribner's Sons, 1940), 1–32.

25. John Howard Yoder, "Armaments and Eschatology," *Studies in Christian Ethics* 1, no. 1 (1988): 58. Cf. John Howard Yoder, *The Politics of Jesus*, 2nd ed. (1972; repr., Grand Rapids, MI: Eerdmans, 1994), 246; and note Stanley Hauerwas, *With the Grain of the Universe: The Church's Witness and Natural Theology*, Gifford Lectures delivered at the University of St. Andrews in 2001 (Grand Rapids, MI: Brazos Press, 2001). For examples of Yoder's elaboration on the social power of nonviolence, see *The Politics of Jesus*, 38–39, 240–41, as well as his extended list of ways that a creative minority can be an effective change agent in history even if it renounces the temptation to force change upon history, as it appears in "Christ, the Hope of the World," in *The Original Revolution: Essays on Christian Pacifism*, Christian Peace Shelf (Scottdale, PA: Herald Press, 1971), 153–60, also reprinted in *The Royal Priesthood: Essays Ecclesiological and Ecumenical*, ed. with an intro. by Michael G. Cartwright, foreword by Richard J. Mouw (Grand Rapids, MI: Eerdmans, 1994), 203–7.

26. To use less religious language, authentic martyrdom is one expression of what political scientist Gene Sharp has identified as key to strategic, active nonviolence. This is the dynamic of "political *jiu-jitsu*" by which nonviolent practitioners absorb but then deflect the violence of an oppressor in such a way that political power rebounds against the regime:

> By combining nonviolent discipline with solidarity and persistence in struggle, the nonviolent actionists cause the violence of the opponent's repression to be exposed in the worst possible light. This, in turn, may lead to shifts in opinion and then to shifts in power relationships favorable to the nonviolent group. These shifts result from withdrawal of support for the opponent and the grant of support to the nonviolent actionists. (Gene Sharp, *The Dynamics of Nonviolent Action*, vol. 3 of *The Politics of Nonviolent Action*, ed. Marina Finkelstein [Boston: Extending Horizons, 1973], 657)

27. On this final point, see Duane K. Friesen and Gerald W. Schlabach, eds., *At Peace and Unafraid: Public Order, Security and the Wisdom of the Cross* (Scottdale, PA: Herald Press, 2005), especially the opening three chapters.

28. For a full account of this shift, see Leo Driedger and Donald B. Kraybill, *Mennonite Peacemaking: From Quietism to Activism* (Scottdale, PA: Herald Press, 1994). For one of my own contributions to this shift, see Gerald W. Schlabach, "Where Are Our Wounds?: A Call for Active Nonviolence in Central America," *Mission Focus* 12, no. 2 (June 1984): 21–24.

29. Benedicto Tapia de Renedo, ed., *Hélder Câmara: Proclamas a la Juventud*, Serie PEDAL, no. 64 (Salamanca: Ediciones Sigueme, 1976), 185–204; Hélder Câmara, *Dom Helder Camara: Essential Writings*, selected with an intro. by Francis McDonagh, Modern Spiritual Masters Series (Maryknoll, NY: Orbis Books, 2009), 12, 85–88, 101–10, 116.

30. This has been the largely untold story of the last century: Indian independence. Regional successes at resistance even in Nazi-occupied Europe.

The overthrow of Marcos through "People Power" in the Philippines. The 1989 Revolution, leading to the breakup of the Soviet empire—what some have called "World War III without the war." The U.S. Civil Rights movement against segregation and KKK terrorism. The end of apartheid in South Africa. The democratic overthrow of Pinochet in Chile. The overthrow of Milosovic in Serbia, doing what NATO bombing couldn't do. The Orange Revolution in Ukraine. The Cedar Revolution in Lebanon. The overthrow of Mubarek in Egypt.

31. Second Vatican Council, *Gaudium et Spes*, §80.

32. Scott Russell Sanders, *Staying Put: Making a Home in a Restless World* (Boston: Beacon Press, 1993), 114.

33. Gerald W. Schlabach, "Beyond Two- Versus One-Kingdom Theology: Abrahamic Community as a Mennonite Paradigm for Engagement in Society," *Conrad Grebel Review* 11, no. 3 (Fall 1993): 205. Chapter 5 in the present book will build toward a restatement of this definition of an Abrahamic community and the grammar of the Gospel it embodies.

34. Daniel Boyarin and Jonathan Boyarin, "Diaspora: Generation and the Ground of Jewish Diaspora," in *Theorizing Diaspora: A Reader*, ed. Jana Evans Braziel and Anita Mannur, Keyworks in Cultural Studies (Malden, MA: Blackwell, 2003), 106.

35. Karl Rahner, "The Present Situation of Christians: A Theological Interpretation of the Position of Christians in the Modern World," in *The Christian Commitment: Essays in Pastoral Theology* (New York: Sheed and Ward, 1963), 26.

36. Philip Jenkins, *The Next Christendom: The Coming of Global Christianity*, 3rd ed. (Oxford; New York: Oxford University Press, 2011).

Chapter 2—pages 31–63

1. See also Second Vatican Council, *Lumen Gentium*, Dogmatic Constitution on the Church (November 21, 1964), §16.

2. Second Vatican Council, *Gaudium et Spes*, §§1–3.

3. Ibid., §§4–9. The word "recoil" appears in §4.

4. The lone footnote in *Evangelii Nuntiandi*, §21 cites chapter 39 of Tertullian's *Apologeticum*, which follows directly upon two chapters in which Tertullian had justified early Christian refusal to participate in affairs of state that involved military bloodshed and violent spectacle, in part because "we acknowledge one all-embracing commonwealth—the world." This is just one of a number of early Christian texts to which we will return in chapter 6 when we review patristic foundations for becoming a Catholic peace church precisely by embracing life in diaspora.

302   *A Pilgrim People*

5. This, at least, is my own working definition. For a survey of some of the problems and debates surrounding the definition of diaspora as a social scientific term see James Clifford, "Diasporas," *Cultural Anthropology* 9, no. 3 (August 1994): 302–38. The very etymology of the term readily and appropriately takes on normative theological import, however. As the Oxford English Dictionary explains, the Greek term, "from *diaspeirein* 'disperse,' from *dia* 'across'+ *speirein* 'scatter' . . . originated in the Septuagint [Greek translation of the Hebrew scriptures] (Deuteronomy 28:25) in the phrase *esē diaspora en pasais basileias tēs gēs* 'thou shalt be a dispersion in all kingdoms of the earth.'" See chapter 4 for a fuller discussion of the conceptual issues and theological reasons for appropriating the term.

6. John Paul II, *Centesimus Annus*, §22.

7. United States Conference of Catholic Bishops, *Harvest of Justice*, introduction.

8. See John Paul Lederach, "On Simplicity and Complexity: Finding the Essence of Peacebuilding," in *The Moral Imagination: The Art and Soul of Building Peace* (New York: Oxford University Press, 2005), 31–40.

9. Second Vatican Council, *Gaudium et Spes*, §84. Also see §23.

10. Drew Christiansen, SJ, "Peacebuilding in Catholic Social Teaching," *Origins* 38, no. 4 (June 5, 2008): 61.

11. While I will be crediting Fr. Christiansen wherever I quote him directly, I wish to acknowledge my debt to him for this entire section. He and I may not agree on every point of interpretation and emphasis, especially insofar as he holds out more hope for the practicability of the just-war tradition than I, yet I cannot imagine writing the current section, or perhaps even this book, if he had not first teased out the steady emergence of a new ethic of peace and war in the Catholic Church. Among his published writings on the topic are the following: "Peacemaking and the Use of Force: Behind the Pope's Stringent Just-War Teaching," *America* 180, no. 17 (May 15, 1999): 13–18; "After Sept. 11: Catholic Social Teaching on Peace and War," *Origins* 32, no. 3 (May 30, 2002): 33, 35–40; "Hawks, Doves and Pope John Paul II," *America* 187, no. 4 (August 12, 2002): 9–11; "Whither the 'Just War'?," *America* 188, no. 10 (March 24, 2003): 7–11; "Benedict XVI: Peacemaker," *America* 197, no. 2 (July 16, 2007): 10–15; "Peacebuilding in Catholic Social Teaching"; "The Ethics of Peacemaking"; "Nonviolence, the Responsibility to Protect and Peacebuilding," *Origins* 41, no. 17 (September 29, 2011): 265–70; "A Vision of Peace: How the Prophetic 'Pacem in Terris' Helped Change the World," *America* 208, no. 12 (April 8, 2013): 11–14. I have also benefited from the following unpublished papers and lectures: "What Is a Peace Church? A Roman Catholic Perspective," paper presented at the International Mennonite-Roman Catholic Dialogue (Karlsruhe, Germany, 2000); "'Never Again War': The Presumption against the Use of Force in Contemporary Catholic Social Teaching and the Diplomacy of the Holy See," unpublished paper (2002);

Notes 303

"Resisting Evil: Recent Catholic Teaching on War, Nonviolence and Peacemaking," lecture (Seattle University, 2003); " 'No, Never Again War': The Evolution of Catholic Teaching on Peace and War," lecture (Santa Clara University, 2004); "John Paul II Peacemaker: A Nonviolent Pope in a Time of Terror," The Thomas Lecture, Saint Meinrad Seminary (Saint Meinrad, IN, 2005).

12. On this question, Christiansen's own thinking appears to have evolved, however. Compare "After Sept. 11," 40, with "Peacebuilding in Catholic Social Teaching," 61. Note also that with the guidance of Pax Christi International, a new effort called the Catholic Nonviolence Initiative has been pressing Pope Francis for an encyclical on "gospel nonviolence" and its implications since April 2016, when it held a conference on "Nonviolence and Just Peace" in Rome with the cosponsorship of the Pontifical Council for Justice and Peace. For a full account of the conference and the debates surrounding it, see Marie Dennis, ed., *Choosing Peace: The Catholic Church Returns to Gospel Nonviolence* (Maryknoll, NY: Orbis Books, 2018). For more information on the Catholic Nonviolence Initiative see https://nonviolencejustpeace.net/. The "Appeal to the Catholic Church to re-commit to the centrality of Gospel nonviolence" that the April 2016 conference issued is available both in the book and on the website.

13. Christiansen, "After Sept. 11," 38.

14. See the second footnote in part II, chapter 5 of Second Vatican Council, *Gaudium et Spes*.

15. For an account of a quietly influential friendship between Catholic peace activists Jean and Hildegard Goss-Mayr, and Cardinal Ottaviani, see Tom Cornell, "How Catholics Began to Speak Their Peace," *Salt of the Earth*, no. 5 (September/October 1996): 17–18. On the role of Ottaviani's speech in favor of what became Part II, Chapter 5, Section 1 of *Gaudium et Spes* on the avoidance of war (§79–82), see Giuseppe Alberigo, ed., *History of Vatican II*, 5 volumes, English version edited by Joseph Komonchak (Maryknoll, NY; Leuven, Belgium: Orbis Books; Peeters, 1996), 5:173–75.

16. Cf. John C. Ford, SJ, "The Morality of Obliteration Bombing," *Theological Studies* 5, no. 3 (September 1944): 261–309. Published as it was while World War II was still raging, Ford's article had initially been a "voice crying in the wilderness," but became increasingly influential in the decades to follow.

17. Second Vatican Council, *Gaudium et Spes*, §27.

18. Ibid., §80.

19. Cf. Francisco de Vitoria, *Comentarios a la Secunda Secundae de santo Tomás*, [1534–1537], ed. Vicente Beltran de Heredia, Biblioteca de Teológos Españoles, vols. 2–6 and 17 (Salamanca: Apartado 17, 1932–52), 2:280. Perhaps aware of the Anabaptists who were his contemporaries in the early sixteenth century, the great Dominican theologian of his day spoke of the

304   *A Pilgrim People*

"haeretici novi" who were citing St. Paul to argue against Christian participation in war. "Sed hoc est haereticum," he wrote dismissively. As recently as 2003, the *New Catholic Encyclopedia's* entry on "Pacifism" (10:744–748) categorized "pacifist sects" with "heretical sects" and concluded that absolute pacifism though not relative pacifism "is still judged irreconcilable with Catholic doctrine."

20. Second Vatican Council, *Gaudium et Spes*, §§78–79.

21. Ibid., §80.

22. A footnote at the end of the call for a reevaluation of war in *Gaudium et Spes* §80 quotes the encyclical *Pacem in Terris* that John XXIII had issued only months before the council's opening: "Therefore in this age of ours, which prides itself on its atomic power, it is irrational to think that war is a proper way to obtain justice for violated rights."

23. Second Vatican Council, *Gaudium et Spes*, §78: "To the extent that people are sinners, the threat of war hangs over them and will so continue until the coming of Christ; but insofar as they can vanquish sin by coming together in charity, violence itself will be vanquished . . ." *Gaudium et Spes*, §82: "But let us not be buoyed up with false hope. . . . The church, however, living with these anxieties, even as it makes these statements, has not lost hope."

24. Following sections 77–82 in *Gaudium et Spes* on peace and war, the document turns to the system of international relations, economic cooperation in pursuit of human development, global dialogue, and the role of Christians in these tasks.

25. Ibid., §82.

26. Ibid., §78.

27. Even the architectonic implications in the metaphor of peace*building* can be a bit misleading, though I myself will employ this increasingly standard term.

28. Paul VI, *Populorum Progressio*, §§76, 87.

29. See Pope John XXIII, *Mater et Magistra* [Christianity and Social Progress], encyclical (May 15, 1961), §§200–211; *Pacem in Terris* [Peace on Earth], encyclical (April 11, 1963), §§130–31; Second Vatican Council, *Gaudium et Spes*, §§23–25. For key examples from the following years see Paul VI, *Populorum Progressio*, §§45–55; Pope John Paul II, *Sollicitudo Rei Socialis*, Encyclical on Social Concern (December 30, 1987), §§9, 26, 36.

30. Alberigo, *History of Vatican II*, I:57, cf. V:623, 638–39.

31. Second Vatican Council, *Gaudium et Spes*, §26.

32. Ibid., §4.

33. Ibid., §58. For an extended commentary on this section and its remarkable prescience concerning the ambiguous dynamics of globalization, see Schlabach, *Unlearning Protestantism*, 193–202.

34. Second Vatican Council, *Gaudium et Spes*, §82.

35. Ibid., §82.

36. Ibid., §83.
37. Pope Paul VI, Address to the United Nations Organization (October 4, 1965), http://www.vatican.va/holy_father/paul_vi/speeches/1965/documents/hf_p-vi_spe_19651004_united-nations_en.html.
38. Paul VI, *Populorum Progressio*, §29.
39. Ibid., §30.
40. Ibid., §31. Cf. the again more-restrictive statement by Pope Paul in *Evangelii Nuntiandi*, apostolic exhortation on Evangelization in the Modern World (December 8, 1975), §37.
41. John Paul II, *Centesimus Annus*, §52, echoing and citing Pope Paul VI, Address to the United Nations Organization (October 4, 1965).
42. NCCB, *The Challenge of Peace*, §§175–76.
43. Ibid., §178.
44. Ibid.
45. This is the clear implication of Ford, "The Morality of Obliteration Bombing," and the sustained argument in Paul Ramsey, *War and the Christian Conscience: How Shall Modern War Be Conducted Justly?*, published for the Lilly Endowment Research Program in Christianity and Politics (Durham, NC: Duke University Press, 1961).
46. NCCB, *The Challenge of Peace*, §99.
47. Unless otherwise noted, this paragraph summarizes the arguments in *The Challenge of Peace*, §§179–84.
48. Ibid., §186.
49. Ibid., §184.
50. Note the skepticism that Pope John Paul expressed in *Centesimus Annus*, §25 toward " those who, in the name of political realism, wish to banish law and morality from the political arena."
51. For an elaboration of the fundamental differences between classical just-war thinking and Christian Realism, see William R. Stevenson, *Christian Love and Just War: Moral Paradox and Political Life in St. Augustine and His Modern Interpreters* (Macon, GA: Mercer University Press, 1987).
52. NCCB, *The Challenge of Peace*, §186.
53. Ibid., §121.
54. Ibid., §120.
55. Ibid., §§221–30.
56. Ibid., §236.
57. United States Conference of Catholic Bishops, *Harvest of Justice*, § I.B.
58. John Paul II, *Centesimus Annus*, §26.
59. Ibid.
60. Ibid., §17.
61. Ibid., §18.
62. Ibid., §19. Likewise, the pope continued in this section, the solution that consumeristic capitalism offered was just as materialistic and contrary

to spiritual values as Marxism, while Marxism offered de-colonized nations shortcuts to national development that would prove illusory.

63. Thanks to prominent "truth and reconciliation commissions," beginning in South Africa in 1995, those two words now often stand together as a pair. Yet in Catholic discourse "truth" and "reconciliation" often remain estranged, championed as they are by different camps. Writing in *Centesimus Annus*, John Paul II had already anticipated why they must not stand estranged.

64. John Paul II, *Centesimus Annus*, §23.
65. Ibid.
66. Ibid., §24.
67. Ibid., §41.
68. Ibid., §25.
69. Ibid.
70. Ibid.
71. Ibid., §51.
72. Ibid.
73. Ibid.
74. Ibid.
75. Ibid., §52.
76. Stanley Hauerwas, *The Peaceable Kingdom: A Primer in Christian Ethics* (Notre Dame, IN: University of Notre Dame Press, 1983), 99. Cf. John Howard Yoder, "The Kingdom as Social Ethic," in *The Priestly Kingdom: Social Ethics as Gospel* (Notre Dame, IN: University of Notre Dame Press, 1984), 80–101.
77. The following section is adapted from the preface to Schlabach and Pfeil, *Sharing Peace*, xi–xviii, and is used with permission.
78. The complete program of the Day of Prayer for Peace in the World, Assisi, January 24, 2002, is available at http://www.vatican.va/special/assisi_20020124_en.html. See especially the "Reading by some of the representatives of a common text of commitment to peace," which is the source for the quotations in the paragraphs that follow.
79. Pope John Paul II, Common Commitment to Peace (*Impegno Comune Per La Pace*), http://www.vatican.va/news_services/liturgy/documents/ns_lit_doc_20020124_assisi-impegno_it.html.
80. Ibid.
81. See Walter Klaassen, *Anabaptism: Neither Catholic nor Protestant* (Waterloo, ON: Conrad Press, 1981). In particular, Anabaptism continued to operate from a more communal understanding of salvation in which participation in the church played an essential role, and insisted on coordinating faith and works in a way quite similar to what the Council of Trent was concluding. Magisterial reformers clearly recognized this affinity, for they regularly denounced the Anabaptists as a "new monkery"—in other words, something that looked too much like monasticism in its tight-knit communities with

strong ethical expectations of all members, even though celibacy was not required of those members.

82. That special relationship of what Christians see as continuity with the ancient faith and people of Israel has led one theologian to call Judaism a "non-non-Christian religion," and has led the Vatican itself to house its Commission for Religious Relations with the Jews not within its Pontifical Council for Interreligious Dialogue, but as a special unit within the Pontifical Council for Promoting Christian Unity.

83. John Paul II, *Centesimus Annus*, §§22–23, 51–52.

84. Among twentieth-century Mennonite historians, Harold S. Bender has stood for many others as the especially influential example, while among twentieth-century Mennonite theologians, John Howard Yoder has stood as the especially prominent one.

85. Mennonite World Conference and Pontifical Council for Promoting Church Unity, "Called Together to Be Peacemakers." The document is also available as Appendix A in Schlabach and Pfeil, *Sharing Peace*, 189–259, and at http://www.vatican.va/roman_curia/pontifical_councils/chrstuni /mennonite-conference-docs/rc_pc_chrstuni_doc_20110324_mennonite _en.html. Additional translations are available at http://www.bridgefolk .net/theology/dialogue. Quotation is from §15.

86. *Called Together to Be Peacemakers*, §20.

87. Ibid.

88. Different kinds of pronouncements by popes, bishops, and Vatican offices enjoy different levels of authority, and the subtleties of infallible vs. definitive vs. authoritative but noninfallible Catholic teaching inevitably invite controversy and disputation. But when the Pontifical Council for Promoting Christian Unity participates in an ecumenical dialogue and issues a final report, those parts of such a document that not only report on deliberations but offer shared theological affirmations carry at least as much authority as pronouncements by other pontifical councils. Furthermore, in the case of *Called Together to Be Peacemakers*, delegates to the Mennonite-Catholic dialogue of 1998–2003 report that the Catholic bishop who co-chaired the dialogue insisted that the Congregation for the Doctrine of the Faith (CDF) vet the document before its publication. Heading the CDF at the time was Cardinal Joseph Ratzinger, soon to become Pope Benedict XVI.

89. To be sure, for the Catholic Church to embrace normative nonviolence does not entirely distance the church from the possibility of justifiable war as a legitimate exception when truly a last resort. But it does strengthen the stringency of just-war thinking.

90. Mennonite World Conference and Pontifical Council for Promoting Church Unity, "A Mennonite and Catholic Contribution to the World Council of Churches' *Decade to Overcome Violence*." The document is also available as Appendix B in Schlabach and Pfeil, *Sharing Peace*, 260–68.

Chapter 3—pages 64–94

1. Mennonite World Conference and Pontifical Council for Promoting Church Unity, "Called Together to Be Peacemakers"; also available as Appendix A in Schlabach and Pfeil, *Sharing Peace*, 189–259.

2. Mennonite World Conference and Pontifical Council for Promoting Church Unity, "A Mennonite and Catholic Contribution to the World Council of Churches' *Decade to Overcome Violence*," section C; also available as Appendix B in Schlabach and Pfeil, *Sharing Peace*, 260–68.

3. Second Vatican Council, *Gaudium et Spes*, §82.

4. The *Catechism of the Catholic Church* notes this ancient tradition in part 3, section 2, §§2064–67, and then goes on to organize its summary of Christian moral teaching accordingly. This approach to Christian ethics is hardly unique to Catholics, however. See for example John Calvin's *Institutes* 2.8.11.

5. See for example *Of the Morals of the Catholic Church*, chapters 26–28; *City of God* 10.3–7, 14.28, 19.14; *On Christian Doctrine* (aka *Teaching Christianity*) 1.35.39, 2.7.10; and Sermon no. 125 on John 5:2. I have written more extensively on Augustine's ethic of love in *For the Joy Set Before Us: Augustine and Self-Denying Love* (Notre Dame, IN: University of Notre Dame Press, 2000) and summarized the structure of his thought in Gerald W. Schlabach and Allan D. Fitzgerald, OSA, "Ethics," in collaboration with Nello Cipriani, OSA, et al., in *Augustine Through the Ages: An Encyclopedia*, gen. ed. Allan D. Fitzgerald, OSA (Grand Rapids, MI: Eerdmans, 1999), 320–30.

6. Augustine did not say this exactly, and yet one of his clearest resolutions to the problematics of how to love neighbor as self was to pair them exactly by stressing that we ought to desire and actively seek exactly the same for both self and neighbor. See *On Christian Doctrine* 1.20.21–22, which climaxes with the following: "So all who love their neighbors in the right way ought so to deal with them that they too love God with all their heart, all their soul, all their mind. By loving them, you see, in this way as themselves, they are relating all their love of themselves and of the others to that love of God, which allows no channel to be led off from itself that will diminish its own flow."

7. See John 4:20-24, where Jesus' conversation with a Samaritan woman alludes to this dispute.

8. Augustine, *De doctrina christiana* 1.28.29. As Oliver O'Donovan has noted, precisely because Augustine wanted to base his ethic solely on Jesus' love commands and not depend on principles from elsewhere that might undermine the principle of universal equality he found there, he had to rely on the limits of time and opportunity in order to sort out and prioritize the multiple demands of "all people." (See Oliver O'Donovan, *The Problem of Self-Love in St. Augustine* [New Haven: Yale University Press, 1980], 122.) Here in this passage, therefore, Augustine did a thought experiment in which he imagined having a surplus available to help one person, but meeting two

people who had equal need, neither of whom was any closer to him than the other. One would simply have to flip a coin to decide whom to help. The lesson, though, was that in some sense the location that places a friend, physical neighbor, or even a family member proximate and his or her needs thus prioritized is ultimately random.

9. Augustine, *City of God*, 19.14. For additional discussions of proximate love by Augustine, see his Homily no. 8 on the First Epistle of John, 8.4, *Ten Homilies on the First Epistle of St. John*, in *Augustine: Later Works*, ed. and trans. John Burnaby, The Library of Christian Classics, vol. 8 (Philadelphia: Westminster Press, 1955), 251–348. See also Raymond Canning, *The Unity of Love for God and Neighbour in St. Augustine* (Heverlee, Belgium: Augustinian Historical Institute, 1993), 168, 219; O'Donovan, *The Problem of Self-Love in St. Augustine*, 121–22.

10. This would be one way to name the concern that drove my earlier book, *Unlearning Protestantism*. See especially chapter 3, "The Practice of Stability."

11. Augustine, *Homilies on the Gospel of John*, vol. 7 of *A Select Library of the Nicene and Post-Nicene Fathers of the Christian Church*, first series, ed. Philip Schaff (Peabody, MA: Hendrickson Publishers, 1994), 65.1.

12. O'Donovan, *The Problem of Self-Love in St. Augustine*, 122.

13. In referring to "traditions of Western Christianity that Augustine has so influenced," I refer not only to mainstream traditions of Roman Catholicism, Lutheranism, and Calvinism, which have all appropriated Augustine's thought, albeit with different emphases. Elsewhere I have argued that even as they have contested key developments in these Augustinian traditions, free church and historic peace church traditions have appropriated Augustinian convictions to do so. See Gerald W. Schlabach, "The Correction of the Augustinians: A Case Study in the Critical Appropriation of a Suspect Tradition," in *The Early Church and the Free Church: Bridging the Historical and Theological Divide*, ed. Daniel H. Williams (Grand Rapids, MI: Eerdmans, 2002), 47–74; and "The Christian Witness in the Earthly City: John H. Yoder as Augustinian Interlocutor," chap. 11 in *A Mind Patient and Untamed: Assessing John Howard Yoder's Contribution to Theology, Ethics, and Peacemaking*, ed. Ben C. Ollenburger and Gayle Gerber Koontz, intro. by Stanley Hauerwas (Telford, PA: Cascadia Publishing House, 2004), 221–44.

14. Augustine, "Letter 138," To Marcellinus [412] in *Letters 100-155* (Epistulae), vol. II/2 of *The Works of Saint Augustine: A Translation for the 21st Century*, ed. Boniface Ramsey, trans. Roland Teske, SJ (Hyde Park, NY: New City Press, 2003), 2.14.

15. Pope John Paul II, Address at the Fiftieth General Assembly of the United Nations Organization (New York, October 5, 1995), §15, http://www.vatican.va/holy_father/john_paul_ii/speeches/1995/october/documents/hf_jp-ii_spe_05101995_address-to-uno_en.html.

310 A Pilgrim People

16. The late Ivan Kauffman, a freelance journalist and cofounder of Bridgefolk, did an exhaustive study of all documents available on the Vatican website in which Popes Paul VI and John Paul II used the phrase "civilization of love." (Ivan Kauffman, "The Civilization of Love: John Paul's Vision for the Third Millennium," unpublished paper [2009].) The total number is at least 229—21 by Paul VI and 208 by John Paul II. Following John Paul's 1993 reflection on the first hundred years of modern Catholic social teaching as well as the momentous events of 1989 in the encyclical *Centesimus Annus*, the pope's employment of the term increased markedly. In the last dozen years of his papacy it appeared in nearly 200 statements; in the year 1999 alone, in the lead-up to Jubilee 2000, it appeared in 33 different statements. John Paul was no doubt expressing his hope as much as he was reporting when he wrote in his 1994 *Letter to Families* that the concept had now "entered the teaching of the Church" and that "today it is difficult to imagine a statement by the Church, or about the Church, which does not mention the civilization of love." Pope John Paul II, *Gratissimam Sane*, Letter to Families (February 2, 1994), §13, http://www.vatican.va/holy_father/john_paul_ii/letters/documents/hf_jp-ii_let_02021994_families_en.html.

17. Pontifical Council for Justice and Peace, *Compendium of the Social Doctrine of the Church*, USCCB Publishing No. 5-692 (Cittá del Vaticano; Washington, DC: Libreria Editrice Vaticana; [distributed by the] United States Conference of Catholic Bishops, 2004).

18. Pope Paul VI, Regina Coeli Address on Pentecost Sunday" (May 17, 1970), http://www.vatican.va/holy_father/paul_vi/angelus/1970/documents/hf_p-vi_reg_19700517_it.html:

> Although to some it may seem strange, Pentecost is an event that also involves the secular world. For it gave rise to a new sociology— one which penetrates the values of the spirit, which forms our hierarchy of values, and which confronts us with the truth, and with the ultimate destiny of humanity. It is this which has given us our belief in the dignity of the human person, and our civil customs, and which above all leads us to resolutely rise above all divisions and conflicts between humans, and to form humanity into a single family of the children of God, free and fraternal. We recall the symbolism at the beginning of this amazing story, of the miracle of many different languages being made comprehensible to everyone by the Spirit. It is the *civilization of love* and of peace which Pentecost has inaugurated—and we are all aware how much today the world still needs love and peace! [emphasis added]

19. Pope John Paul II, *Christifideles Laici*, apostolic exhortation on the Vocation and Mission of the Lay Faithful in the Church and in the World (December 30, 1988), §9.

20. John Paul II, Address at the Fiftieth General Assembly of the United Nations Organization, §1.

21. Ibid., §17.
22. Ibid., §2.
23. Ibid.
24. Ibid., §4.
25. Ibid., §3.
26. Ibid., §12.
27. Ibid.
28. Ibid., §4.
29. Ibid., §13.
30. Ibid.
31. Ibid.
32. Ibid., §5.
33. Ibid., §6.
34. Ibid., §7.
35. Ibid.
36. Ibid., §§7–8.
37. Ibid., §8.
38. Ibid., §1 and §14.
39. Ibid., §3.
40. Ibid., §14.
41. Ibid., §9.
42. Ibid., §§9–10.
43. Ibid., §10.
44. Ibid., §17.
45. Ibid., §3.
46. Ibid., §4.
47. Ibid.
48. Ibid., §7.

Chapter 4—pages 95–130

1. Rahner, "The Present Situation of Christians," 17, 26. In my text I date this essay at 1961, when Rahner first presented it in German, in order to situate it historically as slightly pre-Vatican II.

2. Joseph Cardinal Ratzinger, *God and the World: Believing and Living in Our Time: A Conversation with Peter Seewald*, trans. Henry Taylor (San Francisco: Ignatius Press, 2002), 259.

3. As I wrote the first draft of this chapter in 2013, an unprecedented six of nine justices on the U.S. Supreme Court were Catholic. The other three were Jewish. Remarkably, in light of the Protestant, sometimes anti-Catholic, cultural and political history of the United States, for the first time ever none was Protestant.

4. I am indebted to Stanley Hauerwas for pointing to the significance of the essay by Rahner that I will cite at length in this section. See the opening pages of his article on the challenges of globalization, "A Worldly Church: Politics, Theology of the Church, and the Common Good," *Journal of Law, Philosophy and Culture* 3, no. 1 (Spring 2009): 450–59, also available as chapter 10 of Stanley Hauerwas, *War and the American Difference: Theological Reflections on Violence and National Identity* (Grand Rapids, MI: Baker Academic, 2011), 135–50.

5. Richard P. McBrien, gen. ed., and Harold W. Attridge et al., assoc. eds., *The HarperCollins Encyclopedia of Catholicism* (New York: HarperCollins, 1995), 1077.

6. Rahner, "The Present Situation of Christians," 17. Rahner gave some pages in this essay (pp. 14–17) to distinguishing between "ought" and "must." The distinction is essentially between ontological necessity and historical necessity. The preeminent example is the crucifixion of Jesus Christ, which God did not will as something that "ought" to happen, but did will as something that "must" happen in light of sinful human rebellion in order to redeem humanity.

7. Rahner, "The Present Situation of Christians," 14.

8. Ibid., 17–18.

9. Ibid., 17.

10. Also see Rahner, "The Present Situation of Christians," 23–26, for his discussion of what it will mean for Catholics to live out their Christianity as a minority among many non-Christians.

11. Rahner, "The Present Situation of Christians," 17.

12. If this simply sounds like pre-Vatican II Catholic triumphalism to some readers, they would do well to remember that all Christians commit themselves to some version of this hope whenever they join in the "Our Father" or "Lord's Prayer" and pray, "Your will be done on earth as it is in heaven."

13. While hardly sectarian, Rahner was actually ready to entertain the notion that in a strictly technical sociological sense, the social posture of the church of diaspora is that of a "sect":

> *Sociologically* speaking, the Church of the diaspora has the character of a sect, in contrast to that of a Church of the vast mass of people, a Church *in possession*, and hence, sociologically, confronting the individual not as something constituted and sustained by himself but as independent of him and over against him; the diaspora Church has the advantages that her "sect" character gives her, and the duty constantly to overcome the dangers inherent in it. The Church of the diaspora rests permanently on the good will of her ordinary members. (Rahner, "The Present Situation of Christians," 25–26)

14. Ibid., 18–19.

15. Ibid., 26. Attempting to make Rahner's meaning clearer, I have partly paraphrased a sentence here concerning Christian reactions to being shaken out of their dream. Here is the original: "[W]e often seek, again in a false context and with inappropriate means, to realize this dream-ideal, and so apply ourselves to the wrong point altogether." Cagily, by the way, Rahner then added: "I had better refrain from giving examples."
16. Ibid., 26.
17. Ibid., 27–60.
18. Ibid., 30.
19. Ibid., 34–35, with quotation from p. 35.
20. Stéphane Dufoix, in his book *Diasporas*, trans. William Rodarmor, with a foreword by Roger Waldinger (Berkeley: University of California Press, 2008), seemed to concur. Initially he worried that the term "diaspora" had suffered an inflation that allowed it to be applied to most of the world's peoples (1). Though until the 1950s the term applied strictly to religious communities (17), "in the space of about fifteen years, 'diaspora' has evolved into an all-purpose word used to describe a growing number of populations," with both wide and loose usage (30). But whatever his initial reservations about conceptual imprecision, by the end of his book, Dufoix was concluding that "in its contemporary usage, 'diaspora' is perfectly suited to the modern world. Relieved of its heavy burden of misery, persecution, and punishment, the word nicely fits the changes in the relationship to distance, in view of the quasi disappearance of time in its relationship to space. . . . 'Diaspora' has become a global word that fits the global world" (106, 108).
21. Parag Khanna, "The End of the Nation State?," *New York Times*, October 12, 2013.
22. This is the definition I have offered my students for years, more for pedagogical purposes than for the sake of precise conceptual theory. Note, though, how my definition of globalization coincides with the following description of globalization by one of its leading theorists, Arjun Appadurai ("Disjuncture and Difference in the Global Cultural Economy," in *Theorizing Diaspora: A Reader*, ed. Jana Evans Braziel and Anita Mannur, Keyworks in Cultural Studies [Malden, MA: Blackwell, 2003], 26):

> It takes only the merest acquaintance with the facts of the modern world to note that it is now an interactive system in a sense which is strikingly new. Historians and sociologists, especially those concerned with translocal processes, . . . have long been aware that the world has been a congeries of large-scale interactions for many centuries. Yet today's world involves interactions of a new order and intensity. . . . [F]ew will deny that given the problems of time, distance, and limited technologies for the command of resources across vast spaces, cultural dealings between socially and spatially separated groups have until the last few centuries been bridged at great cost and sustained over time only with great effort. The forces of

314 *A Pilgrim People*

cultural gravity seemed always to pull away from the formation of large-scale ecumenes whether religious, commercial or political, towards smaller-scale accretions of intimacy and interest. . . . Sometime in the last few centuries the nature of this gravitational field seems to have changed.

23. The process is hardly neat, of course, nor is the resulting web of interconnections anything so balanced and symmetrical as classic spider web. The influential theorist of globalization Arjun Appadurai has thus sought to recognize the jagged disjunctures inherent in globalization, as well as the disparate perspectives on globalization that people will have from different locations, by speaking of five "dimensions of cultural flow"—ethnoscapes, technoscapes, financescapes, mediascapes and ideoscapes. If these -scapes all constitute "imagined worlds," that itself reflects another dynamic of globalization: "An important fact of the world we live in today is that many persons on the globe live in such imagined worlds (and not just imagined communities) and thus are able to contest and sometimes even subvert the imagined worlds of the official mind and of the entrepreneurial mentality that surround them." See Appadurai, "Disjuncture and Difference in the Global Cultural Economy," 31–37, with quotations from p. 31.

24. The literature on globalization is itself large and growing. Some sources that I and colleagues have found helpful are: John Tomlinson, *Cultural Imperialism: A Critical Introduction* (London: Pinter Publishers, 1991); Arjun Appadurai, *Modernity at Large: Cultural Dimensions of Globalization*, Public Worlds, vol. 1 (Minneapolis: University of Minnesota Press, 1996); Benjamin R. Barber, *Jihad vs. McWorld: How Globalism and Tribalism Are Reshaping the World*, 1st Ballantine Books ed. (New York: Times Books, 1996); Jerry Mander and Edward Goldsmith, eds., *The Case against the Global Economy: And for a Turn toward the Local* (San Francisco: Sierra Club Books, 1996); R. J. Holton, *Globalization and the Nation-State* (Houndmills, Basingstoke, Hampshire; New York: Macmillan Press; St. Martin's Press, 1998); Fredric Jameson and Masao Miyoshi, eds., *The Cultures of Globalization*, Post-Contemporary Interventions (Durham, NC: Duke University Press, 1998); David Held et al., *Global Transformations: Politics, Economics and Culture* (Stanford, CA: Stanford University Press, 1999); Maryann K. Cusimano, ed., *Beyond Sovereignty: Issues for a Global Agenda* (Boston: Bedford/St. Martin's, 2000); James H. Mittelman, *The Globalization Syndrome: Transformation and Resistance* (Princeton, NJ: Princeton University Press, 2000); Jan Aart Scholte, *Globalization: A Critical Introduction* (Basingstoke; New York: Palgrave, 2000); Peter Dicken, *Global Shift: Reshaping the Global Economic Map in the 21st Century* (New York: Guilford Press, 2003). Insofar as the literature of "diaspora studies" inevitably engages the dynamics of globalization, of course, many other sources that I reference throughout this chapter could be added to this bibliography.

25. John Paul II, Address at the Fiftieth General Assembly of the United Nations Organization, §8. See pp. 86–88 above.

26. Ibid., §7.

27. All quotations in this paragraph are from Daniel Boyarin and Jonathan Boyarin, "Diaspora," 97.

28. Daniel Boyarin, *A Radical Jew: Paul and the Politics of Identity*, Contraversions (Berkeley; London: University of California Press, 1994).

29. Daniel Boyarin and Jonathan Boyarin, "Diaspora," 86–88, with quotations from p. 88. The pages that then follow critique a number of modern and post-modern thinkers and argue that their proposals are not just bad for Jews, but other real non-abstract communities as well. The short and somewhat random list of indigenous peoples at the end of this paragraph is my own, but note that the Boyarins themselves discuss a number of other ethnic and indigenous groups along the way.

30. Ibid., 109–11. Tribalism and universalism are not just Gentile tendencies, but have been part of Judaism's own internal struggles and debates. The Hellenization to which Paul contributed so much was nonetheless a broader form of Jewish universalism.

31. Jonathan Boyarin and Daniel Boyarin, *Powers of Diaspora: Two Essays on the Relevance of Jewish Culture* (Minneapolis: University of Minnesota Press, 2002), vii, 21, 30–31; Daniel Boyarin and Jonathan Boyarin, "Diaspora," 110.

32. Daniel Boyarin and Jonathan Boyarin, "Diaspora," 110.

33. This is of course the claim implied in the title of the book *Powers of Diaspora*. Communities constituted by genealogy and tradition rather than territorial control may be perpetually strengthened through the self-examination required by accountability to the ancestors. And though "everything is permanently at risk" in diaspora, even that offers a paradoxical form of power. For "diasporic consciousness" has the capacity to honestly accept the contingencies of social life that are always present anyway, and does so at those very points where territorial nation-states falsely, dangerously, and often violently tend to suppress identities that compete with nationalism (*Powers of Diaspora*, 4, cf. pp. 9–10).

34. Jonathan Boyarin and Daniel Boyarin, *Powers of Diaspora*, 114–18; Daniel Boyarin and Jonathan Boyarin, "Diaspora," 101. Quotation is from the latter location.

35. Jonathan Boyarin and Daniel Boyarin, *Powers of Diaspora*, 33; Daniel Boyarin and Jonathan Boyarin, "Diaspora," 110.

36. Daniel Boyarin and Jonathan Boyarin, "Diaspora," 110–11.

37. See pp. 58–63.

38. See, for example, Reinhold Niebuhr, "Why the Christian Church Is Not Pacifist."

39. John H[oward] Yoder, *Reinhold Niebuhr and Christian Pacifism* (1955, A Concern Reprint; Scottdale, PA: Concern, n.d.); *The Christian Witness to the State*, Institute of Mennonite Studies Series, no. 3 (Newton, KS: Faith and Life Press, 1964); *The Original Revolution: Essays on Christian Pacifism*, Christian

Peace Shelf (Scottdale, PA: Herald Press, 1971); *The Politics of Jesus; The Priestly Kingdom: Social Ethics as Gospel* (Notre Dame, IN: University of Notre Dame Press, 1984); *Royal Priesthood; For the Nations: Essays Public and Evangelical* (Grand Rapids, MI: Eerdmans, 1997); *The Jewish-Christian Schism Revisited*, ed. Michael G. Cartwright and Peter Ochs, Radical Traditions (Grand Rapids, MI: Eerdmans, 2003).

40. The shape of Yoder's rebuttals to Niebuhr was already present in the work of his teacher Guy F. Hershberger, yet even Hershberger also honed his arguments by learning from Yoder; see Guy F. Hershberger, *War, Peace, and Nonresistance*, 3rd ed., Christian Peace Shelf Selection (Scottdale, PA: Herald Press, 1969), 232–52. For a later Mennonite ethicist who has appropriated Yoder on "middle axioms" and multilingual "translation," see Duane K. Friesen, "In Search of Security: A Theology and Ethic of Peace and Public Order," chap. 2 in *At Peace and Unafraid: Public Order, Security and the Wisdom of the Cross*, ed. Duane K. Friesen and Gerald W. Schlabach (Scottdale, PA: Herald Press, 2005), 37–82. For an appropriation of Yoder that draws out the implications of diaspora most fully (and in conversation with the Boyarins), see Alain Epp Weaver, *States of Exile: Visions of Diaspora, Witness, and Return*, Polyglossia: Radical Reformation Theologies, vol. 3 (Scottdale, PA: Herald Press, 2008), especially chaps. 4–6. Also see Schlabach, "Christian Witness in the Earthly City."

41. Yoder, *For the Nations*, 76, n. 60.

42. Ibid., 1.

43. Ibid., 33–34, 67–68.

44. Yoder, *For the Nations*, 71. Cf. John Howard Yoder, "On Not Being Ashamed of the Gospel: Particularity, Pluralism, and Validation," *Faith and Philosophy* 9, no. 3 (July 1992): 290–91.

45. Yoder, *For the Nations*, 3–5. Yoder prepared and titled *For the Nations* in part to clarify that his own position was less contrarian than his former colleague Stanley Hauerwas's position often appeared to be. Hauerwas, after all, had published *Against the Nations*. (Cf. Yoder's hint of this purpose in footnote 6 on p. 4 of *For the Nations*.) Long-time readers of Yoder, of course, know that he had regularly drawn up lists of the ways that a prophetic minority, creative minority, Abrahamic community, Jeremianic Diaspora community, or any other preferred term for a putatively sectarian group that provides societies-at-large with the resources for constructive social change. See, for example, *Christian Witness to the State*, 18-22; "Christ, the Hope of the World," 203–7; "The Biblical Mandate for Evangelical Social Action," in *For the Nations: Essays Public and Evangelical* (Grand Rapids, MI: Eerdmans, 1997), 184–89; *Body Politics: Five Practices of the Christian Community Before the Watching World* (Nashville, TN: Discipleship Resources, 1992).

46. William Safran, "The Jewish Diaspora in a Comparative and Theoretical Perspective," *Israel Studies* 10, no. 1 (Spring 2005): 36.

47. Dufoix, *Diasporas*, 1, 16–17.
48. Ibid., 1.
49. Jana Evans Braziel and Anita Mannur, "Nation, Migration, Globalization: Points of Contention in Diaspora Studies," ed. Jana Evans Braziel and Anita Mannur, in *Theorizing Diaspora: A Reader*, Keyworks in Cultural Studies (Malden, MA: Blackwell, 2003), 3.
50. Clifford, "Diasporas," 304–6. Clifford appropriates, yet for this reason also critiques, William Safran, "Diasporas in Modern Societies: Myths of Homeland and Return," *Diaspora* 1, no. 1 (1991): 83–99. Safran's later and slightly expanded list of criteria appears in "The Jewish Diaspora," 37:

1. They, or their ancestors, have been dispersed from a specific original "center" to two or more peripheral, or foreign, regions.

2. They retain a collective memory, vision, or myth about their original homeland—its physical location, history, achievements, and, often enough, sufferings.

3. Their relationship with the dominant element of society in the hostland is complicated and often uneasy. They believe that they are not, and perhaps cannot be, fully accepted by their host society and therefore feel partly alienated and insulated from it.

4. They regard their ancestral homeland as their true, ideal home and as the place to which they or their descendants would (or should) eventually return—if and when conditions are appropriate.

5. They continue to relate, personally or vicariously, to that homeland in one way or another, and their ethnocommunal consciousness and solidarity, which reach across political boundaries, are importantly defined in terms of the existence of such a relationship. That relationship may include a collective commitment to the maintenance or restoration of their original homeland and to its independence, safety, and prosperity. The absence of such a relationship makes it difficult to speak of transnationalism.

6. They wish to survive as a distinct community—in most instances as a minority—by maintaining and transmitting a cultural and/or religious heritage derived from their ancestral home and the symbols based on it. In so doing, they adapt to hostland conditions and experiences to become themselves centers of cultural creation and elaboration.

7. Their cultural, religious, economic, and/or political relationships with the homeland are reflected in a significant way in their communal institutions.

Safran himself went on to recognize, however, that "no diaspora, including the Jewish one, conforms completely to the paradigm presented above" (p. 39).

51. Clifford, "Diasporas," 306.

52. Cf. Braziel and Mannur, "Nation, Migration, Globalization," 8–10; Appadurai, "Disjuncture and Difference in the Global Cultural Economy," 42; Avtar Brah, *Cartographies of Diaspora: Contesting Identities*, Gender, Racism, Ethnicity (London; New York: Routledge, 1996), 194.

53. Dufoix, *Diasporas*, 75. Cf. Brah, *Cartographies of Diaspora*, 192–96.

54. See warnings to this effect in Brah, *Cartographies of Diaspora*, 182–84; Clifford, "Diasporas," 313, 315; Braziel and Mannur, "Nation, Migration, Globalization," 16–17.

55. Cf. Appadurai, "Disjuncture and Difference in the Global Cultural Economy," 35.

56. Raymond G. Gordon, ed., *Ethnologue: Languages of the World*, contr. ed. Barbara F. Grimes (Dallas, TX: SIL International, 2005), 15. The total number of living languages at the time of publication was 6,912. "A living language is defined as one that has at least one speaker for whom it is their first language; extinct languages and languages that are used only as a second language are excluded from these counts."

57. The influential social philosopher, anthropologist, and expert on ideologies of nationalism Ernest Gellner worked with the number 8,000; see Gellner, *Nations and Nationalism*, intro. by John Breuilly, New Perspectives on the Past (Ithaca, NY: Cornell University Press, 2008), 42–43. Also using linguistics as one of their most important markers, the authors and compilers of the *World Christian Encyclopedia: A Comparative Survey of Churches and Religions in the Modern World*, 2 vols. (Oxford; New York: Oxford University Press, 2001) put the number of "peoples" or "ethnocultural peoples" at around 12,600 in 2001; see their companion volume, David B. Barrett and Todd M. Johnson, *World Christian Trends, AD 30–AD 2200: Interpreting the Annual Christian Megacensus*, Christopher R. Guidry and Peter F. Crossing, eds. (Pasadena, CA: William Carey Library, 2001), 615–24. William Ury, Senior Fellow of the Harvard Negotiation Project, remarked in passing in a TED talk in October 2010 that there are 15,000 *tribes* in the world; see http://www.ted.com/talks/william_ury.html.

58. The number 800 here is Gellner's upper-range estimate (pretending "for the sake of charity" and argumentation) of the number of "reasonably effective nationalisms on earth," which "have not yet attained their state (and perhaps never will), but which are struggling in that direction and thus have a legitimate claim to be counted among actual, and not merely potential, nationalisms." Gellner's point as well is to de-link nations from nation-states here, for his "rough calculation still gives us only *one* effective nationalism for *ten* potential ones." And one implication is to in turn de-link national identity from the misplaced fear that the drive to construct or preserve nationhood necessarily implies "imposing homogeneity on the popu-

lations unfortunate enough to fall under the sway of authorities possessed by the nationalist ideology." Gellner, *Nations and Nationalism*, 43–44.

59. Appadurai, "Disjuncture and Difference in the Global Cultural Economy," 27. Appadurai explained that the technology of print media, the spread of "print capitalism," and the growth of mass literacy together made possible the "large-scale production of projects of ethnic affinity that were remarkably free of the need for face-to-face communication or even of indirect communication between persons and groups." The "act of reading things together [across great distances] set the stage for movements based on [this] paradox of 'constructed primordialism.'"

60. Daniel Boyarin and Jonathan Boyarin, "Diaspora," 94–96, with quote from p. 96. The Boyarins go on to remark: "There is thus a sense in which the convert becomes the ideal type of the Jew."

61. Alberigo, *History of Vatican II*, I:42, II:16; Pope John XXIII, *Gaudet Mater Ecclesia*, Address at the opening of the Second Vatican Council (October 11, 1962), 4.5, cf. 7.3.

62. Second Vatican Council, *Gaudium et Spes*, §57. Among numerous other Vatican II references to the church as a pilgrim people, see *Lumen Gentium*, §§25, 48; and *Unitatis Redintegratio*, Decree on Ecumenism (November 21, 1964), §3.

63. Brah, *Cartographies of Diaspora*, 180, cf. 182.

64. See my earlier article, "Deuteronomic or Constantinian."

65. Schlabach, "Deuteronomic or Constantinian," 463.

66. See Ochs's editorial commentary in Yoder, *The Jewish-Christian Schism Revisited*, 180. Also see pp. 120, 203–4 there, as well as Peter Ochs, *Another Reformation: Postliberal Christianity and the Jews* (Grand Rapids, MI: Baker Academic, 2011), 146–51, where Ochs concludes: "A dialectical relation between exile and landedness is therefore more representative of classical Jewish life and belief than any clear and unchanging choice for one against the other."

67. Ochs's editorial commentary, Yoder, *The Jewish-Christian Schism Revisited*, 203–4.

68. Daniel Boyarin and Jonathan Boyarin, "Diaspora," 104. Commenting further they insist:

> It is profoundly disturbing to hear Jewish attachment to the Land decried as regressive in the same discursive situations in which the attachment of native Americans or Australians to their particular rocks, trees, and deserts is celebrated as an organic connection to the Earth that "we" have lost. The uncritical valorization of indigenousness (and particularly the confusion between political indigenousness and mystified autochthony) must come under critique, without wishing, however, to deny the rights of native Americans, Australians, and Palestinians to their lands precisely on the basis of real, unmysterious political claims. If, on the other hand,

Jews are to give up hegemony over the Land, this does not mean that the profundity of our attachment to the Land can be denied. This also must have a political expression in the present, in the provision of the possibility for Jews to live a Jewish life in a Palestine not dominated by one ethnic group or another.

69. Ibid., 104.

70. Ibid.

71. Ibid., 106. Cf. Safran, "The Jewish Diaspora," 43–44.

72. Daniel Boyarin and Jonathan Boyarin, "Diaspora," 106–7. So also Elie Wiesel, though more somber about the creative possibilities of exile, traces Jewish exilic life back to its primal beginnings (Elie Wiesel, "Longing for Home," in *The Longing for Home*, ed. Leroy S. Rouner, Boston University Studies in Philosophy and Religion, vol. 17 [Notre Dame, IN: University of Notre Dame Press, 1996], 21), as does Christian theologian Jürgen Moltmann (Jürgen Moltmann, "Shekinah: The Home of the Homeless God," in *The Longing for Home*, ed. Leroy S. Rouner, Boston University Studies in Philosophy and Religion, vol. 17 [Notre Dame, IN: University of Notre Dame Press, 1996], 175). Moltmann describes "exilic religion" as "a prolongation or development of Israel's primal experiences of God."

73. Revelation 21:1. The earthy dimension of a Christian heavenly homeland is all the more necessary for those who dare to take seriously the affirmation of bodily resurrection in 1 Corinthians 15, and in the penultimate line of the Apostles' Creed.

74. Daniel Boyarin and Jonathan Boyarin, "Diaspora," 107.

75. For a summary of the debate around this open question, see Safran, "The Jewish Diaspora," 50–55.

76. This paragraph summarizes in my own way insights from Clifford, "Diasporas," 306–7, 309, 311, 327; and Dufoix, *Diasporas*, 75.

77. See p. 35 in chapter 2.

78. Cf. H. Richard Niebuhr, *Christ and Culture*, Harper Torchbooks/Cloister Library (New York: Harper and Row, 1956), along with Glen H. Stassen, Diane M. Yeager, and John Howard Yoder, *Authentic Transformation: A New Vision of Christ and Culture*, with a previously unpublished essay by H. Richard Niebuhr (Nashville: Abingdon Press, 1996).

79. The *Catechism of the Catholic Church* speaks of the threefold office or mission of Christ in pars. 436, 783, 1241, 1546, and 1581.

80. Ernst Troeltsch, *The Social Teaching of the Christian Churches*, trans. Olive Wyon, intro. by Richard Niebuhr (1931; repr., Chicago: University of Chicago Press, 1981).

81. Richard Niebuhr, *Christ and Culture*.

82. David Tracy, *The Analogical Imagination: Christian Theology and the Culture of Pluralism* (New York: Crossroads, 1981).

83. As my own appropriation of Augustinian categories in a previous and coming chapter probably imply, I am only willing to accept the usefulness

of this last typology if the "neo" in "neo-Augustinian" signals as much discontinuity as it does continuity with St. Augustine himself, thus allowing for the possibility that Augustine's thought might critique contemporary misappropriations put forward in his name. As the following chapter will argue, Augustine's analogical identification of the church with Jews in Babylon, and his turn to Jeremiah 29 at the climax of his long and complex argument in *City of God*, suggests that he not only carried the diasporic sensibility of earlier church fathers into the post-Constantine era, but saw diaspora as the fundamental Christian social posture or strategy from which all other ways of seeking the peace of the earthly city always pivot as merely provisional tactics.

84. Karl Rahner, "Towards a Fundamental Theological Interpretation of Vatican II," *Theological Studies* 40, no. 4 (December 1979): 716–17. Among Rahner's evidence were points such as the following: "Indigenous" bishops had participated in the council for the first time, not simply European missionaries ordained as bishops in other countries. A number of Vatican II decrees gave churches in different regions a degree of independence, most famously *Sacrosanctum Concilium*, the decree on liturgy that shifted worship into the vernacular. Furthermore, most decrees in some way demonstrated the church's sense of responsibility for all humanity. More subtly, the documents of Vatican II attempted to use theological language accessible throughout the world—not just in the specialized Roman Catholic circles long dominated by Neo-Scholasticism. Also subtly but fundamentally, by renouncing instruments of political power in service to Gospel proclamation, especially in the declaration on religious freedom, *Dignitatis Humanae*, the church began to de-link itself from traditional European patterns of church-state relationship. And finally, in its decree on ecumenism, *Unitatis Redintegratio*, the council committed the church to addressing the great obstacle that "the ecclesial division of Christendom . . . constitutes for the spread of Christianity in all the world, in the so-called 'mission countries.'" (Pp. 718–20; quotation from p. 720.)

85. Rahner, "Towards a Fundamental Theological Interpretation of Vatican II," 721.

86. Despite his wide-angle perspective and ecumenical openness to Christian communities beyond the Roman church, Rahner may have still been operating from a somewhat restricted Eurocentric historical perspective here, as I will shortly note. Also, his way of demarking only two major transitions and three epochs of church history will not be satisfying to Protestants who consider the sixteenth-century Reformation epoch-making. Even if he has missed or underestimated certain details, however, at least three things may be said in Rahner's defense: (1) The value of his "macroscopic" survey is precisely that it allows us to pan out from features of church history that may in the long run turn out to have absorbed too much of our attention; (2) caught up in their own internal debates about the legacy of Vatican

II, Catholics have sometimes been slower than Protestants to recognize the council's significance for the entire ecumenical community of churches, precisely along lines such as those Rahner was identifying; so that (3) even if non-Catholics sense a lingering Catholic triumphalism in Rahner's analysis, that analysis nonetheless illuminates deep tectonic shifts affecting all Christian traditions.

87. Rahner, "Towards a Fundamental Theological Interpretation of Vatican II," 717.

88. See Philip Jenkins on what he calls the "myth of Western Christianity" in *The Next Christendom*, 21–33.

89. Rahner, "Towards a Fundamental Theological Interpretation of Vatican II," 717. On p. 716, Rahner also spoke of "a relation of reciprocal interdependence."

90. This is hardly less true fifty, rather than thirty, years after the council, under the pontificate of Francis, who leading scholar of Vatican II Massimo Faggioli calls the first pope truly of the Vatican II era (*Papa Francesco e la "chiesa-mondo"* [Rome: Armando Editore, 2014], 73). Rahner's macroscopic survey should thus give us a wide-angle view that puts continuing "culture wars" concerning the legacy of the council in perspective.

91. Rahner, "Towards a Fundamental Theological Interpretation of Vatican II," 721–23, 727.

92. Ibid., 725.

93. Ibid.

94. Ibid., 725–26.

95. *The Coming of the Third Church: An Analysis of the Present and Future of the Church* (Maryknoll, NY: Orbis Books, 1977). Though Bühlmann and Rahner both saw three major epochs in church history, their divisions were significantly different. Bühlmann's schema identified the First Church as the Eastern church that was preeminent in the first millennium CE, the Second Church as the Western church that was preeminent in the second millennium CE, and the Third Church as the Southern church that was coming into preeminence as the third millennium CE approached. Bühlmann and Rahner's schemas are not mutually exclusive, however, insofar as they address somewhat different questions. Bühlmann's schema is more historical, while Rahner emphasized that while he certainly took church history seriously, he was engaged in a "fundamental theological interpretation" of history and those focused on basic theological shifts that might take centuries to fully manifest themselves.

96. Jenkins, *The Next Christendom*.

97. African Initiated Churches are also known as African Independent Churches.

98. John L. Allen Jr., *The Future Church: How Ten Trends Are Revolutionizing the Catholic Church* (New York: Doubleday, 2009), 10.

Notes   323

99. Pew Forum on Religion and Public Life, *Global Christianity: A Report on the Size and Distribution of the World's Christian Population* (Washington, DC: Pew Research Center, 2011), http://www.pewforum.org/files/2011/12/Christianity-fullreport-web.pdf. Page references in subsequent footnotes are to the full report, available for download on this website. One problem working with the Pew Forum report is that it generally lumps North America, Latin America, and the Caribbean into a single category, "the Americas." To disaggregate overall statistics on the Americas one must carefully study the maps and charts on pp. 12, 43, 71–72, subtract numbers for the United States and Canada, then recalculate percentages. The weighted map on p. 12 is especially important to do this for the year 1910, and thus compare the distribution in the Americas vis-à-vis 2010. My own calculations are confirmed within a negligible margin of error by the Pew Forum's own reaggregation of Christians in the Global South and North in the years 1910 and 2010, as presented on pp. 13–15.

100. Pew Forum on Religion and Public Life, *Global Christianity*, 9.

101. More precisely, the percentages in 1910 were 66.3% in Europe and 27.1% in the Americas, while 0.7% were in the Middle East-North Africa, 4.5% in Asia-Pacific, and 1.4% were in Sub-Saharan Africa, for a total outside Europe and the Americas of 6.6% (Pew Forum on Religion and Public Life, *Global Christianity*, 9). Regarding statistics on the Americas, see note 99 above.

102. More precisely, the percentages in 2010 were 25.9% in Europe and 36.8% in the Americas, while 0.6% were in the Middle East/North Africa, 13.1% in Asia-Pacific, and 23.6% were in Sub-Saharan Africa, for a total outside Europe and the Americas of 37.3% (Pew Forum on Religion and Public Life, *Global Christianity*, 9). Regrouping Latin America and the Caribbean with the rest of the Global South, however, yields the following percentages for 2010: 25.9% in Europe, 12.4% in North America, 24.4% in Latin America and the Caribbean, 0.6% in the Middle East/North Africa, 13.1% in Asia-Pacific, and 23.6% in Sub-Saharan Africa. (Regarding statistics on the Americas, see note 99 above.) Cf. Pew Forum pp. 13–14 on the global distribution of Christians in the Global South and North.

103. Pew Forum on Religion and Public Life, *Global Christianity*, 13, 23.

104. Ibid., 9.

105. Ibid., 23–25.

106. Pew Forum on Religion and Public Life, *Religion in Latin America: Widespread Change in a Historically Catholic Region* (Washington, DC: Pew Research Center, 2014), https://www.pewforum.org/2014/11/13/religion-in-latin-america.

107. Specific numbers are 16.1% of the world Catholic population in Sub-Saharan Africa and 12.0% in Asia-Pacific for a combined total of 28.1%; and 23.9% of the world Catholic population in Europe, 1.2% in Canada, and 6.8% in the United States for a combined 31.9%. See Pew Forum on Religion and

Public Life, *Global Christianity*, 23–25. The Canadian percentage is calculated from a table on p. 79.

108. Jenkins, *The Next Christendom*, 73.
109. Allen, *The Future Church*, 11. Allen continued:

> Americans had eleven cardinals in the conclave that elected Pope Benedict XVI, for example, the same number as all of Africa, even though Africa has twice the Catholic population. Brazil, the largest Catholic country on earth, only had three votes, which works out to one cardinal-elector for every 6 million American Catholics and for every 43 million Catholics in Brazil. Though Catholicism is not a democracy, that sort of discrepancy understandably strikes many Catholics around the world as unfair. (11–12)

110. Jenkins, *The Next Christendom*, 21–24, 45.
111. Ibid., 26–33, with a summary to this effect on p. 30.
112. Ibid., 36–41, 68.
113. Ibid., 55–57.
114. Ibid., 40–43, 47–50, 70.
115. Ibid., 70.
116. Ibid., 70–76, 86–85.
117. Ibid., 55–58.
118. Rahner, "The Present Situation of Christians," 17. See p. 97 above.
119. Pew Forum on Religion and Public Life, *Global Christianity*, 19. Indeed, the Pew Forum report is based on statistics from 232 countries and territories, and of these 158 had Christian majorities in 2010 (13, 19). That figure is somewhat misleading, however, for as the report clarifies, "most of the Christian-majority countries are relatively small: about seven-in-ten have fewer Christians than the Christian-minority country Vietnam (7 million Christians)" (19). Nonetheless, if we are underscoring the (normative) case for a social ethic in which diaspora is church's most basic and guiding paradigm by arguing (descriptively, empirically) that the church lives in diaspora anyway, the Pew Forum data may give us pause.
120. Pew Forum on Religion and Public Life, *Global Christianity*, 25.
121. Rahner, "The Present Situation of Christians," 17, 14.
122. This is true even in William Safran's demanding list of criteria as to what defines a diaspora community. See note 50 above.
123. Or moving to an African example, Zimbabwe is 78.2 percent Christian, two-thirds of its Christians are Roman Catholic, and its prime-minister-then-president for decades, Robert Mugabe, called himself a devout Catholic. With serious doubts about whether Mugabe represented a majority of Zimbabweans, however, many *others* called him a tyrant.
124. One vivid example would be traditionally and still-majority Catholic Guatemala as it has experienced a rapid shift to Protestantism in the 1970s and '80s, contributing to the rise of the neo-Pentecostal military dictator Efraín Rios Montt in 1982. Rios Montt's rule was short-lived and after many

years he was tried for genocide, but other Protestant Pentecostal presidents have followed. Rightly or wrongly, Catholics and Protestants both can feel discriminated against for decades in such a situation of political flux.

125. In order to draw upon a demographic study such as the Pew Forum's, we have had to bracket the question of who is truly a Christian or who is actually living as a Christian. Whether and in what way some Christians have a right to judge others as merely "nominal" Christians in a pejorative sense, social scientists like the demographers at Pew have no choice but to count us *all* as nominal Christians. In other words, nothing in their discipline allows social scientists to sort out theological rivalries—much less make the judgment that not even theologians dare make with confidence as to who is a true Christian in the eyes of God. Thus, all they can do is count those who *name themselves* as Christian in some way, any way—which is what "nominal" means.

126. Paul VI, *Evangelii Nuntiandi*, §21. See my commentary in chapter 2 above, pp. 31–33.

127. See "The Last Debate," chapter 9 in book 5 of *The Lord of the Rings*, which appears in *The Return of the King*, the third volume of the trilogy (actually comprised of six "books" originally published in three physical volumes).

Chapter 5—pages 133–61

1. Francis, *Evangelii Gaudium*, cf. §§45, 49, 87, 111, 181.
2. Ibid., §180.
3. Ibid., §218.
4. Ibid., §236.
5. Ibid., §§217–21.
6. The following sections rework material from chapters 2 and 3 of Gerald W. Schlabach, *To Bless All Peoples: Serving with Abraham and Jesus*, Peace and Justice Series, no. 12 (Scottdale, PA: Herald Press, 1991). Also cf. Gerald W. Schlabach, "Beyond Two- versus One-Kingdom Theology: Abrahamic Community as a Mennonite Paradigm for Engagement in Society."
7. I am aware that a big-picture reading of the biblical story can risk dismissal by some biblical scholars as a pre-critical or even naive reading. At any number of points, specialists may be able to drill down into my survey and contest my overgeneralizations by reminding me of long but still-unsettled scholarly debates. I hope I have left enough hints as to my awareness of debates and technicalities—as, for example, when I implicitly recognize the multilayered authorship of the book of Isaiah—that I may retain the confidence of such specialists. And of course I will be acknowledging a few prominent biblical scholars who buttressed my own confidence when I began years ago to test and elaborate the suggestive theme of "Abrahamic

minorities" from another preacher—Dom Hélder Câmara, archbishop of Recife, Brazil (see *The Desert Is Fertile*, trans. Dinah Livingstone [Maryknoll, NY: Orbis Books, 1974]; *Hélder Câmara y la Justicia: Ideario* [Salamanca: Ediciones Sigueme, 1981]; *Dom Helder Camara: Essential Writings*). In the end, though, I would simply plead that this kind of big-picture synthetic reading has an integrity of its own, at minimum as a thought experiment, and at maximum as the task that is necessary if systematic theology is to appropriate the more specialized work of biblical scholarship.

8. See chapter 3.

9. This section owes a heavy debt to Carlos H. Abesamis, *Where Are We Going, Heaven or New World?*, Foundation Books (Manila, Philippines: Communication Foundation for Asia, 1983), 1–60.

10. Francis, *Evangelii Gaudium*, §131, §230.

11. For a critical analysis of the difficulties of this view from a Catholic philosopher and theologian generally known as a stalwart traditionalist, see Germain Gabriel Grisez, "The True Ultimate End of Human Beings: The Kingdom, Not God Alone," *Theological Studies* 69, no. 1 (March 2008): 38–61.

12. See for example Second Vatican Council, *Lumen Gentium*, §1; *Gaudium et Spes*, §45.

13. John Paul II, "'Peace on Earth to Those Whom God Loves,'" §20.

14. This and the following section rely on Gerhard von Rad, *Genesis: A Commentary*, rev. ed., trans. John H. Marks, Old Testament Library (Philadelphia: The Westminster Press, 1972), 153–54; and Hans Walter Wolff, "The Kerygma of the Yahwist," trans. Wilbur A. Benware, *Interpretation* 20, no. 2 (April 1966): 131–58. In Wolff, see especially pp. 132, 136–37, 139–42, 145–46, 150, 152. Basic to my overall conceptualization of Abrahamic community as a people-for-all-people, fulfilled and recapitulated in Christ as the person-for-all-persons is Oscar Cullmann, *Christ and Time: The Primitive Christian Conception of Time and History*, trans. Floyd V. Filson (1951; repr., London: SCM Press, 1962). Cullmann summarized much in his book on pp. 115–18, where he wrote of "the principle of *representation*": "The principle of this gracious process [of redemptive history] is that of the *election of a minority for the redemption of the whole*" (p. 115), 31–58. In Wolff, see especially pp. 132, 136–37, 139–42, 145–46, 150, 152.

15. Translation is from Wolff, "The Kerygma of the Yahwist," 137–38.

16. Here is where Wolff, "The Kerygma of the Yahwist," is especially illuminating.

17. For my extended reflections on the fundamental challenges of the "Deuteronomic juncture" see Schlabach, "Deuteronomic or Constantinian."

18. Cf. the harsh though understandable emotions expressed in Psalm 137.

19. In Jewish liturgy, the *Shema* continues with the recitation of Deuteronomy 11:13-21 and Numbers 15:37-41 as well.

20. On the role that the book of Isaiah played in Jesus' formation, or at least in the Matthean community as it remembered Jesus' ministry and teaching, see Glen H. Stassen and David P. Gushee, *Kingdom Ethics: Following Jesus in Contemporary Context* (Downers Grove, IL: InterVarsity Press, 2003), 22–30, and Glen H. Stassen, *Living the Sermon on the Mount: A Practical Hope for Grace and Deliverance* (San Francisco: Jossey-Bass, 2006), 21–24.

21. All but one of the sixteen appearances of the term appear in the first thirty-nine chapters of the book of Isaiah, sometimes called First Isaiah.

22. Other references to Israel as God's chosen servant people appear in Isaiah 40–55. See 41:8ff.; 43:10-20; 44:1-2; 45:4; and 48:20. An important passage related in spirit and theology is Isaiah 61–62 (compare 42:1, 4, 7 with 61:1-2).

23. On the overlapping identities of Servant of the LORD in Isaiah, see Gerhard von Rad, *The Theology of Israel's Historical Traditions*, vol. 1 of *Old Testament Theology*, trans. D. M. G. Stalker (New York: Harper and Row, 1962), 258–62. Also see Cullmann, *Christ and Time*, 115–18.

24. This summary is adapted slightly from Schlabach, "Beyond Two- Versus One-Kingdom Theology," 205. Cf. p. 23 in the introductory chapter above.

25. Francis, *Evangelii Gaudium*, §24.

26. Ibid., §114. Of course, Francis also uses the images to which we will return in the following chapter, the Vatican II images of the church as a pilgrim people, sacrament of salvation, and people of God. See §§111–12, 114–15.

27. Note the way that Francis anticipated such risks:

> An evangelizing community gets involved by word and deed in people's daily lives; it bridges distances, it is willing to abase itself if necessary, and it embraces human life, touching the suffering flesh of Christ in others. Evangelizers thus take on the "smell of the sheep" and the sheep are willing to hear their voice. An evangelizing community is also supportive, standing by people at every step of the way, no matter how difficult or lengthy this may prove to be. (*Evangelii Gaudium*, §24)

28. Ibid., §27. In §207, Francis also noted that the community life of the church will break down "if it thinks it can comfortably go its own way without creative concern and effective cooperation in helping the poor to live with dignity and reaching out to everyone."

29. Ibid., §268.

30. Ibid., §§222–25.

31. Also see ibid., §24, where Francis stresses the importance of patience: "An evangelizing community is also supportive, standing by people at every step of the way, no matter how difficult or lengthy this may prove to be. It is familiar with patient expectation and apostolic endurance. Evangelization consists mostly of patience and disregard for constraints of time."

32. Ibid., §§226–30.

328 A Pilgrim People

33. Ibid., §§218–19. Francis cited Paul VI, *Populorum Progressio*, §76, in particular. See also Second Vatican Council, *Gaudium et Spes*, §78.

34. Francis, *Evangelii Gaudium*, §§231–33.

35. Antonio Spadaro, "A Big Heart Open to God: An Interview with Pope Francis," *America* 209, no. 8 (September 30, 2013): 26.

36. Francis, *Evangelii Gaudium*, §231.

37. Ibid., §§98–99.

38. Ibid., §§234–37.

39. John Paul II, "Address at the Fiftieth General Assembly of the United Nations Organization," §7. See pp. 86–87 and 91–92 in chapter 3 above.

40. Francis, *Evangelii Gaudium*, §234.

41. Ibid, §235.

42. Ibid.

43. Ibid., §236.

44. Ibid.

45. Monica Duffy Toft, Daniel Philpott, and Timothy Samuel Shah, *God's Century: Resurgent Religion and Global Politics* (New York: W. W. Norton & Co., 2011), 16.

46. Ibid., 9–10.

47. See chapters 5 and 6 of Toft, Philpott, and Shah, *God's Century*, with summaries on pp. 17–18, 144, 150, and 157–58.

48. See chapters 4 and 7 of Toft, Philpott, and Shah, *God's Century*, with summaries on pp. 17–18, 109–10, 120, 187–88, 196, 200, and 205–06. Also see Daniel Philpott, "What Religion Brings to the Politics of Transitional Justice," *Journal of International Affairs* 61, no. 1 (Fall/Winter 2007): 93–110; "When Faith Meets History: The Influence of Religion on Transitional Justice," in *The Religious in Responses to Mass Atrocity: Interdisciplinary Perspectives*, ed. Thomas Brudholm and Thomas Cushman (Cambridge; New York: Cambridge University Press, 2009), 174–212.

49. Francis, *Evangelii Gaudium*, §224.

Chapter 6—pages 162–96

1. Excerpt from Universal Prayer: Confession of Sins and Prayer for Forgiveness, March 12, 2000.

2. Fairly or not, Stanley Hauerwas and William H. Willimon, *Resident Aliens: Life in the Christian Colony* (Nashville: Abingdon Press, 1989) has elicited this reaction. Complicating its reception is its affirmative use by more conservative voices in the culture wars among Catholics and other Christians in U.S. culture wars, such as Rod Dreher, " 'Resident Aliens' & the Benedict Option," *The American Conservative*, September 1, 2015, http://www.theamericanconservative.com/dreher/resident-aliens-the-benedict-option/.

3. This rare combination of genres is itself telling, insofar as moral exhortation or *parenesis* tends to be socially conservative as it passes down the moral common sense of a community, while apocalypse conveys a heightened sense of urgency and demand for moral change. The very combination indicates Hermas's need to maintain a sense of crisis even as the church found itself settling in for a longer haul than it had expected, or perhaps that for the church to settle in as it moved beyond its first generations was itself the crisis.

4. James S. Jeffers, *Conflict at Rome: Social Order and Hierarchy in Early Christianity* (Minneapolis: Fortress Press, 1991), 114. The text shows many signs of composite authorship, over many decades. Thus, while there is solid evidence for a historical figure named Hermas in the early-to-mid-second century church in Rome, the literary figure of Hermas may also be something of a composite figure. Further, while the text recounts a series of incidents and conversations with Hermas's angelic guardian or "shepherd," it combines the disparate genres of apocalyptic literature and parenesis in such a way that it is hardly a straightforward memoir. But of course it would be anachronistic to expect such a piece of writing from the second century, especially from "a former slave with little education, wealth, or status." If anything, that makes the document all the more remarkable. For as Jeffers goes on to note, "Very few such people in antiquity have left behind a record of their lives and thoughts. Hermas's very ordinariness makes quite probable the representative nature of his work." In any case, a consistent enough set of community concerns is evident that even if "Hermas" were entirely fictional, *The Shepherd of Hermas* would provide an unrivaled window into the life of the Roman Church in its second or third generation. So for convenience, I will speak of Hermas as though he were a singular historical figure. Were a scholarly consensus to emerge that "Hermas" is a composite and thus representational figure, after all, that would actually strengthen my argument that *The Shepherd of Hermas* gives us a window into the lived experience of ordinary Christian laypeople in the second century. In any case, one other indicator in this regard was the popularity of *The Shepherd* in the early church, such that it made it on to some preliminary lists for the New Testament canon.

For additional scholarship on the document, see Carolyn A. Osiek, *Rich and Poor in the* Shepherd of Hermas: *An Exegetical-Social Investigation*, Catholic Biblical Quarterly Monograph Series, no. 15 (Washington, DC: Catholic Biblical Association of America, 1983); Carolyn A. Osiek, "The Genre and Function of the Shepherd of Hermas," *Semeia*, no. 36 (1986): 113–21; Carolyn A. Osiek, *The Shepherd of Hermas: A Commentary*, vol. 4 of *The Disputation: A Theological Debate between Christians and Jews*, Video, ed. Helmut Koester, Message of the Fathers of the Church 1 (Minneapolis: Fortress Press, 1998); D. K. Buell, "Race and Universalism in Early Christianity," *Journal of Early*

Christian Studies 10, no. 4 (2002): 429–68; chapters 10 and 22 of Peter Lampe, *From Paul to Valentinus: Christians at Rome in the First Two Centuries*, ed. Marshall D. Johnson, trans. Michael Steinhauser (Minneapolis: Fortress Press, 2003); and Benjamin H. Dunning, "Foreign Countries and Alien Assets in *The Shepherd of Hermas*," chap. 4 in *Aliens and Sojourners: Self as Other in Early Christianity*, Divinations: Rereading Late Ancient Religion (Philadelphia: University of Pennsylvania Press, 2009), 78–90.

5. See Mandate 10.1.40 and Similitude 8.8.74 of *The Shepherd of Hermas* for indications of the way that the need for business contacts might lead to worldly friendships that might tempt him away from the faith.

6. Scholars have debated the extent to which early Christians such as Hermas, or for that matter the first readers of 1 Peter were actually exiles or otherwise officially marginalized, and thus bore a corresponding legal status, or whether this was mainly a literary device or topos employed for theological and paraenetic or exhortatory purposes. (For a survey of such debates, see Dunning, *Aliens and Sojourners*, 9–15.) But these questions are not decisive for my argument here. My assumption is that actual experiences of migration, deportation, diaspora, and marginalization made the theological metaphor easily recognizable for many in the Christian community such as "Hermas," such that there was a creative feedback loop between legal or social status and religious identity. And there certainly is ample evidence that Hermas had such life experiences. I write, of course, as a theologian and ethicist who shares a twenty-first century version of early Christian writers' normative interests. But I also write as a resident in a neighborhood in a metropolis in which I regularly observe the experience of immigrants (including a few of my students) who must navigate the demands of host and homeland cultures. The affinity between their lived experience and that of "Hermas" is too obvious for me to dismiss the resident alien topos as merely a rhetorical device, even as I appropriate the topos for my own normative theological purposes.

7. J. B. Lightfoot and J. R. Harmer, trans., "The Shepherd of Hermas," in *The Apostolic Fathers*, 2nd ed., ed. and rev. Michael W. Holmes (Grand Rapids, MI: Baker Book House, 1989), Parable (or Similitude) 1.1.50.

8. Ibid.

9. Ibid.

10. Rodney Stark, *The Rise of Christianity: A Sociologist Reconsiders History* (Princeton, NJ: Princeton University Press, 1996), 4–13.

11. Ibid., 13–21. Stark and colleagues had studied the Unification Church, better known as "Moonies," and examined the meticulous records that the Church of Jesus Christ of Latter Day Saints, or "Mormons," have maintained for more than a century and a half. On the one hand, a 40-percent-per-decade rate of growth was quite credible. On the other hand, there was no need for either miraculous explanations of the sort to which even eminent church

historians such as Ramsey MacMullen have defaulted, or the mass conversions that evangelists often aim for. While the Mormons famously send their young people out to do door-to-door evangelism around the world, for example, they know from their records that only one in fifty conversions happens through these strategies. Instead, most happen through contacts among family and friends.

12. Stark, *The Rise of Christianity*, 20.
13. Ibid., 73–94.
14. Ibid., 95–128.
15. Ibid., 163–90.
16. Ibid., 49.
17. For Stark, marginality was a matter of culture more than economic class. See *The Rise of Christianity*, 51–57, and note that in his previous chapter 2 he had argued that early Christianity was not so exclusively a movement of the dispossessed as we have assumed, even if it did break down class and other divisions in unprecedented ways.
18. Stark, *The Rise of Christianity*, 57, citing Wayne A. Meeks, *The First Urban Christians: The Social World of the Apostle Paul* (New Haven: Yale University Press, 1983), and Paul Johnson, *A History of Christianity* (New York: Atheneum, 1976).
19. Though in his erudition, Philo was obviously not representative, he nonetheless offered Stark a "compelling" example of these cross-cultural tensions. Stark, *The Rise of Christianity*, 60–61.
20. Stark, *The Rise of Christianity*, 59. The argument is not that most did or even a majority, but that enough did for the network of Jewish Diaspora to provide many perduring strands in the growing network that constituted the Christian community. Indeed, Stark noted that only a fifth of Diaspora Jews would have needed to become Christians to account for all of Christianity's demographic growth up until the year 250 (69–70), when the trendline of 40 percent growth per decade really starts to arc exponentially upward.
21. Ibid., 50–51, 65–67.
22. Lampe, *From Paul to Valentinus*, 9.
23. Stark, *The Rise of Christianity*, 63.
24. Origen, *Contra Celsum*, trans. Henry Chadwick (1953; repr., Cambridge: Cambridge University Press, 1965), III, 55.
25. Judith Lieu, John North, and Tessa Rajak, eds., *The Jews among Pagans and Christians in the Roman Empire* (London; New York: Routledge, 1992), 6–7, 178–79, 191. I do find the notion of a competitive marketplace of ideas, which the editors pick up from sociologist Peter Berger, a potentially anachronistism from modern capitalism into ancient traditional society. The very notion of diaspora—or better, overlapping diasporas —would allow ancient realities to inform our own instead.

26. Lampe, *From Paul to Valentinus*, 76–79.
27. Ibid., 201.
28. Lieu, North, and Rajak, *The Jews among Pagans and Christians in the Roman Empire*, 115.
29. Chandler H. Im and Amos Yong, eds., *Global Diasporas and Mission*, intro. by Chandler H. Im and Tereso C. Casiño, Regnum Edinburgh Centenary Series, vol. 23 (Oxford Regnum Books International, 2014), 1.
30. James 1:1 likewise begins with greetings to "the twelve tribes in the Dispersion."
31. On the dating of this anonymous document, which is not so much a letter as an apologetic, see J. B. Lightfoot and J. R. Harmer, trans., "The Epistle to Diognetus," in *The Apostolic Fathers*, 2nd ed., ed. and rev. Michael W. Holmes (Grand Rapids, MI: Baker Book House, 1989), 293. For commentaries especially apropos to the issues here, see Denise Kimber Buell, *Why This New Race: Ethnic Reasoning in Early Christianity*, Gender, Theory, and Religion (New York: Columbia University Press, 2005), 29–33, and Benjamin H. Dunning, "Outsiders by Reason of Outdoing: The *Epistle to Diognetus*," chap. 3 in *Aliens and Sojourners: Self as Other in Early Christianity*, Divinations: Rereading Late Ancient Religion (Philadelphia: University of Pennsylvania Press, 2009), 64–77. The Lightfoot/Harmer/Holmes translation is the one I begin with here, while making slight adaptations based on Dunning's translation of chapters 5 and 6, which appears on pp. 65–66.
32. Without claiming that all Christians lived up to *Diognetus*'s portrayal, one can find extensive evidence that the ethical practices and relatively higher moral standards of early Christians were not simply ideals that an apologist might highlight or a preacher might exhort. See Alan Kreider's extensive study of the missionary appeal of Christianity in its first four centuries, *The Patient Ferment of the Early Church: The Improbable Rise of Christianity in the Roman Empire* (Grand Rapids, MI: Baker Academic, 2016).
33. Cf. Dunning, *Aliens and Sojourners*, 74–76.
34. Ibid., 68–69.
35. As Ireneus put it (*Against Heretics* 4.34.4), when the apostles preached God's word throughout the known world, they "caused such a change in the state of things, that [people from many nations] did form their swords and war-lances into plowshares, and changed them into pruning-hooks for reaping the corn, [that is], into instruments used for peaceful purposes, [so that] they are now unaccustomed to fighting, but when smitten, offer also the other cheek." Also see Justin Martyr, *First Apology* 29, *Dialogue with Trypho* 90; Tertullian, *An Answer to the Jews* 3; Origen, *Against Celsus* 5.33; Athanasius, *On the Incarnation of the Word* 52. Tellingly, this line of argument seems to have become an embarrassment and fallen away after the emperor Constantine began the Roman rapprochement with Christianity that first made Christianity legal, and later official. Cf. Alan Kreider, *The Change of Conversion*

and the Origin of Christendom (Harrisburg, PA: Trinity Press International, 1999), 27, 52, 64.

36. Pontius the Deacon, *The Life and Passion of Cyprian, Bishop and Martyr*, in *The Ante-Nicene Fathers*, vol. 7, ed. Alexander Roberts and James Donaldson (Edinburgh: T. & T. Clark, 1873), 11.

37. Gregory of Nazianzen, *Select Orations*, in *A Select Library of the Nicene and Post-Nicene Fathers of the Christian Church*, second series, vol. 7, ed. Philip Schaff and Henry Wace (Peabody, MA: Hendrickson, 1994), XLIII.49.

38. James Clifford's word is "slippage," which he has noted between diasporic theories, discourses, actual historical experiences. Clifford, "Diasporas," 302.

39. Devorah Schoenfeld, " 'You Will Seek from There': The Cycle of Exile and Return in Classical Jewish Theology," chap. 2 in *Theology of Migration in the Abrahamic Religions*, ed. Elaine Padilla and Peter C. Phan, Palgrave Macmillan's Christianities of the World (New York: Palgrave Macmillan, 2014), 27–45.

40. Brah, *Cartographies of Diaspora*, 180.

41. Dale T. Irvin, "Theology, Migration, and the Homecoming," chap. 1 in *Theology of Migration in the Abrahamic Religions*, 17–20. Irvin draws heavily on Thomas A. Tweed, *Crossing and Dwelling: A Theory of Religion* (Cambridge, MA: Harvard University Press, 2006), which emphasizes the migrant experience as formative for all religious experience.

42. Clement of Alexandria, *Exhortation to the Heathen*, in *The Ante-Nicene Fathers*, vol. 7, ed. Alexander Roberts and James Donaldson (Edinburgh: T. & T. Clark, 1873), chap. 10. Translation modernized.

43. Clement of Alexandria, *The Instructor*, in *The Ante-Nicene Fathers*, vol. 7, I.7.

44. Ibid.

45. Clement of Alexandria, *Stromata*, in *The Ante-Nicene Fathers*, vol. 7, 6.5.41–42.

46. Lightfoot and Harmer, "Epistle to Diognetus," 1.1.

47. Buell, *Why This New Race*, 30–31, 84, 138, 151.

48. This echoes the analysis by Jonathan and Daniel Boyarin, upon whom we drew in chapter 4.

49. Buell, *Why This New Race*, 1–2. Also see pp. 41–47 for a full explanation as to why "religion" was not necessarily a separate and more transcendent category but could itself be understood as constitutive of racial or ethnic identity in the ancient world.

50. Ibid., 3, 6, 40–41, 94, 151. Buell's specific reference to rebirth appears on p. 3. Page numbers listed are some of her most important references to the simultaneous fixity and fluidity of race and ethnicity.

51. Ibid., 156.

52. Ibid., 157.

53. Tertullian, *Ad Naciones*, in *The Ante-Nicene Fathers*, vol. 3, ed. Alexander Roberts and James Donaldson (Edinburgh: T. & T. Clark, 1873), I.8. On the spread of Christians into every possible location, also see Tertullian, *The Apology*, in *The Ante-Nicene Fathers*, vol. 3, chap. 37.

54. Tertullian, *The Apology*, chap. 38. Cf. Buell, *Why This New Race*, 4, on this sort of thinking, more widely.

55. Buell's summary of the logic of Origen's universalism (*Why This New Race*, 82) could probably explain Tertullian's as well: "By locating this universalism within a historical narrative of human development, Origen can speak of Christians as both a universally true philosophy and a historically recent *ethnos* that is authorized and legitimized by original human unity. This universalizing argument relies on rather than opposes ethnic reasoning because Origen portrays Christians as the *ethnos* that embodies these universal truths—an *ethnos* that humans from all other *ethnê* can and should join." While this is not identical to the Abrahamic people-for-all peoples model that I am advocating, it is cognate, and does provide a precedent both for insisting that Christians think of themselves as a transnational nation, for relativizing the nationalistic claims of other polities, yet doing so without abandoning social engagement in pursuit of the common good.

56. Origen, *Contra Celsum*, 8.75.

57. Ibid., 8.73.

58. Dunning, *Aliens and Sojourners*, 66.

59. Second Vatican Council, *Gaudium et Spes*, §57.

60. See for example John Dear, *The God of Peace: Toward a Theology of Nonviolence* (Maryknoll, NY: Orbis Books, 1994), 126; Terrence J. Rynne, *Jesus Christ, Peacemaker: A New Theology of Peace* (Maryknoll: New York Orbis Books, 2014), 142–64. For a thorough historical study of the influence of Augustine's just-war thought on subsequent centuries, see Frederick H. Russell, *The Just War in the Middle Ages*, Cambridge Studies in Medieval Life and Thought, 3rd Ser., v. 8 (Cambridge; New York: Cambridge University Press, 1975), the first chapter of which begins with a statement that some will read as ominous: "The die for the medieval just war was cast by St. Augustine, who combined Roman and Judaeo-Christian elements in a mode of thought that was to influence opinion throughout the Middle Ages and beyond" (16). Elsewhere, though, Russell has warned against oversimplifications of Augustine's just-war thought in ways that are "bound to be a distortion that masks his inner turmoil and renders explicit assumptions that were at best implicit in his writings." (Russell, "War," in *Augustine through the Ages: An Encyclopedia*, gen. ed. Allan D. Fitzgerald, OSA [Grand Rapids, MI: Eerdmans, 1999], 876.)

61. For an extended argument to this effect, see Schlabach, "Correction of the Augustinians."

62. This is perhaps the explanation for Terrence Rynne's expressed puzzlement: "What is somewhat difficult to understand is that even as the just war

theory has endured, the foundational teachings of Augustine that shaped his just war theory have been rejected" (Rynne, *Jesus Christ, Peacemaker*, 160). I am less certain than Rynne that the core convictions Augustine articulated have been or need be rejected. But, to be sure, specific teachings by Augustine concerning matters such as predestination, free will, the biological transmission of original sin, or the moral status of even faithful marital sexual relations have had mixed reception even in Christian traditions that recognize Augustine as an authority.

63. The remainder of this section is a rewrite of material originally included in Gerald W. Schlabach, "The Christian Witness in the Earthly City: John H. Yoder as Augustinian Interlocutor," chap. 11 in *A Mind Patient and Untamed: Assessing John Howard Yoder's Contribution to Theology, Ethics, and Peacemaking*, ed. Ben C. Ollenburger and Gayle Gerber Koontz, intro. by Stanley Hauerwas (Telford, PA: Cascadia Publishing House, 2004), 221–44, and is used with permission.

64. Robert Markus, in his influential *Saeculum: History and Society in the Theology of St. Augustine*, 2nd ed. (1970; repr., Cambridge: Cambridge University Press, 1988), may have overstated his case when he portrayed Augustine as laying the basis for political liberalism by desacralizing every temporal order. My intention is not to weigh in on the revisionist debate concerning Markus's thesis, reflected for example in Mark Vessey, Karla Pollmann, and Allan D. Fitzgerald, eds., *History, Apocalypse, and the Secular Imagination: New Essays on Augustine's City of God* (Bowling Green, OH: Philosophy Documentation Center, Bowling Green State University, 1999). Still, I simply cannot imagine how Augustinian political thought can ever do without some sense of the limitations of human politics, whether or not those limitations are now construed to require political liberalism. I thus assume that the summary statements in this paragraph will reflect an uncontroverted consensus however the debate between Markus and his revisionists proceeds.

65. Richard Niebuhr suggested something similar when he noted in *Christ and Culture* that Augustine's *City of God* lacked an ecclesiology to match its philosophy of history. See *Christ and Culture*, 215–16.

66. Cf. Augustine, *The Trinity* 6.5.7, and Oliver O'Donovan's comments in *The Problem of Self-Love in St. Augustine*, 128.

67. Augustine, *City of God* 1.1. The translation I am using is Augustine, *The City of God* (De Civitate Dei), intro. and trans. by William Babcock, notes by Boniface Ramsey, The Works of Saint Augustine: A Translation for the 21st Century, Part I: Books, vols. 6–7 (Hyde Park, NY: New City Press, 2012), though in consultation with the translation by Henry Bettenson, intro. by David Knowles (Harmondsworth, Middlesex, England: Penguin, 1972).

68. These are themes and arguments that run throughout *City of God*, but that Augustine anticipated already in the preface to book one when he noted

"what efforts are needed to persuade the proud how great the power of humility is," in contrast to the pride, arrogance and lust of domination that God was surely resisting according to the promise of James 4:6.

69. Augustine, *The City of God* (De Civitate Dei), 7.32 (quoted).

70. Yoder, "The Original Revolution," in *The Original Revolution: Essays on Christian Pacifism*, 13–33.

71. On this characteristic rhetorical practice, see John Cavadini, "The Structure and Intention of Augustine's *De Trinitate*," *Augustinian Studies* 23 (1992): 103–23; John C. Cavadini, "Time and Ascent in *Confessions* XI," in *Augustine: Presbyter Factus Sum*, papers originally presented at a conference at Marquette University, November 1990, ed. Joseph T. Lienhard, Earl C. Muller, and Roland J. Teske, Collectanea Augustiniana (New York: Peter Lang Publishing, 1993), 171–85.

72. Augustine, *The City of God* (De Civitate Dei), 1.1, 1.33, 2.2.

73. Ibid., 5.12–20.

74. Ibid., 10.1, 19.1–4.

75. Ibid., 10.29.

76. Ibid., 19.5.

77. Augustine, *Letters* 189 and 220.

78. Cf. Robert Dodaro, "Eloquent Lies, Just Wars and the Politics of Persuasion: Reading Augustine's *City of God* in a 'Postmodern' World," *Augustinian Studies* 25 (1994): 77–138.

79. For a masterful argument as to why Augustine's just-war theory falls apart precisely at this point, see Robert L. Holmes, "St. Augustine and the Just War Theory," in *The Augustinian Tradition*, ed. Gareth B. Matthews, Philosophical Traditions, no. 8 (Berkeley: University of California Press, 1998), 332.

80. Augustine, *The City of God* (De Civitate Dei), 19.17.

81. Ibid.

82. Ibid., 19.10, 19.17.

83. Ibid., 19.26.

84. Some of the material in the remainder of this chapter is adapted from Gerald W. Schlabach, "Meeting in Exile: Historic Peace Churches and the Emerging Peace Church Catholic," *Journal of Religion, Conflict, and Peace* 1, no. 1 (Fall 2007), https://www.manchester.edu/docs/default-source/academics/by-major/philosophy-and-religious-studies/journal/volume-1-issue-1-fall-2007/meeting-in-exile.pdf?sfvrsn=4f5b8962_2, and is used with permission.

85. John XXIII, *Gaudet Mater Ecclesia*, 4.5, cf. 7.3.

86. Alberigo, *History of Vatican II*, I.42, cf. II.16.

87. See chapter 4, especially pp. 96–99 and 121–24.

88. Rahner, "Towards a Fundamental Theological Interpretation of Vatican II."

89. Cf. Alberigo, *History of Vatican II*, IV.625.
90. Second Vatican Council, *Lumen Gentium*, §1.
91. Second Vatican Council, *Gaudium et Spes*, §45, quoting *Lumen Gentium*, §7.
92. Second Vatican Council, *Gaudium et Spes*, §57.
93. Ibid., §58.
94. For surveys of the tectonic shifts that have made Christianity a truly global faith, with a center of gravity in the global South, see Andrew F. Walls, "Mission and Migration: The Diaspora Factor in Christian History," *Journal of African Christian Thought* 5, no. 2 (December 2002): 3–11; the first three chapters of Jenkins, *The Next Christendom*; and Pew Forum on Religion and Public Life, *Global Christianity*. As Walls has summarized the result of these shifts,

> The great European migration has left a strange legacy: a post-Christian West and a post-Western Christianity. Christianity was once the religion of confident, technological advance and rising affluence, and sometimes saw these things as a mark of God's favour. Christianity now will increasingly be associated (mostly) with rather poor and very poor people, and with some of the poorest countries on earth. And people from the non-Western world will be the principal agents of Christian mission right across the world. (10)

95. Augustine, *Ep* 138.14–15, to Marcellinus. See earlier discussion of this passage in chapter 3, pp. 76–78.
96. Cf. John Howard Yoder, *When War Is Unjust: Being Honest in Just-War Thinking*, rev. ed., foreword by Charles P. Lutz, afterword by Drew Christiansen (Maryknoll, NY: Orbis Books, 1996), 68–69, 89.
97. Second Vatican Council, *Lumen Gentium*, §48; Second Vatican Council, *Gaudium et Spes*, §§45, 57.
98. Isaiah 65:17-25; 2 Peter 3:12; Revelation 22:1.
99. 1 Corinthians 15.

Chapter 7—pages 199–235

1. Recognizing this are Anthony J Gittins, "Beyond Hospitality? The Missionary Status and Role Revisited," *International Review of Mission* 83, no. 330 (July 1994): 397–416; Christine D. Pohl, *Making Room: Recovering Hospitality as a Christian Tradition* (Grand Rapids, MI: Eerdmans, 1999), 78, 119; Jessica Wrobleski, *The Limits of Hospitality* (Collegeville MN: Liturgical Press, 2012), 34; Deenabandhu Manchala, "Migration: An Opportunity for Broader and Deeper Ecumenism," chap. 8 in *Theology of Migration in the Abrahamic Religions*, ed. Elaine Padilla and Peter C. Phan, Palgrave Macmillan's Christianities of the World (New York: Palgrave Macmillan, 2014), 161; Patrick T. McCormick, "Fair Trade Tourism: Practicing Hospitality and Keeping the

Sabbath in a Foreign Land," in *Living with(out) Borders: Catholic Theological Ethics on the Migration of Peoples*, ed. Agnes M. Brazal and María Teresa Dávila, Catholic Theological Ethics in the World Church (Maryknoll, NY: Orbis Books, 2016), 162–72; Joshua W. Jipp, *Saved by Faith and Hospitality* (Grand Rapids, MI: Eerdmans, 2017), 99, 113–14.

2. "Address at the Fiftieth General Assembly of the United Nations Organization," §7–8. See earlier exposition of this part of the pope's address in chapter 3, pp. 86–88.

3. For a rich reflection on the twin imperatives of the gospel to embed within every culture yet transcend every culture, see Andrew F. Walls, "The Gospel as Prisoner and Liberator of Culture," chap. 1 in *The Missionary Movement in Christian History: Studies in the Transmission of Faith* (Maryknoll, NY: Orbis Books, 1996), 3–15.

4. I am quite sure that I heard this quote on National Public Radio but I have not been able to trace its source. I am thus less than 100 percent certain that the quote came from Iraq rather than Afghanistan, or which anniversary it was. What I am certain of is that the man's memorable words—though perhaps a paraphrase here—were too original for me to have invented them myself.

5. Paul VI, *Populorum Progressio*, §67.

6. John Koenig, *New Testament Hospitality: Partnership with Strangers as Promise and Mission*, Overtures to Biblical Theology, no. 17 (Philadelphia: Fortress Press, 1985), 15–16; Amy G. Oden, *God's Welcome: Hospitality for a Gospel-Hungry World* (Cleveland, OH: Pilgrim Press, 2008), 18–19. For New Testament examples of Abraham in this archetypical role see Matthew 8:11 and Luke 16:19-31. For a Patristic example that cites both, see John Chrysostom's second sermon in *On Wealth and Poverty*, sermons on Lazarus and the rich man, trans. Catharine P. Roth (Crestwood, NY: St Vladimir's Seminary Press, 1984).

7. Jipp, *Saved by Faith and Hospitality*, 3. Jipp cites especially the First Letter of Clement of Rome, chapters 10–12, which pairs the saving faith and saving hospitality not only of Abraham but of Lot and Rahab as well.

8. Jipp, *Saved by Faith and Hospitality*, 80.

9. Ibid., 21.

10. Koenig, *New Testament Hospitality*, 88–91; Pohl, *Making Room*, 20–23, 29-31; Jipp, *Saved by Faith and Hospitality*, 17–18, 31, 82, 92–95.

11. Koenig draws out such connections especially for Luke–Acts. See Koenig, *New Testament Hospitality*, 11–12, 85–86, 91, 106.

12. Koenig, *New Testament Hospitality*, 11. Cf. Jipp, *Saved by Faith and Hospitality*, 28.

13. Koenig, *New Testament Hospitality*, 90–91, 106, 109; Jipp, *Saved by Faith and Hospitality*, 107–14.

14. Pohl, *Making Room*, 5.

15. Chawkat Georges Moucarry, "The Alien according to the Torah," *Themelios* 14, no. 1 (1988): 18.
16. Moucarry listed these examples in "The Alien according to the Torah," 20, n. 30: Exod 12:43, 45; Deut 14:21; 15:3; 17:15; 23:[20].
17. See Moucarry, "The Alien according to the Torah," 18.
18. Matt 5:17; Mark 10:42–44; John 18:36.
19. Pohl, *Making Room*, 5; Amy G. Oden, ed., *And You Welcomed Me: A Sourcebook on Hospitality in Early Christianity* (Nashville: Abingdon Press, 2001), 17–18, 22–23; Lucien Richard, *Living the Hospitality of God* (New York: Paulist Press, 2000), 5–6.
20. Pohl, *Making Room*, 6.
21. Richard, *Living the Hospitality of God*, 78.
22. Jipp, *Saved by Faith and Hospitality*, 80.
23. Ibid., 17–18.
24. Augustine, Sermon 111.4, in *Sermons*, vol. III/4 of *The Works of Saint Augustine: A Translation for the 21st Century*, gen. ed. Edmund Hill (Brooklyn and Hyde Park, NY: New City Press, 1990).
25. Pope Francis, *Laudato Si'*, Encyclical on Care for Our Common Home (May 24, 2015), §67.
26. Revelation 21, cross-referenced with 1 Corinthians 15:28 and Ephesians 1:23.
27. Richard, *Living the Hospitality of God*, 75, 78.
28. Moucarry, "The Alien according to the Torah," 17–20, first published in French in the magazine *Ichthus*, no. 132 (1985): 3–10.
29. Moucarry's comment: "This statement may surprise us since it refers to land that Abraham, by divine promise, could have considered his own. Indeed it reveals to us the noble mind of the patriarch. Abraham had not abandoned his native land in order to receive another in its place. One might think he was waiting for God himself to fulfil his promise. But quite aside from demonstrating his patience and his detachment from material things, Abraham's attitude indicates how the 'father of believers' saw himself in regard to the One who called him. To confess, in effect, that one is an alien on the earth and a guest in God's earthly house is the distinctive mark of a faith that holds God to be the possessor of all things and man to be but a passing shadow" (18).
30. Moucarry, "The Alien according to the Torah," 18.
31. Ibid.
32. 1 Chr 29:13-15. As Moucarry pointed out (p. 19), this same spiritual sensibility echoes through the Psalms, along with its ethical implications. See Psalms 39:12, 69:8, 94:6, 119:19, 146:9.
33. Moucarry, "The Alien according to the Torah," 18. His initial list included thirteen items, but succeeding paragraphs and their footnotes add more. Summarizing, I count at least the following: the Sabbath, the

Sabbatical year, laws regarding the Day of Atonement, sacrificial offerings, prohibition on the consumption of blood, ritual purity, idolatry and blasphemy, the sacred meal, fair and equitable wages, right to glean from the excess of harvests, treatment of those who are unable to pay one's debts, regulation of slavery, atonement for sins, cities of refuge, the law of the talon, and equal access to the courts.

34. Moucarry, "The Alien according to the Torah," 18–19. See Exod 22:21; Exod 23:9; Lev 19:33-34; Deut 10:19; Deut 16:12; Deut 23:8; Deut 24:18, 22; Deut 26:5.

35. Peter C. Phan, "Embracing, Protecting, and Loving the Stranger: A Roman Catholic Theology of Migration," chap. 5 in *Theology of Migration in the Abrahamic Religions*, ed. Elaine Padilla and Peter C. Phan, Palgrave Macmillan's Christianities of the World (New York: Palgrave Macmillan, 2014), 105.

36. Jipp, *Saved by Faith and Hospitality*, 102.

37. Paul VI, *Evangelii Nuntiandi*, §80.

38. John Paul II, Address at the Fiftieth General Assembly of the United Nations Organization, §7–8. For a fuller elaboration of Pope John Paul II's communitarian vision for international relations and human rights see chapter 3, beginning at p. 79.

39. The latter is what Pope Francis speaks of as "the techno-economic paradigm" whose "new power structures" threaten to "overwhelm not only our politics but also freedom and justice" (*Laudato Si'*, §53).

40. John Paul II, Address at the Fiftieth General Assembly of the United Nations Organization, §7.

41. David Hollenbach, "Religion and Political Life," *Theological Studies* 52 (March 1991): 104.

42. I am grateful to Tisha Rajendra, who read a draft of this chapter, for helping me to clarify and sharpen a number of points throughout. Whether or not I have satisfied all of her concerns, I must especially give her credit for the observations in these last two sentences, which are paraphrases of comments in her correspondence to me dated February 1, 2019.

43. This is a key dynamic in the political science of nonviolent movements for social change, as identified by Gene Sharp in *Power and Struggle*, vol. 1 of *The Politics of Nonviolent Action*, ed. Marina Finkelstein (Boston: Extending Horizons, 1973).

44. The arguments of Daniel and Jonathan Boyarin, who figured largely in chapter 4, would move the international system in this direction.

45. To be sure, there is also an opposite assumption at work among political activists who are only comfortable working "prophetically" from the outside, and celebrate the power of marginality, perhaps in order to explain their anxiety that anyone who does get inside "the room where it happens" will be co-opted and almost by definition will be unfaithful to Christ.

46. Reinhold Niebuhr, "Why the Christian Church Is Not Pacifist."

47. This is my way of summarizing the process that took place in the twentieth century by which Mennonites moved from "nonresistance" to "nonviolence" or from "quietism" to "activism." For a summary study of this transformation see Driedger and Kraybill, *Mennonite Peacemaking: From Quietism to Activism*. For a crucial chapter in the transformation, see Theron F. Schlabach, "Race and Another Look at Nonviolent Resistance," chap. 12 in *War, Peace, and Social Conscience: Guy F. Hershberger and Mennonite Ethics*, Studies in Anabaptist and Mennonite History, no. 45 (Scottdale, PA: Herald Press, 2009), 435–71. Also crucial was the growing voice of women in Mennonite theological and pastoral reflection; see Elizabeth G. Yoder, ed., *Peace Theology and Violence against Women*, intro. by Gayle Gerber Koontz, Occasional Papers, no. 16 (Elkhart, IN: Institute of Mennonite Studies, 1992).

48. Troeltsch, *Social Teaching*, 691–706, 993–1002; Richard Niebuhr, *Christ and Culture*, 56; John C. Bennett, *Christian Ethics and Social Policy*, The Richard Lectures at the University of Virginia (New York: Charles Scribner's Sons, 1946), 41–46; and by implication Reinhold Niebuhr, *Moral Man and Immoral Society*, 263–64, and Reinhold Niebuhr, "Why the Christian Church Is Not Pacifist," 4–5.

49. For critiques of the school of thought that has depended on Troeltsch's church/sect typology or Richard Niebuhr's "Christ against culture" type, see Duane K. Friesen, "Normative Factors in Troeltsch's Typology of Religious Association," *Journal of Religious Ethics* 3, no. 2 (Fall 1975): 271–83; Arne Rasmusson, "The Genealogy of the Charge of Sectarianism," in *The Church as Polis: From Political Theology to Theological Politics as Exemplified by Jürgen Moltmann and Stanley Hauerwas* (Notre Dame, IN: University of Notre Dame Press, 1995), 231–47; Stassen, Yeager, and Yoder, *Authentic Transformation: A New Vision of Christ and Culture*; D. Stephen Long, *The Goodness of God: Theology, Church, and the Social Order* (Grand Rapids, MI: Brazos Press, 2001). Also note the introduction to Stanley Hauerwas, *Christian Existence Today: Essays on Church, World and Living in Between* (Durham, NC: The Labyrinth Press, 1988).

50. Richard Niebuhr, *Christ and Culture*, 32.

51. Friesen, "In Search of Security," 46. That Friesen saw the challenges inherent in this social location as requiring the finesse of a diaspora sensibility is clear from chapter titles in his book, *Artists, Citizens, Philosophers: Seeking the Peace of the City*, foreword by Glen Stassen (Scottdale, PA; Waterloo, ON: Herald Press, 2000), which name the role of Christians as simultaneously "Citizens and Aliens," and explore "The Dynamics of Dual Citizenship."

52. Friesen, "In Search of Security," 55.

53. Ibid., 55–56, citing Walter Wink, *Engaging the Powers: Discernment and Resistance in a World of Domination* (Minneapolis: Fortress Press, 1992), 94–95.

54. Friesen, "In Search of Security," 56.

55. Ibid., 57–58, drawing upon Jeffrey Stout, *Democracy and Tradition*, New Forum Books (Princeton, NJ: Princeton University Press, 2004).

56. Friesen, "In Search of Security," 59–60, 68–75. The notion of middle axioms first entered Mennonite ethics through the work of John Howard Yoder in Yoder, *Christian Witness to the State*, 32–44, though he in turn noted its prominence in preparatory materials at the 1948 General Assembly of the World Council of Churches in Amsterdam.

57. Costa Rica, for example, abolished its military in 1948, but it does still maintain a national guard.

58. As John Howard Yoder once summarized such an ethic, it recognizes "duality without dualism" (*Christian Witness to the State*, 31). It is not dualistic because it recognizes only one norm, Jesus Christ, a norm that applies as much to the state as to the church, and in complex impersonal relationships as much as in face-to-face ones. And yet it is realistic about the difference that faith and unbelief regarding Jesus makes—a functional "duality" not an ultimate or ontological "dualism."

59. Friesen, "In Search of Security," 57–58.

60. Friesen worked through examples of both in "In Search of Security," 60–75. Having been an active participant in the development of "just-peacemaking theory" that we will survey toward the end of chapter 8, Friesen's examples largely coincided with the ten "normative practices" outlined in Glen H. Stassen, ed., *Just Peacemaking: The New Paradigm for the Ethics of Peace and War*, 3rd ed. (Cleveland: Pilgrim Press, 2008). But if anything, Friesen's framework allowed him to do a more finely grained casuistry explaining the relative priorities for Christian peacemaking.

61. Pope John XXIII's 1961 encyclical *Mater et Magistra* marks the church's full engagement with modern human rights discourse, but such engagement had been growing for decades. Pope Pius XII's 1952 apostolic constitution *Exsul familia* is the first document in official Catholic moral thought to recognize the right of persons who experience conditions unworthy of human life in their home county to migrate. As Pius's successor, John XXIII quoted Pius in his 1963 encyclical *Pacem in Terris*, stating: "Every human being has the right to freedom of movement and of residence within the confines of his own State. When there are just reasons in favor of it, he must be permitted to emigrate to other countries and take up residence there. The fact that he is a citizen of a particular State does not deprive him of membership in the human family, nor of citizenship in that universal society, the common, world-wide fellowship of men" (§25).

62. Reflecting this sense of pastoral responsibility are documents such as the following: Sacred Congregation of Bishops, *De Pastorali Migratorum Cura*, Instruction on the Pastoral Care of People Who Migrate (August 22, 1969); United States Conference of Catholic Bishops and Conferencia del Episcopado Mexicano, *Strangers No Longer: Together on the Journey of Hope: A Pasto-*

ral Letter concerning Migration from the Catholic Bishops of Mexico and the United States (Washington, DC: United States Conference of Catholic Bishops, 2003); Pontifical Council for the Pastoral Care of Migrants and Itinerant People, *Erga Migrantes Caritas Christi,* Instruction on the Love of Christ towards Migrants (May 3, 2004), as well as annual papal messages for the World Day of Migrants and Refugees. Peter C. Phan has traced the growing sense of pastoral concern that recent popes have felt in "Embracing, Protecting, and Loving the Stranger," 79–88.

63. Pontifical Council for the Pastoral Care of Migrants and Itinerant People, *Refugees: A Challenge to Solidarity* (June 25, 1992), http://www.vatican.va /roman_curia/pontifical_councils/corunum/documents/rc_pc_corunum _doc_25061992_refugees_en.html.

64. Hannah Arendt, *The Origins of Totalitarianism*, intro. by Samantha Power (New York: Schocken Books, 2004), 376, quoted in Tisha M. Rajendra, *Migrants and Citizens: Justice and Responsibility in the Ethics of Immigration*, foreword by Daniel G. Groody, CSC (Grand Rapids, MI: Eerdmans, 2017), 18.

65. Rajendra, *Migrants and Citizens*, 22.

66. Pope Leo XIII, *Rerum Novarum*, Encyclical on the Condition of the Working Classes (May 15, 1891), §13.

67. For a thorough analysis of the way that a Christian family ethic offers a critique of current immigration policy—along with recognition of the ways that idealized visions of family life sometimes do a disservice to migrant women—see the work of Kristin E. Heyer, *Kinship across Borders: A Christian Ethic of Immigration*, Moral Traditions Series (Washington, DC: Georgetown University Press, 2012); "*Familismo* across the Americas: En Route to a Liberating Christian Family Ethic," in *Living with(out) Borders: Catholic Theological Ethics on the Migration of Peoples*, ed. Agnes M. Brazal and María Teresa Dávila, Catholic Theological Ethics in the World Church (Maryknoll, NY: Orbis Books, 2016), 121–31.

68. Cf. David Hollenbach, SJ, "A Future without Borders: Reimagining the Nation-State and the Church," in *Living with(out) Borders: Catholic Theological Ethics on the Migration of Peoples*, ed. Agnes M. Brazal and María Teresa Dávila, Catholic Theological Ethics in the World Church (Maryknoll, NY: Orbis Books, 2016), 223–35.

69. Marianne Heimbach-Steins, "The Ambivalence of Borders and the Challenge of an Ethics of Liminality," in *Living with(out) Borders: Catholic Theological Ethics on the Migration of Peoples*, ed. Agnes M. Brazal and María Teresa Dávila, Catholic Theological Ethics in the World Church (Maryknoll, NY: Orbis Books, 2016), 236–45. Also see Rosemary L. Haughton, "Hospitality: Home as the Integration of Privacy and Community," in *The Longing for Home*, ed. Leroy S. Rouner, Boston University Studies in Philosophy and Religion, vol. 17 (Notre Dame, IN: University of Notre Dame Press, 1996), 204–5.

70. Saskia Sassen, "The Making of Migrations," in *Living with(out) Borders: Catholic Theological Ethics on the Migration of Peoples*, ed. Agnes M. Brazal and María Teresa Dávila, Catholic Theological Ethics in the World Church (Maryknoll, NY: Orbis Books, 2016), 19–20.

71. Heyer, *Kinship across Borders*, 110.

72. Ibid., 24–25; Nancy Pineda-Madrid, "Sex Trafficking and Femicide along the Border: Re-Membering Our Daughters," in *Living with(out) Borders: Catholic Theological Ethics on the Migration of Peoples*, ed. Agnes M. Brazal and María Teresa Dávila, Catholic Theological Ethics in the World Church (Maryknoll, NY: Orbis Books, 2016), 81–87.

73. Heimbach-Steins, "The Ambivalence of Borders," 240. All of this provides additional evidence for my earlier claim that "we all live in diaspora anyway."

74. United States Conference of Catholic Bishops, *Welcoming the Stranger among Us: Unity in Diversity*, pastoral statement (Washington, DC: United States Conference of Catholic Bishops, 2001). Emphasis added.

75. For an additional example in which the right to defend borders risks trumping the human rights of migrants, see Pope Benedict XVI, *Migrations: Pilgrimage of Faith and Hope*, Message for 2013 World Day of Migrants and Refugees (October 12, 2012).

76. William O'Neill, SJ, "The Place of Displacement: The Ethics of Migration in the United States," in *Living with(out) Borders: Catholic Theological Ethics on the Migration of Peoples*, ed. Agnes M. Brazal and María Teresa Dávila, Catholic Theological Ethics in the World Church (Maryknoll, NY: Orbis Books, 2016), 72–73; Heimbach-Steins, "The Ambivalence of Borders," 236, 240–42. Also see Heyer, *Kinship across Borders*, 113.

77. Rajendra, *Migrants and Citizens*, 125, but see the entire chapter 6 from which this quotation is taken, titled "Justice as Responsibility to Relationships." That chapter in turn builds on her biblical survey in chapter 5 of "Justice as Fidelity to the Demands of Relationship."

78. Rajendra, *Migrants and Citizens*, 129–38.

79. In actual not metaphorical languages, this is the problem of "false friends"—words that look like cognates, but are not. A famous example is "embarrassed" in English and "*embarazada*" in Spanish. Embarrassed as they struggle with beginners' Spanish, many English-speaking visitors to Latin America have drawn laughter by mistakenly saying that they are *embarazados*—pregnant!

80. Within the church's own language of biblical hospitality, foundational human dignity, and the lexical priority of the family over the derivative status of the state, "self-defense" might evoke the right of vulnerable families to defend themselves by migrating, with or without legal status. And although Pope Leo XIII has focused our attention on families, the principle here can easily extend to individuals who certainly do not lack human dig-

nity simply because they are single, and who so often are hoping to contribute within family networks that stretch across borders besides.

81. Jessica Wrobleski's book, *The Limits of Hospitality*, testifies to this in numerous ways. Explaining the book's very title, she notes its "double meaning: not only is it the case that hospitality cannot exist without limits, but it is also essential that these limits be formed and informed by the spirit of hospitality that they intend to protect" (xii). See also pp. 13, 21, 31–32, 35, 102, and the entirety of her case study on the Catholic Worker, which constitutes her final chapter (pp. 128–50). Summarizing, she notes at one point that

> although it may appear that there are few limits to the hospitality of the Catholic Worker, even here hospitality cannot exist as total openness or surrender. While the limits of Catholic Worker hospitality generally fall well outside what most people would find tolerable, limits are by no means absent. In many ways these limits reflect the same concerns for identity and security that I have articulated in the previous chapters: there is, ultimately, a distinction between hosts and guests, just as there must be lines drawn "for staff survival" as well as for the safety of all involved.

82. Haughton, "Hospitality," 204–5.

83. Ibid., 208.

84. Though Haughton did not elaborate on this implicit need for borders, she made the conceptual linkage clear in passing when she acknowledged that "hospitality can be dangerous, in the very literal sense that makes people put double locks and spy holes on their doors and in the more profound sense that the breaching of barriers is also a breaking of categories and therefore a harbinger of revolution" ("Hospitality," 208). Later she also noted that hospitality did not mean simply "taking the lock off the door or opening the borders of the country . . . because such actions can destroy the home that makes hospitality possible" (215).

85. Haughton, "Hospitality," 211. Wrobleski makes a similar point in *The Limits of Hospitality*, 102.

86. Haughton, "Hospitality," 211, 215.

87. Ibid., 215.

88. As with every article in Aquinas's *Summa*, ST II-II.66.1 and .2 began with objections to what Aquinas was about to argue. In this case those objections claimed in various ways, citing various biblical and patristic authorities, that God's gift of creation and charge of stewardship to all of humanity requires a pure community of goods or shared ownership. In none of Aquinas's own counterarguments or replies to these objections at the end of each article did Aquinas contest the basic premise of his imagined objectors, however. Rather he showed why additional considerations require—but also guide and limit—the distributive management of common goods through conditionally private ownership. Thus Aquinas prepared for the implications that we will shortly examine in his statement in II-II.66.7: "In cases of need all

things are common property, so that there would seem to be no sin in taking another's property, for need has made it common."

89. See Aquinas, *ST* II-II.66.1, obj. 1 but also replies 1 and 3.

90. Ibid. II-II.66.2: Possession of property "is necessary to human life for three reasons. First because every man is more careful to procure what is for himself alone than that which is common to many or to all: since each one would shirk the labor and leave to another that which concerns the community, as happens where there is a great number of servants. Secondly, because human affairs are conducted in more orderly fashion if each man is charged with taking care of some particular thing himself, whereas there would be confusion if everyone had to look after any one thing indeterminately. Thirdly, because a more peaceful state is ensured to man if each one is contented with his own. Hence it is to be observed that quarrels arise more frequently where there is no division of the things possessed."

91. See the second replies to objections in both II-II.66.1 and .2.

92. Ibid. II-II.66.7.

93. Haughton, "Hospitality," 213.

94. I allude here to two of the foundational practices of conflict transformation: "Separate the people from the problem" and "Focus on interests not positions." See chapter 2 of Roger Fisher and William Ury, *Getting to Yes: Negotiating Agreement without Giving In*, 2nd ed., ed. Bruce Patton (New York: Penguin Books, 1991).

95. Pope Francis, "Migrants and Refugees: Men and Women in Search of Peace," World Day of Peace message (January 1, 2018), §1, http://w2.vatican.va/content/francesco/en/messages/peace/documents/papa-francesco_20171113_messaggio-51giornatamondiale-pace2018.html.

96. Note for example the ways in which Kristin Heyer has both appealed to the conditions required to support families, and warned about ways in which idealized family norms can hurt migrant women in *Kinship across Borders*, 75–78, and "*Familismo* across the Americas."

97. This is what I have elsewhere labeled the "Deuteronomic juncture," in which God's liberated people have come into the land but now are tempted to forget the Lord and become new oppressors. Moses' warnings in this regard are especially direct in Deuteronomy chapter 8. See Schlabach, "Deuteronomic or Constantinian."

98. Wink, *Engaging the Powers*, 65–89; Walter Wink, *The Powers That Be: Theology for a New Millennium* (New York: Doubleday, 1998), 31–36.

99. Cardinal Peter Turkson, "Christian Nonviolence and Just Peace," keynote address, The Catholic Church Moves towards Nonviolence? Just Peace Just War in Dialogue (University of San Diego, 2017), https://youtu.be/1iY__KsrFK0, at 1:18:03. See also the similar language in Rajendra, *Migrants and Citizens*, 93–94, citing John R. Donahue, "Biblical Perspectives on Justice," in *The Faith That Does Justice: Examining the Christian Sources for Social Change*,

ed. John C. Haughey, Woodstock Studies, vol. 2 (New York: Paulist Press, 1977), 69.
100. Rajendra, *Migrants and Citizens*, 93.

Chapter 8—pages 236–73

1. A version of this chapter is also appearing with the title "A 'Manual' for Escaping Our Vicious Cycles: The Political Relevance of Enemy-Love," in *Modern Theology*, pre-published online through Early View in Wiley Online Library, DOI:10.1111/moth.12470 and available at https://rdcu.be/bfWNE. Forthcoming in hard-copy edition of the journal. Used with permission.

2. The most immediate prompt for Pope Francis's 2017 World Day of Peace message was a conference organized by the Catholic peace organization Pax Christi International, which was held in Rome on April 11–13, 2016, and its well-publicized final document. See Pax Christi International, "An Appeal to the Catholic Church to Re-Commit to the Centrality of Gospel Nonviolence," final document of the conference "Nonviolence and Just Peace: Contributing to the Catholic Understanding of and Commitment to Nonviolence," hosted by the Pontifical Council for Justice and Peace (Rome, 2016), http://www.paxchristi.net/sites/default/files/documents/appeal-to-catholic-church-to-recommit-to-nonviolence.pdf.

3. John Paul II, "World Day of Peace Message 2000," §20.

4. Pope Francis, "Nonviolence: A Style of Politics for Peace," Message for the World Day of Peace (January 1, 2017), §6, https://w2.vatican.va/content/francesco/en/messages/peace/documents/papa-francesco_20161208_messaggio-l-giornata-mondiale-pace-2017.html.

5. Ibid., §2.

6. Ibid., §1–4. Quotations from Benedict XVI are from his Angelus message of February 18, 2007, in St. Peter's Square, http://w2.vatican.va/content/benedict-xvi/en/angelus/2007/documents/hf_ben-xvi_ang_20070218.html.

7. Francis, "Nonviolence: A Style of Politics for Peace," §6.

8. ZENIT, "Cardinal Ratzinger on the Abridged Version of Catechism Compendium Expected Out in 2 Years."

9. One such manual in the English-speaking world that went through many editions from the 1930s through the 1950s may illustrate, that of Henry Davis, SJ. Other than organizing his work according to the order of the Decalogue and placing his discussion of self-defense, dueling, and warfare under the heading of the fifth commandment against killing, Davis made no reference to biblical sources at all. See Henry Davis, SJ, *Moral and Pastoral Theology: A Summary*, Heythrop Series (New York: Sheed & Ward, 1952), 54–58; and Henry Davis, SJ, *Moral and Pastoral Theology in Four Volumes*, 7th

ed., rev. and enl., ed. L. W. Geddes, SJ, Heythrop Series., no. 2 (London; New York: Sheed & Ward, 1958), 148–51.

10. Less than a decade before the Second Vatican Council began to rehabilitate conscientious objection to war by recognizing the moral integrity of those who forego violent self-defense in favor of other means (*Gaudium et Spes*, §78), Pope Pius XII in his 1956 Christmas address was, however, suggesting otherwise. After recapitulating the broad requirements for war to be justifiable, he noted: "Therefore a Catholic citizen cannot invoke his own conscience in order to refuse to serve and fulfill those duties the law imposes." Pope Pius XII, *The Major Addresses of Pope Pius XII*, 2 vols., ed. Vincent A. Yzermans (St. Paul: North Central Pub. Co., 1961), 225. And historically, two of the casuists with the greatest influence on Catholic teaching on the ethics of war in the early modern period, Francisco de Vitoria, OP, and Francisco Suárez, SJ, did reject Christian pacifism outright as heretical. Vitoria heroically extended just-war casuistry in order to critique the Spanish Conquest of the Americas, and for that deserves his place as a founder of modern international law. He was not so generous, however with *"isti haeretici novi"* who cite St. Paul against Christian participation in war. (Had he learned of contemporaneous Anabaptists emerging elsewhere in Europe in the 1520s and '30s?) His conclusion: *"Sed hoc est haereticum."* See Vitoria, *Comentarios a la Secunda Secundae de santo Tomás*, v. 2, p. 280, commenting on Aquinas ST II-II.40.1. Suárez likely rejected "the assertion that it is intrinsically evil and contrary to charity to wage war" as heresy in "Disputation XIII: On War (*de Bello*)," excerpted in *The Ethics of War: Classic and Contemporary Readings*, ed. Gregory M. Reichberg, Henrik Syse, and Endre Begby (Malden, MA; Oxford: Blackwell, 2006), 339–70.

11. Reinhold Niebuhr, *Moral Man and Immoral Society*; Niebuhr, "Why the Christian Church Is Not Pacifist."

12. Second Vatican Council, *Lumen Gentium*, §39–42.

13. Second Vatican Council, *Gaudium et Spes*, §78.

14. John Paul II, *Centesimus Annus*, §23.

15. Francis, "Nonviolence: A Style of Politics for Peace," §§2–4.

16. Cf. 2 Corinthians 12:9, but also note Augustine's *Confessions*, book 7, section 18.24 and the following sections.

17. For a window into the faith of the Christian community in its first few decades, I am confining myself to Acts 2. No serious biblical scholars would consider the sermons in the book of Acts to be exact transcripts, of course. Many would suspect that even if the author of Luke and Acts was benefiting from accounts passed down through oral tradition (see Luke 1:1-4; cf. Acts 1:1-2), he overlaid them with his own theological emphases. Nonetheless, Peter's sermon in Acts 2 gives enough signs of its primitive origins for scholars to use it as one among a number of key resources for discerning the outline of earliest Christian proclamation or *kerygma*. (Taken in isolation

from other New Testament texts, for example, the Acts 2:36 affirmation that God had *made* Jesus both Lord and Messiah would seem to support an "adoptionist" understanding of Jesus' relationship to God that later Christian theology would soon find inadequate. This provides strong evidence for its authentic antiquity.) For far more detailed studies identifying the earliest and most basic core of Christian faith, based on texts from throughout the New Testament, see Ben F. Meyer, "The Gospel Literature: Data on Jesus?," chap. 3 in *The Aims of Jesus*, intro. by N. T. Wright, Princeton Theological Monograph Series, vol. 48 (1979; repr., San Jose, CA: Pickwick Publications, 2002), 60–75; Larry W. Hurtado, *At the Origins of Christian Worship: The Context and Character of Earliest Christian Devotion* (Grand Rapids, MI: Eerdmans, 2000), 76–81, 86–97; and above all Hurtado's monumental work, *Lord Jesus Christ: Devotion to Jesus in Earliest Christianity* (Grand Rapids, MI: Eerdmans, 2003), especially pp. 108–18, 179–84, 650–51. I wish to thank my colleague John Martens for help in reviewing this literature.

18. Acts 2:32 has been used for anti-Semitic purposes, since it records Peter bluntly saying to his Jewish listeners: "You crucified and killed [this man, Jesus] by the hands of those outside the law." Yet this very verse conveys the responsibility that the Roman occupiers shared. Crucifixion was their trademark technique of political execution, after all, and it is they who are the ones outside the law or Torah whose hands were required for it to be carried out at all.

19. Peter's own difficulty accepting Jesus as a messiah who would suffer, and his failure to identify with Jesus as he neared death, is a prominent element in the drama of Jesus' ministry and passion. See Mark 8:27-38; Mark 14:28-31, 66-72; and parallels in other gospels.

20. Mark 8:27-34; 10:32-45.

21. Gene Sharp, *The Politics of Nonviolent Action*, 3 vols., ed. Marina Finkelstein (Boston: Extending Horizons, 1973); Gene Sharp, *Social Power and Political Freedom*, Extending Horizons Books (Boston: P. Sargent Publishers, 1980); Erica Chenoweth and Maria J. Stephan, *Why Civil Resistance Works: The Strategic Logic of Nonviolent Conflict*, Columbia Studies in Terrorism and Irregular Warfare (New York: Columbia University Press, 2011).

22. Yoder, "Armaments and Eschatology," 58. Cf. Yoder, *The Politics of Jesus*, 246; and note Hauerwas, *With the Grain of the Universe*.

23. The tempter's suggestion that Jesus turn stones into bread was not simply a way to stave off his own hunger, but coincided with the option to promote his movement through a demagogic appeal to the lowest common denominator of self-interest on the part of the populace. The tempter's suggestion that Jesus throw himself from the pinnacle of the temple in Jerusalem and allow God to save him was not simply a misguided test of faith, but coincided with the option to manipulate the public through spectacle, thus winning a name that had more to do with shallow celebrity than faithful

witness. And when the tempter showed Jesus "all the kingdoms of the world" in an instant and offered to give Jesus "their glory and all this authority," the problem was not only that Jesus would have to bow down to one other than God. More than that, the very kind of power that the tempter offered was incompatible with God's Kingdom—the violence of imperial conquest.

24. John 6:1-15; Matt 21:1-17; Mark 11:1-19; Luke 19:28-48; Matt 26:51-53.

25. For a fuller elaboration of the political implications of Luke 4, see Yoder, "The Kingdom Coming," chapter 2 of *The Politics of Jesus*, 21–59. The reference to "a truly original revolution" derives from the title essay in Yoder, *The Original Revolution: Essays on Christian Pacifism*.

26. In an earlier chapter I cited the work of Rodney Stark (*The Rise of Christianity*) as a source for understanding the spread of early Christianity. On the role that practices of nonviolence played in that growth, see Kreider, *The Patient Ferment of the Early Church*.

27. Cf. pp. 164–67 in chapter 6 on the experience of the second-century Roman Christian Hermas.

28. Alan Kreider, "Changing Patterns of Conversion in the West," in *The Origins of Christendom in the West*, ed. Alan Kreider (Edinburgh: T. & T. Clark, 2001), 17–21; Kreider, *The Patient Ferment of the Early Church*, 251–79.

29. Augustine addressed the question at least in passing both early and late in his career. The issue serves as an illustration as he debates the role of the passions in his early dialogue *The Free Choice of the Will* (De Libero Arbitrio, 386), in *The Teacher, The Free Choice of the Will, Grace and Free Will*, The Fathers of the Church, vol. 59 (Washington, DC: The Catholic University of America Press, 1968), 1.5. And there are hints that he may have modified his position by 413 or 414 in letter 153 to Macedonius, imperial vicar of North Africa (Augustine, "Letter 153," To Macedonius [413–14] in *Letters 100–155* [Epistulae], vol. II/2 of *The Works of Saint Augustine: A Translation for the 21st Century*, ed. Boniface Ramsey, trans. Roland Teske, SJ [Hyde Park, NY: New City Press, 2003], 5.17). But because the first is early and speculative, while the latter is inconclusive, I am relying instead on his succinct but direct letter no. 47 to Publicola in 398.

30. Aquinas, *Summa theologiae* II-II.64.7.

31. Augustine, "Letter 47," To Publicola [398] in *Letters 1-99* (Epistulae), vol. II/2 of *The Works of Saint Augustine: A Translation for the 21st Century*, ed. Boniface Ramsey, trans. Roland Teske, SJ (Hyde Park, NY: New City Press, 2001), 5.

32. David Hollenbach, *Nuclear Ethics: A Christian Moral Argument* (New York: Paulist Press, 1983), 37.

33. Cf. Letter 138 2.9 to Marcellinus, where Augustine remarked that he could speak more briefly to the relationship between the duties of the Christian disciple and the duties of the citizen because he could appeal to Roman

sources themselves, especially Cicero. See Cicero, *De republica* 3 and *De officiis* 1, where his discussions explicitly or implicitly include requirements that war be defensive, be waged as a last resort, be preceded by attempts to achieve recompense for wrongs, be openly declared should those attempts fail, be aimed at a just cause as defined by the pursuit of the common good rather than private goods, be proportionate in the imposition of punishment rather than unlimited retribution, be conducted only by lawfully designated soldiers, and be concluded with a generosity in victory that rests once peace is won rather than multiplying retribution against civilians or combatants who have surrendered.

34. E.g., Letter 185 to Boniface.
35. E.g., Letter 138 to Marcellinus.
36. E.g., Letter 133 to Marcellinus.
37. *Summa theologiae* II-II.40.1.
38. Francisco de Vitoria, "De Indis Recenter Inventis [On the Indians Lately Discovered— 1539]," trans. John Pawley Bate, in *De Indis et de Ivre Belli Relectiones* [On the Indians and on the Law of War], ed. Ernest Nys, Classics of International Law, no. 7 (Washington, DC: Carnegie Institution, 1917), 115–62 [Latin text: 217–68].
39. Hugo Grotius, *Prolegomena to the Law of War and Peace*, 1625, trans. Francis W. Kelsey, intro. by Edward Dumbauld, The Library of Liberal Arts (Indianapolis: Bobbs-Merrill, 1957).
40. Augustine, *Answer to Faustus a Manichean* [Contra Faustum Manichaeum], vol. I/20 of *The Works of Saint Augustine: A Translation for the 21st Century*, ed. Boniface Ramsey, intro., trans., and notes by Roland Teske, SJ (Brooklyn and Hyde Park, NY: New City Press, 2007), 22.75. Due authority, just cause, and right intention are the basic categories that Aquinas identified as necessary for a justifiable war in *Summa theologiae* II-II.40.1. Note, however, that Augustine's main interest was not primarily to lay out a systematic just-war theory, but to counter the Manichaean argument that Old Testament wars showed the God of the Jews to be an evil god or demiurge by demonstrating how wars could be just.
41. A twofold grouping of criteria into *ad bellum* and *in bello* criteria has arguably been implicit since Francisco de Vitoria in the sixteenth century, but only became standard in the twentieth century. See Robert Kolb, "Origin of the Twin Terms Jus Ad Bellum/Jus in Bello," *International Review of the Red Cross*, no. 320 (October 31, 1997), https://www.icrc.org/eng/resources/documents/article/other/57jnuu.htm; and Nicholas Rengger, "The Jus in Bello in Historical and Philosophical Perspective," in *War: Essays in Political Philosophy*, ed. Larry May, with assistance of Emily Crookston (Cambridge; New York: Cambridge University Press, 2008), 30–46.
42. Yoder provided a quite detailed catalog in appendix 5 of the revised edition of *When War Is Unjust*, 147–61 (note that this appendix is *not* available

in the first edition, Augsburg Publishing House, 1984). Also see the 1992 *Catechism of the Catholic Church*, §2307–17, and the United States Conference of Catholic Bishops, *Harvest of Justice*, section I.B.2.

43. Brian Orend, "Justice After War," *Ethics & International Affairs* 16, no. 1 (2002): 43–56; Center for Strategic and International Studies (CSIS) and Association of the United States Army (AUSA), "Post-Conflict Reconstruction Task Framework," in *Laying a Durable Foundation for Post-Conflict Societies*, 37th Conference on the United Nations of the Next Decade, sponsored by The Stanley Foundation (Carmel, CA, 2002); Kenneth R. Himes, OFM, "Intervention, Just War, and U.S. National Security," *Theological Studies* 65, no. 1 (2004): 141–57; Richard P. DiMeglio, "The Evolution of the Just War Tradition: Defining Jus Post Bellum," *Military Law Review* 186 (Winter 2005): 116–63; Robert E. Williams and Dan Caldwell, "Jus Post Bellum: Just War Theory and the Principles of Just Peace," *International Studies Perspectives* 7, no. 4 (November 2006): 309–20; Mark J. Allman and Tobias L. Winright, *After the Smoke Clears: The Just War Tradition and Post War Justice* (Maryknoll, NY: Orbis Books, 2010).

44. Augustine, *Homilies on the First Epistle of John* (Tractatus in Epistolam Joannis Ad Parthos), vol. I/14 of *The Works of Saint Augustine: A Translation for the 21st Century*, ed. Daniel E. Doyle, OSA, and Thomas Martin, OSA, intro., trans., and notes by Boniface Ramsey (Brooklyn and Hyde Park, NY: New City Press, 2008), 8.10. In a book that did much to bring just-war thinking back into Protestant discourse in the second half of the twentieth century, Paul Ramsey argued that even when Aquinas came to justify personal self-defense and developed the principle of double-effect in order to do so, that principle carried Augustine's legacy forward by continuing to recognize the dignity of the enemy. It did so by insisting that one must never directly intend the death of assailants, but only the preservation of one's own life to which their death might be an unintended effect. Disproportionate force would vitiate the act of self-defense as it revealed an intention to kill. And direct attacks on innocents was altogether forbidden. This trajectory was that source of noncombatant immunity, which for Ramsey was the lynchpin of the entire just-war framework. See Ramsey, *War and the Christian Conscience*, 40–46, 56, 59.

45. Even Augustine's arguments for coercive measures against heretics reflected the tug of conscience that Jesus' call to love one's enemies required. Both in that context and in the pastoral guidance he gave to military officers concerning warfare, he repeatedly felt the need to explain why the "correction" of sinful adversaries would also be good for them. Whether one concludes that such arguments constitute legitimate justifications or dubious rationalizations, they demonstrate his abiding recognition of the human dignity of enemies. See Augustine, "Letter 138," 2.9; *Homilies on the First Epistle of John*, 7.8, 9.3–4, 10.7; "The Lord's Sermon on the Mount (*De Sermone*

Domini in Monte)," in *New Testament I and II*, vol. I/15 and I/16 of *The Works of Saint Augustine: A Translation for the 21st Century*, trans. Michael G. Campbell, intro. and notes by Boniface Ramsey (Brooklyn and Hyde Park, NY: New City Press, 2014), 1.18.55, 1.20.63, 1.21.69.

46. For background, see Schlabach, *For the Joy Set Before Us*, especially pages 24–47 and 67–82. Some of this material is also available in Schlabach, "'Love Is the Hand of the Soul': The Grammar of Continence in Augustine's Doctrine of Christian Love," *Journal of Early Christian Studies* 6, no. 1 (Spring 1998): 59–92.

47. Sermon 56 [410–12] §14 in Augustine, *Sermons*. This is not to deny that his Platonic tendency to interiorize moral questions may also have helped him rationalize violence as he shifted his focus on the evils that are truly blameworthy in war from the actual human deaths of those "who are going to die at some time" anyway to "the desire to do harm, cruelty in taking vengeance, a mind that is without peace and incapable of peace, fierceness in rebellion, the lust for domination, and anything else of the sort." Augustine, *Answer to Faustus a Manichean* [Contra Faustum Manichaeum], 22.74.

48. Augustine, *Homilies on the First Epistle of John*, 8.10; Augustine, *The City of God* (De Civitate Dei), 1.35; Augustine, "The Lord's Sermon on the Mount (*De Sermone Domini in Monte*)," 1.18.54.

49. Augustine, "Letter 138," 2.12.

50. I am grateful to the late Glen Stassen for his assistance at various stages in the conceptualization and writing of the arguments in this section and in the following chapter. I first presented these arguments at a session of the annual meeting of the Society of Christian Ethics in 2013, in a paper that later appeared as "'Confessional' Nonviolence and the Unity of the Church: Can Christians Square the Circle?," *Journal of the Society of Christian Ethics* 34, no. 1 (2014): 125–44. Stassen was present at that session and an enthusiastic participant in the discussion that followed. Though I certainly did not expect Stassen to concur with every judgment of mine, he was supportive when I initially shared my core argument with him in 2010, graciously answered numerous questions in the course of my writing, and pointed me in helpful bibliographic directions.

51. Stassen laid out his exegetical evidence in greatest detail for biblical scholars in "The Fourteen Triads of the Sermon on the Mount (Matthew 5:21–7:12)," *Journal of Biblical Literature* 122, no. 2 (Summer 2003): 267–308. His most accessible elaboration for a general audience is *Living the Sermon on the Mount*. Also see Stassen and Gushee, *Kingdom Ethics*; Glen H. Stassen, "Healing the Rift between the Sermon on the Mount and Christian Ethics," *Studies in Christian Ethics* 18, no. 3 (2005): 89–105; and Glen H. Stassen, *A Thicker Jesus: Incarnational Discipleship in a Secular Age* (Louisville, KY: Westminster John Knox Press, 2012). Stassen was not the first to break with the easy assumption of many commentators that the writer of Matthew had

organized the long core of the Sermon on the Mount (5:21–7:12) around a series of dyads or antitheses. Understandably, the repeated formula in Matthew 5, "you have heard it said . . . but I say onto you," has made antithesis a prima facie reading for lay readers and scholars alike. See for example Joachim Jeremias, *The Sermon on the Mount*, trans. Norman Perrin, Biblical Series, no. 2 (1961; repr., Philadelphia: Fortress Press, 1963); Daniel J. Harrington, *The Gospel of Matthew*, Sacra Pagina series, vol. 1 (Collegeville, MN: Liturgical Press, 1991); Ben F. Meyer, *Five Speeches That Changed the World* (Collegeville, MN: Liturgical Press, 1994); Hans Dieter Betz, *The Sermon on the Mount: A Commentary on the Sermon on the Mount, Including the Sermon on the Plain (Matthew 5:3–7:27 and Luke 6:20-49)*, ed. Adela Yarbro Collins, Hermeneia: A Critical and Historical Commentary on the Bible (Minneapolis: Fortress Press, 1995). But even commentators who have assumed the structure of antithesis have noted Jesus' intent to overcome vicious cycles in creative and transformational ways. See Meyer, *Five Speeches That Changed the World*, 46–47, 57; Betz, *The Sermon on the Mount*, 276; Frederick Dale Bruner, *Matthew: A Commentary Vol. 1, The Christbook, Matthew 1–12* (Grand Rapids, MI: Eerdmans, 2004), 207, 246, 248.

52. Stassen, *Just Peacemaking*; Glen H. Stassen, "The Unity, Realism, and Obligatoriness of Just Peacemaking Theory," *Journal of the Society of Christian Ethics* 23, no. 1 (2003): 171–94; Glen H. Stassen, "Just Peacemaking as Hermeneutical Key: The Need for International Cooperation in Preventing Terrorism," *Journal of the Society of Christian Ethics* 24, no. 2 (Fall/Winter 2004): 171–91.

53. Unfortunately, though not surprisingly for an emerging field or perspective, terminology is still being standardized. While specialists may thus debate the subtle advantages of "just peace" or "just peacemaking," and competing meanings for "peacemaking" in military or United Nations circles have prompted still others to prefer "peace*building*," the differences should not distract readers from noticing what all of these proposals share—a desire both to hold together work for justice and work for peace, and hope to transcend tired debates between just-war and pacifist positions. For an early effort to move toward a "just-peace" framework, see the document from the United Church of Christ, "Pronouncement on Affirming the United Church of Christ as a Just Peace Church," Fifteenth General Synod (1985), http://d3n8a8pro7vhmx.cloudfront.net/unitedchurchofchrist/legacy_url/257/just-peace-church-pronouncement-1985.pdf. For a later and much wider statement of ecumenical consensus, see World Council of Churches, *An Ecumenical Call to Just Peace*, received, endorsed and commended for study, reflection, collaboration and common action during the Central Committee meetings in February 2011, Geneva, Switzerland (2011), http://www.overcomingviolence.org/en/resources-dov/wcc-resources/documents/declarations-on-just-peace/ecumenical-call-to-just-peace.html.

54. Glen H. Stassen, *Just Peacemaking: Transforming Initiatives for Justice and Peace* (Louisville, KY: Westminster/John Knox Press, 1992). Chapter 2 is on the Sermon on the Mount, with an initial exposition of its "threefold pattern" on pp. 42–51.

55. The most famous example is probably Jesus' denunciation of the hypocrisy of the religious leaders of his day in Matt 23. In verse 17 of that chapter, he even calls them fools. See also Mark 3:5.

56. For Stassen's complete list of difficulties presented by a dyadic analysis of Matt 5:21-26, see "The Fourteen Triads," 271–72. For a list of problems that the dyadic approach to 5:21-48 in particular presents, see "The Fourteen Triads," 268–69.

57. This is not to say that Jesus owed nothing to the intermediary rabbis who had commented on the Torah. Matthew Goldstone has demonstrated developments and precedents already in Exod 21:14 and in early rabbinic glosses in his article "Murder, Anger, and Altars: The First Matthean Antithesis in Light of Exodus 21:14 and Its Early Rabbinic Interpretation," *Novum Testamentum* 59, no. 4 (2017): 339–54. Jesus was thus part of a tradition by which the rabbis had already transformed "the protagonist in Exod 21:14 from a sanctuary seeker to a person bringing a sacrifice." Still, this very link "draws our attention to the general way in which Jesus is presented as encouraging a person to leave a sacrifice in contrast to the rabbinic attempt to limit the scenarios in which an offering can be interrupted." This underscores Jesus' innovative shift in focus from a casuistry around the recognition of sanctuary for past violence, to the prevention of future cycles of violence.

58. Glen H. Stassen, "The Fourteen Triads," 273, quoting Robert A. Guelich, *The Sermon on the Mount: A Foundation for Understanding* (Waco, TX: Word Books, 1982), 190.

59. That neglected but legitimate translation of *tō ponērō* solves nagging interpretive problems in its own right, by the way. Stassen credits Clarence Jordan for noticing that the dative can be instrumental rather than substantive, and that this better accords with parallel passages in Romans 12:17-21; Luke 6:27-36; 1 Thessalonians 5:15; and the *Didache* 1.4-5. See Stassen, "The Fourteen Triads," 281–82; *Living the Sermon on the Mount*, 89–91.

60. Stassen, "The Fourteen Triads," 279–81; Stassen, *Living the Sermon on the Mount*, 89–98. See also Wink, *Engaging the Powers*, 175–94; "Breaking the Spiral of Violence," in *The Powers That Be*, 84–97.

61. Wink, *The Powers That Be*, 98–111; Stassen, *Living the Sermon on the Mount*, 91–95.

62. Cf. Glen H. Stassen, "Transforming Initiatives of Just Peacemaking Based on the Triadic Structure of the Sermon on the Mount," Matthew section, Society of Biblical Literature (2006), 1 and 5, https://www.sbl-site.org/assets/pdfs/Stassen_Transforming.pdf: "Direct copying, unimaginative and literalistic transposition from Jesus' social context to ours is anachronistic.

But on the other hand, developing an allegedly Christian ethic that evades the way of Jesus is hardly Christian. . . . I suggest we employ a hermeneutical method of analogy, asking what practice or practices in our context corresponds to and carries out Jesus' command to go and make peace with our adversary. A method of analogy is not an unimaginative and legalistic act of obedience. Nor is it an unimaginative assertion that Jesus' or Matthew's context was different from ours and therefore Jesus' teaching does not apply. Nor is it to reduce the teaching to a thin principle not fleshed out in disciplined practice. Rather it is to ask what kind of practice in our context functions as implementation of the intention in Jesus' teaching in first-century context. . . . The transforming initiatives all command us not simply to comply but to invent a surprising initiative."

63. Recognizing this are W. D. Davies and Dale C. Allison, *Critical and Exegetical Commentary on the Gospel according to Saint Matthew: In Three Volumes*, International Critical Commentary on the Holy Scriptures of the Old and New Testaments (Edinburgh: T. & T. Clark, 1988), 506, 549–50; Betz, *The Sermon on the Mount*, 267. As Davies and Allison wrote: "The content of 5.21, 27, 31, 33, and 43 can be derived in every instance from the [Old Testament]. . . . It is not necessary to rifle extracanonical literature for parallels."

64. Take, for example, an abused wife, and the wisdom needed by those working for her safety. Bringing to the surface a hatred she may need in order to "get the hell out" of the abusive relationship may be one of those transitory tasks on the way to truth-telling and whatever healing is possible. Indeed, it may already begin the diagnosis of complicated vicious cycles.

65. Fittingly, for example, the verses that Stassen associated with Jesus' diagnoses of vicious cycles often use continuous action participles in Greek, not the imperatives one would expect if Jesus had intended to place his accent there. Instead, the Greek imperatives almost always come where triadic analysis would expect, within the transforming initiatives. In other evidence, to discern fourteen triads matches the 3 x 14 number of generations in Jesus' genealogy in Matthew 1, and thus Matthew's affinity for numerology in general. (Cf. Davies and Allison, *Critical and Exegetical Commentary on the Gospel according to Saint Matthew*, 85.) And then there is Stassen's cogent explanation of the dogs, swine, and pearls in Matthew 7:6, which has long befuddled interpreters to the point of despair. See Stassen, "The Fourteen Triads," 289, citing Ulrich Luz, *Matthew 1-7: A Commentary*, trans. Wilhelm C. Linss (Minneapolis: Augsburg, 1989), 419.

66. Though not a New Testament scholar *per se*, Stassen's detailed exegesis was published in the highly selective *Journal of Biblical Literature* in 2003 and he received an enthusiastic response when he presented his exegesis to the Matthew section of the Society of Biblical Literature in 2006. In an October 16, 2012, email to me, Stassen commented: "At the conclusion of the [2006] panel, the moderator declared: 'Well we have reached one consensus:

the Sermon on the Mount is transforming initiatives.' Many NT scholars have spoken to me in agreement. No NT scholar that I know of has either written or spoken against it." Dale C. Allison, a leading scholar of the Gospel of Matthew, has explicitly accepted Stassen's correction of his own interpretation (Dale C. Allison, "The Configuration of the Sermon on the Mount and Its Meaning," in *Studies in Matthew: Interpretation Past and Present* [Grand Rapids, MI: Baker Academic, 2005], 183; also see Bruner, *Matthew*, 207). This wide reception of Stassen's exegesis includes historic peace church scholars. For example, the long-time dean of Mennonite New Testament scholars, Willard M. Swartley, has offered a full-throated endorsement of Stassen's interpretation. In his major book on New Testament peace theology, *Covenant of Peace*, Swartley called Stassen's "structural analysis . . . impressive and persuasive" and went on to explain: "Stassen's tightly argued contribution, considering other major scholarly efforts to understand the Sermon's structure, is most helpful, for his emphasis on the transforming initiatives puts the Sermon directly into the service of peacemaking." See Swartley, *Covenant of Peace: The Missing Piece in New Testament Theology and Ethics* (Grand Rapids, MI: Eerdmans, 2006), 65–66. Also see pp. 426–27.

67. John XXIII, *Mater et Magistra*, §219.

68. John XXIII's strong reference to "individuals" is in fact somewhat exceptional here. Catholic social teaching tends to use the word "persons" instead because the term widens the focus from atomized one-by-one humans in a way that allows recognition that each one is who one is through relationships. "Persons" are embedded in social matrices in a way that "individuals" conceptually are not. For an insightful reflection on the distinction see Rowan Williams, "What Is a Person?," in *Being Human: Bodies, Minds, Persons* (Grand Rapids MI: Eerdmans, 2018), 28–47.

69. Second Vatican Council, *Gaudium et Spes*, §19.

70. Ibid., §12.

71. Ibid., §24.

72. Ibid., §25. Section 30 elaborates the contemporary implications of this view of the human person still further: "The pace of change is so far-reaching and rapid nowadays that it is imperative that no one, out of indifference to the course of events or because of inertia, would indulge in a merely individualistic morality. The best way to to fulfill one's obligations of justice and love is to contribute to the common good according to one's means and the needs of others, and also to promote and help public and private organizations devoted to bettering the conditions of life." Also see Paul VI, *Populorum Progressio*, §17.

73. Francis, *Evangelii Gaudium*, §178; see also §§87 and 115.

74. For further confirmation for how this communitarian metaphysic has given Catholic social teaching its coherence, see Michael J. Schuck, *That They Be One: The Social Teaching of the Papal Encyclicals 1740–1989* (Washington,

DC: Georgetown University Press, 1991), with summary statements to this effect on pp. 92, 157, 180–88.

75. George Herbert Mead, *Mind, Self, and Society: From the Standpoint of a Social Behaviorist*, in *Works of George Herbert Mead*, vol. 1, ed. and intro. by Charles W. Morris (1934; repr., Chicago: University of Chicago Press, 1962).

76. Merlin Donald, *A Mind So Rare: The Evolution of Human Consciousness* (New York: Norton, 2001). See also Merlin Donald, *Origins of the Modern Mind: Three Stages in the Evolution of Culture and Cognition* (Cambridge, MA; London: Harvard University Press, 1991); "Human Cognitive Evolution: What We Were, What We Are Becoming," *Social Research* 60, no. 1 (1993): 143–70; "Mimetic Theory Re-Examined, Twenty Years after the Fact," in *Evolution of Mind, Brain, and Culture*, ed. Gary Hatfield and Holly Pittman (Philadelphia: University of Pennsylvania Museum of Archaeology and Anthropology, 2013), 169–92.

77. Robert N. Bellah, *Religion in Human Evolution: From the Paleolithic to the Axial Age* (Cambridge, MA: Belknap Press of Harvard University Press, 2011).

78. Along with Mead, Donald, and Bellah, corresponding analysis could also come from René Girard and the "Girardians" he has influenced. Fairly or unfairly, Girard is sometimes taken to be a bit of a cult figure. Theologian and former Anglican archbishop Rowan Williams, while appreciative of Girard's thought, implicitly acknowledged this when he noted that Girard "continues to inspire and exasperate in almost equal measure" and expressed hope that the volume he was introducing would make it "that much harder to see (and dismiss) Girard as an exotic intellectual outlier" (Rowan Williams, foreword to Pierpaolo Antonello and Paul Gifford, eds., *Can We Survive Our Origins? Readings in René Girard's Theory of Violence and the Sacred*, Studies in Violence, Mimesis, and Culture [East Lansing: Michigan State University Press, 2015], xi). Knowing this, both as I have done research to prepare for and have written the following pages, I have depended first and foremost on other sources, mainly adding Girardian sources for color. I would describe my own intellectual relationship here in much the way that anthropologist Scott Atran has: "Without being a Girardian or even knowing Girard's theory intimately, I've often found my paths crossing with his" (Antonello and Gifford, *Can We Survive Our Origins?*, 233).

79. Mead, *Mind, Self, and Society*, 42.

80. Mead seemed to assume a relatively early development of language, which was then key to further developments (*Mind, Self, and Society*, 51–59). Donald argues that while self-consciousness is a product of culture, culture could develop quite well through kinetic mimesis and quite primitive vocalization without the abstractions of language beginning to develop until quite late (*A Mind So Rare*, 274, 279–80, 291–94). Joseph Henrich seems to concur with Donald; see Henrich, *The Secret of Our Success: How Culture Is*

Driving Human Evolution, Domesticating Our Species, and Making Us Smarter (Princeton, NJ; Oxford: Princeton University Press, 2016), 232–34.

81. On becoming "objects to ourselves," see Mead, *Mind, Self, and Society*, 136, 138, 140–41. Merlin Donald ("Mimetic Theory Re-Examined," 183) elaborates on the same essential insight:

> For the mammalian brain, the emergence of mimetic capacity in hominin evolution was not a small innovation. It was a radical change. Previously, in every known mammalian species, the brain's action systems were focused outside, on the environment, rather than internally, on action itself. Animals could move, chase, hold, chew, and so on, in flexible and clever ways. But they could not focus on their own actions in detail in order to evaluate and improve them. In effect, mimesis requires an actor to attend to the exact form of his own actions in fine detail, and to parse his own movements, in order to bring a performed action sequence into conformity with an imagined ideal. This imagined ideal of movement might originate in the acts of another actor, or in the event structure of the environment. It could even originate in an event structure that was completely imaginary. In either case, in order to achieve this, the anterior and posterior cerebral cortices had to interact in a way that was evolutionarily new.

82. Though he did not cite either Mead or Donald, Joseph Henrich has independently confirmed their essential insights in *The Secret of Our Success*:

> The key to understanding how humans evolved and why we are so different from other animals is to recognize that we are a *cultural species*. Probably over a million years ago, members of our evolutionary lineage began learning from each other in such a way that culture became cumulative. That is, hunting practices, tool-making skills, tracking know-how, and edible-plant knowledge began to improve and aggregate—by learning from others—so that one generation could build on and hone the skills and know-how gleaned from the previous generation. . . . The secret of our species' success resides not in the power of our individual minds, but in the *collective brains* of our communities. Our collective brains arise from the synthesis of our cultural and social natures—from the fact that we readily learn from others (are cultural) and can, with the right norms, live in large and widely interconnected groups (are social). (3, 5)

83. Or more precisely: "The organization of the social act has been imported into the organism and becomes then the mind of the individual. It still includes the attitudes of others, but now highly organized, so that they become what we call social attitudes rather than roles of separate individuals. This process of relating one's own organism to the others in the interactions that are going on, in so far as it is imported into the conduct of the individual with the conversation of the 'I' and the 'me,' constitutes the self." Mead, *Mind, Self, and Society*, 178–79. Also see pp. 171–77, 197–98, and 214.

84. Duncan Morrow has explicitly drawn these threads together in summarizing René Girard's theory:

> At the heart of the mimetic hypothesis is the rediscovery of relatedness as the core of human existence. Not only does everything and everyone exist in relationships, but relationships are foundational to being, rather than the other way around. Behind, before, and around each person is the "given" of relationality. Or, put another way, there is no human being outside some given nexus of relationships. Our only questions can be: "with whom?," "in which mode?," and "with what fruits?"

Duncan Morrow, "Northern Ireland: Breaking the Inheritance of Conflict and Violence," in *Can We Survive Our Origins? Readings in René Girard's Theory of Violence and the Sacred*, ed. Pierpaolo Antonello and Paul Gifford, Studies in Violence, Mimesis, and Culture (East Lansing: Michigan State University Press, 2015), 186.

85. See Donald, "Mimetic Theory Re-Examined," 179–83; Bellah, *Religion in Human Evolution*, 123–25. Donald summarizes the ways that archeological evidence from stonecutting confirms mimetic theory on pp. 179–80:

> These findings confirm the following conclusions about mimesis. (1) At this early stage, hominins could *rehearse and refine* action. This confirms the most fundamental postulate of mimesis theory, that hominins advanced beyond primates in their ability to refine skill very early in their evolution. (2) The species could also *transmit and maintain* skills accurately across generations through a combination of imitation and practice, and possibly pedagogy as well. (3) The species was already moving toward a *group cognitive strategy*, in which the talents of individuals were transformed into shared \180 resources within a group of hominins. (4) Because mimetic expression is regulated by essentially the same neuro-cognitive system that produces skill, it is very likely that hominins at this early stage had evolved a degree of *communicative capability*, especially in the domain of vocal modulations and whole-body gesticulation. This may well have been an exaptation, as initially proposed. The research of the past 20 years thus strengthens and enriches the original proposal for an archaic mimetic adaptation very early in the hominin scenario.

86. Note the recurrence of mimetic scenarios involving aggression, bullying, violence, dogfights, etc., in Mead, *Mind, Self, and Society*, 14–15, 20, 42–49, 53–56, 63, 66, 147, 181. Also note Donald, *A Mind So Rare*, 180–81, and Bellah, *Religion in Human Evolution*, 119, 130.

87. John Gardner and John R. Maier, trans., *Gilgamesh: Translated from the Sîn-Leqi-Unninnī Version*, with assistance of Richard A. Henshaw (New York: Alfred A. Knopf, 1984). For an accessible, interpretive rendering of the story, a modern English speaker might wish to consult Herbert Mason, *Gilgamesh: A Verse Narrative* (New York: New American Library, 1972).

88. Of necessity, I am abbreviating the story here. Also contributing to the humanization of Enkidu, already before he meets Gilgamesh, is his first sexual encounter, with a prostitute sent from the city to lure him and prepare him for social life. Modern critical analysis might identify yet another kind of vicious cycle here. One aspect of Gilgamesh's tyranny has been his demand for "first-night privilege"—sleeping with the brides of Uruk prior to their weddings. To counter one kind of sexual exploitation the community has employed another.

89. Mason, *Gilgamesh*, 24.

90. Ibid., 40–41. See Gardner and Maier, *Gilgamesh*, 145–47, for the textual basis of Mason's interpretation.

91. For an excellent summary of the scapegoating mechanism according to Girard see Antonello and Gifford, *Can We Survive Our Origins?*, xxix–xxxii.

92. Donald, "Mimetic Theory Re-Examined," 189.

93. Mead, *Mind, Self, and Society*, 173, 176–78.

94. Ibid., 217.

95. Ibid., 214. But see pp. 214–18 for Mead's full discussion of "the social creativity of the emergent self."

96. Donald, *A Mind So Rare*, 299–300.

97. What Duncan Morrow has said of René Girard's thought points to an arguable implication of mimetic theory more widely: "Among the many uncomfortable conclusions of Girard's insights is that, *pace* all dissenters, Jesus *matters*—albeit in a manner inverse to the triumphalist, militant proclamation of ex-Christendom. We might struggle with this, as might our critics, were it not for the fact that Jesus is for humanity before humanity is for Jesus." Morrow, "Northern Ireland," 188.

98. Witness a version of the phrase in the iconic science-fiction series Star Trek, specifically in the 1991 movie *Star Trek VI: The Undiscovered Country*.

99. Leon Marincowitz, "South Africa: Positive Mimesis and the Turn toward Peace," in *Can We Survive Our Origins?*, 223–31.

100. Girardians sometimes speak of "bad mimesis" and "good mimesis," or moving "from negative to positive mimesis." See Antonello and Gifford, *Can We Survive Our Origins?*, 191–92, 198–99, 228.

101. Francis, "Nonviolence: A Style of Politics for Peace," §1.

102. See Stassen, *Just Peacemaking*, 20–22, for an overview of the connections between a triadic interpretation of the Sermon on the Mount and the normative practices of just-peacemaking theory. See Stassen, "Transforming Initiatives of Just Peacemaking," for a collation of nine of the ten just-peacemaking practices with transforming initiatives in the Sermon on the Mount and elsewhere in the Gospel of Matthew.

103. Stassen, "Transforming Initiatives of Just Peacemaking," 5–6.

104. The list here is hardly exclusive, but simply reflects the tactics used as examples on pp. 44–56 of Stassen, *Just Peacemaking*.

105. Stassen, "Transforming Initiatives of Just Peacemaking," 6–7.
106. Stassen, *Just Peacemaking*, 59–64.
107. Stassen, "Transforming Initiatives of Just Peacemaking," 3–5.
108. Ibid., 9–10.
109. Stassen, *Just Peacemaking*, 102.
110. Rudolph Nelson et al., *Precarious Peace: God & Guatemala*, Video recording (Worcester, PA: Gateway Films; Distributed by Vision Video, 2003).
111. In these last few sentences I have summarized a list of "seven essential ingredients of Christian peacemaking" through transforming initiatives that appears on p. 22 of Stassen, *Just Peacemaking*.
112. Stassen, "Transforming Initiatives of Just Peacemaking," 8–9.
113. Jonathan Schell, "No More Unto the Breach," two-part series, *Harper's* 306, no. 1834–35 (March and April 2003): I:46.
114. Stassen, "Transforming Initiatives of Just Peacemaking," 8.
115. See ibid., 7–8, for Stassen's discussion of how this just-peacemaking practice responds in a more general way to Jesus' teachings in the Sermon on the Mount, by seeking to "include your enemies in the community of neighbors."
116. See ibid., for Stassen's discussion of how this just-peacemaking practice responds in a more general way to Jesus' teachings in the Sermon on the Mount, by seeking to "include your enemies in the community of neighbors."
117. Ibid., 10.
118. See for example John Paul II, "World Day of Peace Message 2000," §20.
119. Tapia de Renedo, *Hélder Câmara: Proclamas a la Juventud*, 189. I have made translations of the speech from which this quote is taken—"Un pacto digno"—along with two others at http://courseweb.stthomas.edu/gwschlabach/docs/manitese.htm.
120. Augustine, "Letter 138," 2.11–12.

Chapter 9—pages 274–94

1. Gerald W. Schlabach, "Just War? Enough Already," *Commonweal* 144, no. 11 (June 16, 2017): 9–14.
2. See Gerald W. Schlabach, "Just Policing, Not War," *America* 189, no. 1 (July 7–14, 2003): 19–21; "Just Policing: How War Could Cease to Be a Church-Dividing Issue"; Schlabach, *Just Policing, Not War*.
3. Tertullian, *On Idolatry*, in *The Ante-Nicene Fathers*, vol. 3, ed. Alexander Roberts and James Donaldson (Edinburgh: T. & T. Clark, 1873), 19.
4. Second Vatican Council, *Gaudium et Spes*, §78–79.
5. NCCB, *The Challenge of Peace*, §§116–19.
6. See p. 58 and following in chapter 1 above.

7. In the United States, others have recognized the peace witness of the church and related issues of nonviolence and war as potentially having confessional status at least since the late 1980s, when the Commission on Faith and Order of the National Council of Churches placed these matters in its program of studies. Key consultations ensued in Oak Brook, Illinois (1990), Douglastown, New York (1991), and Notre Dame, Indiana (1995). For documentation see Marlin Miller and Barbara Nelson Gingrich, eds., *The Church's Peace Witness* (Grand Rapids, MI: Eerdmans, 1994); Jeffrey Gros and John D. Rempel, eds., *The Fragmentation of the Church and Its Unity in Peacemaking* (Grand Rapids, MI: Eerdmans, 2001).

8. See Marlin E. Miller, "Toward Acknowledging Together the Apostolic Character of the Church's Peace Witness," in *The Church's Peace Witness*, 196–207. Put less politely than usual, for a rigorous Christian pacifist in a historic peace church, those who claim to be Christians and also claim to have justifiable reasons for killing other human beings are at best unfaithful, and at worst may not be Christians at all. Matters are usually *not* put so impolitely, of course. To recognize one another as "separated brothers and sisters" across lines of denomination and tradition is surely a good thing, after all. In the long run of church history, those lines have sometimes been literal battle lines. Thus, ecumenical generosity itself contributes to a more peaceable world. That Christians who do not agree on last resort can nonetheless join together in first-resort strategies for just peacemaking is likewise welcome. But however much practical collaboration helps create the conditions for further dialogue and unity, alone it does not yet do all the dialogue that may be necessary to name a principled unity that is not merely pragmatic.

9. Schlabach, *Unlearning Protestantism*, 168–73, 191–92.

10. Paul Ramsey, *Speak Up for Just War or Pacifism: A Critique of the United Methodist Bishops' Pastoral Letter "In Defence of Creation,"* epilogue by Stanley Hauerwas (University Park: Pennsylvania State University Press, 1988).

11. See pp. 267 and following for a survey of the ten normative practices of just-peacemaking theory.

12. For an explicit statement to this effect see Stassen and Gushee, *Kingdom Ethics*, 150. Also see Stassen, *Just Peacemaking: Transforming Initiatives*, 236, 254; "Just Peacemaking as Hermeneutical Key," 171–72.

13. Community and State World Conference on Church, "Report of the Section on the Universal Church and the World of Nations," Oxford, United Kingdom, July 12–26, 1937, in *On Earth Peace: Discussions on War/Peace Issues between Friends, Mennonites, Brethren, and European Churches, 1935–75*, ed. Donald Durnbaugh (Elgin, IL: The Brethren Press, 1978), 35.

14. See Mark Thiessen Nation, *John Howard Yoder: Mennonite Patience, Evangelical Witness, Catholic Convictions* (Grand Rapids, MI: Eerdmans, 2006), 17–18, 77ff.; and Donald Durnbaugh, ed., *On Earth Peace: Discussions on War/*

Peace Issues between Friends, Mennonites, Brethren, and European Churches, 21–23, along with primary documents in chapters 9–12, 21 of the latter.

15. Second Vatican Council, *Gaudium et Spes,* §§78, 80.

16. NCCB, *The Challenge of Peace,* §74.

17. The United Methodist Council of Bishops, *In Defense of Creation: The Nuclear Crisis and a Just Peace,* Foundation Document (Nashville: Graded Press, 1986), 33.

18. Glen H. Stassen, ed., *Just Peacemaking: Ten Practices for Abolishing War,* 1st ed. (Cleveland: Pilgrim Press, 1998). Revised and with a somewhat more circumspect subtitle, the book is now in its third edition: *Just Peacemaking: The New Paradigm for the Ethics of Peace and War,* 3rd ed. (Cleveland: Pilgrim Press, 2008).

19. Mennonite World Conference and Pontifical Council for Promoting Church Unity, "Called Together to Be Peacemakers."

20. Mennonite World Conference and Pontifical Council for Promoting Church Unity, "A Mennonite and Catholic Contribution to the World Council of Churches' *Decade to Overcome Violence,*" introduction.

21. "The Fragmentation of the Church and Its Unity in Peacemaking: A Report," June 13–17, 1995, University of Notre Dame, in *The Fragmentation of the Church and Its Unity in Peacemaking,* ed. Gros and Rempel, §4.

22. Stassen, *Just Peacemaking: Ten Practices,* 26.

23. Mennonite World Conference and Pontifical Council for Promoting Church Unity, "Called Together to Be Peacemakers," §152. Cf. also §180.

24. Ibid., §187, summarizing §147–85.

25. Mennonite World Conference and Pontifical Council for Promoting Church Unity, "A Mennonite and Catholic Contribution to the World Council of Churches' *Decade to Overcome Violence,*" III.3. For still more examples of continuing irresolution among recent documents, see also: Consultation on the Apostolic Faith and the Church's Peace Witness, "A Summary Statement," October 27–29, 1991, Douglaston, New York, in *The Church's Peace Witness,* ed. Miller and Gingrich, VI; and "The Fragmentation of the Church and Its Unity in Peacemaking: A Report," §18.

26. International Ecumenical Peace Convocation, "Glory to God and Peace on Earth: The Message of the International Ecumenical Peace Convocation" (Kingston, Jamaica, 2011), http://www.overcomingviolence.org/en/resources-dov/wcc-resources/documents/presentations-speeches-messages/iepc-message.html. Also see the preparatory document, World Council of Churches, *An Ecumenical Call to Just Peace,* §§21–22.

27. John Howard Yoder, "Radical Reformation Ethics in Ecumenical Perspective," *Journal of Ecumenical Studies* 15, no. 4 (Fall 1978): 660.

28. Gerald W. Schlabach, "Just Policing: How War Could Cease to Be a Church-Dividing Issue," in *Just Policing: Mennonite-Catholic Theological Colloquium 2002,* ed. Ivan J. Kauffman, Bridgefolk Series, no. 2 (Kitchener, ON:

Pandora Press, 2004), 19–75. A more definitive revised version of that essay was later published with the same title in the *Journal of Ecumenical Studies* 41, no. 3–4 (Summer-Fall 2004): 409–30. Also see Schlabach, *Just Policing, Not War*.

29. Joseph E. Capizzi, "War Remains Church Dividing," in *Just Policing: Mennonite-Catholic Theological Colloquium 2002*, ed. Ivan J. Kauffman, Bridgefolk Series, no. 2 (Kitchener, ON: Pandora Press, 2004), 76–88.

30. See note 50 in the previous chapter.

31. Francis, "Nonviolence: A Style of Politics for Peace," §6.

32. Vatican Radio, "Holy See Ratifies Treaty on the Prohibition of Nuclear Arms" (September 21, 2017), http://www.archivioradiovaticana.va/storico/2017/09/21/holy_see_ratifies_treaty_on_the_prohibition_of_nuclear_arms/en-1338124.

33. See, for example "The Fourteen Triads," which in other ways is Stassen's most thorough rendering of his exegesis. A chart on p. 275 does not so much define traditional righteousness as offer a merely functional way of identifying it within each triad.

34. John H[oward] Yoder, *Nevertheless: The Varieties and Shortcomings of Religious Pacifism*, Christian Peace Shelf Series (Scottdale, PA: Herald Press, 1971), 25–26.

35. See Duane Friesen's elaboration on this process in *Christian Peacemaking & International Conflict: A Realist Pacifist Perspective*, foreword by Stanley Hauerwas, Christian Peace Shelf Selection (Scottdale, PA: Herald Press, 1986), 170–72. See also John Howard Yoder, *Christian Attitudes to War, Peace, and Revolution*, ed. Theodore J. Koontz and Andy Alexis-Baker (Grand Rapids, MI: Brazos Press, 2009), 345; John Howard Yoder, "Just War Tradition: Is It Credible?," *Christian Century* 108, no. 9 (March 13, 1991): 298; Duane K. Friesen, "Peacemaking as an Ethical Category: The Convergence of Pacifism and Just War," in *Ethics in the Nuclear Age: Strategy, Religious Studies, and the Churches*, ed. Todd Whitmore (Dallas: Southern Methodist University Press, 1989), 176–77.

36. George Weigel, "Moral Clarity in a Time of War," *First Things* 128 (January 2003): 23; James Turner Johnson, "Just War, as It Was and Is," *First Things*, no. 149 (January 2005): 18–19. For an influential articulation of the presumption-against-war thesis to which Weigel and Turner Johnson have objected, see James F. Childress, "Just-War Criteria," in *Moral Responsibility in Conflicts: Essays on Nonviolence, War, and Conscience* (Baton Rouge: Louisiana State University Press, 1982), 63–94. The thesis gained authoritative traction when U.S. Catholic bishops adopted it in *The Challenge of Peace*, §§70–79. For a defense of the thesis, see Richard B. Miller, "Aquinas and the Presumption against Killing and War," *Journal of Religion* 82, no. 2 (April 2002): 173–204. For a Mennonite exchange with Weigel, see the June 2003 (58:2) issue of *Mennonite Life*, available at http://tools.bethelks.edu/mennonitelife/2003June.

37. John Howard Yoder, "Just War and Nonviolence: Disjunction, Dialogue, or Complementarity?," in *The War of the Lamb: The Ethics of Nonviolence and Peacemaking*, ed. Glen Harold Stassen, Mark Thiessen Nation, and Matt Hamsher (Grand Rapids, MI: Brazos Press, 2009), 85–87.

38. Ibid.

39. See Yoder's remarkable and uncharacteristically first-person account of why he had so long and so arduously dialogued with just-war Christians, even though he remained unconvinced of the ultimate "credibility" of just-war theory and pessimistic about it being consistently applied: "Gordon Zahn Is Right: Going the Second Mile with Just War," in *The War of the Lamb: The Ethics of Nonviolence and Peacemaking*, ed. Glen Harold Stassen, Mark Thiessen Nation, and Matt Hamsher (Grand Rapids, MI: Brazos Press, 2009), 109–16.

40. Yoder, "Gordon Zahn Is Right," 109–10. Cf. Yoder, *Christian Attitudes to War, Peace, and Revolution*, 127.

41. John Howard Yoder, *The War of the Lamb: The Ethics of Nonviolence and Peacemaking*, ed. Glen Harold Stassen, Mark Thiessen Nation, and Matt Hamsher (Grand Rapids, MI: Brazos Press, 2009), 97.

42. Yoder, *Christian Attitudes to War, Peace, and Revolution*, 341–46.

43. See, for example, Yoder, "A Theological Critique of Violence," in *The War of the Lamb*, ed. Stassen et al., 27–42.

44. Yoder, *Christian Attitudes to War, Peace, and Revolution*, 344–45.

45. Second Vatican Council, *Gaudium et Spes*, §80.

46. Cornell, "How Catholics Began to Speak Their Peace."

47. After getting no response when he first wrote to Ottaviani in the Vatican, Cornell recounts, Goss traveled in 1950 to Rome, and managed to get the cardinal's attention by shouting past the Swiss Guards, "*Bellum omnino interdicendum*, your Eminence!" Ottaviani's friendship with Jean Goss soon expanded to include his wife, Hildegard Goss-Mayr, as well, who shared Jean's strong and winsome faith but also had a doctorate in philosophy that won the couple even more respect.

48. On the role of Ottaviani's speech in favor of what became part II, chapter 5, section 1 of *Gaudium et Spes* on the avoidance of war (§79–82), see Alberigo, *History of Vatican II*, 5:173–75.

49. Though he does not frame the challenges in quite this way, John D. Rempel struggles with them as he names the gap between Mennonite ecclesiology and its claims concerning what it means to be a historic peace church vis-à-vis the realities of Mennonite practice, in his own chapter of Gros and Rempel, *The Fragmentation of the Church and Its Unity in Peacemaking*, 34–47.

50. Schlabach, *Just Policing, Not War*; Schlabach, "Just Policing: How War Could Cease to Be a Church-Dividing Issue"; Schlabach, "Just Policing, Not War."

51. Wink, *The Powers That Be: Theology for a New Millennium*, 136–43.
52. I allude to Yoder's posthumous book, *The Jewish-Christian Schism Revisited*.

Bibliography

Abesamis, Carlos H. *Where Are We Going, Heaven or New World?* Foundation Books. Manila, Philippines: Communication Foundation for Asia, 1983.

Alberigo, Giuseppe, ed. *History of Vatican II.* 5 volumes. English version edited by Joseph Komonchak. Maryknoll, NY: Orbis Books; Leuven, Belgium: Peeters, 1996–2006.

Alexander, Paul. *Peace to War: Shifting Allegiances in the Assemblies of God.* The C. Henry Smith Series, vol. 9. Telford, PA: Cascadia; Scottdale, PA: Herald Press, 2009.

Allen, John L., Jr. *The Future Church: How Ten Trends Are Revolutionizing the Catholic Church.* New York: Doubleday, 2009.

Allison, Dale C. "The Configuration of the Sermon on the Mount and Its Meaning." In *Studies in Matthew: Interpretation Past and Present*, 173–215. Grand Rapids, MI.: Baker Academic, 2005.

Allman, Mark J., and Tobias L. Winright. *After the Smoke Clears: The Just War Tradition and Post War Justice.* Maryknoll, NY: Orbis Books, 2010.

Andraos, Michel. "Becoming a Christian, Becoming a Peacemaker." *New Theology Review* 18, no. 3 (August 2005): 32–40.

Antonello, Pierpaolo, and Paul Gifford, eds. *Can We Survive Our Origins? Readings in René Girard's Theory of Violence and the Sacred.* Studies in Violence, Mimesis, and Culture. East Lansing: Michigan State University Press, 2015.

Appadurai, Arjun. "Disjuncture and Difference in the Global Cultural Economy." In *Theorizing Diaspora: A Reader*, edited by Jana Evans Braziel and Anita Mannur. Keyworks in Cultural Studies, 25–48. Malden, MA: Blackwell, 2003.

———. *Modernity at Large: Cultural Dimensions of Globalization.* Public Worlds, vol. 1. Minneapolis: University of Minnesota Press, 1996.

Arendt, Hannah. *The Origins of Totalitarianism.* Introduction by Samantha Power. New York: Schocken Books, 2004.

Augustine. *Answer to Faustus a Manichean* [Contra Faustum Manichaeum]. Vol. I/20 of *The Works of Saint Augustine: A Translation for the 21st Century*. Edited by Boniface Ramsey. Translated, with an introduction and notes by Roland Teske, SJ. Brooklyn and Hyde Park, NY: New City Press, 2007.

———. *The City of God* (De Civitate Dei). Translated, with an introduction by William Babcock, notes by Boniface Ramsey. In *The Works of Saint Augustine: A Translation for the 21st Century, Part I: Books*, vols. 6–7. Hyde Park, NY: New City Press, 2012.

———. *The City of God*. Translated by Henry Bettenson, with an introduction by David Knowles. Harmondsworth, Middlesex, England: Penguin, 1972.

———. *The Free Choice of the Will* (De Libero Arbitrio). In *The Teacher, The Free Choice of the Will, Grace and Free Will*. The Fathers of the Church, vol. 59, 63–241. Washington, DC: The Catholic University of America Press, 1968.

———. *Homilies on the First Epistle of John* (Tractatus in Epistolam Joannis Ad Parthos). Vol. I/14 of *The Works of Saint Augustine: A Translation for the 21st Century*, edited by Daniel E. Doyle, OSA, and Thomas Martin, OSA. Translated, with an introduction and notes by Boniface Ramsey. Brooklyn and Hyde Park, NY: New City Press, 2008.

———. *Homilies on the Gospel of John*. Vol. 7 of *A Select Library of the Nicene and Post-Nicene Fathers of the Christian Church*. First series. Edited by Philip Schaff, 1–452. Peabody, MA: Hendrickson, 1994.

———. "Letter 138." To Marcellinus [412] in *Letters 100–155* (Epistulae). Vol. II/2 of *The Works of Saint Augustine: A Translation for the 21st Century*, edited by Boniface Ramsey, translated by Roland Teske, SJ, 225–37. Hyde Park, NY: New City Press, 2003.

———. "Letter 153." To Macedonius [413–14] in *Letters 100–155* (Epistulae). Vol. II/2 of *The Works of Saint Augustine: A Translation for the 21st Century*, edited by Boniface Ramsey, translated by Roland Teske, SJ, 390–404. Hyde Park, NY: New City Press, 2003.

———. "Letter 47." To Publicola [398] in *Letters 1-99* (Epistulae). Vol. II/2 of *The Works of Saint Augustine: A Translation for the 21st Century*, edited by Boniface Ramsey, translated by Roland Teske, SJ, 187–91. Hyde Park, NY: New City Press, 2001.

———. "The Lord's Sermon on the Mount (*De Sermone Domini in Monte*)." In *New Testament I and II*. Vol. I/15 and I/16 of *The Works of Saint Augustine: A Translation for the 21st Century*, translated by Michael G.

Campbell, introduction and notes by Boniface Ramsey, 9–129. Brooklyn and Hyde Park, NY: New City Press, 2014.

———. *Of the Morals of the Catholic Church*. Vol. 4 of *A Select Library of the Nicene and Post-Nicene Fathers of the Christian Church*. First series. Edited by Philip Schaff. Reprint ed., 37–63. Peabody, MA: Hendrickson, 1994.

———. *On Christian Doctrine*. Translated with an introduction by D. W. Robertsonn Jr. The Library of Liberal Arts. New York: Macmillan, 1958.

———. *Sermons*. Vol. III/1–11 of *The Works of Saint Augustine: A Translation for the 21st Century*. Edmund Hill, gen. ed. Brooklyn and Hyde Park, NY: New City Press, 1990.

———. *Teaching Christianity*. [De doctrina christiana]. Edited by John E. Rotelle. Translated, with an introduction and notes by Edmund Hill. The Works of Saint Augustine, vol. 11. Hyde Park, NY: New City Press, 1996.

———. *Ten Homilies on the First Epistle of St. John*. In *Augustine: Later Works*, edited and translated by John Burnaby. The Library of Christian Classics, vol. 8, 251–348. Philadelphia: Westminster Press, 1955.

Barber, Benjamin R. *Jihad vs. McWorld: How Globalism and Tribalism Are Reshaping the World*. 1st Ballantine Books ed. New York: Times Books, 1996.

Barrett, David B., and Todd M. Johnson. *World Christian Trends, AD 30–AD 2200: Interpreting the Annual Christian Megacensus*. Edited by Christopher R. Guidry and Peter F. Crossing. Pasadena, CA: William Carey Library, 2001.

Barrett, David B., George T. Kurian, and Todd M. Johnson. *World Christian Encyclopedia: A Comparative Survey of Churches and Religions in the Modern World*. 2 vols. Oxford; New York: Oxford University Press, 2001.

Bellah, Robert N. *Religion in Human Evolution: From the Paleolithic to the Axial Age*. Cambridge, MA: Belknap Press of Harvard University Press, 2011.

Benedict XVI, Pope. Angelus. February 18, 2007. http://w2.vatican.va/content/benedict-xvi/en/angelus/2007/documents/hf_ben-xvi_ang_20070218.html.

———. "*Migrations: Pilgrimage of Faith and Hope*." Message for 2013 World Day of Migrants and Refugees, October 12, 2012.

Bennett, John C. *Christian Ethics and Social Policy*. The Richard Lectures at the University of Virginia. New York: Charles Scribner's Sons, 1946.

Betz, Hans Dieter. *The Sermon on the Mount: A Commentary on the Sermon on the Mount, Including the Sermon on the Plain (Matthew 5:3–7:27 and Luke 6:20-49)*. Edited by Adela Yarbro Collins. Hermeneia: A Critical and Historical Commentary on the Bible. Minneapolis: Fortress Press, 1995.

Bordoni, Linda. "Pope Francis: 'Death Penalty Inadmissible.'" *Vatican News Service*. August 2, 2018. https://www.vaticannews.va/en/pope/news/2018-08/pope-francis-cdf-ccc-death-penalty-revision-ladaria.html.

Boyarin, Daniel. *A Radical Jew: Paul and the Politics of Identity*. Contraversions. Berkeley; London: University of California Press, 1994.

Boyarin, Daniel, and Jonathan Boyarin. "Diaspora: Generation and the Ground of Jewish Diaspora." In *Theorizing Diaspora: A Reader*, edited by Jana Evans Braziel and Anita Mannur. Keyworks in Cultural Studies, 85–118. Malden, MA: Blackwell, 2003.

Boyarin, Jonathan, and Daniel Boyarin. *Powers of Diaspora: Two Essays on the Relevance of Jewish Culture*. Minneapolis: University of Minnesota Press, 2002.

Brah, Avtar. *Cartographies of Diaspora: Contesting Identities*. Gender, Racism, Ethnicity. London; New York: Routledge, 1996.

Braziel, Jana Evans, and Anita Mannur. "Nation, Migration, Globalization: Points of Contention in Diaspora Studies." Edited by Jana Evans Braziel and Anita Mannur. In *Theorizing Diaspora: A Reader*. Keyworks in Cultural Studies, 1–22. Malden, MA: Blackwell, 2003.

Bruner, Frederick Dale. *Matthew: A Commentary. Vol. 1: The Christbook, Matthew 1–12*. Grand Rapids, MI: Eerdmans, 2004.

Buell, D. K. "Race and Universalism in Early Christianity." *Journal of Early Christian Studies* 10, no. 4 (2002): 429–68.

Buell, Denise Kimber. *Why This New Race: Ethnic Reasoning in Early Christianity*. Gender, Theory, and Religion. New York: Columbia University Press, 2005.

Bühlmann, Walbert. *The Coming of the Third Church: An Analysis of the Present and Future of the Church*. Maryknoll, NY: Orbis Books, 1977.

Canning, Raymond. *The Unity of Love for God and Neighbour in St. Augustine*. Heverlee, Belgium: Augustinian Historical Institute, 1993.

Capizzi, Joseph E. "War Remains Church Dividing." In *Just Policing: Mennonite-Catholic Theological Colloquium 2002*, edited by Ivan J. Kauffman. Bridgefolk Series, no. 2, 76–88. Kitchener, ON: Pandora Press, 2004.

Catechism of the Catholic Church (2nd ed.). Washington, DC: Libreria Editrice Vaticana—United States Conference of Catholic Bishops, 2000.

Cavadini, John C. "Time and Ascent in *Confessions* XI." In *Augustine: Presbyter Factus Sum*, edited by Joseph T. Lienhard, Earl C. Muller, and Roland J. Teske. Collectanea Augustiniana, 171–85. New York: Peter Lang Publishing, 1993. Papers originally presented at a conference at Marquette University, November 1990.

Cavadini, John. "The Structure and Intention of Augustine's *De Trinitate.*" *Augustinian Studies* 23 (1992): 103–23.

Câmara, Hélder. *The Desert Is Fertile.* Translated by Dinah Livingstone. Maryknoll, NY: Orbis Books, 1974.

———. *Dom Helder Camara: Essential Writings.* Selected with an introduction by Francis McDonagh. Modern Spiritual Masters Series. Maryknoll, NY: Orbis Books, 2009.

———. *Hélder Câmara y la Justicia: Ideario.* Salamanca: Ediciones Sigueme, 1981.

Center for Strategic and International Studies (CSIS), and Association of the United States Army (AUSA). "Post-Conflict Reconstruction Task Framework." In *Laying a Durable Foundation for Post-Conflict Societies.* 37th Conference on the United Nations of the Next Decade, sponsored by The Stanley Foundation. Carmel, California, 2002.

Chenoweth, Erica, and Maria J. Stephan. *Why Civil Resistance Works: The Strategic Logic of Nonviolent Conflict.* Columbia Studies in Terrorism and Irregular Warfare. New York: Columbia University Press, 2011.

Childress, James F. "Just-War Criteria." In *Moral Responsibility in Conflicts: Essays on Nonviolence, War, and Conscience,* 63–94. Baton Rouge: Louisiana State University Press, 1982.

Christiansen, Drew, SJ. "After Sept. 11: Catholic Social Teaching on Peace and War." *Origins* 32, no. 3 (May 30, 2002): 33, 35–40.

———. "Benedict XVI: Peacemaker." *America* 197, no. 2 (July 16, 2007): 10–15.

———. "The Ethics of Peacemaking: The Genesis of *Called Together to Be Peacemakers, Report of the International Mennonite-Catholic Dialogue* (2004)." *Journal of Ecumenical Studies* 45, no. 3 (Summer 2010): 385–416.

———. "Hawks, Doves and Pope John Paul II." *America* 187, no. 4 (August 12, 2002): 9–11.

———. "John Paul II Peacemaker: A Nonviolent Pope in a Time of Terror." The Thomas Lecture. Saint Meinrad Seminary. Saint Meinrad, IN, 2005.

———. "'Never Again War': The Presumption against the Use of Force in Contemporary Catholic Social Teaching and the Diplomacy of the Holy See." Unpublished paper, 2002.

———. "'No, Never Again War': The Evolution of Catholic Teaching on Peace and War." Lecture. Santa Clara University, 2004.

———. "Nonviolence, the Responsibility to Protect and Peacebuilding." *Origins* 41, no. 17 (September 29, 2011): 265–70.

———. "Peacebuilding in Catholic Social Teaching." *Origins* 38, no. 4 (June 5, 2008): 60–63.

———. "Peacemaking and the Use of Force: Behind the Pope's Stringent Just-War Teaching." *America* 180, no. 17 (May 15, 1999): 13–18.

———. "Resisting Evil: Recent Catholic Teaching on War, Nonviolence and Peacemaking." Lecture. Seattle University, 2003.

———. "A Vision of Peace: How the Prophetic 'Pacem in Terris' Helped Change the World." *America* 208, no. 12 (April 8, 2013): 11–14.

———. "What Is a Peace Church? A Roman Catholic Perspective." Paper presented at the International Mennonite-Roman Catholic Dialogue. Karlsruhe, Germany, 2000.

———. "Whither the 'Just War'?" *America* 188, no. 10 (March 24, 2003): 7–11.

Chrysostom, John. *On Wealth and Poverty*. Sermons on Lazarus and the rich man. Translated by Catharine P. Roth. Crestwood, NY: St Vladimir's Seminary Press, 1984.

Clement of Alexandria. *Exhortation to the Heathen*. In *The Ante-Nicene Fathers*. Vol. 7. Edited by Alexander Roberts and James Donaldson. Edinburgh: T. & T. Clark, 1873.

———. *The Instructor*. In *The Ante-Nicene Fathers*. Vol. 7. Edited by Alexander Roberts and James Donaldson. Edinburgh: T. & T. Clark, 1873.

———. *Stromata*. In *The Ante-Nicene Fathers*. Vol. 7. Edited by Alexander Roberts and James Donaldson. Edinburgh: T. & T. Clark, 1873.

Clifford, James. "Diasporas." *Cultural Anthropology* 9, no. 3 (August 1994): 302–38.

Consultation on the Apostolic Faith and the Church's Peace Witness. "A Summary Statement." October 27–29, 1991, Douglaston, New York. In *The Church's Peace Witness*, edited by Marlin Miller and Barbara Nelson Gingrich, 208–15. Grand Rapids, MI: Eerdmans, 1994.

Cornell, Tom. "How Catholics Began to Speak Their Peace." *Salt of the Earth*, no. 5 (September/October 1996): 17–18.

Cullmann, Oscar. *Christ and Time: The Primitive Christian Conception of Time and History*. Translated by Floyd V. Filson. 1951. Reprint, London: SCM Press, 1962.

Cusimano, Maryann K., ed. *Beyond Sovereignty: Issues for a Global Agenda*. Boston: Bedford / St. Martin's, 2000.

Davies, W. D., and Dale C. Allison. *Critical and Exegetical Commentary on the Gospel according to Saint Matthew: In Three Volumes*. International Critical Commentary on the Holy Scriptures of the Old and New Testaments. Edinburgh: T. & T. Clark, 1988.

Davis, Henry, SJ. *Moral and Pastoral Theology: A Summary*. Heythrop Series. New York: Sheed & Ward, 1952.

———. *Moral and Pastoral Theology in Four Volumes*. Seventh edition, revised and enlarged. Edited by L. W. Geddes, SJ. Heythrop Series, no. 2. New York: Sheed & Ward, 1958.

Dear, John. *The God of Peace: Toward a Theology of Nonviolence*. Maryknoll, NY: Orbis Books, 1994.

Dennis, Marie, ed. *Choosing Peace: The Catholic Church Returns to Gospel Nonviolence*. Maryknoll, NY: Orbis Books, 2018.

Dicken, Peter. *Global Shift: Reshaping the Global Economic Map in the 21st Century*. New York: Guilford Press, 2003.

DiMeglio, Richard P. "The Evolution of the Just War Tradition: Defining Jus Post Bellum." *Military Law Review* 186 (Winter 2005): 116–63.

Dodaro, Robert. "Eloquent Lies, Just Wars and the Politics of Persuasion: Reading Augustine's *City of God* in a 'Postmodern' World." *Augustinian Studies* 25 (1994): 77–138.

Donahue, John R. "Biblical Perspectives on Justice." In *The Faith That Does Justice: Examining the Christian Sources for Social Change*, edited by John C. Haughey. Woodstock Studies, vol. 2, 68–112. New York: Paulist Press, 1977.

Donald, Merlin. "Human Cognitive Evolution: What We Were, What We Are Becoming." *Social Research* 60, no. 1 (1993): 143–70.

———. "Mimetic Theory Re-Examined, Twenty Years after the Fact." In *Evolution of Mind, Brain, and Culture*, edited by Gary Hatfield and Holly Pittman, 169–92. Philadelphia: University of Pennsylvania Museum of Archaeology and Anthropology, 2013.

———. *A Mind So Rare: The Evolution of Human Consciousness*. New York: Norton, 2001.

———. *Origins of the Modern Mind: Three Stages in the Evolution of Culture and Cognition*. Cambridge, MA; London: Harvard University Press, 1991.

Dreher, Rod. "'Resident Aliens' & the Benedict Option." *The American Conservative*, September 1, 2015. http://www.theamericanconservative.com/dreher/resident-aliens-the-benedict-option/.

Driedger, Leo, and Donald B. Kraybill. *Mennonite Peacemaking: From Quietism to Activism*. Scottdale, PA: Herald Press, 1994.

Dufoix, Stéphane. *Diasporas*. Translated by William Rodarmor, with a foreword by Roger Waldinger. Berkeley: University of California Press, 2008.

Dunning, Benjamin H. *Aliens and Sojourners: Self as Other in Early Christianity*. Divinations: Rereading Late Ancient Religion. Philadelphia: University of Pennsylvania Press, 2009.

———. "Foreign Countries and Alien Assets in *The Shepherd of Hermas*." Chap. 4 in *Aliens and Sojourners: Self as Other in Early Christianity*. Divinations: Rereading Late Ancient Religion, 78–90. Philadelphia: University of Pennsylvania Press, 2009.

———. "Outsiders by Reason of Outdoing: The *Epistle to Diognetus*." Chap. 3 in *Aliens and Sojourners: Self as Other in Early Christianity*. Divinations: Rereading Late Ancient Religion, 64–77. Philadelphia: University of Pennsylvania Press, 2009.

Durnbaugh, Donald, ed. *On Earth Peace: Discussions on War/Peace Issues between Friends, Mennonites, Brethren, and European Churches, 1935–75*. Elgin, IL: The Brethren Press, 1978.

Epp Weaver, Alain. *States of Exile: Visions of Diaspora, Witness, and Return*. Polyglossia: Radical Reformation Theologies, vol. 3. Scottdale, PA: Herald Press, 2008.

Erikson, Erik H. *Gandhi's Truth: On the Origins of Militant Nonviolence*. New York: W. W. Norton, 1969.

Faggioli, Massimo. *Papa Francesco e la "chiesa-mondo."* Rome: Armando Editore, 2014.

Fisher, Roger, and William Ury. *Getting to Yes: Negotiating Agreement without Giving In*. 2nd ed. Edited by Bruce Patton. New York: Penguin Books, 1991.

Flannery, Austin, ed. *Vatican Council II: Constitutions, Decrees, Declarations; The Basic Sixteen Documents*. Collegeville, MN: Liturgical Press, 2014.

Ford, John C., SJ. "The Morality of Obliteration Bombing." *Theological Studies* 5, no. 3 (September 1944): 261–309.

"The Fragmentation of the Church and Its Unity in Peacemaking: A Report." June 13–17, 1995, University of Notre Dame, in *The Fragmentation of the Church and Its Unity in Peacemaking*, edited by Jeffrey Gros and John D. Rempel, 220–27. Grand Rapids, MI: Eerdmans, 2001.

Francis, Pope. *Evangelii Gaudium* [The Joy of the Gospel]. Apostolic exhortation. November 24, 2013.

———. *Laudato Si'*. Encyclical on care for our common home. May 24, 2015.

———. "Migrants and Refugees: Men and Women in Search of Peace." Message for the World Day of Peace. January 1, 2018. http://w2.vatican.va/content/francesco/en/messages/peace/documents/papa-francesco_20171113_messaggio-51giornatamondiale-pace2018.html.

———. "Nonviolence: A Style of Politics for Peace." Message for the World Day of Peace. January 1, 2017. https://w2.vatican.va/content/francesco/en/messages/peace/documents/papa-francesco_20161208_messaggio-l-giornata-mondiale-pace-2017.html.

Friesen, Duane K. *Artists, Citizens, Philosophers: Seeking the Peace of the City.* With a foreword by Glen Stassen. Scottdale, PA; Waterloo, ON: Herald Press, 2000.

———. *Christian Peacemaking & International Conflict: A Realist Pacifist Perspective.* With a foreword by Stanley Hauerwas. Christian Peace Shelf Selection. Scottdale, PA: Herald Press, 1986.

———. "In Search of Security: A Theology and Ethic of Peace and Public Order." Chap. 2 in *At Peace and Unafraid: Public Order, Security and the Wisdom of the Cross*, edited by Duane K. Friesen and Gerald W. Schlabach, 37–82. Scottdale, PA: Herald Press, 2005.

———. "Normative Factors in Troeltsch's Typology of Religious Association." *Journal of Religious Ethics* 3, no. 2 (Fall 1975): 271–83.

———. "Peacemaking as an Ethical Category: The Convergence of Pacifism and Just War." In *Ethics in the Nuclear Age: Strategy, Religious Studies, and the Churches*, edited by Todd Whitmore. Dallas: Southern Methodist University Press, 1989.

Friesen, Duane K., and Gerald W. Schlabach, eds. *At Peace and Unafraid: Public Order, Security and the Wisdom of the Cross.* Scottdale, PA: Herald Press, 2005.

Gardner, John, and John R. Maier, trans. *Gilgamesh: Translated from the Sîn-Leqi-Unninnī Version.* With the assistance of Richard A. Henshaw. New York: Alfred A. Knopf, 1984.

Gellner, Ernest. *Nations and Nationalism.* Introduction by John Breuilly. New Perspectives on the Past. Ithaca, NY: Cornell University Press, 2008.

Gittins, Anthony J. "Beyond Hospitality? The Missionary Status and Role Revisited." *International Review of Mission* 83, no. 330 (July 1994): 397–416.

Godrej, Farah. "Nonviolence and Gandhi's Truth: A Method for Moral and Political Arbitration." *The Review of Politics* 68, no. 2 (Spring 2006): 287–317.

Gordon, Raymond G., ed. *Ethnologue: Languages of the World.* Contributing editor Barbara F. Grimes. Dallas, TX: SIL International, 2005.

Gregory of Nazianzen. *Select Orations.* In *A Select Library of the Nicene and Post-Nicene Fathers of the Christian Church.* Second series, vol. 7. Edited by Philip Schaff and Henry Wace. Peabody, MA: Hendrickson, 1994.

Grisez, Germain Gabriel. "The True Ultimate End of Human Beings: The Kingdom, Not God Alone." *Theological Studies* 69, no. 1 (March 2008): 38–61.

Gros, Jeffrey, and John D. Rempel, eds. *The Fragmentation of the Church and Its Unity in Peacemaking*. Grand Rapids, MI: Eerdmans, 2001.

Grotius, Hugo. *Prolegomena to the Law of War and Peace*. 1625. Translated by Francis W. Kelsey, with an introduction by Edward Dumbauld. The Library of Liberal Arts. Indianapolis: Bobbs-Merrill, 1957.

Harrington, Daniel J. *The Gospel of Matthew*. Sacra Pagina Series, vol. 1. Collegeville, MN: Liturgical Press, 1991.

Hauerwas, Stanley. *Christian Existence Today: Essays on Church, World and Living in Between*. Durham, NC: The Labyrinth Press, 1988.

———. *The Peaceable Kingdom: A Primer in Christian Ethics*. Notre Dame, IN: University of Notre Dame Press, 1983.

———. *War and the American Difference: Theological Reflections on Violence and National Identity*. Grand Rapids, MI: Baker Academic, 2011.

———. *With the Grain of the Universe: The Church's Witness and Natural Theology*. Gifford Lectures delivered at the University of St. Andrews in 2001. Grand Rapids, MI: Brazos Press, 2001.

———. "A Worldly Church: Politics, Theology of the Church, and the Common Good." *Journal of Law, Philosophy and Culture* 3, no. 1 (Spring 2009): 450–59.

Hauerwas, Stanley, and William H. Willimon. *Resident Aliens: Life in the Christian Colony*. Nashville: Abingdon Press, 1989.

Haughton, Rosemary L. "Hospitality: Home as the Integration of Privacy and Community." In *The Longing for Home*, edited by Leroy S. Rouner. Boston University Studies in Philosophy and Religion, vol. 17, 204–16. Notre Dame, IN: University of Notre Dame Press, 1996.

Heimbach-Steins, Marianne. "The Ambivalence of Borders and the Challenge of an Ethics of Liminality." In *Living with(out) Borders: Catholic Theological Ethics on the Migration of Peoples*, edited by Agnes M. Brazal and María Teresa Dávila. Catholic Theological Ethics in the World Church, 236–45. Maryknoll, NY: Orbis Books, 2016.

Held, David, Anthony McGrew, David Goldblatt, and Jonathan Perraton. *Global Transformations: Politics, Economics and Culture*. Stanford, CA: Stanford University Press, 1999.

Henrich, Joseph. *The Secret of Our Success: How Culture Is Driving Human Evolution, Domesticating Our Species, and Making Us Smarter*. Princeton, NJ; Oxford: Princeton University Press, 2016.

Hershberger, Guy F. *War, Peace, and Nonresistance*. 3rd ed. Christian Peace Shelf Selection. Scottdale, PA: Herald Press, 1969.

Heyer, Kristin E. "*Familismo* across the Americas: En Route to a Liberating Christian Family Ethic." In *Living with(out) Borders: Catholic Theological Ethics on the Migration of Peoples*, edited by Agnes M. Brazal and María Teresa Dávila. Catholic Theological Ethics in the World Church, 121–31. Maryknoll, NY: Orbis Books, 2016.

———. *Kinship across Borders: A Christian Ethic of Immigration*. Moral Traditions Series. Washington, DC: Georgetown University Press, 2012.

Himes, Kenneth R., OFM. "Intervention, Just War, and U.S. National Security." *Theological Studies* 65, no. 1 (2004): 141–57.

Hollenbach, David, SJ. "A Future without Borders: Reimagining the Nation-State and the Church." In *Living with(out) Borders: Catholic Theological Ethics on the Migration of Peoples*, edited by Agnes M. Brazal and María Teresa Dávila. Catholic Theological Ethics in the World Church, 223–35. Maryknoll, NY: Orbis Books, 2016.

Hollenbach, David. *Nuclear Ethics: A Christian Moral Argument*. New York: Paulist Press, 1983.

———. "Religion and Political Life." *Theological Studies* 52 (March 1991): 87–106.

Holmes, Robert L. "St. Augustine and the Just War Theory." In *The Augustinian Tradition*, edited by Gareth B. Matthews. Philosophical Traditions, no. 8, 323–44. University of California Press, 1998.

Holton, R. J. *Globalization and the Nation-State*. Houndmills, Basingstoke, Hampshire; New York: Macmillan Press; St. Martin's Press, 1998.

Huebner, Chris K. *A Precarious Peace: Yoderian Explorations on Theology, Knowledge, and Identity*. Waterloo, ON: Herald Press, 2006.

Hurtado, Larry W. *At the Origins of Christian Worship: The Context and Character of Earliest Christian Devotion*. Grand Rapids, MI: Eerdmans, 2000.

———. *Lord Jesus Christ: Devotion to Jesus in Earliest Christianity*. Grand Rapids, MI: Eerdmans, 2003.

Im, Chandler H., and Amos Yong, eds. *Global Diasporas and Mission*. Introduction by Chandler H. Im and Tereso C. Casiño. Regnum Edinburgh Centenary Series, vol. 23. Oxford Regnum Books International, 2014.

International Ecumenical Peace Convocation. "Glory to God and Peace on Earth: The Message of the International Ecumenical Peace Convocation." Kingston, Jamaica, 2011. http://www.overcomingviolence.org/en/resources-dov/wcc-resources/documents/presentations-speeches-messages/iepc-message.html.

Irvin, Dale T. "Theology, Migration, and the Homecoming." Chap. 1 in *Theology of Migration in the Abrahamic Religions*, edited by Elaine Padilla and Peter C. Phan. Palgrave Macmillan's Christianities of the World, 7–25. New York: Palgrave Macmillan, 2014.

Jameson, Fredric, and Masao Miyoshi, eds. *The Cultures of Globalization*. Post-Contemporary Interventions. Durham, NC: Duke University Press, 1998.

Jeffers, James S. *Conflict at Rome: Social Order and Hierarchy in Early Christianity*. Minneapolis: Fortress Press, 1991.

Jenkins, Philip. *The Next Christendom: The Coming of Global Christianity*. 3rd ed. Oxford; New York: Oxford University Press, 2011.

Jeremias, Joachim. *The Sermon on the Mount*. Translated by Norman Perrin. Biblical Series, no. 2. 1961. Reprint, Philadelphia: Fortress Press, 1963.

Jipp, Joshua W. *Saved by Faith and Hospitality*. Grand Rapids, MI: Eerdmans, 2017.

John Paul II, Pope. Address at the Fiftieth General Assembly of the United Nations Organization. New York (October 5, 1995). http://www.vatican.va/holy_father/john_paul_ii/speeches/1995/october/documents/hf_jp-ii_spe_05101995_address-to-uno_en.html.

———. *Centesimus Annus*. Encyclical on the Hundredth Anniversary of Rerum Novarum. May 1, 1991.

———. *Christifideles Laici*. Apostolic exhortation on the Vocation and Mission of the Lay Faithful in the Church and in the World. December 30, 1988.

———. *Evangelium Vitae*. [Gospel of Life]. Encyclical. March 25, 1995.

———. *Gratissimam Sane*. Letter to Families. February 2, 1994. http://www.vatican.va/holy_father/john_paul_ii/letters/documents/hf_jp-ii_let_02021994_families_en.html.

———. "No Peace without Justice; No Justice without Forgiveness." Message for the World Day of Peace. January 1, 2002.

———. "An Ever-Timely Commitment: Teaching Peace." Message for the World Day of Peace. January 1, 2004.

———. " 'Peace on Earth to Those Whom God Loves!' " Message for the World Day of Peace. January 1, 2000.

———. *Sollicitudo Rei Socialis*. Encyclical on Social Concern. December 30, 1987.

John XXIII, Pope. *Gaudet Mater Ecclesia*. Address at the opening of the Second Vatican Council. October 11, 1962.

———. *Mater et Magistra* [Christianity and Social Progress]. Encyclical. May 15, 1961.

———. *Pacem in Terris* [Peace on Earth]. Encyclical. April 11, 1963.

Johnson, James Turner. "Just War, as It Was and Is." *First Things*, no. 149 (January 2005): 14–24.

Johnson, Paul. *A History of Christianity*. New York: Atheneum, 1976.

Kauffman, Ivan. "The Civilization of Love: John Paul's Vision for the Third Millennium." Unpublished paper, 2009.

Khanna, Parag. "The End of the Nation State?" *New York Times*, October 12, 2013.

Klaassen, Walter. *Anabaptism: Neither Catholic nor Protestant*. Waterloo, ON: Conrad Press, 1981.

Koenig, John. *New Testament Hospitality: Partnership with Strangers as Promise and Mission*. Overtures to Biblical Theology, no. 17. Philadelphia: Fortress Press, 1985.

Kolb, Robert. "Origin of the Twin Terms Jus Ad Bellum/Jus in Bello." *International Review of the Red Cross*, no. 320 (October 31, 1997). https://www.icrc.org/eng/resources/documents/article/other/57jnuu.htm.

Kreider, Alan. *The Change of Conversion and the Origin of Christendom*. Harrisburg, PA: Trinity Press International, 1999.

———. "Changing Patterns of Conversion in the West." In *The Origins of Christendom in the West*, edited by Alan Kreider, 3–46. Edinburgh: T. & T. Clark, 2001.

———. *The Patient Ferment of the Early Church: The Improbable Rise of Christianity in the Roman Empire*. Grand Rapids, MI: Baker Academic, 2016.

La Civiltà Cattolica. "Modern War and the Christian Conscience." Editorial. Translated by William Shannon. *Origins* 21, no. 28 (December 19, 1992): 450–55.

Lampe, Peter. *From Paul to Valentinus: Christians at Rome in the First Two Centuries*. Edited by Marshall D. Johnson. Translated by Michael Steinhauser. Minneapolis: Fortress Press, 2003.

Lederach, John Paul. "On Simplicity and Complexity: Finding the Essence of Peacebuilding." In *The Moral Imagination: The Art and Soul of Building Peace*, 31–40. New York: Oxford University Press, 2005.

Leo XIII, Pope. *Rerum Novarum*. Encyclical on the Condition of the Working Classes. May 15, 1891.

Lieu, Judith, John North, and Tessa Rajak, eds. *The Jews among Pagans and Christians in the Roman Empire*. London; New York: Routledge, 1992.

Lightfoot, J. B., and J. R. Harmer, trans. "The Epistle to Diognetus." In *The Apostolic Fathers*, 2nd ed., edited and revised by Michael W. Holmes, 189–290. Grand Rapids, MI: Baker Book House, 1989.

———, trans. "The Shepherd of Hermas." In *The Apostolic Fathers*, 2nd ed., edited and revised by Michael W. Holmes, 189–290. Grand Rapids, MI: Baker Book House, 1989.

Long, D. Stephen. *The Goodness of God: Theology, Church, and the Social Order*. Grand Rapids, MI: Brazos Press, 2001.

Luz, Ulrich. *Matthew 1–7: A Commentary*. Translated by Wilhelm C. Linss. Minneapolis: Augsburg, 1989.

Manchala, Deenabandhu. "Migration: An Opportunity for Broader and Deeper Ecumenism." Chap. 8 in *Theology of Migration in the Abrahamic Religions*, edited by Elaine Padilla and Peter C. Phan. Palgrave Macmillan's Christianities of the World, 155–71. New York: Palgrave Macmillan, 2014.

Mander, Jerry, and Edward Goldsmith, eds. *The Case against the Global Economy: And for a Turn toward the Local*. San Francisco: Sierra Club Books, 1996.

Marincowitz, Leon. "South Africa: Positive Mimesis and the Turn toward Peace." In *Can We Survive Our Origins? Readings in René Girard's Theory of Violence and the Sacred*, edited by Pierpaolo Antonello and Paul Gifford. Studies in Violence, Mimesis, and Culture, 223–31. East Lansing: Michigan State University Press, 2015.

Markus, R. A. *Saeculum: History and Society in the Theology of St. Augustine*. 2nd ed. 1970. Reprint, Cambridge, England: University Press, 1988.

Mason, Herbert. *Gilgamesh: A Verse Narrative*. New York: New American Library, 1972.

McBrien, Richard P., gen. ed., and Harold W. Attridge et al., assoc. eds. *The HarperCollins Encyclopedia of Catholicism*. New York: HarperCollins, 1995.

McCormick, Patrick T. "Fair Trade Tourism: Practicing Hospitality and Keeping the Sabbath in a Foreign Land." In *Living with(out) Borders: Catholic Theological Ethics on the Migration of Peoples*, edited by Agnes M. Brazal and María Teresa Dávila. Catholic Theological Ethics in the World Church, 162–72. Maryknoll, NY: Orbis Books, 2016.

McManus, Philip, and Gerald Schlabach, eds. *Relentless Persistence: Nonviolent Action in Latin America*. With a foreword by Leonardo Boff. Philadelphia: New Society Publishers, 1991.

Mead, George Herbert. *Mind, Self, and Society: From the Standpoint of a Social Behaviorist*. In *Works of George Herbert Mead*. Vol. 1. Edited and introduced by Charles W. Morris. 1934. Reprint, Chicago: University of Chicago Press, 1962.

Meeks, Wayne A. *The First Urban Christians: The Social World of the Apostle Paul*. New Haven: Yale University Press, 1983.

Mennonite World Conference, and Pontifical Council for Promoting Church Unity. "Called Together to Be Peacemakers: Report of the International Dialogue between the Catholic Church and Mennonite World Conference, 1998–2003." *Information Service* 2003-II/III, no. 113 (2004): 111–48.

———. "A Mennonite and Catholic Contribution to the World Council of Churches' *Decade to Overcome Violence*." Report from Mennonite–Catholic Conference, Rome, October 23–25, 2007. http://www.overcomingviolence.org/fileadmin/dov/files/iepc/Mennonite_and_Catholic_contribution_to_DOV.pdf.

Meyer, Ben F. *Five Speeches That Changed the World*. Collegeville, MN: Liturgical Press, 1994.

———. "The Gospel Literature: Data on Jesus?" Chap. 3 in *The Aims of Jesus*, with a new introduction by N. T. Wright. Princeton Theological Monograph Series, vol. 48, 60–75. 1979. Reprint, San Jose, CA: Pickwick Publications, 2002.

Miller, Marlin E. "Toward Acknowledging Together the Apostolic Character of the Church's Peace Witness." In *The Church's Peace Witness*, edited by Marlin Miller and Barbara Nelson Gingrich, 196–207. Grand Rapids, MI: Eerdmans, 1994.

Miller, Marlin, and Barbara Nelson Gingrich, eds. *The Church's Peace Witness*. Grand Rapids, MI: Eerdmans, 1994.

Miller, Richard B. "Aquinas and the Presumption against Killing and War." *Journal of Religion* 82, no. 2 (April 2002): 173–204.

Mittelman, James H. *The Globalization Syndrome: Transformation and Resistance*. Princeton, NJ: Princeton University Press, 2000.

Moltmann, Jürgen. "Shekinah: The Home of the Homeless God." In *The Longing for Home*. Edited by Leroy S. Rouner. Boston University Studies in Philosophy and Religion. Vol. 17, 170–84. Notre Dame, IN: University of Notre Dame Press, 1996.

Morrow, Duncan. "Northern Ireland: Breaking the Inheritance of Conflict and Violence." In *Can We Survive Our Origins? Readings in René Girard's Theory of Violence and the Sacred*, edited by Pierpaolo Antonello and Paul Gifford. Studies in Violence, Mimesis, and Culture, 169–89. East Lansing: Michigan State University Press, 2015.

Moucarry, Chawkat Georges. "The Alien according to the Torah." *Themelios* 14, no. 1 (1988): 17–20.

Nation, Mark Thiessen. *John Howard Yoder: Mennonite Patience, Evangelical Witness, Catholic Convictions*. Grand Rapids, MI: Eerdmans, 2006.

National Conference of Catholic Bishops (NCCB). *The Challenge of Peace: God's Promise and Our Response*. Washington, DC: United States Catholic Conference, 1983.

Nelson, Rudolph, Shirley Nelson, Martin E. Marty, Dennis Smith, Paul Jeffrey, Matt Samson, Gr and Gr Projects, Quest Productions, and Catticus Corporation. *Precarious Peace: God & Guatemala*. Video recording. Worcester, PA: Gateway Films. Distributed by Vision Video, 2003.

Niebuhr, H. Richard. *Christ and Culture*. Harper Torchbooks/Cloister Library. New York: Harper and Row, 1956.

Niebuhr, Reinhold. *Moral Man and Immoral Society*. Reprint ed. The Scribner Lyceum Editions Library. New York: Scribner's, 1960.

———. "Why the Christian Church Is Not Pacifist." In *Christianity and Power Politics*, 1–32. New York: Charles Scribner's Sons, 1940.

O'Donovan, Oliver. *The Problem of Self-Love in St. Augustine*. New Haven: Yale University Press, 1980.

O'Neill, William, SJ. "The Place of Displacement: The Ethics of Migration in the United States." In *Living with(out) Borders: Catholic Theological Ethics on the Migration of Peoples*, edited by Agnes M. Brazal and María Teresa Dávila. Catholic Theological Ethics in the World Church, 67–77. Maryknoll, NY: Orbis Books, 2016.

Ochs, Peter. *Another Reformation: Postliberal Christianity and the Jews*. Grand Rapids, MI: Baker Academic, 2011.

Oden, Amy G., ed. *And You Welcomed Me: A Sourcebook on Hospitality in Early Christianity*. Nashville: Abingdon Press, 2001.

———. *God's Welcome: Hospitality for a Gospel-Hungry World*. Cleveland, OH: Pilgrim Press, 2008.

Orend, Brian. "Justice After War." *Ethics & International Affairs* 16, no. 1 (2002): 43–56.

Origen. *Contra Celsum*. Translated by Henry Chadwick. 1953. Reprint, Cambridge: Cambridge University Press, 1965.

Osiek, Carolyn A. "The Genre and Function of the Shepherd of Hermas." *Semeia*, no. 36 (1986): 113–21.

———. *Rich and Poor in* The Shepherd of Hermas: *An Exegetical-Social Investigation*. Catholic Biblical Quarterly Monograph Series, no. 15. Washington, DC: Catholic Biblical Association of America, 1983.

———. *The Shepherd of Hermas: A Commentary*. Vol. 4 of *The Disputation: A Theological Debate between Christians and Jews*. Video. Edited by Helmut Koester. Message of the Fathers of the Church 1. Fortress Press, 1998.

Paul VI, Pope. *Evangelii Nuntiandi*. Apostolic exhortation on Evangelization in the Modern World. December 8, 1975.

———. "If You Want Peace, Work for Justice." Message for the Day of Peace. January 1, 1972.

———. *Populorum Progressio*. Encyclical on the Development of Peoples. March 26, 1967.

———. Regina Coeli Address on Pentecost Sunday. May 17, 1970. http://www.vatican.va/holy_father/paul_vi/angelus/1970/documents/hf_p-vi_reg_19700517_it.html.

———. Address to the United Nations Organization. October 4, 1965. http://www.vatican.va/holy_father/paul_vi/speeches/1965/documents/hf_p-vi_spe_19651004_united-nations_en.html.

Pax Christi International. "An Appeal to the Catholic Church to Re-Commit to the Centrality of Gospel Nonviolence." Final document of the conference "Nonviolence and Just Peace: Contributing to the Catholic Understanding of and Commitment to Nonviolence." Hosted by the Pontifical Council for Justice and Peace. Rome, Italy, 2016. Http://www.paxchristi.net/sites/default/files/documents/appeal-to-catholic-church-to-recommit-to-nonviolence.pdf.

Pew Forum on Religion and Public Life. *Global Christianity: A Report on the Size and Distribution of the World's Christian Population*. Washington, DC: Pew Research Center, 2011. http://www.pewforum.org/files/2011/12/Christianity-fullreport-web.pdf.

Phan, Peter C. "Embracing, Protecting, and Loving the Stranger: A Roman Catholic Theology of Migration." Chap. 5 in *Theology of Migration in the Abrahamic Religions*, edited by Elaine Padilla and Peter C. Phan. Palgrave Macmillan's Christianities of the World, 77–110. New York: Palgrave Macmillan, 2014.

Philpott, Daniel. "What Religion Brings to the Politics of Transitional Justice." *Journal of International Affairs* 61, no. 1 (Fall/Winter 2007): 93–110.

———. "When Faith Meets History: The Influence of Religion on Transitional Justice." In *The Religious in Responses to Mass Atrocity: Interdisciplinary Perspectives*, edited by Thomas Brudholm and Thomas Cushman, 174–212. Cambridge; New York: Cambridge University Press, 2009.

Pineda-Madrid, Nancy. "Sex Trafficking and Femicide along the Border: Re-Membering Our Daughters." In *Living with(out) Borders: Catholic Theological Ethics on the Migration of Peoples*, edited by Agnes M. Brazal and María Teresa Dávila. Catholic Theological Ethics in the World Church, 81–90. Maryknoll, NY: Orbis Books, 2016.

Pius XII, Pope. *The Major Addresses of Pope Pius XII*. 2 volumes. Edited by Vincent A. Yzermans. St. Paul: North Central Pub., 1961.

Pohl, Christine D. *Making Room: Recovering Hospitality as a Christian Tradition*. Grand Rapids, MI: Eerdmans, 1999.

Pontifical Council for Justice and Peace. *Compendium of the Social Doctrine of the Church*. USCCB Publishing No. 5-692. Cittá del Vaticano; Washington, DC: Libreria Editrice Vaticana; [distributed by the] United States Conference of Catholic Bishops, 2004.

Pontifical Council for the Pastoral Care of Migrants and Itinerant People. *Erga Migrantes Caritas Christi*. Instruction on the Love of Christ towards Migrants (May 3, 2004). http://www.vatican.va/roman_curia/pontifical_councils/migrants/documents/rc_pc_migrants_doc_2004 0514_erga-migrantes-caritas-christi_en.html.

———. *Refugees: A Challenge to Solidarity*. June 25, 1992. http://www.vatican.va/roman_curia/pontifical_councils/corunum/documents/rc_pc_corunum_doc_25061992_refugees_en.html.

Pontius the Deacon. *The Life and Passion of Cyprian, Bishop and Martyr*. In *The Ante-Nicene Fathers*. Vol. 7. Edited by Alexander Roberts and James Donaldson. Edinburgh: T. & T. Clark, 1873.

Rahner, Karl. "The Present Situation of Christians: A Theological Interpretation of the Position of Christians in the Modern World." In *The Christian Commitment: Essays in Pastoral Theology*, 3–37. New York: Sheed and Ward, 1963.

———. "Towards a Fundamental Theological Interpretation of Vatican II." *Theological Studies* 40, no. 4 (December 1979): 716–27.

Rajendra, Tisha M. *Migrants and Citizens: Justice and Responsibility in the Ethics of Immigration*. With a foreword by Daniel G. Groody, CSC. Grand Rapids, MI: Eerdmans, 2017.

Ramsey, Paul. *Speak up for Just War or Pacifism: A Critique of the United Methodist Bishops' Pastoral Letter "In Defence of Creation."* Epilogue by Stanley Hauerwas. University Park: Pennsylvania State University Press, 1988.

———. *War and the Christian Conscience: How Shall Modern War Be Conducted Justly?* Published for the Lilly Endowment Research Program in Christianity and Politics. Durham, NC: Duke University Press, 1961.

Rasmusson, Arne. "The Genealogy of the Charge of Sectarianism." In *The Church as Polis: From Political Theology to Theological Politics as Exemplified by Jürgen Moltmann and Stanley Hauerwas*, 231–47. Notre Dame, IN: University of Notre Dame Press, 1995.

Ratzinger, Joseph, Cardinal. *God and the World: Believing and Living in Our Time: A Conversation with Peter Seewald.* Translated by Henry Taylor. San Francisco: Ignatius Press, 2002.

Rengger, Nicholas. "The Jus in Bello in Historical and Philosophical Perspective." In *War: Essays in Political Philosophy*, edited by Larry May, with the assistance of Emily Crookston, 30-46. Cambridge; New York: Cambridge University Press, 2008.

Richard, Lucien. *Living the Hospitality of God.* New York: Paulist Press, 2000.

Russell, Frederick H. *The Just War in the Middle Ages.* Cambridge Studies in Medieval Life and Thought, 3d Ser., v. 8. Cambridge; New York: Cambridge University Press, 1975.

———. "War." In *Augustine through the Ages: An Encyclopedia*, Allan D. Fitzgerald, OSA, gen. ed. Grand Rapids, MI: Eerdmans, 1999.

Rynne, Terrence J. *Jesus Christ, Peacemaker: A New Theology of Peace.* Maryknoll, NY: Orbis Books, 2014.

Sacred Congregation of Bishops. "De Pastorali Migratorum Cura." Instruction on the pastoral care of people who migrate. August 22, 1969.

Safran, William. "Diasporas in Modern Societies: Myths of Homeland and Return." *Diaspora* 1, no. 1 (1991): 83–99.

———. "The Jewish Diaspora in a Comparative and Theoretical Perspective." *Israel Studies* 10, no. 1 (Spring 2005): 36–60.

Sanders, Scott Russell. *Staying Put: Making a Home in a Restless World.* Boston: Beacon Press, 1993.

Sassen, Saskia. "The Making of Migrations." In *Living with(out) Borders: Catholic Theological Ethics on the Migration of Peoples*, edited by Agnes M. Brazal and María Teresa Dávila. Catholic Theological Ethics in the World Church, 11–22. Maryknoll, NY: Orbis Books, 2016.

Schell, Jonathan. "No More unto the Breach." Two-part series. *Harper's* 306, no. 1834–1835 (March and April 2003): 33–46, 41–55.

Schlabach, Gerald W., ed. and lead author. *Just Policing, Not War: An Alternative Response to World Violence.* With Drew Christiansen, SJ, Ivan Kauffman, John Paul Lederach, Reina C. Neufeldt, Margaret R. Pfeil, Glen H. Stassen, and Tobias Winright. Collegeville, MN: Liturgical Press, 2007.

———. "Anthology in Lieu of System: John H. Yoder's Ecumenical Conversations as Systematic Theology." Review essay on *The Royal Priesthood: Essays Ecclesiological and Ecumenical* by John Howard Yoder and Michael G. Cartwright (ed.). *Mennonite Quarterly Review* 71, no. 2 (April 1997): 305–9.

———. "Augustine's Hermeneutic of Humility: An Alternative to Moral Imperialism and Moral Relativism." *Journal of Religious Ethics* 22, no. 2 (Fall 1994): 299–330.

———. "Beyond Two- Versus One-Kingdom Theology: Abrahamic Community as a Mennonite Paradigm for Engagement in Society." *Conrad Grebel Review* 11, no. 3 (Fall 1993): 187–210.

———. "Capitalizing Church: On Finding Catholicism Inevitable." *Conrad Grebel Review* 34, no. 3 (Fall 2016): 284–302.

———. "Catholic and Mennonite: A Journey of Healing." In *Sharing Peace: Mennonites and Catholics in Conversation*, edited by Gerald W. Schlabach and Margaret Pfeil, foreword by Msgr. John A. Radano, 159–78. Collegeville, MN: Liturgical Press, 2013.

———. "The Christian Witness in the Earthly City: John H. Yoder as Augustinian Interlocutor." Chap. 11 in *A Mind Patient and Untamed: Assessing John Howard Yoder's Contribution to Theology, Ethics, and Peacemaking*, edited by Ben C. Ollenburger and Gayle Gerber Koontz, with an introduction by Stanley Hauerwas, 221–44. Telford, PA: Cascadia Publishing House, 2004.

———. "'Confessional' Nonviolence and the Unity of the Church: Can Christians Square the Circle?" *Journal of the Society of Christian Ethics* 34, no. 1 (2014): 125–44.

———. "Continuity and Sacrament, or Not: Hauerwas, Yoder, and Their Deep Difference." *Journal of the Society of Christian Ethics* 27, no. 2 (Fall–Winter 2007): 171–207.

———. "The Correction of the Augustinians: A Case Study in the Critical Appropriation of a Suspect Tradition." In *The Early Church and the Free Church: Bridging the Historical and Theological Divide*, edited by Daniel H. Williams, 47–74. Grand Rapids, MI: Eerdmans, 2002.

———. "Deuteronomic or Constantinian: What Is the Most Basic Problem for Christian Social Ethics?" In *The Wisdom of the Cross: Essays in Honor of John Howard Yoder*, edited by Stanley Hauerwas, Chris K. Huebner, Harry Huebner, and Mark Thiessen Nation, 449–71. Grand Rapids, MI: Eerdmans, 1999.

———. *For the Joy Set Before Us: Augustine and Self-Denying Love*. Notre Dame, IN: University of Notre Dame Press, 2000.

———. "Just Policing: How War Could Cease to Be a Church-Dividing Issue." In *Just Policing: Mennonite-Catholic Theological Colloquium 2002*, edited by Ivan J. Kauffman. Bridgefolk Series, no. 2, 19–75. Kitchener, ON: Pandora Press, 2004.

———. "Just Policing: How War Could Cease to Be a Church-Dividing Issue." *Journal of Ecumenical Studies* 41, no. 3–4 (Summer–Fall 2004): 409-30.

———. "Just Policing, Not War." *America* 189, no. 1 (July 7-14, 2003): 19–21.

———. "Just War? Enough Already." *Commonweal* 144, no. 11 (June 16, 2017): 9–14.

———. " 'Love Is the Hand of the Soul': The Grammar of Continence in Augustine's Doctrine of Christian Love." *Journal of Early Christian Studies* 6, no. 1 (Spring 1998): 59–92.

———. "Meeting in Exile: Historic Peace Churches and the Emerging Peace Church Catholic." *Journal of Religion, Conflict, and Peace* 1, no. 1 (Fall 2007). https://www.manchester.edu/docs/default-source/academics/by-major/philosophy-and-religious-studies/journal/volume-1-issue-1-fall-2007/meeting-in-exile.pdf?sfvrsn=4f5b8962_2.

———. "Must Christian Pacifists Reject Police Force?" Chap. 5 in *A Faith Not Worth Fighting for: Addressing Commonly Asked Questions about Christian Nonviolence*, edited by Tripp York and Justin Bronson Barringer. The Peaceable Kingdom Series, no. 1, 60–84. Eugene OR: Cascade Books, 2012.

———. "Only Those We Need Can Betray Us: My Relationship with John Howard Yoder and His Legacy." Interviewed by Paul Martens and Jonathan Tran, 2014. http://www.geraldschlabach.net/2014/07/10/only-those-we-need-can-betray-us-my-relationship-with-john-howard-yoder-and-his-legacy/.

———. *To Bless All Peoples: Serving with Abraham and Jesus*. Peace and Justice Series, no. 12. Scottdale, PA: Herald Press, 1991.

———. *Unlearning Protestantism: Sustaining Christian Community in an Unstable Age*. Grand Rapids, MI: Brazos Press, 2010.

———. "Where Are Our Wounds? A Call for Active Nonviolence in Central America." *Mission Focus* 12, no. 2 (June 1984): 21–24.

———. "You Converted to What? One Mennonite's Journey." *Commonweal* 134, no. 11 (1 June 2007): 14–17.

Schlabach, Gerald W., and Margaret Pfeil, eds. *Sharing Peace: Mennonites and Catholics in Conversation*. Forward by Msgr. John A. Radano. Collegeville, MN: Liturgical Press, 2013.

Schlabach, Gerald W., and Allan D. Fitzgerald, OSA. "Ethics." In collaboration with Nello Cipriani, OSA, Robert Dodaro, OSA, David G. Hunter, John Langan, SJ, and Robert A. Markus. In *Augustine through the Ages: An Encyclopedia*, Edited by Allan D. Fitzgerald, OSA, 320–30. Grand Rapids, MI: Eerdmans, 1999.

Schlabach, Theron F. "Race and Another Look at Nonviolent Resistance." Chap. 12 in *War, Peace, and Social Conscience: Guy F. Hershberger and Mennonite Ethics*. Studies in Anabaptist and Mennonite History, no. 45, 435–71. Scottdale, PA: Herald Press, 2009.

Schlabach, Theron F., and Richard T. Hughes, eds. *Proclaim Peace: Christian Pacifism from Unexpected Quarters*. Urbana: University of Illinois Press, 1997.

Schoenfeld, Devorah. " 'You Will Seek from There': The Cycle of Exile and Return in Classical Jewish Theology." Chap. 2 in *Theology of Migration in the Abrahamic Religions*, edited by Elaine Padilla and Peter C. Phan. Palgrave Macmillan's Christianities of the World, 27–45. New York: Palgrave Macmillan, 2014.

Scholte, Jan Aart. *Globalization: A Critical Introduction*. Basingstoke; New York: Palgrave, 2000.

Schuck, Michael J. *That They Be One: The Social Teaching of the Papal Encyclicals 1740–1989*. Washington, DC: Georgetown University Press, 1991.

Second Vatican Council. *Gaudium et Spes*. Pastoral Constitution on the Church in the Modern World. 1965. In Austin Flannery, ed. *Vatican Council II: Constitutions, Decrees, Declarations; The Basic Sixteen Documents*. Collegeville, MN: Liturgical Press, 2014.

———. *Lumen Gentium*. Dogmatic Constitution on the Church. November 21, 1964. In Austin Flannery, ed. *Vatican Council II: Constitutions, Decrees, Declarations; The Basic Sixteen Documents*. Collegeville, MN: Liturgical Press, 2014.

———. *Unitatis Redintegratio*. Decree on Ecumenism, November 21, 1964. In Austin Flannery, ed. *Vatican Council II: Constitutions, Decrees, Declarations; The Basic Sixteen Documents*. Collegeville, MN: Liturgical Press, 2014.

Sharp, Gene. *The Dynamics of Nonviolent Action*. Vol. 3 of *The Politics of Nonviolent Action*. Edited by Marina Finkelstein. Boston: Extending Horizons, 1973.

———. *The Politics of Nonviolent Action*. 3 vols. Edited by Marina Finkelstein. Boston: Extending Horizons, 1973.

———. *Power and Struggle*. Vol. 1 of *The Politics of Nonviolent Action*. Edited by Marina Finkelstein. Boston: Extending Horizons, 1973.

———. *Social Power and Political Freedom*. Extending Horizons Books. Boston: P. Sargent Publishers, 1980.

Spadaro, Antonio. "A Big Heart Open to God: An Interview with Pope Francis." *America* 209, no. 8 (September 30, 2013): 26.

Stark, Rodney. *The Rise of Christianity: A Sociologist Reconsiders History*. Princeton, NJ: Princeton University Press, 1996.

Stassen, Glen H., ed. *Just Peacemaking: Ten Practices for Abolishing War*. 1st ed. Cleveland: Pilgrim Press, 1998.

———, ed. *Just Peacemaking: The New Paradigm for the Ethics of Peace and War*. 3rd ed. Cleveland: Pilgrim Press, 2008.

———. "The Fourteen Triads of the Sermon on the Mount (Matthew 5:21–7:12)." *Journal of Biblical Literature* 122, no. 2 (Summer 2003): 267–308.

———. "Healing the Rift between the Sermon on the Mount and Christian Ethics." *Studies in Christian Ethics* 18, no. 3 (2005): 89–105.

———. "Just Peacemaking as Hermeneutical Key: The Need for International Cooperation in Preventing Terrorism." *Journal of the Society of Christian Ethics* 24, no. 2 (Fall/Winter 2004): 171–91.

———. *Just Peacemaking: Transforming Initiatives for Justice and Peace*. Louisville, KY: Westminster/John Knox Press, 1992.

———. *Living the Sermon on the Mount: A Practical Hope for Grace and Deliverance*. San Francisco: Jossey-Bass, 2006.

———. *A Thicker Jesus: Incarnational Discipleship in a Secular Age*. Louisville, KY: Westminster John Knox Press, 2012.

———. "Transforming Initiatives of Just Peacemaking Based on the Triadic Structure of the Sermon on the Mount." Matthew section. Society of Biblical Literature, 2006. https://www.sbl-site.org/assets/pdfs/Stassen_Transforming.pdf.

———. "The Unity, Realism, and Obligatoriness of Just Peacemaking Theory." *Journal of the Society of Christian Ethics* 23, no. 1 (2003): 171–94.

Stassen, Glen H., and David P. Gushee. *Kingdom Ethics: Following Jesus in Contemporary Context*. Downers Grove, IL: InterVarsity Press, 2003.

Stassen, Glen H., Diane M. Yeager, and John Howard Yoder. *Authentic Transformation: A New Vision of Christ and Culture*. With a previously unpublished essay by H. Richard Niebuhr. Nashville: Abingdon Press, 1996.

Stevenson, William R. *Christian Love and Just War: Moral Paradox and Political Life in St. Augustine and His Modern Interpreters*. Macon, GA: Mercer University Press, 1987.

Stout, Jeffrey. *Democracy and Tradition*. New Forum Books. Princeton, NJ: Princeton University Press, 2004.

Suárez, Francisco. "Disputation XIII: On War (*de Bello*)." Excerpted in *The Ethics of War: Classic and Contemporary Readings*, edited by Gregory M. Reichberg, Henrik Syse, and Endre Begby, 339–70. Malden, MA; Oxford: Blackwell, 2006.

Swartley, Willard M. *Covenant of Peace: The Missing Piece in New Testament Theology and Ethics*. Grand Rapids, MI: Eerdmans Pub., 2006.

Tapia de Renedo, Benedicto, ed. *Hélder Câmara: Proclamas a la Juventud*. Serie PEDAL, no. 64. Salamanca: Ediciones Sigueme, 1976.

Tertullian. *Ad Naciones*. In *The Ante-Nicene Fathers*. Vol. 3. Edited by Alexander Roberts and James Donaldson. Edinburgh: T. & T. Clark, 1873.

———. *The Apology*. In *The Ante-Nicene Fathers*. Vol. 3. Edited by Alexander Roberts and James Donaldson. Edinburgh: T. & T. Clark, 1873.

———. *On Idolatry*. In *The Ante-Nicene Fathers*. Vol. 3. Edited by Alexander Roberts and James Donaldson. Edinburgh: T. & T. Clark, 1873.

Thiel, John E. *Icons of Hope: The "Last Things" in Catholic Imagination*. Notre Dame, IN: University of Notre Dame Press, 2013.

Toft, Monica Duffy, Daniel Philpott, and Timothy Samuel Shah. *God's Century: Resurgent Religion and Global Politics*. New York: W. W. Norton & Co., 2011.

Tolkien, J. R. R. *The Lord of the Rings*. 50th Anniversary ed. Boston: Houghton Mifflin, 2004.

Tomlinson, John. *Cultural Imperialism: A Critical Introduction*. London: Pinter Publishers, 1991.

Tracy, David. *The Analogical Imagination: Christian Theology and the Culture of Pluralism*. New York: Crossroads, 1981.

Troeltsch, Ernst. *The Social Teaching of the Christian Churches*. Translated by Olive Wyon, with an introduction by Richard Niebuhr. 1931. Reprint, Chicago: University of Chicago Press, 1981.

Turkson, Peter, Cardinal. "Christian Nonviolence and Just Peace." Keynote address. The Catholic Church Moves towards Nonviolence? Just Peace Just War in Dialogue. University of San Diego, 2017. https://www.youtube.com/watch?v=1iY__KsrFK0.

Tweed, Thomas A. *Crossing and Dwelling: A Theory of Religion*. Cambridge, MA: Harvard University Press, 2006.

United Church of Christ. "Pronouncement on Affirming the United Church of Christ as a Just Peace Church." Fifteenth General Synod, 1985. http://www.ucc.org/justice/advocacy_resources/pdfs/just-peace/just-peace-church-pronouncement-1985.pdf.

The United Methodist Council of Bishops. *In Defense of Creation: The Nuclear Crisis and a Just Peace*. Foundation Document. Nashville: Graded Press, 1986.

United States Conference of Catholic Bishops. *The Harvest of Justice Is Sown in Peace*. Washington, DC: USCCB, 1993.

———. *Welcoming the Stranger among Us: Unity in Diversity.* Pastoral statement. Washington, DC: United States Conference of Catholic Bishops, 2001.

United States Conference of Catholic Bishops, and Conferencia del Episcopado Mexicano. *Strangers No Longer: Together on the Journey of Hope: A Pastoral Letter concerning Migration from the Catholic Bishops of Mexico and the United States.* Washington, DC: United States Conference of Catholic Bishops, 2003.

Vatican Radio. "Holy See Ratifies Treaty on the Prohibition of Nuclear Arms." September 21, 2017. http://www.archivioradiovaticana.va/storico/2017/09/21/holy_see_ratifies_treaty_on_the_prohibition_of_nuclear_arms/en-1338124.

Vessey, Mark, Karla Pollmann, and Allan D. Fitzgerald, eds. *History, Apocalypse, and the Secular Imagination: New Essays on Augustine's City of God.* Bowling Green, OH: Philosophy Documentation Center, Bowling Green State University, 1999.

Vitoria, Francisco de. *Comentarios a la Secunda Secundae de santo Tomás.* [1534–1537]. Edited by Vicente Beltran de Heredia. Biblioteca de Teológos Españoles, vols. 2–6 and 17. Salamanca: Apartado 17, 1932–52.

———. "De Indis Recenter Inventis [On the Indians Lately Discovered —1539]." Translated by John Pawley Bate. In *De Indis et de Ivre Belli Relectiones* [On the Indians and on the Law of War], edited by Ernest Nys. Classics of International Law, no. 7, 115–62 [Latin text: 217–68]. Washington: Carnegie Institution, 1917.

von Rad, Gerhard. *Genesis: A Commentary.* Rev. ed. Translated by John H. Marks. Old Testament Library. Philadelphia: The Westminster Press, 1972.

———. *The Theology of Israel's Historical Traditions.* Vol. 1 of *Old Testament Theology.* Translated by D. M. G. Stalker. New York: Harper and Row, 1962.

Walls, Andrew F. "The Gospel as Prisoner and Liberator of Culture." Chap. 1 in *The Missionary Movement in Christian History: Studies in the Transmission of Faith,* 3–15. Maryknoll, NY: Orbis Books, 1996.

———. "Mission and Migration: The Diaspora Factor in Christian History." *Journal of African Christian Thought* 5, no. 2 (December 2002): 3–11.

Waltner Goossen, Rachel. "'Defanging the Beast': Mennonite Responses to John Howard Yoder's Sexual Abuse." *Mennonite Quarterly Review* 89, no. 1 (January 2015): 7–80.

Weigel, George. "Moral Clarity in a Time of War." *First Things* 128 (January 2003): 20–27.

Wiesel, Elie. "Longing for Home." In *The Longing for Home*, edited by Leroy S. Rouner. Boston University Studies in Philosophy and Religion, vol. 17, 17–29. Notre Dame, IN: University of Notre Dame Press, 1996.

Williams, Robert E., and Dan Caldwell. "Jus Post Bellum: Just War Theory and the Principles of Just Peace." *International Studies Perspectives* 7, no. 4 (November 2006): 309–20.

Williams, Rowan. "What Is a Person?" In *Being Human: Bodies, Minds, Persons*, 28–47. Grand Rapids MI: Eerdmans, 2018.

Wink, Walter. "Breaking the Spiral of Violence." In *The Powers That Be: Theology for a New Millennium*, pp. 84–97. New York: Doubleday, 1998.

———. *Engaging the Powers: Discernment and Resistance in a World of Domination*. Minneapolis: Fortress Press, 1992.

———. *The Powers That Be: Theology for a New Millennium*. New York: Doubleday, 1998.

Wolff, Hans Walter. "The Kerygma of the Yahwist." Translated by Wilbur A. Benware. *Interpretation* 20, no. 2 (April 1966): 131–58.

World Conference on Church, Community and State. "Report of the Section on the Universal Church and the World of Nations." Oxford, United Kingdom, July 12–26, 1937, in *On Earth Peace: Discussions on War/Peace Issues Between Friends, Mennonites, Brethren, and European Churches, 1935–75*, edited by Donald Durnbaugh, 33–37. Elgin, IL: The Brethren Press, 1978.

World Council of Churches. *An Ecumenical Call to Just Peace*. Received, endorsed and commended for study, reflection, collaboration and common action during the Central Committee meetings in February 2011, Geneva, Switzerland. http://www.overcomingviolence.org/en/resources-dov/wcc-resources/documents/declarations-on-just-peace/ecumenical-call-to-just-peace.html.

Wrobleski, Jessica. *The Limits of Hospitality*. Collegeville MN: Liturgical Press, 2012.

Yoder, Elizabeth G., ed. *Peace Theology and Violence against Women*. With an introduction by Gayle Gerber Koontz. Occasional Papers, no. 16. Elkhart, IN: Institute of Mennonite Studies, 1992.

Yoder, John Howard. "Armaments and Eschatology." *Studies in Christian Ethics* 1, no. 1 (1988).

———. "The Biblical Mandate for Evangelical Social Action." In *For the Nations: Essays Public and Evangelical*, 180–98. Grand Rapids, MI: Eerdmans, 1997.

———. *Body Politics: Five Practices of the Christian Community Before the Watching World*. Nashville, TN: Discipleship Resources, 1992.

———. "Christ, the Hope of the World." In *The Original Revolution: Essays on Christian Pacifism*. Christian Peace Shelf, 140–76. Scottdale, PA: Herald Press, 1971.

———. *Christian Attitudes to War, Peace, and Revolution*. Edited by Theodore J. Koontz and Andy Alexis-Baker. Grand Rapids, MI: Brazos Press, 2009.

———. *The Christian Witness to the State*. Institute of Mennonite Studies Series, no. 3. Newton, KS: Faith and Life Press, 1964.

———. *For the Nations: Essays Public and Evangelical*. Grand Rapids, MI: Eerdmans, 1997.

———. "Gordon Zahn Is Right: Going the Second Mile with Just War." In *The War of the Lamb: The Ethics of Nonviolence and Peacemaking*, edited by Glen Harold Stassen, Mark Thiessen Nation, and Matt Hamsher, 109–16. Grand Rapids, MI: Brazos Press, 2009.

———. *The Jewish-Christian Schism Revisited*. Edited by Michael G. Cartwright and Peter Ochs. Radical Traditions. Grand Rapids, MI: Eerdmans, 2003.

———. "Just War and Nonviolence: Disjunction, Dialogue, or Complementarity?" In *The War of the Lamb: The Ethics of Nonviolence and Peacemaking*, edited by Glen Harold Stassen, Mark Thiessen Nation, and Matt Hamsher, 85–92. Grand Rapids, MI: Brazos Press, 2009.

———. "Just War Tradition: Is It Credible?" *Christian Century* 108, no. 9 (March 13, 1991): 295–98.

———. "The Kingdom as Social Ethic." In *The Priestly Kingdom: Social Ethics as Gospel*, 80–101. Notre Dame, IN: University of Notre Dame Press, 1984.

———. *Nevertheless: The Varieties and Shortcomings of Religious Pacifism*. Christian Peace Shelf Series. Scottdale, PA: Herald Press, 1971.

———. "On Not Being Ashamed of the Gospel: Particularity, Pluralism, and Validation." *Faith and Philosophy* 9, no. 3 (July 1992): 285–300.

———. *The Original Revolution: Essays on Christian Pacifism*. Christian Peace Shelf. Scottdale, PA: Herald Press, 1971.

———. "The Original Revolution." In *The Original Revolution: Essays on Christian Pacifism*. Christian Peace Shelf, 13–33. Scottdale, PA: Herald Press, 1971.

———. *The Politics of Jesus*. 2nd ed. 1972. Reprint, Grand Rapids, MI: Eerdmans, 1994.

———. *The Priestly Kingdom: Social Ethics as Gospel*. Notre Dame, IN: University of Notre Dame Press, 1984.

———. "Radical Reformation Ethics in Ecumenical Perspective." *Journal of Ecumenical Studies* 15, no. 4 (Fall 1978): 247–661.

———. *Reinhold Niebuhr and Christian Pacifism*. 1955. A Concern Reprint. Scottdale, PA: Concern, n.d.

———. *The Royal Priesthood: Essays Ecclesiological and Ecumenical*. Edited, with an introduction by Michael G. Cartwright and a foreword by Richard J. Mouw. Grand Rapids, MI: Eerdmans, 1994.

———. "A Theological Critique of Violence." In *The War of the Lamb: The Ethics of Nonviolence and Peacemaking*, edited by Glen Harold Stassen, Mark Thiessen Nation, and Matt Hamsher, 27–42. Grand Rapids, MI: Brazos Press, 2009.

———. *The War of the Lamb: The Ethics of Nonviolence and Peacemaking*. Edited by Glen Harold Stassen, Mark Thiessen Nation, and Matt Hamsher. Grand Rapids, MI: Brazos Press, 2009.

———. *When War Is Unjust: Being Honest in Just-War Thinking*. Rev. ed. With a foreword by Charles P. Lutz and an afterword by Drew Christiansen. Maryknoll, NY: Orbis Books, 1996.

ZENIT. "Cardinal Ratzinger on the Abridged Version of Catechism Compendium Expected Out in 2 Years." *ZENIT News Agency*, May 2, 2003. https://zenit.org/articles/cardinal-ratzinger-on-the-abridged-version-of-catechism/.

Index

1989 Revolution, 50, 53–55, 83, 90–91, 301

Abesamis, Carlos H., 326
abolition of war, 43
abortion, 38, 156–57
Abraham (Abram), 4, 22, 94, 102, 110, 113, 136, 141–45, 147–48, 153, 171, 178, 180, 191, 203, 207, 218, 244, 271, 286, 338–39
Abrahamic community, Abrahamic communities, 22–23, 110, 133, 143, 153–54, 160, 193, 301, 316, 326; a.k.a. Abrahamic minorities, 19, 22, 271, 326; as the deep grammar of the Gospel and the biblical drama, 23, 25, 133, 135–36, 145, 153–54, 161, 301; —, and Pope Francis, 135–36, 160
Abrahamic tension, ix, 23, 25, 87, 92, 94, 99, 107, 143–47, 179, 210
accompaniment, 32, 267
accountability, 16, 76, 78, 124, 130, 218–19, 288, 315
acculturation, 23, 60, 108, 153
activism, xi, xiii, 3–4, 6–7, 18, 20, 41, 44, 50, 57, 63, 79, 135, 139, 181, 195, 199, 213, 217, 236, 280–81, 288, 290, 300, 303, 340–41
adoptionism, 349
advocacy, xv, 4, 18, 60, 73, 93, 103, 135, 202, 212–16, 219–27, 231–32, 244–45, 253, 279, 284, 288, 334
Afghanistan, 58, 338

afterlife, the, 168, 297
agriculture, 65, 140, 204, 262
Aguirre, Gilberto, xi
Alabama, USA, 266
Alberigo, Giuseppe, 303–4, 319, 336–37, 366
Alexandria, Egypt, 24, 108, 175, 333
allegiance. *See* loyalty, allegiance
Allen, John L., Jr., 124, 126, 322, 324
Allison, Dale C., 356–57
Allman, Mark J., 352
Americans, 121, 201, 231, 324
Americas, 250, 323, 348
Amish, 60, 298
Amsterdam, Netherlands, 342
Anabaptism, Anabaptists, ix, xii, xiv, 59–60, 298, 303, 306, 341, 348
Anabaptist Mennonite Biblical Seminary (AMBS), 295
anarchism, 246
anathema, 38
angels, 52, 140, 164–65, 174, 329
anger, 252, 254–55, 258, 355
Answer to Faustus a Manichean, 351, 353
anthropology, 87, 210, 318, 358; cultural, 262; neuro-, 260, 262, 273; relational, 235
anti-clericalism, 128
antitheses. *See* dyads, dyadic analysis
antiwar activism, 217, 289
Antonello, Pierpaolo, 358, 360–61
apartheid, 211, 266, 301

396

Apologeticum, 301
Appadurai, Arjun, 112, 313–14, 318–19
Aquinas, Thomas, xi, 2, 43, 77, 229–30, 239, 249–50, 345–46, 348, 350–52, 365
Arendt, Hannah, 221, 343
Argentina, 160
arms reduction, 268, 270–71, 274
asceticism, 178–79
Asia, 59, 108, 125, 171, 173, 323, 326
assimilation, assimilationism, 17, 21, 23, 33, 101, 104, 108–9, 118, 143–44, 147, 151, 153, 163, 165, 179–80, 214–15, 217, 221
Assisi, Italy, 58–59, 61–63, 306
Athanasius, 332
atheism, 51, 55
Athenians, 175
Atran, Scott, 358
atrocities, 178, 289, 328
Augustine of Hippo, xi, xiv, 69–78, 114, 163, 174, 181–90, 194, 196, 206, 249–52, 271, 273, 297, 305, 308–9, 321, 334–37, 339, 348, 350–53, 362
Augustinianism, Augustinians, 120, 183, 186, 309, 320–21, 334–36
Australia, 103, 319
authoritarianism, 84, 159
autochthony, 116, 319

Babel, 140–41
Babylon, Babylonian exile, 24–25, 105, 129, 145–47, 149, 163–64, 188, 190, 200, 214, 233, 321
banishment, 173–74
banquet, eschatological, 137, 204
baptism, 1, 26, 29, 59, 98, 102, 128, 200, 247
barbarians, 75, 152
Barber, Benjamin R., 314
Barrett, David B., 318
Beatitudes, the, 236–37, 239, 265
Bellah, Robert N., 260, 358, 360

Bender, Harold S., 307
Benedict XVI, Pope, 14, 95, 197, 237–38, 302, 307, 324, 344, 347
Bennett, John C., 341
Bent, Norman, xi
Berbers, 103
Berger, Peter, 331
Bergoglio, Jorge, Cardinal, SJ. *See* Francis, Pope
Berrigan, Daniel, SJ, 6, 289
Berrigan, Philip, 289
Betz, Hans Dieter, 354, 356
biculturalism. *See* hybridity, hybrid identities
Birmingham, Alabama, USA, 266
blasphemy, 340
Boniface, Count, 187, 351
Bontrager, Herman, x
borders, boundaries, 15, 21, 26, 58, 64–65, 72, 75, 86, 92–93, 99–101, 103, 109, 112, 127, 136, 177, 199, 201, 206, 209, 216, 222–31, 233, 262, 317, 338, 343–46
Bordoni, Linda, 299
Boundary Waters Canoe Area Wilderness, Minnesota, USA, 223
Boyarin, Daniel and Jonathan, 24, 102–5, 113, 116–17, 301, 315–16, 319–20, 333, 340
Boyle, John, xiii
Brady, Bernard, xiii
Brah, Avtar, 115, 174, 318–19, 333
Brandt, Willy, 268
bravery, 83, 91
Brazal, Agnes M., 338, 343–44
Braziel, Jana Evans, 301, 313, 317–18
Brazil, xi, 6, 19, 125, 271, 324, 326
Bridgefolk, xii, 17, 310, 364–65
Bruner, Frederick Dale, 354, 357
Buddha, the, 264
Buddhism, 58
Buell, Denise Kimber, 176, 329, 332–34
Buenos Aires, Argentina, 134

398 A Pilgrim People

Bühlmann, Walbert, OFM, 124, 322
bullying, 360

Cahill, Lisa Sowle, xiii
Cain, 255–56, 293
Caldwell, Dan, 352
caliphate, Islamic, 110
Called Together to be Peacemakers, 12–13, 61, 63, 274, 281, 299, 307–8, 364
calling. *See* vocation
Calvin, John, 59, 77, 119, 308
Calvinism, 250, 309
Canada, 223, 323–24
Canning, Raymond, 309
canon law, 124
canonization, 247
capital punishment, 14, 76, 299
Capizzi, Joseph, 365
Cappadocia, 173
Caribbean, 125, 257, 264, 323
Carvalho, Corrine, xiii
Cartwright, Michael G., 316
Cassius Dio, 170, 332
casuistry, casuists, 265
Catechism of the Catholic Church, 308, 320, 352
Catholic Nonviolence Initiative (CNI), xiii
Catholic Peacebuilding Network (CPN), xiii
Catholic social teaching, 7–8, 16, 20, 27, 31, 35–36, 43, 50–51, 57, 62, 65, 79–80, 82, 85, 88, 94, 104, 118, 128–29, 134, 160, 215–16, 220, 222, 225, 233, 259, 274–75, 302–3, 310, 357
Catholic Worker, 345
Catholicism, Roman Catholic Church: official teaching, xii, 7, 15, 31, 34, 36–37, 39–40, 43, 45–49, 51, 56, 62, 80, 85, 110, 122–23, 134, 190, 216, 221–22, 224–25, 238, 240, 250, 276–77, 280–82, 290–91, 307, 342–43, 357; scandal in, 1–4, 276

Cavadini, John, xi, 336
Cavanaugh, William, xiii
Câmara, Dom Hélder, Archbishop, xi, 6, 19, 22, 271, 300, 326, 362
Cedar Revolution, 301
Celsus, 169, 178, 332
Centesimus Annus, 50–52, 55–56, 91, 240, 297, 302, 305–7, 310, 348
Central America, x, xvi, 7, 300
CEPAD, xi
Charismatic movement, 124
Charlottesville, Virginia, USA, 211–12
Chenoweth, Erica, 244, 349
Childress, James F., 365
Chile, 301
China, 266, 268
Christendom, 26, 97, 124, 130, 162, 181, 321, 361
Christianity and Social Progress, 304
Christian Realism. *See* realism, Realism: Christian
Christiansen, Drew, SJ, xii, 36–37, 39, 296, 298, 302–3, 337
Christifideles Laici, 310
Chrysostom, John, 170, 338
Church of the Brethren, 10, 60, 363–64
Church, the: as friend accompanying humanity, 42, 233; as global, 15–16, 21, 26–27, 35, 57, 65, 90, 94–95, 101–2, 113, 121, 124–26, 199; as hospital, 184, 277; as household of God, 13; as no longer a cultural region, 122; as pilgrim people, 2, 15, 23–27, 33, 79, 104, 110, 114, 131, 133, 136, 153, 155, 161, 163, 174, 189–90, 192, 214, 234–35, 319, 327; renewal of, 20, 133, 154; as sacrament of salvation and human unity, 23, 35–36, 131, 136, 139, 153, 162–63, 171–72, 185, 190–92, 327; as sign and instrument of peace, 63, 191, 193;

as transnational nation, 106–7, 111–12, 163, 170, 175, 177, 179, 200, 217, 234, 275, 334; unity of, 1, 9, 15–16, 61–62, 90, 123–24, 136, 156, 158, 163, 172, 191, 193, 274, 276–79, 281, 283, 286, 291, 294, 363
Cicero, 250, 351
circumcision, 113, 143, 205
citizenship, 26, 114, 164, 172, 174–75, 180, 188, 194, 196, 200, 204, 222, 275, 341–42
civil disobedience, 225, 230, 234, 267
Civil Rights Movement, USA, 19, 237, 266, 301
civilization, 65, 79
civilization of love, 42, 56, 64–65, 79–80, 83, 85–86, 88, 90–92, 94, 157, 310
clash of civilizations, 41, 58, 85–86, 93, 96, 122, 261–63, 265, 269–70, 293
Clement of Alexandria, 175–76, 333
Clement of Rome, 338
clergy, 98, 204, 240
Clifford, James, 108, 302, 317–18, 320, 333
climate change, 100, 136
coercion, 18, 76, 83, 90, 102, 105, 213, 246, 248, 352
Cold War, 1, 34, 41, 44, 48, 55, 210, 253, 280
colonialism, 92–93, 126–27; post- 84
common good, the, xv, 3, 5, 7, 19–20, 23, 34, 42–44, 56–57, 68, 76–77, 82, 85, 93, 96, 98, 105, 129, 135–36, 140, 146, 154, 158, 180, 193, 200–201, 214, 216, 218, 229, 233, 249, 275, 280, 334, 351, 357
commonwealth of humanity, 33, 163, 178, 222, 301
communism, 41, 51, 53, 55, 237
communitarianism, 17, 86, 340, 357
compassion, 92, 98, 142, 243, 258
Compendium of the Social Doctrine of the Church, 79, 310

Conferencia del Episcopado Mexicano, 342
conflict transformation, conflict resolution, 8, 49, 54, 268, 298, 346
Confucianism, 58
Congregation for the Doctrine of the Faith (CDF), 307
Connor, "Bull," 266
conquest, 10, 79, 92–93, 208, 211, 250, 348, 350
conscientious objection, 10, 17, 39, 277, 280, 291, 348
conscription, military, 17
Constantine, 32, 78, 188–90, 247, 321, 332
Constantinianism, xiv, 247, 319, 326, 346
consumerism, consumer capitalism, 51, 57, 210, 232, 305
counterculturalism, 17, 32, 96, 105, 120, 128–29, 152, 163, 179, 215
Contra Celsum, 331, 334
Contra Faustum Manichaeum, 351, 353
contraception, 156
conversion, converts, 34, 56, 76, 113, 127, 164, 167–68, 212, 252, 277, 290, 296, 319, 331–32, 350
Coptic Orthodoxy, 123
Cornelius, 123
Cornell, Tom, 290, 303, 318, 366
Costa Rica, 342
Council of Trent, 190, 306
covenant, covenanted identity, 94, 142–43, 145–46, 357
covetousness, 66
cowardice, 56
creative minorities, xv, 4, 19, 148, 150, 185, 300, 316
creatureliness, 207
creeds, 138, 196, 218, 243, 320
cross, the, 26, 56, 63, 106, 114, 242, 244, 267, 295, 300, 316
crucifixion, 13, 33, 59, 114, 140, 152, 243–44, 312, 349

cruelty, 76, 353
crusades, 10, 138, 195, 287–88
Cuban Missile Crisis, 38
Cullmann, Oscar, 326–27
cultural imperialism. *See* imperialism: cultural
cultures. *See* multiculturalism; vulnerable communities, cultures and peoples
Cushman, Thomas, 328
Cusimano, Maryann K., 314
Cyprian, 99, 173, 333

Daniel (biblical), 129, 146, 164, 188, 200, 214, 233
David, King, Davidic monarchy, 24, 145, 208
Davies, W. D., 356
Davis, Henry, SJ, 347
Day, Dorothy, 6, 39, 278, 290
De Civitate Dei, 335–36, 353
De Indis Recenter Inventis, 351
De Libero Arbitrio, 350
De Sermone Domini in Monte, 353
Dear, John, 334
death penalty. *See* capital punishment
Decade to Overcome Violence, 62, 281–82, 299, 307–8, 364
Decalogue, 66, 347
Decree on Ecumenism, 319
deforestation, 136
demagoguery, 349
democracy, democratization, 18, 50, 83–84, 121, 128–29, 159, 218, 269, 301, 324, 342
demography, demographic trends, 121, 125, 127, 232, 325, 331
Dennis, Marie, xiii, 303
Deuteronomic juncture, 326, 346
dialogue and negotiation, 34, 42, 54, 89–90, 134, 260, 273, 304
Dialogue with Trypho, 332
diaspora, xv, 23–27, 29, 31, 33–36, 94–101, 103–9, 111–21, 127–29, 146–47, 149, 155, 158–59, 162–63, 167–68, 170, 174, 177, 179–80, 188–91, 193, 196, 199–200, 213–15, 217, 225, 227, 233–35, 275, 292, 301–2, 312–21, 324, 330–33, 337, 341, 344; as conceptual framing device, 23–27, 31–36; creative tensions of life in, 25, 99, 107, 147, 179, 200; and globalization, 25, 94–95, 99, 101, 111, 118–19, 127, 314; Jeremianic model, xvi, 316; Jewish, 24, 103, 105, 108, 113, 116, 162–63, 168, 170, 191, 301, 316–17, 320, 331; and political theory, 103–4, 111, 116, 129, 215–16; power of, 103, 105, 120–21, 129–30, 213, 315
Dicastery for Promoting Integral Human Development, xiii
Dicken, Peter, 314
dictatorship, dictators, 41, 137, 201, 280, 324
Didache, 355
Dignitatis Humanae, 321
DiMeglio, Richard P., 352
Diognetus, 171–72, 174, 176, 179–80, 189, 332–33
disarmament, 41, 43, 45, 285
discernment, xii, 11, 39, 119, 179, 236, 238, 273, 275, 282, 341
discipleship, 10, 13, 17, 59, 62, 118, 128, 240, 247, 259, 264, 274, 292, 353
discourses, ethical. *See* translation across ethical systems
dispersal, dispersion, 24, 33, 100, 103, 107–9, 112, 114, 116, 118, 127, 141, 149, 171–72, 302, 317, 332
displacement, 109, 113, 116, 148, 202, 244, 344
dissent, 78, 361
diversity-in-unity, unity-in-diversity, 88, 90, 156, 221, 276–77
Dodaro, Robert, 336

Index 401

domination, 42, 79, 95, 103, 117, 144, 149, 152, 155, 184, 186, 208, 211–12, 226, 245, 336, 341, 353
Dominicans, 303. *See also* Aquinas, Thomas
Donahue, John R., 346
Donald, Merlin, 260, 263–64, 358–61
Donatism, 75–76
doublemindedness, 165
Douglass, James, 290
downtrodden, the, 137
Dreher, Rod, 328
Driedger, Leo, 300, 341
dualism, 172, 342
duality without dualism, 342
Dufoix, Stéphane, 109, 313, 317–18, 320
Dunning, Benjamin H., 179–80, 330, 332, 334
Durnbaugh, Donald, 363
dyads, dyadic analysis, 252, 254, 283–84, 354–55

ecclesiology, xiv–xv, 2, 4, 6, 22, 57, 62, 90, 99, 107, 113, 158–59, 163, 170, 177, 180, 183–85, 193–94, 199–200, 215, 217, 267, 278, 284, 291–92, 335, 366; diaspora, 106–9, 111–21, 170, 199; as integral to Christian peacemaking, 2–3, 5–6, 153, 234, 267
eclecticism, 187
ecology, human, 269
economics, 56, 88, 116, 314
ecumenism, ecumenical dialogue, xi, xiv, 10–11, 16–17, 60–62, 194, 253, 276–82, 284, 286, 288–89, 292, 297, 307, 319, 321–22, 337, 354, 363–65
egotism, 45, 52, 64, 70, 80, 144, 195, 226, 240, 268, 349
Egypt, 24, 66, 108, 144, 204, 208–9, 266, 301
Eliot, T. S., 1, 189–90, 199
elitism, 129, 131

enemies, 13, 22, 34–35, 55, 69, 74–78, 93, 101, 152, 181–82, 184, 194–95, 197, 230–31, 237, 239, 241, 244, 248–49, 252–53, 255, 257–59, 261–66, 268–70, 272, 275, 277, 347, 352, 362. *See also* love: of enemy
enforcement, 223, 225, 246
Enlightenment, the, 92, 211, 239
entrepreneurship, 85, 100, 232, 314
epidemics, 167
epistemology, 297
Epp Weaver, Alain, xii, 316
Erga Migrantes Caritas Christi, 343
Erikson, Erik H., 297
escapism, 115
eschatology, 155, 184–85, 191, 258, 300, 349; eschatological tension, 23, 139, 184–85
Escobar, Rafaél, x
Essenes, 257
ethics: Christian, xv, 8, 18–19, 22, 25, 27, 34, 36, 47, 65–67, 79, 99, 104, 107, 116, 128, 199, 253, 258, 280, 291, 308; development, x; of power, 129; social, xv, 8, 19, 25, 27, 36, 47, 57, 65, 79, 99, 104, 107, 116, 118, 128, 139, 163, 214–15, 291, 306, 316; utilitarian, 83; virtue, 73; of war and peace, 36, 47, 269, 278, 280
Ethiopian Orthodoxy, 123
ethnic cleansing, 213
ethnic reasoning, 176–77, 332, 334
ethnicity, ethnic groups, 93, 103, 106–7, 168, 176, 318, 333
Eucharist, 20, 203
Eurocentrism, 122–23, 321
Europe, 25, 51–52, 59–60, 81, 86, 91, 96–97, 105, 108–9, 122–26, 162, 170, 202, 216, 232, 237, 280, 300, 321, 323, 337, 348, 363–64
euthanasia, 38
Evangelicals, 194
Evangelii Gaudium, 131, 133, 153–54, 199, 296–97, 325–28, 357

Evangelii Nuntiandi, 29, 31–32, 128, 301, 305, 325, 340
evangelism, 154, 331
Evangelium Vitae, 299
evangelization, 5, 29, 31, 110, 123, 128, 131, 133, 154, 167, 209, 252, 305, 327
evil, evils, 14, 20, 37, 44, 48, 56, 69, 75, 77, 102, 130, 197, 218, 231, 233, 241–42, 248, 250, 252–53, 256, 258, 262, 267, 272, 303, 348, 351, 353
exceptions, moral, role of, 9, 12–14, 44, 129, 247–49, 252, 275, 278–79, 282–83, 307
excommunication, 279, 294
exile, exiles, 24, 32, 99, 105, 109, 116, 145–49, 163–64, 171, 173, 175, 179–80, 183, 188–89, 193, 200, 207, 214, 233, 235, 316, 319–20, 330, 333
exodus, 148–49, 205
Exsul familia, 342
Ezra, 150

Faggioli, Massimo, xiii, 322
fair trade, 337
Finnegan, Amy, xiii
Fisher, Roger, 346
Fitzgerald, Allan D., OSA, 308, 334–35
Flores, Isaías, x
Flores, Ovidio, x
force: military, 12; police 12, 219; use of 2, 12, 20, 26, 37, 39, 46, 49–50, 53–55, 58, 97, 102, 109, 115, 119, 139, 159, 181, 201, 212, 219, 231, 236, 238, 241, 249–51, 253, 277, 285, 300, 302, 352. *See also* coercion; enforcement; nonviolence: power of
Ford, John C., SJ, 303, 305
forgiveness, 7, 37, 47, 58, 131, 162, 170, 218, 241, 253, 268, 296–97, 328
formation of peacemakers, 3–5, 8–9, 49, 56–57, 150, 217, 234, 267, 271, 275
Francis of Assisi, 58
Francis, Pope, 14, 62, 131, 133–36, 138, 153–58, 160, 199, 206, 231–33, 236–41, 260, 266, 269, 277, 285, 296–97, 299, 303, 322, 325–28, 339–40, 346–48, 357, 361, 365
Free Choice of the Will, 350
freedom, inseparable from truth, 51–52, 55, 57, 81–82, 88
Friesen, Duane K., xii, 217–20, 227, 295, 300, 316, 341–42, 365
fundamentalism, 16, 156, 242

Gandhi, Mahatma, 3, 157, 237, 297
Gardner, John, 360–61
Gaudet Mater Ecclesia, 319, 336
Gaudium et Spes, 7, 32, 38, 42, 48, 50, 191–92, 240, 290, 296–97, 301–4, 308, 319, 326, 328, 334, 337, 348, 357, 362, 364, 366
Gbowee, Leymah, 237
Gellner, Ernest, 318–19
genealogy, 102, 111, 113, 117, 141, 315, 341, 356
Geneva, Switzerland, 22, 136, 140–41, 143–44, 150, 203, 326; CU, 5
genius, phenomenon of, 264
genocide, 26, 37–38, 102, 258, 325
Gentiles, 64, 72, 75, 113, 119, 122–23, 151–52, 163, 169, 171, 175, 195, 244, 265, 269–70, 315
geopolitics, 41–42, 45, 50, 83, 266, 268
Germany, 125, 212, 268, 302
ghettoization, 98, 104, 110
Gilgamesh Epic, The, 262–63, 265, 270, 360–61
Girard, René, 263, 358, 360–61
Girardians, 358, 361
Gittins, Anthony J., 337
global Christianity, 16, 26, 110, 118, 124–26, 323–24, 337

Global South, 26–27, 41, 84, 121, 124–26, 133, 135, 323
globalism, 21–22, 314
globalization, 15, 25, 35, 41–42, 51, 65, 80, 85–86, 88, 90, 94–95, 99–101, 104, 108, 111–12, 115, 117–19, 124, 127, 133–34, 157, 190, 209–11, 270, 304, 312–14, 317–18
Gnosticism, gnosis, 116, 150
Godrej, Farah, 297
Golden Rule, 93
Goldsmith, Edward, 314
Goldstone, Matthew, 355
Gorbachev, Mikhail, 50
Goshen College, x
Gospel: Abrahamic shape of, 150–51, 160; as challenging, 21, 25–26, 78, 97–98, 135; joy of, 138, 160; peace at the heart of, 13, 63–64, 274, 277; vision of peace, 13, 33, 63–64, 134, 156, 217, 274. *See also* evangelism; evangelization; inculturation; proclamation of the Gospel
Gospel of Life, The, 299
Gospel of Matthew, 64, 75, 129, 200, 205, 237, 248, 252–54, 256–57, 279, 283–85, 291, 327, 353–54, 356
Goss, Jean, 6, 39, 290, 303, 366
Goss-Mayr, Hildegard, xi, 6, 39, 290, 303, 366
governance, xv, 42–43, 76, 100, 181, 233, 246, 270
Gratissimam Sane, 310
Greeks, 175
Gregory Nazianzen, 173
Grisez, Germain Gabriel, 326
Groody, Daniel G., 343
Grotius, Hugo, 250, 351
Guatemala, x, 11, 211, 268, 324, 362
Guelich, Robert A., 355
guesthood, 2, 199, 201–2, 205, 208–9, 211, 213, 227, 230–31; ethic of, 201–2, 213, 235; metaphysics of, 205–9; and policy advocacy, 214, 226–34; practices of, 199, 213; resistance to, 200, 206–7, 209, 211–12; spirituality of, 208
Gushee, David P., 327, 353, 363
Gypsies. *See* Roma, the

Hamilton, the musical, 214
Harrington, Daniel J., 354
Harvest of Justice is Sown in Peace, The, 49–50, 250, 296, 302, 305, 352
hatred, 12, 56, 75–76, 255–58, 265, 356
Hauerwas, Stanley, 57, 300, 306, 312, 316, 328, 341, 349, 363, 365
Haughton, Rosemary, 227–30, 343, 345–46
heaven and earth, new, 117, 137, 140, 207
Hebrews: ancient, 6–7, 66, 105, 140, 164, 202, 207
Heidegger, Martin, 96
Hellenization, 108, 168–69, 315
Henrich, Joseph, 358–59
heresy, 10, 39, 72, 304, 332, 348, 352
Hermas, 164–67, 171, 174, 189, 329–30, 350
hermeneutics: of analogy, 356; of charity, 22; of suspicion, xiv
heroism, 19, 34, 39, 63, 75, 78, 197, 219, 232, 277, 280, 348
Herr, Robert, and Judy Zimmerman, xii
Hershberger, Guy F., 18–19, 316, 341
Heyer, Kristin E., 343–44, 346
Higueros, Mario, 11
Himes, Kenneth R., OFM, 352
Hispanics, 195
historic peace churches (HPCs). *See* peace church: historic peace churches; Church of the Brethren; Mennonitism, Mennonites; Quakers

holiness, 162, 259, 277; personal, 39, 49, 240; universal call to, 13, 63–64, 239–41, 244–45, 248, 272, 285, 293, 303, 347
Hollenbach, David, SJ, 211, 249, 340, 343, 350
Hollerich, Michael, xiii
Holocaust, the, 220
Holton, R. J., 314
Holy Spirit, 3, 33, 79, 138, 184, 190, 243–44
homeland, 24, 33, 83, 99, 114–18, 147, 149, 163, 165–66, 171–75, 192, 195, 211, 317, 320, 330; heaven as, 114–17, 133, 137–38, 174–75, 180, 182, 184–85, 188, 192, 195–96, 297, 320
homelessness, 67–68, 166, 199, 202, 227, 320
homicide. *See* killing, homicide
homogenization, 21, 88, 100–102, 104, 106, 136, 156, 210
homosexuality, 156
Honduran Mennonite Church, x
Honduras, x
hospitality, xvi, 94, 110, 142, 144, 152, 173, 177, 199–209, 211, 213–16, 218, 226–31, 337–40, 343–46; ancient codes of, 142, 209; biblical, 200, 202–9, 227; character of, 201–2; in the Christian tradition, 200, 202–3, 227; ethic of, 110, 211–12, 226, 230; houses of, 227, 345; and identity, 211–12, 231; and ownership, 206–7, 211, 227–30, 345; politics of, 199–201, 213–22, 224–35; practices of, 173, 177, 199–200, 218, 228; as source of security, 94, 144. *See also* guesthood
household of God, 106
Huebner, Chris K., 297
Hughes, Richard T., 298
humanitarian intervention, 37, 281
humanization, 256, 262, 361

human rights. *See* rights: human
Hurtado, Larry W., 349
Hussein, Saddam, 201
Hutterites, 60, 298
Hutus, 1
hybridity, hybrid identities, 109, 119, 165, 168

idealism: accusations of, 43, 55, 79, 158–59, 241, 253, 258–59, 284; political 79
identity: Abrahamic, paradox of, 23, 34, 110, 115, 120, 136, 145, 152–54, 158; Christian or Catholic, 10, 26, 93, 129, 174, 176, 211, 218, 233; complicating not suppressing, 212–13; diaspora, 34–35, 94, 105–6, 109, 112, 117–18, 168, 170, 174, 176–77, 179–80, 190, 193, 200, 233; dual or bicultural, 109, 119, 164–66, 168, 193; ethnic, 9; and globalization, 86, 100–101, 122; Jewish, 103; local, 199; oppositional, 217, 246, 263; peace church, peacemaking, ix, 13, 106, 153, 193, 277, 298; preservation of, 33, 87, 93–94, 105, 134, 154, 200, 210–12, 223–24, 230–31, 318, 345; primary or core, 5, 10, 33–34, 113, 118, 146, 218. *See also* covenant, covenanted identity; ethnicity; hybridity, hybrid identities; loyalty, allegiance; nationalism; particularity; patriotism; race; tribalism
idolatry, 66, 99, 112, 119, 147, 164, 188, 200, 214, 233, 243–44, 340, 362
illiteracy, 84
Im, Chandler H., 170, 332
imagination, role of, 6, 29, 42, 50, 64, 79, 85, 103, 120, 137, 158, 174, 183, 257, 265, 267, 292, 294, 298, 314, 355–56, 359

immigrants. *See* migrants
immigration policy, xiii, 211, 215–16, 220–21, 225, 227, 232, 234, 343. *See also* hospitality: politics of
imperialism, 22, 34, 36, 41, 50, 54–55, 78–79, 81, 83, 92–94, 96, 102, 110, 126, 143, 145–46, 177–78, 183–84, 188–89, 246–47, 297, 301, 314, 350; cultural, 22, 94, 102, 110, 126
incarnation, 2, 9, 116, 157, 184, 192, 203, 205, 242–43, 273, 332, 353
inculturation, 2, 15–16, 20, 36, 90, 110, 123, 127, 152–53, 158, 200
independent initiatives, 268
India, 115, 300
indigenous peoples, 7, 103, 116, 199, 201, 211–12, 315, 319
individualism, 85–86, 97, 134, 157, 259, 357
Indochina, 217
Indonesia, 58
industrialization, 44, 50
infanticide, 173
injustice, 4, 9, 14, 18, 21, 43–44, 50, 57, 63, 136, 152, 180, 183, 197, 202, 237, 241, 250, 267–68, 277, 282, 285, 290
Inquisition, the, 38, 290
institutionalization, 43, 90–91, 159, 270
Instruction on the Love of Christ towards Migrants, 343
integrationism, 159
interdependence, 7, 42–43, 65, 82, 104, 123, 207, 269, 322
interiorization of ethics, 7, 120, 254, 321
intermarriage, 72, 150
International Ecumenical Peace Convocation, Kingston 2011, 282
internationalism, 287
interreligious dialogue, 32, 58–60, 89, 307
Iraq, 201, 209, 250, 338

Ireneus, 332
Irvin, Dale T., 174, 333
Isaiah, 140, 147–51, 173, 245, 325, 327, 337
Islam, 58, 93, 110, 203
Israel, ancient, 3, 24, 65, 67, 108, 113–14, 116, 119, 144–45, 147–50, 204–5, 207–8, 242, 289, 307, 320, 327
Israel, modern, 102, 116, 174, 265–66
Italian Peninsula, 114
Italy, 125, 290

Jamaica, 62, 364
Jameson, Fredric, 314
Jeffers, James S., 329
Jefferson, Thomas, 211
Jenkins, Philip, 26, 124, 126–27, 301, 322, 324, 337
Jeremias, Joachim, 354
Jerusalem, 71, 145, 147, 178, 189, 204, 245–46, 266, 349
Jesuits, 36, 96
Jesus Christ: according to the Gospel of Matthew, 257, 279, 283, 285, 291, 327, 355; as hinge of history, 272; Jesus of Nazareth, 9, 78, 147, 150, 242–43, 273; source of nonviolence, 9–10, 33, 55, 78, 243, 293. *See also* lordship of Christ; natural law: Christic reading of
Jewish people, 24, 72, 102–5, 108–10, 113, 116, 145, 149, 168–70, 175–76, 188, 212, 232, 243–44, 307, 315, 319–21, 329, 331–32, 351
jingoism, 74, 112, 209
Jipp, Joshua W., 203, 209, 338–40
John Paul II, Pope, 5, 14, 34, 36, 45, 48, 50, 54, 56–61, 64–65, 79–80, 86, 88, 90–91, 101, 133, 139, 154, 162, 200, 210–12, 233, 237, 240, 260, 296–97, 299, 302–7, 309–10, 314, 326, 328, 340, 347–48, 362
John the Baptist, 48, 169

John XXIII, Pope, 20, 37, 39, 42, 114, 190, 259, 304, 319, 336, 342, 357
Johnson, James Turner, 365
Johnson, Paul, 331
Johnson, Todd M., 318
Jordan, Clarence, 355
Jubilee (biblical), 204, 206, 208
Jubilee Year 2000, 5, 162
Judah, 145, 147
Judaism, 24, 60, 66, 102–5, 107, 113, 116–17, 145–46, 162, 168–70, 174, 176, 203, 257, 307, 315; Judaic studies, 116
just peace, 11, 62, 159, 219, 253, 270, 275, 282, 291, 293, 303, 346–47, 352, 354, 364
just peacemaking, 234, 253, 259, 267–71, 275–76, 279–81, 285, 291, 293–94, 342, 354–55, 361–64; normative practices, 234, 267–71, 279, 281, 342, 361, 363
just policing, xiii, 9, 20, 275, 283, 293, 296, 299, 362, 364–66
just war theory, just war tradition, xiii, xv, 9–10, 12, 14, 37–38, 41, 43–49, 53, 62, 181, 194, 219, 238–39, 241, 247, 249–51, 253, 255, 270–71, 275–80, 282–89, 291–94, 302, 305, 307, 334–37, 346, 348, 351–52, 354, 362–63, 365–66; case for, 245–52; criteria; —, civilian and noncombatant immunity, 46, 251, 351–52; —, comparative justice, 250; —, jus ad bellum, 250–51, 351; —, jus in bello, 250–51, 285, 351–52; —, jus post bellum, 250; —, just cause, 130, 250–51, 277, 285, 351; —, last resort, 20, 37, 41, 50, 219, 225, 230, 251, 274–75, 307, 351, 363; —, legitimate or due authority, 250, 351; —, probability of success, 251; —, proportionality, 46, 251; —, right intention, 250–51, 351;
growing skepticism concerning in Catholic teaching, 10, 14, 37–38, 45–46, 48–49, 62, 238, 249, 275, 282, 284–85, 288–89, 307; pacifist use of, xv, 9–10, 48, 219, 241, 278, 284, 286–89, 291, 366; stringent, 49, 278, 288, 302
justice: as condition of peace, 7, 11, 40–41, 51, 54, 58, 63, 134–35, 158, 251, 268–69, 296; criminal, 217; definition of, ix, 235; economic, 13, 63, 150, 202, 274; egalatarian, 134; God's 143, 234, 258; limits of, 183; relational, 235; rough, through balance of power, 240; rules of, 68; social, 7, 16, 67–68, 73, 140, 176, 245; through forgiveness, 7; toward migrants, 221–22, 226, 233

Kauffman, Ivan, xii, 310, 364–65
Khan, Khan Abdul Ghaffar, 237
Khanna, Parag, 313
killing, homicide, 1, 56, 76–77, 104, 140, 194, 239, 245, 249, 263, 275–77, 279, 283, 288, 347, 349, 352, 363, 365
King, Martin Luther, Jr., 19, 237, 266
kingdom of God. *See* Reign of God
Kingston, Jamaica, 282
Klaassen, Walter, 306
Klassen, John, Abbot, OSB, xii
Klein, Michael, xiii
Koenig, John, 203, 338
Kolb, Robert, 329
Kraybill, Donald B., 300, 341
Kraybill, Paul, 59–60
Kreider, Alan, xii, 332, 350
Krisetya, Mesach, 58–59
Kroc Institute for International Peace Studies, University of Notre Dame, xiii
Kropf, Marlene, xii
Ku Klux Klan (KKK), 301

LaCugna, Catherine, xi
Lakota, the, 103
Lamech, 255, 286, 288, 293
Lampe, Peter, 169, 330–32
languages, ethical. *See* translation across ethical systems
Latin America, x–xi, 41, 59, 96, 125, 128, 201, 323, 344. *See also* Caribbean; Central America
Laudato Si', 206, 269, 339–40
laxism, 119
Lazarus, 140, 169, 338
Lebanon, 301
Lederach, John Paul, 302
legalism, 66, 242, 356
Leo XIII, Pope, 50, 52, 222, 300, 343–44
lex talionis, 255–56, 289
Leyerle, Blake, xi
liberalism, 85, 92, 102–3, 109, 269, 335
liberation, 16, 41, 209; God as liberator, 66, 209; messianic, 242; movements for, 41, 50–51, 91; nonviolent, 149, 245, 258–59; theology of, 16, 41
Liberia, 237
libertarianism, 81, 83
Lieu, Judith, 331
linguistics, 111, 227, 318
literalism, 242, 355
liturgy, 10, 113, 119, 138, 157, 192, 218, 306, 321, 326
lobbying, 10, 121
localization, 157
Long, D. Stephen, 341
Lord of the Rings, The, 130, 325
lordship of Christ, 3, 9, 23, 26, 33, 55, 59, 95, 98, 112, 114, 151, 153, 243–44, 277
Louisville Institute, xiv
love: of enemy, 75, 197, 252, 259, 265; —, political relevance of, xv, 18, 105, 214, 241, 259–65, 267; of God, 68, 70–71, 76–77, 138, 308;
of neighbor, 35, 52, 56, 65–73, 75–80, 93, 101, 104, 112, 118, 181, 184, 194–95, 230, 248–49, 252, 255, 257, 275, 308; of one's own kind, 93, 99, 200, 245, 264–65, 269–70; proximate, 73–75, 92, 112, 249, 309; of self, 52, 65, 69–71, 73, 76–77, 181, 186, 209, 249, 252; of temporal goods, 69–70, 73, 181, 249, 252; trinitarian shape of, 78, 184, 260; undiscriminating, 75
loyalty, allegiance, 3, 22, 26, 33–34, 36, 59, 93, 107, 109–10, 112, 119, 147, 159, 164–66, 169, 174, 178–79, 185, 189, 194–95, 224, 233, 275, 278
Lucien, Richard, 205, 207, 339
Lumen Gentium, 133, 191, 240, 301, 319, 326, 337, 348
Luther, Martin, 59, 77
Lutheranism, 309
Luz, Ulrich, 356

Maccabees, 149
Maciel, Creuza, xi
MacMullen, Ramsey, 331
magisterium, the, 15, 37, 62, 80, 276
Maier, John R., 360–61
malnutrition, 84
mammals, 359
Manchala, Deenabandhu, 337
Mandela, Nelson, 266
Mander, Jerry, 314
Manichaeism, 351, 353
Manila, Philippines, 5
Manualism, 301, 313, 317–18, 347
Mao Zedong, 266
Marcellinus, 77, 187, 271, 309, 337, 350–51
Marcos, Ferdinand, 301
marginality, marginalization, 96, 103, 126, 151, 168, 202, 212–13, 270, 330–31, 340
Marincowitz, Leon, 361
Markus, Robert A., 335
Martens, John, xiii, 349

Marxism, 53–54, 306
Mason, Herbert, 314
Mater et Magistra, 259, 304, 342, 357
materialism, 305
materiality, 139
Maurin, Peter, 6
Maya, the, 211
McCarthy, Eli, xiii
McCormick, Patrick T., 337
McDonagh, Francis, 300
McManus, Philip, xi, 295
Mead, George Herbert, 260–61, 263–64, 358–61
Medieval period, 97, 181, 334
Mediterranean, 24, 149, 152
Meeks, Wayne A., 331
Mennonite Central Committee (MCC), x, xii, 60, 295
Mennonite World Conference (MWC), 11–12, 58–59, 61–62, 274, 281, 299, 307–8, 364
Mennonitism, Mennonites, x, 10, 12–13, 17–19, 59–63, 104–5, 217, 219–20, 277, 281, 288, 292, 298–99, 341, 363–64
mercy, 26, 72, 76–77, 107, 119–20, 131, 143, 152, 156, 237, 277
Merton, Thomas, 6, 289
messiah, 104, 148, 150, 174, 242–44, 349
metaphysics, 184, 203, 205–6
Methodism, Methodists, 57, 278, 280, 363–65
methodology, 22, 103, 181–83, 234
Mexico, 342–43
Meyer, Ben F., 349, 354
Micah, 173
middle axioms, 219, 232–33, 316, 342
migrants, 29, 31–33, 68, 96, 100, 144, 157, 165, 199, 202, 208–9, 214–16, 220–22, 224–27, 230–33, 330, 333, 343–44, 346–47; undocumented, 100, 224–25, 230. *See also* immigration policy

migration, 86, 99, 115, 174, 194, 208, 210, 224–25, 230, 235, 317–18, 330, 333, 337–38, 340, 343–44
militaries, military action, 12–13, 17, 37, 40, 46, 50, 52–53, 76, 83, 130, 144, 187, 244, 247, 250–52, 268, 275, 280–81, 284–85, 289, 301, 352, 354. *See also* force: military
militarism, 51, 219
Miller, Marlin E., 363
Milosovic, Slobodan, 301
mimesis, mimetic action, 260–64, 266, 358–61
Minucius Felix, 32
Miskito, the, 7
missiology, 170, 174
missionary work, missionaries, 22, 92, 98, 122, 126–27, 133, 154, 169, 194, 204, 321, 332, 337–38
Mittelman, James H., 314
Miyoshi, Masao, 314
modernity, 32, 42, 96, 159, 314
Modestus, 173
Moltmann, Jürgen, 320, 341
monasticism, 6, 187, 306
monotheism, 110
Montanists, 178
Moonies, 330
moral theology, 35, 65, 67, 73, 240–41. *See also* ethics: Christian
Moravians, xi, 11
Mormons, 330–31
Morrow, Duncan, 360–61
Moses, 66–67, 102, 147, 152, 204, 208, 257, 286, 346
Moucarry, Chawkat Georges, 207–8, 339–40
Mubarek, Hosni, 301
Mugabe, Robert, 324
Muhammad, 110
multiculturalism, 106
Murdi, the, 103
Muslims, 109–10, 211, 237
mutually assured destruction (MAD), 45

Nairobi, Kenya, 5
National Conference of Catholic Bishops (USA). *See* United States Conference of Catholic Bishops (USCCB)
nationalism, 1, 26, 34, 51, 64, 74, 79, 84–85, 101, 112, 144, 150, 159, 177, 179, 200, 209–11, 244, 275, 315, 318–19, 334
nationhood, 107, 109–12, 318
nations, defined in contrast with nation-states, 85–89, 101, 111–12
Native Americans, 319
nativism, 210–11
natural law, 25, 48, 63, 216, 220–21, 226, 228–30, 239–40, 244, 253, 259, 272–73, 284, 286; Christic reading of, 272; and "the grain of the universe," 19, 244, 300, 349
Navajo, the, 103
Nazareth, 9, 78, 147, 150, 203, 242–43, 245, 273
Nazism, 268, 300
negotiation. *See* dialogue and negotiation
Nehemiah, 150
Nelson Gingrich, Barbara, 363–64
Nelson-Pallmeyer, Jack, xiii
neuroanthropology, 260, 262, 273
neuroscience, 260, 273
Nicaragua, x–xi
Niebuhr, H. Richard, 119, 217, 320, 335, 341
Niebuhr, Reinhold, xv, 18, 104–5, 214, 240, 299, 315–16, 341, 348
Niebuhrianism, 105, 264
Nigeria, 125
Nisly, Weldon, xii
Nixon, Richard, 266, 268
Noah, 137, 141–42
nomads, nomadic life, 24, 94, 116–17, 144, 235, 262
nonresistance, 19, 256, 316, 341
nonviolence: active, 9–10, 13–14, 19–20, 36–37, 41, 47, 53–54, 57, 60, 62–63, 83, 90–91, 236, 238, 240, 256, 258, 274, 276, 278, 280, 282, 285, 293, 300; confessional, 10, 277, 284–85, 289, 293, 353, 363; conflicting through, 4, 8, 49, 156, 256, 274, 276; as the ethic of Jesus, 9–15, 18–19, 33–36, 55, 63, 105, 154, 181, 195–96, 231, 237, 242, 248, 258, 271, 273, 277, 293, 298, 302, 334; as first resort, 13, 278, 363; Gandhian, 19, 41, 244; Gospel, 237–38, 242, 266, 285, 346; institutionalizing, 91, 270; and just war as twin traditions, 10, 48, 238, 276, 280, 288, 351, 366; normative, xii, 12–15, 35, 53, 62, 274, 282, 291, 307; power of, 20, 53, 55, 60, 194, 237–38, 242, 252, 266, 271–72, 278, 300, 340; in public affairs, 36, 50, 215, 238, 240; and solidarity, 63, 81, 83, 90, 274, 300; strategic, 49, 54, 83, 90, 212–13, 231, 233, 257, 267, 275, 277–78, 300, 349; toward the truth, 9, 25, 54, 297
North America, x, 17, 27, 60, 103, 123, 125–26, 170, 217, 323
North Atlantic Treaty Organization (NATO), 301
Norway, 268
Nostra Aetate, 32

O'Donovan, Oliver, 74, 308–9, 335
O'Neill, William, SJ, 344
Oceania, 133
Ochoa, Juan Angel, x
Ochs, Peter, 116, 316, 319
Oden, Amy, 338–39
On Social Concern, 304
On the Condition of the Working Classes, 343
option for the poor, preferential, 233
Orange Revolution, 301
Orend, Brian, 333

Origen, 178–79, 331–32, 334
original sin, 55, 335
Oromo, the, 103
Osiek, Carolyn A., 329
Ottaviani, Alfredo, Cardinal, 38, 290–91, 303, 366
ownership, private property, 206–7, 211, 227–30, 345

Pacem in Terris, 302, 304, 342
pacifism, xv, 9–10, 14, 17–18, 20, 39, 47–48, 62, 105, 129, 184, 194, 219, 241, 247, 253, 258, 270, 275–80, 282–91, 293–94, 297–99, 304, 315, 341, 348, 354, 363, 365; case for Christian, 9–10, 242–45; Catholic, 39, 277–78, 289
paganism, 164, 169, 178, 195, 247, 331–32
Palawah, the, 103
Palestine, first-century, 108, 116, 149, 168, 266, 285, 320
Palestinians, 102, 319
papacy, the, 60, 79, 134, 160, 310
Parajón, Gustavo, xi
paroikoi. See resident aliens, *paroikoi*
particularity, 2, 21–22, 87, 89, 92–94, 101–2, 117, 157, 160, 176, 178, 200, 210–12, 221, 226, 316
particularity and universality, creative tension between, 87, 91, 93, 157, 200, 210–11
passivity, 48, 139, 213, 237, 256
pastors, pastoral leadership, xiv, 15–16, 18, 34, 43–44, 75, 124, 158, 160, 184, 187, 199, 220–21, 224, 241, 250, 275, 277–78, 292, 294, 341–43, 352; pastoral accommodation, 277
paternalism, 202
patriarchy, 167
patriotism, 74, 112, 202
patristics, xi, 32, 163, 170, 174, 177, 301, 338, 345

Paul, the apostle, 102–3, 114, 151–53, 169, 174, 196, 204, 209, 244, 256, 304, 315, 348
Paul VI, Pope, 2, 29, 31–33, 40–41, 43–44, 64, 79–80, 128, 202, 209, 296, 304–5, 310, 325, 328, 338, 340, 357
Pauline thought, 102–3
Pax Christi International, xiii, 6, 303, 347
peace: in Catholic social teaching, 7, 35–36, 43, 94, 118, 160, 274–75; definition of, 7–8, 40, 51–53, 63, 134, 155; —, author's, 8; as eirene, 7; as pax, 7; as shalom, 6–7, 13, 40, 105, 129, 146–47, 219; theology of; —, Catholic, xii, 6, 33, 36–37, 40, 48–49, 57, 65, 88, 90, 154, 160, 217, 275, 282, 291, 299, 334, 341, 357
peace church: Catholic, 2, 8, 12, 14–17, 25, 33, 35, 41, 45, 48, 63, 102, 118, 154, 182, 196, 276, 292, 298, 301; definition of, 9–15; —, author's, 13; historic peace churches (HPCs), 10–11, 16–17, 58, 60, 62, 104, 185, 215, 217, 220, 276–78, 280, 282, 285, 287–88, 291–93, 298, 309, 357, 363, 366
peacemaking, peacebuilding, x, xii–xiii, 2–9, 12–14, 16–18, 22, 26, 34, 36–37, 40–44, 48–49, 52, 54, 56–57, 60–64, 94, 104, 111, 128–29, 134–35, 137, 140, 153–60, 181–83, 193, 197, 199–200, 209, 212, 217, 219, 233–41, 244, 250, 252–53, 258–59, 266–72, 274–76, 279–82, 285, 287, 291, 293–94, 296, 298–300, 302–4, 307–9, 334–35, 341–42, 354–55, 357, 361–66; spirituality of, 49, 62
Pelagianism, 292
Pentagon, the, 58

Pentateuch, 113
Pentecost, 190, 218, 242–44, 310
Pentecostalism, 124, 127–28, 190
people-building, peacemaking as, 153–54, 156–57, 160, 271
peoplehood, 23, 134, 143, 153, 155, 176
persecution, 18, 62, 75, 98, 127–28, 137, 153, 167, 172–73, 232, 253, 313
Pew Forum on Religion and Public Life, 125, 127–28, 323–25, 337
Pfeil, Margaret, xii, 299, 306–8
Phan, Peter C., Fr., 209, 340, 343
Philippines, 41, 301, 326
philosophy, philosophers, 7, 48, 78, 92, 96, 155, 160, 172, 178, 185–87, 200, 220, 227, 248, 252, 272, 318, 326, 334
Philpott, Daniel, 159, 328
pietism, 11
pilgrimage, pilgrims, ix, 2, 15–17, 21, 23, 94, 114, 131, 134–35, 145, 155, 163, 174, 180, 182, 185, 189, 192–93, 195, 209, 235, 344
Pineda-Madrid, Nancy, 344
Pinochet, Augusto, 301
Pius XII, Pope, 37, 342, 348
Platonism, 186–87, 252, 353
pluralism, 123, 316, 320
Pohl, Christine D., 204–5, 337–39
Poland, 50, 83, 87, 91, 211–12, 268
policing, xiii, 9, 12, 20, 76, 219, 246, 266, 275, 283, 293, 296, 299, 362, 364–66; as distinct from soldiering and war making, 76; nonlethal, 246. *See also* just policing
policymaking, 3, 5, 8, 129, 135, 158, 214, 223–24, 226, 232, 236, 246, 251, 284, 288, 290
political jiu-jitsu, 267, 300
political relevance, xv, 18, 36, 50, 105, 214, 241, 259, 264, 266
Pollmann, Karla, 335

polyhedron, Pope Francis's, 134, 136, 158
Pontius the Deacon, 173, 333
Populorum Progressio, 40, 44, 202, 296, 304–5, 328, 338, 357
Porter, Jean, xi, xiv
poverty, the poor, 11, 13, 40–41, 51, 57, 63, 73, 84, 121, 134, 150, 155, 157–58, 199–200, 202–3, 205, 229–30, 233, 245, 269, 274, 290, 327, 338
Powers, Gerard, xiii
pragmatism, 187, 279, 285, 363
presumption against war and violence, 37, 49, 250–51, 288, 302, 365
primordialism, 112, 319
private property. *See* ownership, private property
proclamation of the gospel, 32, 123, 128, 134
Prolegomena to the Law of War and Peace, 351
propaganda, 91, 218
prophetic critique, prophets, 5, 16, 19–20, 67, 74, 119–20, 135, 140, 145, 147–48, 218, 233, 246, 270, 278, 298
prophetic minorities. *See* creative minorities
Protestantism, xi, 110, 125, 128, 194, 304, 309, 321–22, 324–25, 363
protests, 6, 54, 213, 254
prudence, prudential judgment, 73, 194
Publicola, 249, 350

Quakers, 10, 60, 288
Quetico Provincial Park, Ontario, Canada, 223
quietism, 300, 341
Qumran, 257

rabbinic Judaism, 25, 103–4, 116–17, 145, 162, 168, 286, 355
Rabin, Yitzhak, 265

race, racial identity, 18, 74, 93, 99, 106, 149, 151, 158, 163, 175–78, 193, 202, 271, 333
racism, 136, 176, 318
Radical Reformation, 59–60, 316, 364. *See also* Anabaptism, Anabaptists
Rahner, Karl, SJ, 25, 29, 95–98, 107, 118, 121–24, 127–28, 190, 301, 311–13, 321–22, 324, 336
Rajak, Tessa, 331–32
Rajendra, Tisha, xiii, 221, 226, 235, 340, 343–44, 346–47
Ramsey, Paul, 278, 305, 352, 363
Rasmusson, Arne, 341
rationalism, 239
Ratzinger, Joseph, Cardinal. *See* Benedict XVI, Pope
Reagan, Ronald, 50, 83
realism, Realism, 8, 45–47, 52, 55, 79, 82–83, 94, 104, 136, 214, 216, 219, 234, 239, 241, 253, 258–59, 267, 284, 305, 342, 354; Christian, 47, 104, 214, 305; political, 4–5, 47, 55, 79, 305
reason, 92, 211, 218, 272
Recife, Brazil, 6, 326
reconciliation, 12–13, 19, 22, 52–54, 63–64, 106, 136, 152, 156, 158–59, 173, 176–77, 213, 254, 258, 274, 281, 294, 297–98, 306; of Jew and Gentile, 151–52; reconciled diversity, 136, 156
refugees 109, 199–200, 202, 211–12, 220–22, 225, 231, 343–44, 346
Reign of God 23, 49, 55, 80, 98, 134, 137, 192, 214, 219, 234, 286, 293
relativism, moral, 216, 278, 288, 297
religion: and colonialism, 122; as discredited, 3; role in peacemaking, 58–61, 89, 92, 102, 104, 109–10, 123, 125–26, 158–59, 211, 271, 276; wars of, 1, 250
Rempel, John D., 363–64, 366
Rengger, Nicholas, 351
Rerum Novarum, 50, 222, 297, 343

resident aliens, *paroikoi*, 145, 163–65, 170–74, 177, 179–80, 188–89, 204, 206–8, 215, 235, 328, 330
responsibility to protect, 282, 302
ressourcement, 160, 163, 172, 182
resurrection, 8, 26, 98, 138–40, 145, 196, 242–44, 320
revelation, 184, 192, 229, 247, 272
revolution, x, 41, 43–44, 50, 53–55, 81, 83, 90–91, 95, 124, 185, 197, 237, 241, 243, 245–46, 265, 283, 301, 315, 322, 336, 345, 350, 365–66; just: 43–44; nonviolent, 41; violent, 44, 81, 83, 91
rights: communal, 85–87, 111, 210; defense of, 11, 13, 37, 39, 44, 50–51, 63, 84, 211, 240, 250; human, 11, 13, 37, 39, 50–52, 63, 81–82, 84, 86–90, 92, 134, 155–56, 200, 210, 216, 220–24, 258, 269–70, 274, 281, 284, 340, 342, 344; migrant, 204–5, 211, 216, 220–24, 229–31; of nations, 86–87, 210; religious freedom, 51, 76, 89, 130; right to have rights, 221–22; rights of difference, 102–4. *See also* self-defense
rigorism, 119, 253, 277, 292
Rios Montt, Efrain, 324
Roma, the, 115
Roman empire, emperors, 32, 75, 78, 96, 122, 138, 162, 167, 169, 176, 181, 183–84, 188–89, 243, 246–47
Romero, Oscar, Archbishop, 6
Roosevelt, Franklin Delano, 10
Rugby World Cup, 266
rule of law, 8, 56
Russell, Frederick H., 334
Russian dolls, 136, 148, 154, 193
Rwanda, 1, 26
Rynne, Terrence J., 334–35

Sabbath, 66, 338–39
sacramentality, 2, 34, 59, 139, 171, 191–93, 296

sacraments, 62, 133, 191, 193, 247.
    See also Church, the: as sacrament of salvation and human unity
Sacrosanctum Concilium, 321
Sadat, Anwar, 266
Safran, William, 316–17, 320, 324
salvation history, ix, 22, 110, 129, 135–36, 142, 150, 153, 162, 191, 207, 286, 293
Samaritans, 71–72, 265, 308
San Salvador, El Salvador, 6
Sanders, Scott Russell, 21, 301
Santiago, Chile, 5
Sarah (Sarai), 94, 110, 136, 141, 144–45, 147, 178, 180, 203, 207
Sassen, Saskia, 344
saturation bombing, 38, 303, 305
Scandinavia, 257
scapegoating, 263, 270, 361
Schell, Jonathan, 362
Schlabach, Theron F., x, 298, 341
Schoenfeld, Devorah, 333
Scholte, Jan Aart, 314
Schuck, Michael J., 357
Scripture, scriptures, 2–3, 10, 24, 108, 113, 137, 145, 147, 162, 164, 193, 203, 207, 218, 240, 243, 257, 273, 283, 302, 356
Scrooge syndrome, 228
Second Vatican Council, xi, 2, 7, 10, 15–16, 20–21, 23, 31–32, 35, 37–43, 45, 48–49, 61, 64, 76, 90, 96, 104, 110, 114, 121–24, 130, 133, 136, 139, 155, 160, 163, 171–72, 174, 180, 182–83, 185, 190–91, 193, 195, 233, 236, 239–40, 259, 274, 277, 280, 290–91, 296–97, 301–4, 308, 311–12, 319, 321–22, 326–28, 334, 336–37, 348, 357, 362, 364, 366
sectarianism, 19, 22, 96, 101, 103, 129, 159, 163, 166, 178, 200, 214, 312, 316, 341
secularization, 128

segregation, racial, 301
self-defense: national, 37, 41, 49, 52, 255, 268, 273, 277, 280, 344, 347–48; personal, 224–25, 249, 273, 277, 280, 347–48, 352
self-interest. *See* egotism
SEMILLA (Anabaptist-Mennonite Seminary in Central America), x
sentimentality, 216, 257, 268
separatism, 96, 150, 166, 178, 217
Septuagint, 24, 107–8, 243, 302
Serbia, 301
Sermon on the Mount, 10, 231, 236–37, 239–42, 252–54, 256, 258, 266–67, 272, 278–79, 283, 285–87, 289, 292, 327, 352–57, 361–62; as a "manual" for peacemaking, 236–37, 239–42, 252–53, 266, 272
servanthood, 140, 149, 151–53
Servicio Paz y Justicia (SERPAJ), xi
sexual abuse, xiv–xv, 1, 295
Shah, Timothy Samuel, 159, 328
Sharp, Gene, 244, 267, 300, 340, 349
Shema, the, 146, 326
Shepherd of Hermas, The, 164–67, 171, 174, 329–30
shirking, charge of, 17–18
Siebert, Steve, xiv
Sikhs, 58
Skudlarek, William, OSB, xii
slavery, 205
Society of Biblical Literature, 355–56
Socrates, 264
soldiering, soldiers, 76–77, 181, 201, 249, 256, 275, 290, 351
solidarity, x–xi, 1, 5, 13, 16, 21–22, 27, 29, 31–32, 34–35, 49, 51, 56, 63, 65, 68–69, 73, 78, 80–85, 89–91, 93, 101, 109–10, 117–19, 129, 136, 156, 176, 180, 202, 209, 220, 226–27, 230, 232, 249, 265, 270, 274–75, 300, 317, 343; global, 22, 35, 65, 68, 73, 78, 80, 117–18; —, Christian, x, 1, 16, 22, 35, 65, 110, 180, 227; human, 32, 49, 51,

414 A Pilgrim People

63, 78, 90, 180, 202; pan-African, 232; pan-Arab, 232
Solidarność, Solidarity Movement in Poland 50, 83
Sollicitudo Rei Socialis, 304
Somalis, 195
soteriology, 291
South Africa, 211, 232, 301, 306, 361
sovereignty, 88, 103–5, 223, 225, 314; spiritual, 88
Soviet Union, Soviet empire, 36, 41, 50, 55, 81, 83, 91, 212, 268, 301
Spadaro, Antonio, SJ, 328
Spain, 125
spiritual but not religious, 3
Star Trek, 361
Stark, Rodney, 167–69, 330–31, 350
Stassen, Glen, xii, 253–54, 256–59, 267, 279, 283–86, 289, 292, 320, 327, 341–42, 353–57, 361–66
state, the, 51, 88, 109, 222, 287, 344
statecraft, 135
statehood, 24, 87
statelessness, 221, 223
Stephan, Maria J., 244, 349
Stevenson, William R., 305
stewardship, 229, 345
Stoesz, Edgar, x
Stoicism, 187–88, 250
Stout, Jeffrey, 342
strangers, 78, 106, 142, 144, 171, 173, 200, 203–8, 220, 223–24, 229–30, 338, 340, 342–44
Stromata, 333
Suárez, Francisco, 348
Summa theologiae, 229, 350–51
supersessionism, 113
Supreme Court, United States, 311
sustainability, 4, 45, 65, 111, 269–70
Swartley, Willard M., 357
Swiss Guards, 290, 366
Switzerland, 59, 354
synagogues, 150, 168–70, 245
syncretism, 156
Syria, 123, 211–12

Talmud, the, 25, 119
Tapia de Renedo, Benedicto, 300, 362
technocratic control, techno-economic paradigm, 129, 340
technology, 32, 42, 49, 74, 100, 167, 210, 223, 270, 313, 319, 337
temple, Jerusalem, 147, 245, 349
Ten Commandments. *See* Decalogue
terrorism, 41, 43, 45, 58, 91, 137, 159, 301, 303, 349, 354
Tertullian, 32, 168, 177–78, 275, 301, 332, 334, 362
theocracy, 109, 112
Theodosius, 181, 188–89
theology, theologians, 1–2, 6, 10, 12, 15–16, 18, 22, 25, 32–37, 39–41, 48–49, 52, 57, 59–63, 65–67, 69–70, 73, 77–78, 94, 96, 107, 112–14, 116–18, 120–24, 129, 150, 159–60, 163, 169–70, 177, 181–84, 189, 200, 202, 209, 218, 237, 239, 241–42, 244, 252, 259–60, 272, 276, 279, 286, 290–92
Thiel, John E., 297
Thiessen Nation, Mark, 363
third race (*genos*), 175–76
Tillich, Paul, xv
Toft, Monica Duffy, 159, 328
Tolkien, J. R. R., 130
Tomlinson, John, 314
toolmaking, 261
Torah, the, 102, 113, 145–46, 204, 207–8, 259, 286, 339–40, 349, 355
torture, 38, 47, 137, 173, 185
totalitarianism, 21, 34, 41, 50–52, 57, 81, 85, 90–91, 220, 285, 343
tourism, 337
Tractatus in Epistolam Joannis Ad Parthos, 352
Tracy, David, 120, 320
traditionalism, 6, 290, 326
trafficking, human, 38, 344
transforming initiatives, 253–54, 257–59, 264–72, 283, 285–86, 291, 293–94, 355–57, 361–63

translation across ethical systems, 93, 215–21, 224–30, 233–34, 266–67, 285, 316
transnationality, 109, 317
triads, triadic exegesis, 252–55, 257, 259, 283, 285–86, 289, 291–93, 353, 355–56, 361, 365
tribalism, 1, 22, 26, 87, 92–93, 101–3, 159, 177, 200, 211, 255, 275, 314–15
tricksters, 257
Trinity, the, 9, 131, 242–43, 260, 335
triumphalism, 192, 211, 272–73, 312, 322, 361
Troeltsch, Ernst, 119–20, 320, 341
Turkson, Peter, Cardinal, ix, 235, 346
Tutsis, 1
typology, typologies, 119–20, 217, 321, 341
tyranny, tyrants, 20, 41, 43–44, 49, 82, 138, 262, 324, 361

ubuntu, 7
Ukraine, 301
Ultramontanism, 110
ummah, Islamic, 110
umunthu, 7
unborn, the, 136
Unitatis Redintegratio, 319, 321
unity-in-diversity. *See* diversity-in-unity, unity-in-diversity
United Methodist Council of Bishops, USA, 280, 363–64
United Nations, 43, 79–81, 85–86, 88–91, 101, 111, 157, 210, 221, 270, 305, 309–10, 314, 328, 338, 340, 352, 354
United States, x, 10–11, 36, 41, 45–46, 82, 96, 110, 121, 126, 202, 216, 221, 224, 226, 231–32, 250, 268, 280, 311, 323, 343, 363
United States Conference of Catholic Bishops (USCCB), 224, 296–97, 302, 305, 310, 342–44, 352, 362, 364

universalism, universalizing projects, 92, 102–3, 176–77, 315, 329, 334. *See also* particularity and universality, creative tension between
Ury, William, 318, 346
utilitarianism, 83–84, 90, 244, 253
utopias, 6–8, 79, 138

Vatican II. *See* Second Vatican Council
vengeance: desire for, 258, 286
veterans, 67
vicious cycles, 236, 241, 253–61, 263–66, 270–72, 283–86, 289–94, 347, 354, 356, 361
Vietnam, 209, 280, 288–89, 324
violence, xv, 7–10, 12–14, 18–19, 32, 39, 41, 43–44, 49, 53–56, 58, 62–63, 79, 81, 89, 93, 102, 129, 134, 138–40, 152, 155, 157, 159, 173, 178, 197, 200, 213, 219, 223, 231, 237–38, 240–41, 244–46, 248, 251–53, 255–56, 263, 267, 274, 277–78, 281–83, 285, 288, 291, 293, 296–97, 299–300, 304, 307–8, 341, 350, 353, 355, 358, 360, 364, 366; cycles of 43, 53, 231, 241, 245, 252–53, 285, 291, 355; institutionalized, 43; inter-religious, 12, 44, 58, 159, 274–75, 278, 282; nation-state, 54, 268, 282; recourse to, 8–10, 14, 19, 44, 129, 277; suppression of conflict through, 7
virtues for nonviolence, peacemaking, just peacebuilding, 14, 35, 49, 73, 83, 151, 218, 239–41, 259, 265, 267, 272. *See also* holiness
Vitoria, Francisco de, 250, 303, 348, 351
vocation, xv–xvi, 5–7, 12–13, 23, 25, 34–36, 49, 63–64, 70–71, 78, 80, 93, 99, 115, 118, 129, 136, 142, 151, 153, 158, 178, 180, 191–92, 218, 233, 237, 239–40, 250, 271, 274, 293, 296, 298, 310

von Rad, Gerhard, 326–27
Vrudny, Kimberly, xiii
vulnerable communities, cultures and peoples, 20, 22, 34, 36, 42, 86, 88–89, 107, 123, 177, 195, 204, 212–13, 220

Waltner Goossen, Rachel, 295
wars, warfare, 14, 38–39, 47, 49, 102, 155, 179, 255, 269, 275, 278, 280, 282, 288–90, 347, 349, 352; Catholic reappraisal of, xi–xiii, 21, 39–41, 43, 182, 236, 238, 280, 284, 290–91; Christian participation in, 1–2, 10, 14, 76–77, 173, 181, 194–95, 249–52, 255, 280, 284, 304, 348; destruction of, 14, 38–39, 45, 251, 271, 285; modern, 14, 38–39, 43, 236, 280, 284, 287, 289, 291, 299, 305; of religion, 1, 250
Warsaw (Poland) Ghetto, 268
Washington DC, USA, 5, 58
wealth, the wealthy, 85, 134, 166, 229, 329, 338
Weigel, George, 365
West, the, 50, 69, 82, 102, 183, 350
Whitmore, Todd, xi, 365
Wiesel, Elie, 320
Williams, Rowan, Archbishop, 357–58
Willimon, William H., 328
Wilson, Woodrow, 285

Wink, Walter, 234, 341, 346, 355, 367
Winright, Tobias, xii, 352
witness, communal and lived, 3, 13, 15–16, 19, 22, 29, 31–34, 50, 54–55, 57, 59–61, 104, 128, 150, 157, 162, 184–85, 190, 215, 218, 276–77, 280–82, 294
Wojda, Paul, xiii
Wojtyła, Karol. *See* John Paul II, Pope
Wolff, Hans Walter, 326
works of mercy, 152
World Council of Churches (WCC), 62–63, 280–82
World Day of Peace, 5, 41, 62, 231, 236, 238, 241, 285, 296, 346–47, 362
Wrobleski, Jessica, 337, 345

xenophobia, 220, 231

Yoder, Elizabeth G., 341
Yoder, John Howard, xiv–xv, 18, 105, 185, 282, 287–89, 295, 297, 300, 306–7, 315–16, 319, 336–37, 341–42, 349–51, 363–67
Yong, Amos, 332

Zahn, Gordon, 39, 366
Zealots, 149
Zimbabwe, 324
Zionism, 116